# THE PROTESTANT MIND
## OF THE ENGLISH REFORMATION,
### 1570-1640

*St. Paul,* REMBRANDT

# THE
# PROTESTANT MIND
# OF THE
# ENGLISH
# REFORMATION
# 1570 · 1640

✝ ✝ ✝

BY CHARLES H. GEORGE

AND

KATHERINE GEORGE

✝ ✝ ✝

PRINCETON, NEW JERSEY
PRINCETON UNIVERSITY PRESS
1961

TO DAVID HILLES GEORGE

*beloved son*

# PREFACE

―――――――――――――――――――✝ ✝ ✝―――――――――――――――――――

THE plan and nature of this book are described in the Introduction. The sources from which this study was constructed are indicated in the footnotes and bibliography. We have given in the first footnote reference to each item all necessary bibliographical information; some of the more formidable titles have been abbreviated and, to avoid repetition, London will be understood as the place of publication unless another city is specified. We have decided to retain the original spelling and generally charming vagaries of capitalization and punctuation in our sources: they are never confusing to a modern reader and they suit much better than modern orthography the structure of Elizabethan rhetoric.

Most of the fossilized record of the Protestant consciousness in the era of Reformation consists of sermons, theological works, and devotional tracts which from 1520 until the later seventeenth century poured forth from the presses of Europe—a flood of ink and paper that in itself constitutes a cultural revolution. Since we intend not a history of the English Reformation but an analysis of Protestant ideology at flood tide, our *terminus a quo* precludes consideration of the early, minority Protestantism (set in fresh perspective by A. G. Dickens, *Lollards and Protestants in the Diocese of York, 1509-1558*, 1959) and even such familiar classics of Protestant literature as Cranmer's liturgical thought and the *Apologia* of John Jewel.

The key to the modernity of the Protestant temper is perhaps its compulsive articulation, repetitive, insecure, aggressive, searching in print for answers that eluded the private gropings of sensitive men caught in an age of frightening tension and irresolvable conflict. Compared to the confessional genius of the succeeding age of Pepys, Boswell, and Rousseau, the epoch of Protestant reform is disappointingly lacking in diaries, letters, autobiographies—the sources of greatest intimacy in revealing men and culture. But the profusion of seemingly formal treatises for public and traditional consumption do, by their intensely ambitious desire to communicate the whole heart of the Christian dilemma in the new age, allow us to perceive the deeper and private roots of the Protestant ego and its culture. Our concern in this study must be primarily with the formal elements in Protestant culture; yet the casual and unconscious, however difficult to document, are never far from our sources or, we trust, our awareness.

The Social Science Research Council made it possible for us to complete our reading to this end in the British Museum for the year 1955 to 1956. We are indebted to them and to a benefaction from June Oakes, Katherine George's mother, for the indispensable generosity that helped make this book a reality. Assistant Chancellor John Geise of the University of Pittsburgh very kindly provided funds for the typing of the entire manuscript. Alice Linton, secretary in the history department, has also given valuable typing assistance.

It will be clear from the text footnotes throughout how great is our debt to others who have written about England in the age of Donne. We have tried to write a critical synthesis as well as our own interpretations of the sources. We should like to acknowledge the helpfulness of Professors George Fowler, Leland Baldwin, and Robert Colodny of the history faculty of the University of Pittsburgh, who read critically large sections of the manuscript.

All scholars who have worked in the library of the British Museum will know the debt of gratitude we owe this superb staff. Finally, we should like to express our appreciation for the splendid services of Princeton University Press, particularly the invaluable editorial work of Miss Judy Walton.

C.H.G.

K.G.

# CONTENTS

————————✝ ✝ ✝————————

# CONTENTS

THE PROTESTANT MIND
OF THE ENGLISH REFORMATION,
1570-1640

# INTRODUCTION

✝✝✝

"It is hardly possible to exaggerate the importance of
the sermon in the seventeenth-century world."
—Douglas Bush, *English Literature in the Earlier
Seventeenth Century,* 1600-1660, 296

✝✝✝

This book has been written to satisfy a desire for exploring
the fascinating world of religious ideas and in the hope of
probing the frontiers which relate religious precepts to social
aspects of the historical process. Protestantism particularly interests us because it is not only a complicated and moving confession in itself, but also one which came into being as a religious viewpoint in a period of unusually rapid and profoundly
revolutionary social change. The Protestant mind was challenged in a unique way, therefore, to make morally and
spiritually comprehensible a pattern of civilization that had no
precedent, a pattern we label "modern." The result was that
Protestantism itself was inevitably a "modern" outlook in that
it was pressed upon by all of the forces, social, economic, political, cultural, which were the components of the complete pattern of change; yet Protestantism was also self-consciously a
conservative, even reactionary, affirmation of an ancient religious viewpoint expressed in a canon of Scripture thousands of
years old. Protestantism was both antimedieval and antimodern.
It rejected the sacramental, institutional, hierarchical Christianity which was the work of the medieval churchmen and,
yet more vehemently, the secularized and fragmented culture
of modern intellectuals. The literature produced by this dramatic historical tension is a compelling, richly instructive experience.

In more specific terms, we hope by this book to throw light
upon some vexed and intriguing problems of modern historiog-

raphy. We are concerned to see in what ways the Protestantism
of England was related to the eruption of the Great Rebellion
of 1640-1660. The English and Dutch revolutions are the only
modern revolutions undertaken in essentially Christian cultures,
and with explicitly and intensely Christian justifications. This
is interesting, and leads to a second and subsidiary purpose in
our book: to see to what extent—if any—the term "puritan"
has meaning as a label for a distinct theological and ethical
position in the English Protestant Church. Finally (and most
important) we hope to reveal in decisive detail the nature of
the Protestant Ethic, in this its formative and also its culminating period, when Protestantism retained the moral and intellectual initiative in English society.

The plan of our book follows, we trust, the logic of our inquiry. In Part I we attempt to state as accurately as possible
the position of the major representatives of Church of England
dogma in regard to that vast and general area of theology which
is humanistically rather than theistically or cosmologically
oriented. Our effort is to establish firmly the theological bedrock
of English Protestant conviction concerning man and his place
in the world and in eternity. Even though we largely ignore
in this discussion the disputed intricacies of relationship between the English and various continental schools, and reduce
almost to their simplest extremes the distinctions between English and Catholic conceptual systems, Part I is necessarily long
and abstract. For, as a whole generation of contemporary scholars have demonstrated, theology constitutes the fundamental
intellectuality of the seventeenth-century *Weltanschauung*.
Therefore, we must achieve a full and reliable definition of
English theology—within the limits of the domain we have
chosen to survey—and such a definition will falsify the English
clerical mind, and thus English Protestantism as well, if it presents this body of thought as simple or entirely self-consistent,
or as intelligible on any but its own peculiar terms.

Once this basic level of English Protestantism has been dis-
sected and analyzed, we consider, in Part II, the specific social
and institutional character of the ideology of the English pulpit.
Here again we leave polemics to footnotes and try, without

benefit of preconceptions, to arrive at conclusions from the sources. Finally, in Part III, we present a statement, extracted from our examination of the many relevant strands of thought, which seeks to assess the reality and significance of the religious dissension within English Protestantism during these decades which precede a so-called "puritan" revolt.

The literature we have under survey consists of hundreds of sermons and other religious publications of English divines in the seven decades from the statutory enactment of England's Protestant creed in the Thirty-Nine Articles to the outbreak of revolution—the thought of roughly three generations of the creative and most vital life of English Protestantism. We believe, quite a posteriori, that this literature reflects a "mind"; thus the title of our book. Though of course our "Protestant mind" need not be accepted as an entity, we have written of it from many angles and in many differing perspectives. But we do insist that insofar as there is a "Protestant mind," it is truly approached only through the clergy. Many laymen are a part of the Protestant religious outlook, but no group of laymen as such are reliably "Protestant" in the ideal sense we are investigating. Nor do laymen as a group write from a consistent religious orientation. Indeed, the failure to convert laymen to a deeply felt Protestant view of life resulted in the tragically rapid disintegration of the Protestant outlook. Thus English lawyers, businessmen, poets, adventurers, politicians, and gentry are perhaps more intimately related to the Protestant mind than the medieval barons and burghers were to the Catholic mind; yet the prime and final source of the ideology, of the vast interrelated synthesis of God, man, and society, is clerical. Christian ideology and clericalism are historically quite inseparable.

Perhaps the most troublesome single problem in writing of the realities of Protestantism in prerevolutionary England is that of the understandable passion of modern scholars to define the word "puritan" in terms which will explain the revolutionary developments in seventeenth-century English society: everything from the political revolution to the new science has been seen as a development from the "puritan" ethos.

The logical inadequacies of many of these efforts will be

dealt with in the course of this book; what concerns us at the very outset is a semantic difficulty. All of us working with religious and cultural materials in this period must use the word "puritan" because contemporaries used it. But when contemporaries used the word, their meaning was a function of a specific context. Archbishop Laud's famous list, the visitation of Bishop Chaderton in 1604 in the diocese of Lincoln and of Bishop Neile in the same diocese in 1614, the occasional efforts made by the Judges of Assize to enforce the Declaration of Sports, King James exhibiting his anxiety concerning Presbyterian extremism at Hampton Court in 1604—in such varieties of specific usage can the word be understood. It may mean that the individual or group described is any enemy to be vilified, a political opponent, a decrier of dancing on Sunday, an adversary of the canons of 1604, a hypocrite in business transactions, a pompous ass, or a subverter of all things English and a general factionist. Before the Revolution the term was almost invariably pejorative, and if one knows the circumstances surrounding its use, one may easily enough understand why the word is used and what is communicated by that use. But the conclusion arising from detailed knowledge of the prerevolutionary uses of the term is that "puritan" is the "x" of a cultural and social equation: it has no meaning beyond that given it by the particular manipulator of an algebra of abuse. All societies have such symbols. And for the cultural historian it is neither surprising nor confounding to find that the same divine is labelled differently by observers as different as Thomas Fuller and Samuel Clarke, for instance. William Perkins, the most important English divine, is a saintly and godly leader in the opinion of both King James and William Prynne; John Wilkins, Cromwell's brother-in-law, when compiling a list of divines for the godly to read for their "practical divinity," includes Lancelot Andrewes, the leading court preacher of the early 1600's.

It is by now commonplace enough for historians to admit, as Professor Eusden does in his recent monograph, that there is "no such thing as a 'Puritan party' . . . in the political life of the time" and that there is no distinctive "puritan" ecclesiasticism, "doctrinal or organizational";[1] but the general tendency is still to follow William Haller's lead in insisting that the only basic and usable definition of "puritanism" distinguishes a core of Calvinist theology, especially a unique interpretation of the doctrine of predestination, from the other varieties of Protestantism in England.[2] "It was still Calvinism," Professor Eusden insists, "which set them [the "puritans"] apart from their Anglican colleagues, who were beginning to espouse liberal, Arminian tendencies."[3] Since we cannot accept this definition, and since we feel certain it is not supported by any significant contemporary evidence,[4] we are in the position—semantically very awkward—of being occasionally forced to use a word whose meaning must always be a function of a particular frame of reference and must always, therefore, involve qualification by adjectives or contextual influences. For we find ourselves responding to this issue of "puritanism," as it comes to our time through the sermon literature we have read, somewhat as Pope Urban VIII responded in the period itself. "The Catholic clergy," the Pope commanded in a letter to his nuncio in England, "are to desist from that foolish, nay rather illiterate and childish, custom of distinction in the Protestant and Puritan doctrine, as if Protestantism were a degree nearer to the Catholic faith."[5] Thus we cannot make a list of "puritans" on any doctrinal basis—a good share of our study will be devoted to demonstrating that no such list is possible—and we have discovered no other set of adequately-defining elements.

The splendid Robert Bolton, as an intense advocate of "purity of heart, holinesse of affections, and unspottednesse of life,"[6] is certainly a "puritan." He accepts the designation, most happily, from the standpoint of logical consistency, when it means simply St. John's "clean through the word." But the same word

---

[1] See John D. Eusden, *Puritans, Lawyers, and Politics in Early Seventeenth-Century England* (New Haven, Connecticut, 1958), p. 11.

[2] *Ibid.*, pp. 18-25.

[3] *Ibid.*, p. 40.

[4] See Peter Heylyn's *Cyprianus Anglicus* (1668), p. 203, for Dr. Samuel Brooke's opinion that Predestination was the root of Laud's troubles.

[5] O. Ogle and W. H. Bliss, eds., *Calendar of the Clarendon State Papers* (Oxford, 1872), I, 191.

[6] Robert Bolton, *The Workes* (4 vols.; 1631-1641), I, 87.

is applied equally to Bishop Downham (a leading proponent of divine right episcopacy), and is extended at last to that generous breadth which enables Bellarmine to call King James a puritan.[7] We must beg the reader's indulgence, then, for not providing the traditional categories of distinction in the Protestant mind: we hope to give him, instead, a truer view of its real configurations. To do so will require some use of the word "puritan," to be sure, and here we shall be concerned with the meaning of the word for two different groups: for the English Protestant divines themselves and their contemporaries, and (with the question of the validity of the word always foremost in our minds) for modern scholars in the field. The real truth of the label must be sought, we feel, primarily in the age of its origin and active usage, and it is here that we are most aware of its essential pejorative intention. Hence the Great Rebellion of 1640-1660 may indeed be called a "puritan" revolution, in the tautological sense at least, for this word, more than any other which was available to the time and place, sums up the substance and reality of revolutionary movements everywhere: the whole dynamic syndrome of moral and practical animus and opposition by which one social system is demolished to make way for the construction of another.

Even though the Protestant mind is alone the central concern of our study, it is impossible to define this mind without some consideration of and comparison with the mind of Roman Catholicism. Thus we are again confronted with a problem of distinguishing between religious ideologies, but in this case the fact of decisive difference is never for a moment in any doubt. For Protestantism, by its very name, indicates its nature as contention and protest. To understand an ideological protest, whatever its type or content, one must obviously be conversant to some degree with the conceptual system against which

---

[7] *Ibid.*, pp. 244-45. Cf. William Bradshaw, *English Puritanisme* (1605); Henry Parker, *A Discourse Concerning Puritans* (1641); William Baxter, *The Christian Directory* (1677-78), Parts II and IV; C. H. Firth, ed., *Stuart Tracts, 1603-1693* (Westminster, 1903), pp. 234-46 for "The Interpreter"; and Clarendon, *The History of the Rebellion and Civil Wars in England* (7 vols.; Oxford, 1839), I, 146-57. See also "Puritanism: a Panel," *Church History* (June, 1954); C. V. Wedgwood, *The King's Peace, 1637-1641* (1955), p. 95.

the protest is directed. We do not presume to claim anything like the same familiarity with the Roman Catholicism of any period as that which we have come to possess with the English Protestantism of the sixteenth and seventeenth centuries. We are well aware, therefore, of the adventurous and hence necessarily tentative quality of the comparisons we make.

Our discussions of Roman Catholicism are based upon three primary areas or kinds of information. There are, first, the descriptions of the distinctive qualities of Roman Catholic thought which are generally recognized in scholarly circles to be valid; these have come to us by means of thorough study of all the major secondary sources and a wide sampling of the primary sources. Then there are the characterizations of the Roman Catholic position, used with due allowance for the prejudice involved, which are prominent in the process of argumentation within English Protestant sermon literature itself. Third, there are the writings of St. Thomas Aquinas, with which we do possess a first-hand and detailed acquaintance and which we have used extensively throughout this book. Time and again, we find occasion to indicate the novelty or significance of an English Protestant opinion by matching it with Thomistic doctrine on the matter.

Our special dependence upon the Thomistic corpus is surely justified, we feel, in view of the eminent place the Angelic Doctor occupies in the theological structure of Roman Catholicism. If one theologian is to be selected as representative of the faith of Rome, St. Thomas is beyond all doubt that one. The most important Roman Catholic theologians of the period of Protestantism's emergence and first triumphs, Bellarmine and Suárez, both, incidentally, Jesuits, are also both self-acknowledged and devoted Thomists; though differences of emphasis and minor viewpoint certainly exist between them and the master they try to interpret for their later and more troubled age, the essential form and content of their ideology are securely founded in and bounded by the teachings of the great medieval saint and scholar. And since it is our particular interest to analyze the social theory of English Protestantism against the background of what may be loosely called a medieval outlook, and to thereby determine as accurately as possible the degree and nature of Protestantism's modernity, we turn more readily to the Thomistic system because of its very origin in a thirteenth-century world and its special quality as a summation and intellectual synthesis of that world. It is our contention, finally, that despite the many adjustments which it has been forced to make over the last four or five hundred years to the pummeling assaults of social, economic, and intellectual change, Roman Catholicism, even into our present age, clings with considerable stubbornness to the form it possessed when it was preeminent as an institution and a body of thought in the West. Beyond any other single man, therefore, St. Thomas speaks best for this particular tradition—whether one views it in the time of its primary dominance over the mind of Western man, in its mortal combat with a second type of Western Christianity, or in this latest time when, for whatever it is worth against the surge of modern secularism, St. Thomas has been officially assigned in the Encyclical of Leo XIII to stand for all eternity as a spokesman and a guardian for the truths of his church.

A few words of caution may be appropriate at this point to the nonspecialist reader who approaches this religious literature for the first time. It is often a very arrogant and wordy literature. Our preachers, remember, *know* all of the important Truths. Their task is to convince by exhortation, not by reason. Further, and as a consequence, though we shall constantly be searching out the new, the shifting emphasis, the "weight" of ideas amidst a great and cumbersome bulk of opinion, none of our divines will admit to innovation or discovery. All Truth, Beauty, and Goodness are of the golden past, of the Garden of primal beneficence, at very latest in the Primitive Church and Gospel revelation. Therefore, the radical and innovating idea is always explicitly "reactionary," a return. Finally, the literature dealt with here is extremely, sometimes unbearably, serious. Partly this is true of all religious literature (death is not a very amusing subject), but it must also be realized that the intellectuals of the sixteenth and seventeenth centuries were accorded a most extraordinary prestige and valuation by their social betters, and the result of this flattery was an intensity of involvement and address, a heady feeling of dedication to leadership in the realm of ideas, quite alien to the intellectuals of our later epochs of modernity.

There are two small matters of method we should perhaps say something about. We have done the research and writing for this book jointly because of our common and complementary interests, because of the bulk of reading necessary, and because by constantly discussing and revising we have been able to have greater confidence in our presentation and interpretations of the many subtle problems that riddle with perplexity the crucial period of our study. The second matter of method relates to the large amount of quoted material. We have commonly quoted rather than paraphrased, on the principle that the words of the original are more convincing and often more interesting than methodical précis. Many of our divines write well; and in any case, the nuances of emotion and meaning are best preserved in their own baroque language and cadence, even if the quoted passages lack literary éclat by the standards of our Hemingway-infested modes of expression.

## I I

We have little space for either the amenities of biographical sketches or the less dispensable narration of the political and social events and trends which constitute the living, affective environment in which English Protestantism thrived. The melancholy aspect of writing intellectual history is precisely the danger of dealing with ideas in a social vacuum. We are, however, fortunate in our concentration upon the epoch 1570-1640, for this is one of the most assiduously and intelligently reconstructed periods in the history of any society. There is the *Dictionary of National Biography*, J. E. Neale on the Elizabethan essentials, S. R. Gardiner's monumental political narrative to 1642, and the articles of the *Economic History Review* for basic economic background.

Obviously, we cannot summarize even the rudiments of this knowledge as it applies to our subject. But we can rest confident that anyone wanting to read our book can easily get at the background against which it is most meaningful.[8]

Many of the social, economic, and political facts of the period will be found solidly implanted in the thought we are describing and analyzing. We trust enough of this rawer stuff of history will be in our quotations and our explanations to satisfy the discriminating. In general, the joy of writing intellectual, and especially religious, history is that no other class of documents of historical specialization reveals so total a fund of historical experience, is so nearly the embodiment of both "climate of opinion" and forces of social control.

Still, it may be appropriate in these lines of introduction to very briefly state what seem to us the principal elements in the historical complex within which the English Protestant mind came into being. First, it is well to say that King Henry's Reformation of the 1530's had not been "Protestant," but dynastic, anticlerical, and national in character. Indeed, when Elizabeth came to the throne in 1558, England was far less Protestant in its theology and sacramental practice than France; for France had a very large Calvinist minority that had penetrated not only the towns but also the nobility and the court, while England's Protestants were more placidly "Lutheran," both less aggressive and far less numerous. Elizabeth was herself a religious Politique, like her Medici counterpart in France. But from the continent a new generation of Bucerian and Calvinist enthusiasts returned from the exile and smell of martyrdom that had marked the reign of Catholic Mary and her consort, Philip of Spain. Their zeal and ability were matched by the folly of the Catholic hierarchy in excommunicating and plotting the deposition and murder of probably the most popular and indispensable ruler in English history. The result was an English church which not only rejected the authority of the Catholic hierarchy at Rome, but created a morale of true independence, and indeed of attack, in relationship to the entire spirit of Catholicism. And the more

[8] There is a competent textbook in *The Oxford History of England* series for the Elizabethan period by J. B. Black, *The Reign of Queen Elizabeth* (1936); but, unhappily, the series volume on *The Early Stuarts, 1603-1660* (1937) by Godfrey Davies is unsatisfactory.

this temper of attack on Catholicism as a whole took possession of England, the more the work of Calvin and the Calvinists appealed to her intellectuals.

In this complicated process, at once patriotic, adventurous, and genuinely pious, the Protestant mind came into being. It was psychologically rooted in *The Book of Martyrs*, in the bull *Regnans in excelsis*, and above all in the excitement of Lutheran and Calvinist theology. Once this continental Protestant theology seized the imaginations of English intellectuals, these people quickly displayed, as we hope our book will demonstrate, the extraordinary quality of all English intellectual life in this amazing epoch of cultural activity. English sermons and theological treatises and polemical tracts and religious poetry add up to a cultural peak nearly as imposing as those thrown up in the drama, science, and lay literature generally.[9] We cannot *explain* the genius of our period: an age that produces Shakespeare, Donne, and Bacon; that was probably the most brilliant period in English music; that gave the world its most beautifully written Bible; that brought the architectural charm of Inigo Jones—such an age cannot be explained, only admired and loved.

But if we cannot entirely explain the genesis or genius of the Protestant mind, if we cannot isolate the magical chemistry of its life and vitality and quality, we can analyze the nature of that mind as an existential phenomenon. We can also suggest its relevance to certain historically obvious characteristics of our period, aside from the most striking fact of the general level of cultural activity which has excited the wonder of intellectuals at least since Dryden. For a prime instance, we may note (though economic historians still worry over the precise relations of prices to rents, industrial growth to commercial expansion, "improving" estate management to "feudal" estate management, bourgeoisie to gentry, and so on) the generally indisputable economic

[9] See the fine volume in *The Oxford History of English Literature* by Douglas Bush: *English Literature in the Earlier Seventeenth Century, 1600-1660* (New York, 1952); C. S. Lewis, *English Literature in the Sixteenth Century* (Oxford, 1954), of the same series, is interesting but less reliable. Basil Willey, *The Seventeenth Century Background* (New York, 1955) remains indispensable. The best book dealing with the richness of popular culture is still Louis B. Wright, *Middle-Class Culture in Elizabethan England* (Ithaca, N.Y., 1935).

muscle developing in English society. The expansion of the new coal and the older textile industries, the successes of trading companies and piracy, the precocious beginnings of London's entrepôt enterprise, the inflation in prices and probably also in rents, the increase of agricultural productivity, particularly in wool growing, the population increase—all of this new wealth certainly created an unprecedented "economic surplus" that made possible a renaissance of thought and art.

The social results of this economic upsurgence are at once obvious and the object of acrimonious debate.[10] That is, to most historians it is clear that there is a crucial and revolutionary social difference between the fifteenth and seventeenth centuries: that one social situation is still essentially "feudal" while the other is either "modern" or, at the very least, antifeudal.[11] The barons rule England, quite beyond the possibility of effective challenge, in 1440; by 1640 they are incapable of controlling even the House of Commons. The bourgeoisie-gentry, in their revolutionary county committees, could afford to pay for a war against the barons which would have bankrupted the entire economy of England a few generations earlier.

On looking at legal and political history during our period, we discover a parallel quickening of institutional and ideational growth. Amid a proliferation of legal techniques, new courts, and law books, the common law smashed through ecclesiastical, civil, and administrative rivals to a victory of towering dimensions. In Sir Edward Coke the age found one of its giants, and the coming revolution a brilliantly articulate champion. Meantime, there proceeded that amazing remaking of the medieval parliament, which A. B. White's admirable phrase has characterized as "self-

10 See R. H. Tawney, "The Rise of the Gentry, 1558-1640," *Economic History Review*, XI, No. 1 (1941), and his "Harrington's Interpretation of his Age," Proceedings of the British Academy (1941); an attempted refutation, successful on some points but inconsistently argued, is H. R. Trevor-Roper, "The Gentry, 1540-1640," *Economic History Review Supplements*, I (1953). The most interesting new evidence since Tawney went to work on the manors (J. A. Cooper, "The Counting of Manors," *op.cit.*, VIII [1956]) is properly critical of Tawney's use of the manor as an economic unit; information regarding the rise of a county capitalism is provided by E. Kerridge, "The Movement of Rent, 1540-1640," *Economic History Review*, VI, No. 1 (1953), in which we see impressive corroboration of the social thesis that capitalist farmers were progressing at a significant rate in profit accumulation.

11 See Trevor-Roper, "The Social Origins of the Great Rebellion," *History Today* (June, 1955).

government at the king's command," into an instrument of class power directed against king, court, and the barons themselves. We still await the final word from Professor Notestein on the actualities of this process by which, first, parliament revolutionized its relations with the crown, and, second, the House of Commons seized the political initiative from the king's councillors and the House of Lords.[12] But that a constitutional revolution was being worked is not in doubt; the only question by the 1640's was whether the *de facto* revolt of the Commons could be accepted by the monarchy and the feudality.

Finally, and most immediately our concern, there is the institutional church. We have no great space to consider it as an institution. But again we are fortunate, for the brilliant recent monograph by Christopher Hill enlightens us about all of the key problems of the church as an institution; it is a work that supplements, and corrects, the labors of R. G. Usher for the Elizabethan church.[13] The dominating institutional problem of the national Protestant church in England (as, in a way, it had been the dominant institutional problem of the Roman Catholic Church everywhere since the thirteenth century) was money. "The root of all evil" to the preachers; but more certainly the root of the church's weakness. The hierarchy of the national Protestant church were faced by an economic crisis: ecclesiastical livings were overwhelmingly in the control of laymen, a control sanctified in the law and sacrificing to personal economic ends the income from manors needed to finance a godly, preaching ministry. To end pluralism, nonresidency, and simony, to reform the petty and antagonizing tyrannies of parish economies, the hierarchy needed, as Laud clearly saw, to recover these lay impropriations. But any such effort at economic reform of the church was opposed by common law and parliament. Thus the hierarchy of the church were forced by economic circumstances into ever-closer ties with the monarchy. Here alone in the state they could get support for the sort of radical economic reform proposed by Archbishop Laud. Socially, the bishops were allied

---

[12] See J. E. Neale, *Elizabeth I and her Parliaments* (2 vols.; 1953-1957) and Wallace Notestein, *The Winning of the Initiative by the House of Commons* (1924).

[13] Christoper Hill, *Economic Problems of the Church* (Oxford, 1956); R. G. Usher, *The Reconstruction of the English Church* (2 vols.; New York, 1910).

with the gentry and townsmen: typically, they were recruited from bright university scholars whose families were farmers or tradesmen. Thus their social prestige was wholly a function of their bureaucratic position. They were never peers, never "blood" cousins to royalty. But as "new men," ambitious men, climbing the treacherous paths to preferment, their socially middle-class character was often altered by the ancient tradition of working with the king (the church was of course still an integral part of government), and by these more recently compelling pressures for increased church income to meet the universal cry for more able and dedicated parish rectors.

And, though we believe it to be intrinsically more emotionally integrated and ambitious than the Catholic mind which preceded it, the Protestant mind, because of its unusual sensitivity to this world of man's history, because of its magnificent gamble on the saint-in-the-world, was peculiarly the victim of these restless, relentless, constantly accelerating patterns of social change in England. The great divines, Perkins, Hall, Hooker, Adams, Donne and their fellows, of this last epoch of religious genius, labored mightily and brilliantly to surmount with imagination the chasm dividing the ethos of gospel Christianity from the emerging world of capitalism, statism, and science. Above all, they struggled to prevent the new economics, the new politics, the "new Philosophy which calls all in doubt," from resulting in secularism. To keep all the new problems thrown up by the new history relevant to the Christian drama of salvation in eternity—this is the basic, the ultimate concern of the Protestant mind confronting the crucial developments of the seventeenth century. What great talents, very hard work, absolute dedication could do to salvage this relevance which Catholic institutionalism had forfeited, the Protestant divines of England did, and did splendidly. Their failures, their final and total defeat, are one sure measure of the revolution which has created our world.

# I I I

Our conclusion concerning the revolutionary impact of English religion is in many ways a negative one. On the one hand, we feel that few of the critical issues facing Cromwell and the revolutionaries were created by Protestantism; nor did Protestantism have solutions for their problems. Protestantism (and "puritanism") had no ecclesiastical polity to recommend (John Milton or Richard Baxter illustrates this indecision, based primarily upon indifference, as does the whole subsequent history of Protestant confessions); no political or constitutional recommendations; no positive economic theory. The great issues of the revolution—political liberalism, imperialism, legalism, democracy, nationalism, capitalism, and so on—were overwhelmingly issues of that middle-class and lay culture which had developed so precociously in England.

Yet the great revolution led by Pym and Cromwell and fought by inspired common folk (no *lumpenproletariat* these) would have been impossible in a Catholic England. For, to attack openly and successfully the most ancient and sanctified institutions and traditions in the land required, in a religious age, psychological resources that no Catholic culture could have provided. A good argument could be made for the fact that revolution in Catholic France was long delayed by the necessity for a secular idealism because a Catholic Christian society could not produce revolutionaries who were not also heretics. In the seventeenth century, the powerful and respectable classes who were to be leaders of revolution had to feel that God was on their side.[14] Protestantism made it *possible* for the English gentry to revolt against their church and state not as heretics, but as the godly representatives of Protestant orthodoxy and Christian conscience.

The contribution of Protestantism to the revolution of 1640-1660 was more positive than this, but, as we shall see, it was almost entirely unintended as a contribution. The situation in 1640 in law, economics, social relations, and politics was potentially so explosive, so much revolution was thrusting up through the crust of convention and status, that open defiance of court and nobility required only those deep reserves of motivation which religion provided for seventeenth-century man. A psychol-

14 See B. C. Poland, *French Protestantism and the French Revolution* (Princeton, 1957), for the insignificance of Protestant psychology in the ultimate revolution against the old regime. The Frondeurs of 1649-1652 lacked a religious rationale fully as much as they lacked a constitutional program and skillful leadership.

ogy of asseveration and daring was needed, passion and a conviction of Truth were required, martyrs and heroes must be forth-
coming from inferior social classes. Many of the very basic elements of the Protestant mind we shall be analyzing were the stuff
of this historically momentous spirit of defiance: the Protestant idea of sainthood, the idea of vocation, the authority of
conscience.

The Protestant pulpit generated moral earnestness and the
duty and courage of decision. More important, in aggressively
disintegrating the moral authority of class codes, especially the
codes of chivalric and ecclesiastic hierarchy, Protestantism left
the ruling elites without their ancient and ultimately essential
monopoly of the Christian Ideal Type, without control of the
cultural heroes of English society. The prowess, loyalty, and
largesse of chivalry, the asceticism, isolation, and sacramental
magic of church, were defiantly and totally rejected for the
Worker in a Calling. The social and political result, however
unintended, was to undermine the sanctity of existing social
privilege and to open the way for a new class code which could,
and would, appropriate for its own this central dogma of the
calling as the determinant of social prestige.

Above all, for the needs of a revolutionary social effort, the
saint of Protestantism "kann nicht anders"; his egotism is absolute in its relation to a personal, transcendent God. He appre-
hends God not mediatorially through an institutional church
and its traditions, but directly through Scripture and experience.
Nor is he isolated like the Catholic mystic who experiences God
directly; his experience is as social, as communicable as it is
authoritative. The resulting self-confidence and intense moral
commitment created the psychological stamina needed for revolution in England. Cromwell is the ultimate, the superb lay product of that psychology confronting the revolutionary decisions
thrown up by generations of economic and social change now
brought to crisis. A Catholic mind could not conceivably have
dared the ego to challenge church, traditions, and status. But
Cromwell is a Protestant saint. Neither monk nor priest nor
knight, but a Protestant Man, whole, intense, activist, pious as
the Elect, a citizen by calling, relying in terrible, challenging

moments of great decision upon the counsel of other citizen-saints, and decisively upon his conscience. He is thus splendidly above existing social fiat, yet intimately related to his fellow revolutionaries. Even thought differences immediately arise amongst them, the godly share the confidence in conscience and decision which makes revolutionary activity possible and successful.

*PART I*

THE BASIC STRUCTURE OF THE ENGLISH

PROTESTANT MIND

"Honour not the malice of thine enemy so much, as to say, thy misery comes from him: Dishonour not the complexion of the times so much, as to say, thy misery comes from them; justifie not the Deity of Fortune so much, as to say, thy misery comes from her; Finde God pleased with thee, and thou hast a hook in the nostrils of every Leviathan, power cannot shake thee, Thou hast a wood to cast into the waters of Marah, the bitternesse of the times cannot hurt thee, thou hast a Rock to dwell upon, and the dream of a Fortune which cannot overturn thee. But if the Lord be angry, he needs no Trumpets to call in Armies, if he doe but . . . hisse and whisper for the flye, and the Bee, there is nothing so little in his hand, as cannot discomfort thee, discomfit thee, dissolve and pour out, attenuate and annihilate the very marrow of thy soul."

—John Donne, *L Sermons* (1649), 170

# CHAPTER 1

## THE ENGLISH PROTESTANT

## AND HUMAN NATURE

"And will God say to me, *Confide fili*, My son be of good cheer, thy sins are forgiven thee? Does he mean all my sins? He knows what original sin is, and I do not, and will he forgive me sin in that root, and sin in the branches, original sin, and actual sin too? He knows my secret sins, and I do not, will he forgive my manifest sins, and those sins too? . . . Will his mercy dive into my heart, and forgive my sinful thoughts there? . . . Will he contract himself into himself and meet me there, and forgive my sins against himself, and scatter himself upon the world, and forgive my sins against my neighbor, and imprison himself in me, and forgive my sins against my self?"

—JOHN DONNE, *Works*, II, 67

### I. The Problem of Salvation

A TASK OF PECULIAR DIFFICULTY confronts the student of Christianity who, lacking the Christian's predispositions to belief, attempts to define either the viewpoint of Christianity as a whole toward the basic problems of human nature and destiny, or even the viewpoint of a particular Christian group toward a particular problem or set of problems. To be sure, the pronouncements contained in any Christian doctrine tend, by virtue of their religious character, to be insistent and emphatic; and yet, as soon as one begins to analyze many if not most of these pronouncements, one finds that they exist not as granitic structures of demonstration and logical consistency, but as mere points of argumentative attachment in a sea of tensions and contradictions. For every thesis there is an equally valid antithesis, and however thoroughly Christianity as faith may appear to the believer to have accomplished the needed synthesis, Christianity as logic or philosophy appears, to the neutral observer, still to hover uncertainly between two antagonistic poles. In the historic succession of doctrines and sects, Christian philosophy may move nearer one pole or the other but it never succeeds in eliminating either or in truly reconciling both.

Thus Christianity has combined, with more or less effective camouflaging of the resultant inconsistencies, two contradictory views of human beings and human nature: the view that adulates and the view that condemns. On the side of adulation, the anthropocentrism of Christianity is so apparent as barely to require comment: a universe whose whole focus and rightful overseer is man; a God whose last and chief masterwork man has been, and whose very superiority to His human product is a further guarantee of that human's superiority over all or almost all other forms of creation; an eternity of time in which the human soul may luxuriate in its existence and self-consciousness, forever immune to the dreaded power which follows all ordinary forms of life and strikes them into dust at last. These expectations, as baldly stated here, might well be products of an egomaniac's dream, and yet they are all supported by Christianity as basic tenets, not subject to doubt or dispute in any area of the orthodox Christian complex. Only the devastating inquiries of science, and the reevaluation of man's place in nature they have compelled, have brought in recent times a certain awareness of the extent of the presumption involved.

This adulatory view by man of himself is, then, one of the poles of an important—perhaps the most important or basic—tension of ideas in Christianity. Its great significance as a concept is perhaps more fully realized when it is pointed out that the presumptions and demands which constitute it are best summed up in Christian terms by that single, extremely focal word, salvation. All that man's superiority to ordinary nature ultimately means, all that his godlikeness means, all that his triumph over death means—what more or less is this than man's salvation? Salvation from nature, salvation as supernature—is this not the true substance of man's dream of glory for himself?

But not all men are destined to be saved. This, too, is a fundamental tenet of every form of Christianity which can be rated as orthodox. Indeed, it is generally assumed in Christianity, and is the unequivocal judgment of the Gospels, that only the few are to be saved while the many will be damned. On the other side of the hope which saves, therefore, is the fear which condemns. Or, one might simply say that on the other side of life is death, for again and again in Christian literature damnation is presented in the figure of death, just as salvation is presented in the figure of eternal life. Thus we are met at the very threshold of the Christian structure of ideas by that primary anxiety which springs from the tragic fact that, born to self-consciousness, man is also born to die.

Man was not meant to die, however; he was not created to die. Having been fashioned after the image of God, he was intended instead to participate fully in God's own immortality. After this fashion speaks the hope in Christianity, for it is most feasible to assert the ultimate saving of some on the basis of God's original intention that salvation should appertain to all. But how has it come to pass that damnation is also a factor, and the dominant factor—since most men will be damned—in human destiny? How has death gained its empire over man? The answer is quick and definite: death happened, damnation happened because man through sin rejected the gift of life which God had given him. Man killed himself, as it were. And from this point we move, in the Christian system, into the extensive exposition of the nature and gravity of human sin.

Damnation and death with its linkage to sin on the one side, and salvation and life with its linkage to virtue on the other—cannot the entire mass of Christian philosophy be ultimately reduced to these two great antagonisms? The problem for the Christian becomes, then, the avoidance of the first and the achieving of the second. The choice is simple, but the way is hard. It is hard because it lies essentially beyond the capacity of human nature, which is hopelessly corrupted by sin and given to death. It can only be found and followed to the end through the interposition of supernature: the interposition of God. No branch of Christianity asserts or assumes that human nature can find its own salvation. Rather, in all men, whether they are numbered among the virtuous few or the wicked many, their human nature, insofar as it is human or natural, is to some degree an enemy or an obstacle to salvation. For man in the Christian view stands at a half-way point between the natural and the supernatural universes and partakes of both realms; he is a composite of the spirit which reaches for life and of the flesh which is hopelessly mired in death. The exact character of the relationship between flesh and spirit, the exact degree of separation and antagonism and the exact intensity of the conflict may be variously formulated in various schools of Christianity, but always there is the acknowledgement that man must somehow transcend what he observes to be his nature if he is to achieve what he desires; for nature perishes and man desires eternal life.

By the most direct of logical pathways the dualism in the Christian view of human nature leads to the fundamental and focal problem of salvation, and the doctrinal and institutional differences in Christianity may all be expected to reflect or involve some difference of approach or emphasis within this basic area of concern. The major difference in Western Christendom, that between Roman Catholicism and Protestantism, could be entirely subsumed, were a broad enough sweep of related matters undertaken, under this single heading of salvation: the degree and kind of its availability and the most suitable or reliable techniques for attaining to it. Therefore, before proceeding into a more detailed analysis of the subject matter of this chapter—human nature in its religious or salvation-seeking character as defined by English Protestantism—it appears desirable to consider briefly some of the general qualities which distinguish a Protestant from a Roman Catholic doctrine of salvation.

The Protestant attack upon the Roman Catholic doctrine of salvation may be initially organized in terms of two complexes of impulse: (1) Protestant revivalism and (2) Protestant personalism. Moved by the first impulse, the Protestant condemned the Roman Catholic for making the road to salvation misleadingly broad and easy, for opening it so wide and smoothing it so thoroughly that rather than being an incline to heaven it became a chute to hell. Moved by the second impulse, the Protestant condemned the Roman Catholic for an opposite error: for artificially obstructing and narrowing that essential highway of the soul with ritualistic minutiae, discriminatory distinctions of ecclesiastical rank, and arbitrary counsels of perfection.

Viewed from any objective standpoint Protestantism must be acknowledged to be a species of Christian revivalism—a cry for the intensification and purification of religious belief and practice so that the way to salvation might be more surely found and maintained. The repeated cycle of decline and revival is well established in Christianity. Decline from an initial level of expectation and achievement is, it would appear, inevitable in a movement which at once made enormous and entirely personal demands upon the moral and spiritual capacities of an individual and, at the same time, tried to embrace the universe in a formalized and compulsive institutional framework. The life and function of a religious faith is the provision to believers of an escape from death and a relative assurance of salvation. What is the essence of religious decline, in consequence, but the cheapening of this reward so that it becomes available to the adherent at a lower rate of exchange? In the institutionalized faith, whether Christian or non-Christian, this lower rate of exchange is usually or principally expressed by two kinds of currency, both readily comprehensible and measurable and both admirably attesting the loyalty to itself which an institution must have if it is to survive: the first currency is ritual, the proper performance of the ceremonies of the cult; and the second is obedience to a more-or-less limited list of commandments for correct or moral behavior in the society with which the religion is affiliated. The concern in both instances is for outward conformity, and while the serviceability of religion as an important part of a system of social control is altogether retained, there is, intellectually or ethically, a kind of return to the compulsive and mechanical procedures which are the hallmark of religions of early civilizations and primitive cultures.

The church, moreover, as an institution and an agency of control, is to some degree directly antagonistic to overenthusiasm or overintensity of religious zeal. It becomes a vested interest among other vested interests, and its leadership becomes integrated with the political, economic, and social leadership of society. The

whole structure presses toward stability and toward the routin-
ized and bureaucratized processes which best assure stability. It
is a parodox not without validity in the history of Christianity
that the more vigorous the institution, the less vigorous the faith.

This is the pattern of decline in Christianity, but there is
equally a pattern of revival. And if the first may in general
be attributed to the weight of Christian institutionalization, the
second may be attributed to the living doctrine which, despite
all, continues to survive beneath such institutional incrustation.
The appeal of the Christian revival is always more or less the
same: away from the relaxed to the intense, away from the mechanical to the vital, away from the outward, which may have its
inward association, to the inward, which must have its outward
fruit. And the same, too, is the model which the Christian revival
holds up for emulation—the vigor of Christian life in the Gospel image, the intensity of faith that brought forth the martyrs
and built the catacombs.

It has often been pointed out that in the West much of the
force of this recurrent revivalism was, at least for a long period,
channeled off into especially-designated circuits of religious life
and thus safely contained within the dominant institution of the
Roman Catholic Church. A double standard of Christian living,
presumed to coincide considerably with the institutional division
between lay and cleric, was consciously defined and accepted.
Though it remained a possible attainment for both orders of
Christian society, it is hard to avoid the conclusion, on examining the institutional structure and the ideology of medieval Roman Catholicism, that salvation was conceived to be more immediately and, proportionally, more commonly within the range
of achievement of the clergy, both secular and regular, than of
the laity. Vibrancy of religious life was not entirely lacking in
lay circles, but the masterly layering of religious life which the
Roman Catholic Church accomplished did assure that most of
the dramas of revival and decline would be played out within
clerical confines and would, as a consequence, be less a threat to
the institution as a whole.

Where many or most of the nominal adherents of the medieval
Christian church are concerned, it is no doubt unjustified to

speak of movements of either religious revival or decline. These people existed on the lower strata of a civilization which was itself still new and uncertainly expanding in much of Europe, and the pattern of their lives and thus the nature of their religious comprehensiveness were essentially primitive. They had nowhere from which to decline and they did not yet possess the cultural resources to be stimulated by the subtler and profounder aspects of Christianity into religious revival. Hence, when seeking sources for the great Christian revival of the sixteenth and seventeenth centuries, in both its Protestant and its Catholic phases, one should perhaps look first to the simple thousand-year spread of civilization which lay behind it, and should speak not so much of revival as of an initial and fresh awakening to some of the gifts which that civilization had to offer.

The second characteristic quality of Protestantism—what we have called its personalism—is, in a sense, only an aspect or a corollary of its revivalism. At any rate, the viewpoints involved are intimately intertwined and both work together to give Protestantism its assertive vigor and sharp combative edge. As Protestant revivalism may be summed up, albeit crudely, in Luther's denial of the doctrine of indulgences, so Protestant personalism may be summed up in Luther's insistence on the priesthood of all believers; and as Protestant revivalism attacked the Roman Catholic double standard of Christian living at the lower level— the undue relaxation and cheapening of the Christian message to the laity—so Protestant personalism attacked the same double standard at its upper level—the undue valuation and exclusiveness of the Christian message to the clergy.

In pursuing this latter argument, Protestant personalism brought under attack as well the mediatorial position and function of the Roman Catholic clergy. The Roman Catholic conception of the priest was seen as a denial both of a privilege and a responsibility which rightfully belonged to the whole Christian community. As no man could achieve salvation for another, so no man could presume, by virtue of an office, to intervene between the salvation-seeking soul and its Creator. Each Christian individual must be his own priest, therefore; he must make his own spiritual oblations and go to God for and by himself, unhindered by institutional obstacles and, in the long run, un-helped by institutional aids.

The device of the double standard, then, which had in one period been a source of stability and unity to Roman Catholicism, now became, by an irony of history, a principal basis for disturbance and schism. For both Protestant revivalism and Protestant personalism asserted the single standard for all Christian men. As there was one salvation, so there was only one way to it. And because of the combination of social and intellectual forces from which Protestantism emerged, this way had to be equally accessible to all human beings in all stations and performing all the functions of the life of a very complex society. The greatest intensity of religious life to be achieved in all the ordinary routines of society—this is the Protestant proclamation, and it was at once an opportunity and a challenge.

The peaks of religious experience were made accessible to great groups of people who had hitherto, by the necessities of their occupations, been excluded from the endeavor to attain them. Here lay the opportunity. But these peaks remained as truly peaks and as difficult of conquest as they had ever been. Here lay the challenge. It was from this new or, perhaps more accurately, revived need to state the utmost requirements of religious life in terms compatible with the performance of ordinary duties in the world that the formulation of the Protestant doctrine of spiritual life in the world arose. Different though this doctrine was from that established in medieval Roman Catholicism, there was no real break in it with the universal Christian assumption that those who wish truly to live with God must, to some extent or in some way, live separate from the world; that even while they are in the world, they cannot be entirely of it. The world still remained, in the Protestant view, primarily a place of trial and sojourn for the God-directed soul. The very activism of the Protestant—indeed, his refusal to cut himself off institutionally from the world—creates a pressure of special intensity toward interiorizing religious life, toward so profound a deepening and strengthening of the life of the spirit that the inward may not only stand as a bulwark against the outward but may also penetrate and sanctify it. Thus the test of the validity of religious conviction becomes not so much a question of what one does as of how or why ones does it.

At the end, as at the beginning, of this brief analysis of Christianity as a complex of ideas about man and man's fate, we therefore encounter another polarization or tension of principles. But we can readily see that this last dichotomy between a realm of worldly trial and a realm of godly security (and it remains a dichotomy—still a division between a City of Man and a City of God—even in the most world-penetrating forms of Protestantism) is a further aspect or reflection of one of those few great dichotomies lying at the base of Christianity from which there is no escape for any orthodox form of the faith and to which all Christian argument and doctrine may finally be reduced. For the division between a City of Man and a City of God is merely a particular formulation of that division between nature and supernature or between death and salvation which all Christianity acknowledges.

## II. Sin

We turn now from the breadth of this introductory discussion to focus on the religious teachings which comprise the essence of English Protestantism as it existed during the seven decades under scrutiny. But the larger context can never be forgotten. It will always be necessary to refer for purposes of comparison and perspective to Protestantism in general, Roman Catholicism in general, and ultimately to Christianity in general. As always in human ideas and affairs, the part cannot be understood unless the whole is also to some extent encompassed.

We shall begin first with English Protestant ideas about man as an entity in himself and in relationship to God—the ideas and problems which are central to religious philosophy, since they lead straightway into the question of man's salvation. These ideas form, after all, a necessary basis for the less directly and completely religious concepts of English Protestantism about man's relationship to his fellows and about the structure and functions of man's society. It is obvious that in the religious frame of reference what man as the child of God may signify is of far greater moment than what man as the child of man entails. Three terms, sin, faith, and predestination, serve as convenient headings under which to include and channel English Protestant pronouncements on human nature and the problem of man's salvation. Each one of these terms, in addition, designates a sharp and definite point of difference between English Protestantism and the Roman Catholicism of the period.

A stronger statement of the negative view of human nature— of its essential slavery to sin—is recognized to be one of the classifying characteristics of Protestantism. It may be wondered why this should be so. Why should a new form of Christianity, intensely proselytizing in its purposes, include as one of its qualities an especially dark and despairing interpretation of man's natural capacities? Is not such an interpretation more likely to repel than to attract? And yet, as we have seen, the negative view is inherent in orthodox Christianity. It is a pole for one of the tensions which we have been considering and, as such, can never be eliminated as long as Christianity remains wholly true to its Gospel origins. Its intensification in Protestantism is in part simply a consequence or an accompaniment of what may be called Protestantism's intensification of Christianity; this in turn is a consequence or an accompaniment of Protestantism's quality as a movement of Christian revival.

There is, in addition, Protestantism's specific quarrel with Roman Catholicism's double standard in the pursuit of salvation and with the relaxation of demands presumed to be characteristic of the lower level of this double standard—the level at which the majority of Christians had of necessity to live. At this lower level, techniques—rituals and devices of automatic performance—had, in the Protestant view, been substituted for the wholesale inner regeneration and the rigorous outer discipline by which alone the salvation of any one in any position of life could be achieved. To Protestant critics, Roman Catholic errors in this category appeared to have a twofold origin: they arose, first, from overoptimism regarding the ability of human nature to achieve its own salvation, and, second, from overconfidence regarding the effectiveness of institutional devices in the stimulation of the process. Thus to assert the profundity of human sin and the magnitude of human depravity was to strike a decisive blow against this entire structure of Catholic institutionalism and this conscious or unconscious deception of the salvation seeking.

Yet another point of reference and disagreement for Protestantism's assertions on sin and human nature was provided by the Thomistic analysis of the subject. The achievement of St. Thomas in this as in other areas of philosophy consisted principally in the brilliance of his ability to obscure and compose antitheses by constructing from them an ordered hierarchy of lesser and greater values. One after the other of the tensions which have been cited as inherent in Christianity the Angelic Doctor succeeded to a large extent in philosophically taming, as it were, so that one element of opposition moved in docile subordination to the other. Thus St. Thomas matched in ideology something of the ordered sequence of subordinate and superior which characterized the massive institution he served. His patterning of human nature follows closely the Aristotelian, of course. Both involve first, the separation of the base from the noble elements, the animal from the human, the physical from the mental, the sensitive and emotional from the rational, the fleshly from the spiritual; and, second, the construction from these ingredients of a three-fold division of human nature into vegetative, sensitive, and rational levels, or simply into body, soul, and spirit. Thus an ordered sequence is arranged, stretching, as it were, from earth to heaven and bringing a kind of end to the conflict between nature and supernature by linking them together in a single organic relationship. Sin itself is integrated by the Thomistic system into human nature, and into God's universe as well, as being in both instances the necessary darkness to set off the light of virtue.

Protestantism certainly does not altogether deny this integrating or unifying effort, which is, to be sure, as much a part of Christianity as the dualisms we have been considering. For since one God is the creator of all things in the Christian universe, all distinctions and oppositions must ultimately be encompassed by any Christian philosophy in this single source of creativity and law. What we are dealing with again are differences of emphasis and not of content. The primary purpose of St. Thomas was to reconcile antagonistic principles and to synthesize discordances, so that the harmonious structure of Christian philosophy might match and support the harmonious structure of Christian institutionalism. Being universal, the Christian church was expected to embrace the sinner and the damned—to rest, in fact, on the basis of the sinner and the damned even while it provided a stimulus to virtue and a guide to salvation for the few who were able to benefit from such aid. The watchword was stability and the pattern was hierarchy. Though its massive foundations rested on the earth, the pyramid moved upward by firm and graduated steps until its point was lost to ordinary human view in the clouded immensity of God's own realm. Thomistic philosophy likewise was universal and graduated—a pyramid of ideas to match the institutional pyramid.

Protestantism, in rejecting the pyramidal institution of Roman Catholicism, rejected also much of the pyramidal philosophy with which that institution was peculiarly associated. It put in the forefront of its concern not synthesis but conflict, not the ordered sequence of elements in human nature but the antagonism between flesh and spirit. It did this certainly in part because its principal purpose, at least initially, was not to support an established institutionalism but to break from one. It emphasized, therefore, not the harmony of God's universe but the great disharmony between good and evil, not the graduated series of little differences which bound nature to supernature, but the infinitude of distinction which separated salvation from damnation. It emphasized sin. And it sought by these means to shock the indifferent and to stimulate the slothful that all Christians might endeavor to their utmost to achieve the inheritance of salvation which assuredly waited for the righteous. It emphasized sin, in short, because its first purpose as a religion was not to build or maintain an institution but to evangelize.

Pronouncements concerning human nature which come from the English pulpit during the period surveyed in this study are fairly consistently Protestant in tone, in accordance with the pattern of Protestantism delineated above. On the sinfulness of

man, the thoughts which Calvin in particular had developed
on the subject and even the phrases he had used are echoed
again and again in these sermons. Thus the doctrine that total
depravity is the natural state of man may be said to have been
at this time the orthodoxy of English Protestantism. Richard
Sibbes declares: ". . . let us labour to have as deepe conceits in
our understandings, as we can of that mystery of sinfulnesse
that is in us, and that mysterie of misery. It is not to be conceived, the cursed state we are in by nature. It is not to be conceived what a depth of corruption is in this heart of ours, and
how it issues out in sinfull thoughts, and speeches, and actions
every day."[1]

Joseph Hall observes more succinctly that "man is nothing
but defect, error, ignorance, injustice, impotence, corruption."[2]
And James Ussher remarks that human beings are all by nature
"stinking corpses" who "go in that broad wide way that leads
to damnation" and are dead and damned in their "foul and
filthy condition."[3] Quotations of this type and spirit could be
multiplied many times from the literature. Some English theologians (Perkins and Bolton, for instance) may spend more
time and passion on the subject, and others (Hooker and Andrewes) less, but an opposition viewpoint can hardly be said
to exist, except perhaps by implication from certain other arguments.[4]

The Protestant, to be sure, emphasizes sin not pessimistically
or for the sake of sin as such, but evangelically or for the sake
of salvation: so that the Christian soul may be adequately aware
of the strength of the enemy within himself which he must
successfully combat if he is to attain his goal. Since man, as he
lives in the flesh and in the world, is an amalgam of two an-

[1] Richard Sibbes, *The Fountaine Opened* (1638), pp. 39-40.
[2] Joseph Hall, *The Works* (4 vols.; 1628-1662), IV, 108.
[3] James Ussher, *Eighteen Sermons Preached in Oxford* (1659), pp. 62-63.
[4] The greater relative frequency with which the names of certain divines appear
throughout this study (Perkins is probably the most frequently-cited author) is
a function merely of the greater volume and extensiveness of their commentary.
We have always been very careful, however, to use quotations which are typical of
opinion among all English Protestants, and when differences of thought or emphasis have been detected, we have always noted it and tried to label the deviant
positions as accurately as possible ("puritan," "Arminian," "conservative," "separatist," etc.).

tagonistic principles, of nature and supernature, he is hopelessly divided within himself and can know no peace but only inevitable and unceasing warfare. The typically Protestant, or, even more narrowly, the typically Calvinist concern for this conflict is fully reflected in English theological writings. At least two entire treatises are devoted to the subject: William Perkins's "Of the combat of the flesh and spirit" and the fourth and last part of John Downame's *The Christian Warfare*, which is similarly titled, "The Conflict Betweene the Flesh and the Spirit."[5] Downame carefully defines his terms. The word flesh, he states, denotes "those reliques of corruption, which after regeneration, doe still remaine in us . . . or that part of a Christian which is unregenerate and continually fighteth against the spirit."[6] Spirit, on the other hand, is "the new man, or the regenerate part of the Christian, which is nothing else but a created qualitie of wisedome, holinesse and righteousness, whereby we are in the whole man renewed unto God's image; which continually fighteth against, and in the end over-commeth the flesh with all the lusts thereof."[7] He takes care to distinguish between his Protestant view of the nature of the combatants in this warfare and the "erroneous conceit of the Papists, who by the flesh understand the body, and the sensuall facultie" and by the spirit "the intellectual faculties, the minde, reason . . . and so affirme this to be the fight betweene the flesh and spirit, when as the body and sensitive parts doe rebell . . . against the understanding and reason. . . ."[8] Ussher specifically concurs with Downame's definition of the distinction between flesh and spirit (the flesh, he says, is "the corruption of our nature wherein we were borne and conceived"); he notes, as does Downame, that this corruption continues to exist in the Christian "so long as we carry the outward flesh about us," and to obstruct and spoil the workings of the spirit which God gives to the regenerate.[9]

[5] William Perkins, *The Workes* (3 vols.; 1612-1613), I; John Downame, *The Christian Warfare* (1634).

[6] Downame, *ibid*, p. 1018.

[7] *Ibid.*, p. 1019.

[8] *Ibid.*, p. 1023.

[9] Ussher, *A Body of Divinitie* (1645), p. 336.

Not that "natural man" or the "flesh" is altogether denied by English Protestantism the possession of positive attributes. It has already been observed many times that, caught as it is between the poles of numerous antitheses, orthodox Christian argumentation tends to be a complex of contradictions. English Protestantism certainly contains its full share of such ambivalences, and one of these we encounter here. Ussher makes a clear statement of the two-fold orientation of the Protestant view of human nature or of "natural man": "Taking nature (in the common sense of Scripture) for that hereditary corruption that cleaveth to all the sons of Adam . . . no good worke hath any ground or help from nature, but is altogether contrary thereto. . . . But if we understand by nature . . . the created abilities of soule and body, as the light of reason, liberty of the will, motion of the bodily members, etc. we acknowledge nature not to be the principall mover or guide . . . but the things moved and guided by grace in well doing."[10]

Perkins describes "natural man" as a completely functioning compound of soul and body in whom may be present "all the ornaments of man, yet so as without grace: such as are, strength of bodie, and minde, memorie, knowledge of arts and sciences, civill policie and vertues, as Justice, Prudence, Temperance, discretion to discerne what is mete to be done, what not. . . ."[11] A distinction must be drawn, Perkins emphasizes, between nature, which "is from God" and in itself is good, and the corruption of nature, which is owing to man's fall; these two, though they "may be indeede distinguished . . . cannot now be separated." It is a sin, therefore, to be a "natural man," "not because a man hath nature in him . . . but because his whole nature, is tainted with originall sinne."[12]

One of the valid bases for differentiation between Protestantism and the officially, if not popularly dominant stream of Roman Catholic theology, represented by the works and viewpoint of St. Thomas Aquinas,[13] is the greater valuation placed by Ro-

---

[10] Ussher, *op.cit.,* p. 338.     [11] *Works,* III, 574.     [12] *Ibid.*

[13] We are dealing here with another of the unavoidable contradictions in orthodox Christianity, and all the specific theologies are relative positions along a common line of argument. Thus St. Thomas Aquinas begins his *Summa Theologica* (I, q. 1, a. 1, c.) with the admission that the truths of Christianity are

man Catholicism on the efficacy of reason as an aid in achieving religious truth and personal salvation. Whereas Thomistic Catholicism tends to except reason from the corruption of human nature, or at least to put it in a special category, Protestantism in general and English Protestantism in particular conceive, as we have seen, that all human capacities and talents are of the flesh fleshly and share in the same burden of sin. Downame specifically attacks Catholic theologians on this issue and declares that they unduly "magnifie and extoll" the intellectual faculties.[14]

In any discussion of the ancient controversy on the relative contributions of faith and reason to securing and maintaining doctrinal soundness, English Protestantism insists upon its unqualified preference for faith. Lancelot Andrewes writes: "The Manichees held that error, that by cunning and reason we should come to God and not by faith; which opinion is next unto atheism. . . . Now then we must prove that faith is the best way, and reason the worst." In defense of his position, Andrewes employs an argument which has certain obvious sociological consequences in terms of equalizing the opportunities for salvation among different ranks. "If by knowledge only and reason," he observes, "we could come to God, then none should come but they that are learned and have good wits, and so the way to God should be as if many should go one journey, and because some can climb over hedges and thorns, therefore the way should be made over hedges and thorns; but God hath made His way *viam regiam*, 'The King's Highway.' "[15] William Laud likewise explains that God has resolved "to bring mankind to their last happiness by faith, and not by knowledge, that so the weakest among men may have their way to blessedness open. And certain it is, that many weak men believe themselves into

---

ultimately founded in revelation and faith. Yet he immediately asserts as well that the entire area of sacred doctrine constitutes a science, indeed, the noblest of the sciences; in the understanding of it, accessible through study and argument, the highest wisdom consists. The emphasis, relative to Protestantism and even to other schools within the Roman Catholic tradition (the Franciscan, for example), is clearly intellectualistic.

[14] Downame, *op.cit.*, p. 1023.

[15] Lancelot Andrewes, *Works* (11 vols.; Oxford, 1841-1854), II, 21.

heaven and many over-knowing Christians lose their way thither
while they will believe no more than they can clearly know."[16]
Hall expresses a similar sentiment more succinctly: "The deepest philosopher that ever was (saving the reverence of the
Schools) is but an ignorant sot, to the simplest Christian."[17]

But the position of English Protestantism, relative to Thomistic Catholicism, is by no means absolutely derogatory of reason. It is most certainly not the position of the extreme non-
rationalists in the Christian tradition who follow Tertullian's
stubborn contention, *Credo quia impossible est.* Rather, it is
closer to the middle ground of Anselm's *Credo ut intelligam,*
and it finds considerable employment for reason as the hand-
maiden of faith. Moreover, cautiously but insistently, English
Protestant divines attack the validity of the miracle. While the
essential Gospel miracles are of course defended, the age of
miracles is declared to be decisively past. There is no longer
need for miracles because the Gospel is well and truly taught in
England, because Christians are now richly endowed with "reason and civility," and because "no hardness of heart is enough
to justify a toleration of these 'devout deceits' or 'holy lies' "
practiced by the Roman Catholic Church.[18] John Donne even
suspects that God would not stoop to miracles because "truly
nothing can be done against the order of nature."[19] Unhappily,
Protestant suspicion of miracles does not extend, except for
isolated cases, to a rejection of witchcraft, though injunctions
to caution in trial and judgment form a notable part of what
discussion of witchcraft there is.[20]

While vigorously maintaining the supremacy of God's gift
of faith over man's power of reason (as, in the long run, what
Christian creed does not?), English Protestantism insists with
equal stoutness that of man's natural capacities it is reason
which is the chief and best. Reason is conceived to be the natural

---

[16] William Laud, *The Works* (7 vols.; Oxford, 1847-1860), II, 120.

[17] Hall, *Works,* I, 35. Cf. John Donne, *Works* (6 vols.; 1839), II, 265; IV, 346.

[18] See Ussher, *op.cit.,* pp. 442-43; Perkins, *Works,* III, 37-38; 239; 249; Donne, *Works,* V, 82; Donne, *Essays in Divinity* (ed. A. Jessopp, 1855), p. 212.

[19] *Ibid.,* p. 203.

[20] See Ussher, *op.cit.,* p. 280; Perkins, *op.cit.,* pp. 608-643; Richard Greenham, *The Works* (1612), pp. 821-822, dissented on the validity of witchcraft.

basis, not only for knowledge or the pursuit of truth, but also for the light or law of nature or for conscience: for the natural ability, insofar as it existed, to choose between right and wrong. "In the understanding power of the soule," Robert Bolton observes, "there are two naturall and originally implanted habits. 1. One, whereby it is . . . moved . . . to assent to the first principles, which serve to the speculation of truth. . . . 2. Another, whereby it is inforced to allow the general notions and principles of doing of things . . . the rules and principles of well doing. . . . From whence . . . the whole decalogue of God's commandements is deduced. . . ."[21]

Indeed, we hear a good deal in these sermons about a "light of nature" by which all men are able to know and are held accountable for knowing certain primary facts of the universe (the fact, for instance, that there is a God) as well as the basic laws of right and wrong. "The light of nature," Perkins states, "is that light, which the view and consideration of the creatures both in generall and particular, affordeth unto man,"[22] and by it one may not only prove the existence of God but in accordance with its possession "every man is bound to know the law."[23] The same author further urges that, if one wishes to test the continuing validity of a judicial law drawn from the Old Testament, one should investigate to see "if it follow necessarily . . . from the light, principles, and conclusions of nature. . . . This law is more than Judiciall: for it is a Rule of common honestie: practised in those countries, by the light of nature, where the written law was never known. And things good and honest which nature teacheth, are morall and must be done."[24]

In a mood of controversy—he was involved in opposing what he considered to be the overdependence on Scripture by a faction in the Church of England—Richard Hooker makes what is perhaps the most emphatic statement in defense of reason and natural law in the literature. Reason he interprets, however, in what may be termed a humanistic rather than a scholastic

---

[21] Robert Bolton, *A Three-Fold Treatise* (1634), p. 69. For an interesting discussion of the relationship of Protestantism to science, see R. Hooykoos, "Science and Reformation," *Cahiers d'Histoire Mondiale,* III (1956), 109-38.

[22] Perkins, *Works,* II, 51.

[23] *Ibid.,* 5.      [24] *Ibid.,* 252.

fashion, as a force which offers a continuous and needed challenge to authority of all kinds, whether of learning or position. "For men to be tied and led by authority," he writes, "as it were with a kind of captivity of judgment, and though there be reason to the contrary not to listen unto it, but to follow like beasts the first in the herd, they know not nor care not whether, this were brutish. . . . 'Companies of learned men' be they never so great and reverend, are to yield unto Reason; the weight whereof is no whit prejudiced by the simplicity of his person which doth allege it, but being bound to be sound and good, the bare opinion of men to the contrary must of necessity stoop and give place."[25] On the specific issue of the authority of Scripture, he declares: ". . . the will of God which we are to judge our actions by, no divine in the world ever denied to be in part made manifest even by the light of nature and not by Scripture alone."[26] He proceeds further to assert the strength and importance of the law of nature, "which is an infallible knowledge imprinted in the minds of all the children of men, whereby both general principles for directing of human actions are comprehended, and conclusions derived from them; upon which conclusions groweth in particularity the choice of good and evil in the daily affairs of this life."[27]

Hooker felt it necessary to defend reason and the "light of nature" from certain types of attack within his own church; yet, were there not in English Protestantism as a whole a willingness to give these qualities a role of considerable significance as positive elements in human nature, there would be no problem of the virtuous heathen or the Christian hypocrite. "Let us take notice (for the shaming of many Christians)," Bolton admonishes, "of many noble and honest acts and endowments of many heathen men, which they attained by the rules of reason and precepts of moralitie."[28] Arthur Dent asserts that "Papists, Heathen Poets, and Philosophers" may exhibit "curtesie, kindnesse, good nourture, good nature . . . learning, wit, and pol-

[25] Richard Hooker, *The Works* (2 vols.; Oxford, 1890), I, *Ecclesiastical Polity*, Book II, Chapter vii, 5-6.
[26] Hooker, *Ecclesiastical Polity*, III, viii, 3.
[27] *Ibid.*, II, vii, 5-6.
[28] *op.cit.*, pp. 66-68.

licie."[29] The unregenerate, both pagan and Christian, may even excell some of the true children of God in such qualities, particularly as these concern affability and social graciousness.[30] Arthur Hildersam declares that "natural man" may actually be ethically indistinguishable from regenerate man.[31]

Thus "natural man" may be, in every formal sense of the word, a Christian—indeed, a Protestant Christian. "The Church is, then, *full*," Andrewes sadly acknowledges, "and (God knowes) *a few true hearers*: the rest are but a sort of Sermon-Hypocrites. . . . And of this Scenicall, theatricall, histrionicall godlinesse, there is a good store abroad in the world. . . ."[32]

Bolton, who divides the reprobate into three types, the notorious sinner, the "grosse hypocrite," and the "formall hypocrite," even claims for individuals in this last grouping some of the inward graces which might be thought appropriate only to the child of God. "For we suppose his heart [the heart of the formal hypocrite]," he declares, "to be seasoned with goodnesse of nature and civill honesty, to have tasted of the general graces of God's Spirit. . . . His heart will . . . be affrighted at . . . Atheisme, Cruelty, Drunkennesse, Adultery . . . but notwithstanding . . . it will let the imaginations loose to much idlenesse and vanity . . . but especially into the endless maze of worldly care and earthly-mindednesse."[33]

English Protestantism is agreed, therefore, that the "natural man," the reprobate, may go far in the practice of external virtue. With the aid of those sources of supernatural enlightenment, the Gospels and the ministry of the Word, he may even for a time become or seem to himself and to others a good Christian. But he does not achieve salvation; he can never achieve salvation. All the natural talents and virtues which man may possess cannot of themselves bring him what from the religious standpoint he desires most of all: eternal life. In themselves, moreover, they are appearances only, which serve to conceal and belie the underlying reality of sin. "A naturall man,"

29 Arthur Dent, *The Plaine Man's Path-way to Heaven* (1601), p. 17.
30 *Ibid.*, p. 22.
31 Arthur Hildersam, *CVIII Lectures Upon the Fourth of John* (1632), p. 174.
32 Andrewes, *XCVI Sermons* (1629), 232.
33 *The Workes* (4 vols.; 1631-1641), IV, 125.

John Preston writes, "may pay a certain debt of duetie and obedience to God, but he paies it in counterfeit coine that hath the stampe, and colour, and similitude of true coine, yet it consists . . . but of base mettall."[34] Hence civil honesty is "but glorious iniquite,"[35] and the virtues of the heathen, however considerable, are dismissed as "glorious sins, beautifull abominations."[36] Even the good that may be found in human nature, though limited in its scope and objectives, is not so much to be credited to human nature as such as to the guiding and restraining hand of God. Thomas Adams, who has asserted that the seeds of all sins are equally in all men because original sin is the material of all sins and all men alike are born in original sin, explains that the difference in the actual practice of sins arises "not from more or lesse corruption, but from more or lesse limitation." He continues: "God restraineth nature, but that is no thankes to nature. Something we ascribe to corporall constitution, something to civill education, something to secular vocation, something to nationall custome, something to rationall discretion, all to the limiting grace of God, that corrects nature from running into divers sinnes, without which, any man would commit any sinne, even the most horrid that ever the world brought forth. . . . There is not the same eruption in all, there is in all the same corruption. . . . This every man that knowes himselfe knowes to be true."[37]

And thus we have come full circle and return to the point at which we started—the dominance of sin in human nature. For whatever concessions may be made to human reason or to other of man's natural talents, it is certainly the consensus of the English Protestant pulpit of this period that human nature is of itself essentially dead and lost in sin. We doubt that stronger statements of this concept could be found anywhere in Christian argumentation. "Every man is by nature dead in sin as a loathsome carrion," Ussher writes.[38] "The nature of man . . . is the worst of all natures except the Devell," Dent declares, "yea,

[34] John Preston, *Sermons* (1630), 33.
[35] Downame, *op.cit.*, 34.
[36] *Op.cit.*, 18.
[37] Thomas Adams, *The Works* (1629), pp. 1187-1188.
[38] Ussher, *Divinitie*, p. 143.

worse than the nature of beasts."[39] "Loe sinfull is man in his whole race," Sebastian Benefield affirms, "sinfull in his conception, sinfull in his birth; in every deed, word, and thought wholly sinfull . . . by nature the vassall, and slave of sinne."[40]

## III. Faith

In the view of English Protestantism, the natural talents of man are not only insufficient for the accomplishment of salvation but insufficient even to aid materially in the process. Left to his own nature, corrupted by sin as it is, every man would infallibly perish and be damned. What force is it, then, which enters into this natural situation and preserves at least some of its participants from the death which by nature is the proper inheritance of all? From the standpoint of God, the giver, it is grace; from the standpoint of man, the receiver, it is faith—faith in God, and more specifically in Christ, the son of God, by whose resurrection the resurrection of the faithful is prefigured.

The concept that God's grace and man's faith are essentials of salvation—are, indeed, the only real essentials of salvation—is universal in all Christianity. One is really stating in another way the basic Christian proposition that man is an amalgam of nature and supernature and that, while nature dies, supernature, truly given, properly possessed, assures immortality. It is once again only differences of emphasis, which, logically speaking, are not great, that separate Protestantism and Catholicism on this issue. Relative to Catholicism, Protestantism emphasizes the externality of grace, its total dependence on God's will, and the internality of faith, its total dependence on an individual's personal rapport with God. In other terms: Protestantism, in the first instance, emphasizes predestination, while Catholicism gives a greater place to man's so-called free will in the acquisition of grace; in the second instance, Protestantism emphasizes faith as such, in its full and perhaps hidden inwardness, while Catholicism pays greater heed to the observable and measurable

[39] Dent, *A Pastime for Parents* (1606), pp. 31-32.
[40] Sebastian Benefield, *A Commentarie . . . of the Prophecy of Amos* (Oxford, 1613), p. 31.

productivity of works, both as indicators of faith and as efficacious aids to grace. Catholicism, in short, tends to build a
ladder of carefully marked degrees between nature and supernature,[41] while Protestantism notes the gulf and speaks primarily
of the needed wholesale leap or catching up between one realm
and the other. "Faith," writes Perkins, "is a supernaturall gift
of God in the minde, apprehending the saving promise with
all the promises that depend on it."[42] For Ussher, faith is
"nothing else but supernaturall action . . . of God in man."[43]
Since faith is so emphatically defined as the peculiar link between divinity and man, as the very embodiment in man of the
supernatural, it is little wonder that the English pulpit of this
period should with an almost unanimous voice assert the unqualified priority of faith as a cause or condition of justification,
and the unqualified priority of justification as a cause or condition of sanctification in the practice of good works.

A corollary of this doctrine of the absolute priority of faith
is the rejection of the merit of any works as such. We have already seen something of the character of this concept in discussing the English Protestant conviction of the fundamental
and ineradicable sinfulness of man and of all his natural acts.
Hooker summarizes the doctrine: "The best things we do have
somewhat in them to be pardoned. How then can we do anything meritorious and worthy to be rewarded? . . . We acknowledge a dutiful necessity of doing well, but the meritorious dignity of well-doing we utterly renounce."[44] Perkins pursues the
conscious quarrel with Roman Catholicism which is involved.
"The Popish Church," he writes, "placeth merits within man,
making two sorts thereof: the merit of the person, and the merit
of the worke." Adherents of English Protestantism, however,

---

[41] We encounter here simply another instance of the peculiar fascination of
Roman Catholic theology and philosophy with hierarchy and degrees. To the
extensiveness and vigor of this tendency the writings of St. Thomas Aquinas
stand as full and eloquent testimonials. There is no aspect of Thomistic philosophy—theological, metaphysical, ethical, or social—which is not permeated with
concern for establishing order on the basis of graded inequalities. For a statement
of the principle as applied to the whole structure of nature and the universe,
see Aquinas, *Summa Contra Gentiles*, Bk. III, ch. 71.

[42] *Works*, I, 124.

[43] *Divinitie*, p. 199.

[44] Hooker, *Works*, II, 609.

"renounce all personall merits, that is, all merits within the person of any meere man . . . And . . . renounce all merit of workes, that is all merit of any worke done by any meere man whatsoever."[45]

There is a much stronger tendency in Protestantism than in Thomistic Catholicism to think of the Pauline and Augustinian pattern of sudden conversion as a usual method of discovering one's spiritual destiny in life and of regeneration or a relatively immediate and total reorientation of life as the product of such conversion. The relatively personalistic or noninstitutional character of Protestantism is no doubt a factor in this as in so many other differences between the older and newer creed. The man who has found true and justifying faith is a "new creature," says Ussher;[46] he is "begotten again."[47] The very term "regenerate" signifies the rebirth through justifying faith from the death of sin to the life of godliness while still in the flesh and the world. "For as in the first birth," John Robinson declares, "the whole person is born again."[48]

And yet the English Protestant allows also for degrees of faith. He allows first, of course—as we have seen in our discussion of the Christian hypocrite—for a distinction between a common or temporary faith which does not save and a true faith which does. But there can be differences, too, within this saving faith, and these are essentially differences of strength or confidence. "Justifying faith," Perkins explains, "is a gift whereby we apprehend Christ and his benefits." Of this apprehension and hence of this faith there are two degrees, a weak and a strong, and it appears in the course of Perkins' argument that a "weak" faith, the mere "endeavour to apprehend," the "will to believe with an honest heart," is the best which the

45 *Works*, I, 574-75.
46 Ussher, *Eighteen Sermons*, p. 387.
47 Ussher, *ibid.*, p. 336.
48 John Robinson, *The Works* (3 vols.; 1851), I, 24-25. Robinson was probably the major intellectual among the separatists. He did brilliantly with the Leyden congregation and was later the admired preacher to the New England Mayflower group. We shall use him as an exponent of the left-wing of English Protestant thought because he shares, as most of the other separatists do not, the orthodox Calvinist theology of the English Church. In this sense, of course, the "puritans," insofar as they are purists, are theologically more removed from the separatists than is such a man as Donne, or even Laud!

majority of Christians can hope to attain in the life of the world.[49]

The saving quality of true faith, however, is not affected by its strength or weakness. The assurance is given again and again by English Protestant divines that a small amount of genuine faith suffices for salvation, and whole treatises (as Perkins' *Mustard Seed* and Sibbes's *Bruised Reede and Smoaking Flax*) are devoted to this exemplification of God's mercy to weak Christians.

When saving faith enters into human nature, it results in the regeneration or sanctification of that nature. The process consists of two parts, "Mortification, or dying unto sin," as Ussher states it, and "Vivification, or quickning unto newness of life, by the power of the resurrection of Christ."[50] Thus, just as fully as in the Catholic view, repentance for sins and the practice of good works are essential in the Christian life. But what is the Protestant definition of a good work? Perkins states it briefly: "A good worke is a worke commanded of God, and done by a man regenerate in faith, for the glorie of God in man's good." The works of the Papists, he continues, are "sinnes before God," not through any failure of the acts as such but through a misdirection of their proper purposes; they are performed to satisfy God's justice and to merit heaven for the benefit of the perpetrators, rather than broadly and impersonally to glorify God in the general good of men.[51]

Good works, therefore, are absolutely essential to salvation. "Are good workes so needfull," Ussher inquires, "that without them we cannot be assured of salvation?" "Yes," he answers himself, "for though good workes doe not worke our salvation in any part; yet because they that are justified are also sanctified, they that doe no good workes, doe declare that they neither are justified nor sanctified, and . . . cannot be saved."[52] "We hold good works necessary to Salvation," Andrewes states, "and that faith without them saveth not."[53] "We teach a necessity," William Gouge concurs, "of practising, of doing good workes. . . .

---

[49] *Works*, II, 208-09.  
[51] *Works*, III, 30.  
[53] *Works*, XI, 29.  
[50] Ussher, *op.cit.*, p. 202.  
[52] Ussher, *op.cit.*, p. 34.

47

And we acknowledge them to be so necessary, as without them we cannot be saved."[54]

English Protestant insistence on the necessity of good works could readily provide the basis for an emphasis on acts of faith and precision of behavior which would rival the utmost legalism of Judaism and the utmost perfectionism of the Catholic tradition. And, in fact, this tendency was to some extent developed and realized by certain aspects or representatives of English Protestantism. "This is the reason that few are saved," Sibbes writes, "because they content themselves with easie, dull and drowsie performances. . . . When they had rather loose the advantage of that which will bring everlasting good to their soules, then loose the petty commodities of this world and yet think themselves good Christians, what a delusion is this? It is the violent only that are successful, *they take it* [salvation] *by force*."[55] Preston declares that ". . . a man is not right borne till he come to *walke exactly* with God, till he be willing to performe every duty, and willing to shunne every sinne that hee knowes . . . otherwise what is the power of Religion, if wee onely doe duties that are facile and easie, to which we have no contrary disposition . . . but herein is the power of Religion . . . to turne the course of nature, to obey God when a man finds the greatest difficulties . . . otherwise the truth is, wee serve the flesh and not God. . . ."[56]

"Are not God's children his Saints?" Edward Dering asks. "If I feele not the spirit of God, to sanctifie more and more my hart . . . how can I say I am the childe of God? . . . except thou love righteousnesse even as thou lovest thy soule . . . thou hast been but an idle hearer of the word of truth. . . . They are Christs, which have crucified the flesh. . . ."[57]

But there were always at least two ideological obstacles in Protestantism, and hence in English Protestantism, to the assertion that a doctrine of the perfect life, in the pattern of the upper level of Catholicism's double standard of Christian living, is a feasible or even desirable goal for the salvation-seeking

[54] William Gouge, *The Saints Sacrifice* (1652), p. 16.
[55] Sibbes, *Beames of Divine Light* (1639), p. 260.
[56] Preston, *Sermons*, p. 100.
[57] Edward Dering, *XXVII Lectures* (1614), pp. 324-34.

individual. One obstacle was the assumption of the omnipresence of sin in human nature, even in regenerate human nature. No man, while he carried the burden of the flesh with him, was perfect, and therefore he could not live a perfect Christian life. And the term "saint" was extended much more broadly and generously by Protestants than by Catholics, because it was applied in some sense to all the regenerate. By this very fact, it could not involve the same measure or quality of exaltation beyond the common level of humanity which Catholic usage implied. The Protestant saint had not annihilated sin; he did not even maintain steady dominion over it; he was merely in a position, thanks to the grace vouchsafed him by God, to engage in more or less equal combat with it. Perfect righteousness, Downame explains, "is altogether impossible to our corrupt nature," and God therefore only requires of us "that wee strive and labour to attaine unto it."[58]

No man, consequently, may avoid sin altogether. Indeed, the regenerate man may commit sins which outwardly appear to be as heinous as any committed by the unregenerate. "A wicked man," Perkins points out, "when he sinneth in his heart he giveth full consent to the sinne: but the godly though they fall into the same sinnes with the wicked, yet they never give full consent: for they are in their mindes, coils, and affections partly regenerate and partly unregenerate, and therefore their wils doe partly will, and partly abhorre that which is evill. . . ."[59]

"When any regenerate man sinneth," Preston writes, "it is not he that doth it, but the sinne that is there";[60] and the godly man, though he relapse into sin, "yet still he gets ground of his sinne, even by every relapse," and he never falls back "to the allowance of any sinne."[61] But the fact remains that, in contradiction to the Catholic tradition of the saint with its emphasis on the practice of counsels of perfection, the Protestant "saint" can sin or, at least to some extent, must sin.

More important than this is the repeated insistence that since the goodness of a work is wholly determined by the internal

[58] Downame, *op.cit.*, p. 296.    [59] *Works*, I, 372.
[60] *Breast-Plate*, p. 196.
[61] *The New Covenant* (1630), pp. 250-55.

source of the work in faith, rather than by the external quantity or kind of work, the smallest, the humblest, the most obscure work which springs from true faith is equal to the greatest which can have no greater origin. Preston declares: "It is an errour among the Papists, to thinke that to give almes, to crucifie the flesh and to use that hardly, to fast, and the like, that these are the onely and the most glorious actions: They are exceeding wide; good actions are nothing else but to doe the will of the *Lord,* and to bring forth fruit. . . . Every action that you doe is that fruit which *God* lookes for. Therefore, to doe the *Lords* will is to doe a good worke. Now by this you may see what a large field you have for good works, in what calling soever you are set, though it bee never so meane a place you have."[62]

And the intent is sometimes as good as the deed. Thus Perkins contends that "if any man have a willingnes and a desire to obey all God's commandments, he hath the spirit; and hee who hath the spirit is in Christ, and he who is in Christ shall never see damnation."[63] Because, finally, it is only God's gift of grace which makes possible a virtuous life in this world and everlasting life in the next, the English Protestant tends to define Christian perfection simply in terms of the possession of grace, with its concomitant effects, rather than through any rigid standards of observable performance.

There is a sense, then, in which Protestantism brought to its adherents a lighter rather than a heavier yoke than had been laid upon Catholics who were seriously intent upon salvation. Certainly this view of itself as a liberator from unnecessary or impossible demands upon the human spirit is an important part of the apologetics of English Protestantism. One of the manifestations of the theme is the doctrine of the two covenants, the "covenant of works" and the "covenant of grace." The covenant of works, Andrewes explains, was "the one made between God and Adam, on God's part to perform him paradise, on Adam's part to perform obedience; but Adam having strength to do this, and abusing the same, incurred the forfeiture of this covenant, which was the danger of hell and the penalty of death."

[62] *Breast-Plate,* 208-09.
[63] *Works,* I, 372.

The covenant of grace or faith, on the other hand, is the new covenant that was made with the coming of Christ, "that Christ to God should make perfection, to us should restore that we had lost; and on our side, that we should perform perfect obedience but by Christ. . . ."[64] "How doth this Covenant [of Grace] differ from that of works?" asks Ussher. He answers: "Much every way; for, first, in many points the Law may be conceived by reason; but the Gospell in all points is farre above the reach of man's reason. Secondly, the Law commandeth to doe good, and giveth no strength, but the Gospell enableth us to doe good. . . . . Thirdly, the Law promised life onely; the Gospell righteousnesse also. Fourthly, the Law required perfect obedience, the Gospell the righteousnesse of Faith. . . . Fifthly, the Law revealeth sin, rebuketh us for it, and leaveth us in it, but the Gospell doth reveale unto us the remission of sins, and freeth us from the punishment belonging thereunto. Sixthly, the Law is the ministery of wrath, condemnation and death: the Gospell is the ministery of grace, Justification and life. Seventhly, the Law was grounded on man's own righteousnesse, requiring every man in his own person perfect obedience . . . but the Gospell is grounded on the righteousnesse of Christ. . . ."[65]

[64] *Works*, II, 62. Perry Miller, "The Marrow of Puritan Divinity," *Publications of the Colonial Society of Massachusetts*, XXXII (1937), 256-90, argues that, though the idea of covenant theology was generally Protestant, the "puritans," especially Preston, gave it a special legal twist, derived from "the common-law conception of the covenant, the idea of a formal agreement of legal validity . . ." (N., p. 258) and that this concept "succeeded in reconciling all contradictions, smoothing out all inconsistencies, securing a basis for moral obligation and for assurance of salvation while yet not subtracting from God's absolute power . . ." (p. 262). We feel English Calvinism established no such highroad to assured salvation by "law of nature" and "clear reason"; nor do we find much evidence of Calvinist opinion that "there need be very little difference between the performances of a saint and the acts of a sinner; the difference will be in the aims and aspirations of the saint and in the sincerity of his effort. The proof of election will be in the trying, not the achieving" (p. 284). On the contrary (Miller also contradicts his own thesis about puritan morality, pp. 272-74), salvation (by covenant) is the ultimate mystery, a function entirely of inscrutable will and power, and therefore apprehended *solely* by Faith. As Donne put it, ". . . though our natural reason, and human arts serve to carry us to the hill, to the entrance of the mysteries of religion, yet to possess us of the hill itself, and to come to such a knowledge of the mysteries of religion, as must save us, we must leave our natural reason and human arts at the bottom of the hill, and climb up only by the light, the strength of faith" (*Works*, II, 265). Cf. E. H. Emerson, "Calvin and Covenant Theology," *Church History* (June, 1956).
[65] Ussher, *Divinitie*, p. 159.

Perkins makes the usual distinction between the two covenants of law and grace and observes that "the law is mercilesse. . . .
all such as . . . have begunne to . . . believe, let them be of good
comfort. For they . . . are dead to the law, and under grace, having a Lord, who is also their mercifull Saviour, who will give
them protection against the terrours of the law, and spare them
as a father spares his child that serves him and not breake them
though they be but as weake and bruised reedes, and as smoking
flare."[66] "Christ," the same author asserts, "hath redeemed us
from the curse of the law . . . neither hell, nor death, nor Satan,
hath any right or power over us, so be it we do unfainedly believe
in Christ."[67]

As is obvious from the type of defensive argument employed,
the Catholic attack on Protestantism in general or English Protestantism in particular was levelled not at the overexactitude or
preciseness of moral standards in the rival faith, but at the laxity
conceived to be the concomitant of the emphasis on faith, rather
than on the merit of works, as the essential element in salvation.
Furthermore, when toward the end of this period a decisive split
occurred within the Church of England, and a king's or bishop's
party stood on one side and what is known as a puritan party
stood on the other, Laud, the leader of the former party, followed
the same strategy in combat. He did, to be sure, inveigh against
the strict Sabbatarianism of the puritans and their wholesale ban
on play-going, but in regard to morality in general, it was the
threat of puritan indifference and not puritan preciseness which
he condemned. One notes the presence of this concern in the following article of the Canons and Constitutions for the church
published in Aberdeen in 1636: "It is manifest, that the superstition of former ages is turned unto great profaneness, and that
people for the most part are grown cold in doing any good, es-
teeming that good works are not necessary; therefore shall all
presbyters, as their text giveth occasion, urge the necessity of good
works to their hearers."[68]

Still more specifically and sharply, in his argument against the
charges of Lord Saye and Sele at the time of his indictment be-

[66] Perkins, *Works*, II, 213.      [67] *Ibid.*, p. 237.
[68] Laud, *Works*, V, Part II, 590.

fore the House of Commons in 1641, Laud declares: ". . . Mr. Pryn himself (who hath been a great stickler in these troubles of the church) says expressly, 'Let any true saint of God be taken away in the very act of any known sin, before it is possible for him to repent; I make no doubt or scruple of it, but he shall as surely be saved as if he had lived to have repented of it.' . . . So, according to this divinity, the true saints of God may commit horrible and crying sins, die without repentance, and yet be sure of salvation; which teareth up the very foundations of religion, induceth all manner of profaneness into the world, and is expressly contrary to the whole current of Scripture."[69]

But Christianity as a whole is intensely involved with the assertion and maintenance of ethical standards. Thus when one segment of Christianity finds itself in conflict with another, it will almost inevitably use as a stock item of aggression and defamation the claim that the tenets of the opposition sect are in some way undermining the foundations of morality. The contrary claim—that excessive demands of a genuinely moral nature are being made—is almost impossible to imagine as part of the armoury of internecine Christian warfare.

## IV. Predestination

Sin, faith, and predestination—around these three terms we have been attempting to cluster the ideas of English Protestantism concerning man's personal character and destiny. We have dealt with the first two and we come now to the third and last. What has been said generally of sin and faith—that these ideas can only be considered relatively and comparatively since they exist everywhere in Gospel Christianity and are matters always of a kind of trembling compromise between antitheses—holds even more emphatically for predestination. The Christian God is omniscient and omnipotent. He has created all, he governs all; he foreknows all, and hence in an ultimate sense he must predestine all. Yet, the problem of salvation and damnation, which is the focus of the Christian's religious concern, would have for him no solution and no real significance if God's will were di-

[69] *Works*, VI, Part I, 132-33.

rectly and absolutely deterministic of man's fate. Thus if there is to be any point at all to the existence of religion, man must be acknowledged to have some capacity to choose between alternatives; in some fashion or in some degree, he must be granted the possession of free will. Christianity once again has to make room in a single ideology for the simultaneous existence of two opposites.

It is a truism that relative to Roman Catholicism, on one side, and Anabaptism and certain other radical Protestant sects, on the other, both Lutheran and Calvinist Protestantism emphasize predestination rather than free will. Calvinism makes a somewhat more emphatic statement of its predestinarian convictions than does Lutheranism and hence, of the major Christian creeds, it can be safely said to occupy the extreme position on this issue. On these doctrines, the English Protestantism of the period under survey can be located somewhere between Lutheranism and Calvinism and, though there are some differences and disputes within it, probably nearer in general to Calvinism than to Lutheranism. The seventeenth article of the Thirty-Nine Articles of the Church of England, which enunciates Church of England doctrine on the predestinarian question, does exhibit some concern with possible abuses of the concept, but its principal purpose and impact is certainly to establish the firm opposition of this church to any suggestion of Pelagian or semi-Pelagian ideas.[70]

Predestination, rather than reprobation, is the subject of this article and of the major part of associated commentary in the literature; but, even where double predestination is not specifically stated (the predestination of some to salvation, the reprobation of others to damnation), it is always implied. The good exist only in terms of the simultaneous existence of the bad, and between the two extremes there is no middle ground.

It is the usual corollary of the predestinarian doctrine that, proportionately speaking, the few are saved and the many are damned. "For the house will not stand empty long," Andrewes

[70] For the interesting political background of this first official dose of Calvinism in the English church, see J. E. Neale, "Parliament and the Articles of Religion, 1571," *English Historical Review* (Vol. LXVIII, 1953).

declares. "One spirit or other, holy or unholy, will enter and take
it up. We see the greatest part of the world by far are entered
upon and held by the unholy spirit . . . for they are many."[71]
Thomas Morton similarly states that "not all mankind is restored
to life, but only a fewe, that it might appeare how unapt man is
made by sinne."[72] "To whom doth God reveal and apply the
Covenant of Grace?" Ussher inquires, and then replies: "Not to
the world, but . . . to the Elect and chosen. . . . though the proclamation of Grace be generall . . . yet most men refuse or neglect
God's goodnesse by reason of the naughtinesse of their hearts . . .
[and] abide without recovery in the state of sin and death . . .
[and] run on in sin deservedly unto condemnation."[73]

The concern which might understandably arise even among
the faithful about the nature of a deity who so ruthlessly repudiated the majority of mankind is met by a standard argument,
stated here in brief by Robinson: "First, we know, that all by
nature and of themselves are subject to sin and condemnation,
and so might in justice have been left of God, without remedy
of redemption. If, then, it had been but just with God to have
left all in that state of sin and misery, into which they have cast
themselves, it is then mere mercy, that he hath chosen any in his
Son, or given him for any."[74] Thus English Protestantism clearly
affirms the point that, since all men are by nature sinful and are
therefore justly damned, the saved owe their salvation entirely
to God's grace and arbitrary choice. And, indeed, when one considers the enormity of the gulf between damnation and salvation,
it is easy to see the logic and the appeal of a viewpoint which
failed to find in the observable differences of human nature and
human behavior an explanation for the selection of some for
salvation and the rejection of many more. There is an element
of pity and humanitarianism, after all, in the comment which
springs naturally from the Protestant, who notes the mass of the
damned as they wind downward toward their doom, that, "There
but for the grace of God go I."

[71] Andrewes, *Works*, VI, 191.
[72] Thomas Morton, *A Treatise of the Threefolde State of Man* (1956), 21.
[73] Ussher, *Divinitie*, 186.
[74] Robinson, *Works*, I, 327.

And yet, as in any Christian argument, provision also had to be made for the existence and activity of man's free will. English Protestantism certainly does make such provision, to the satisfaction of its own apologists at least, and this at the very time that the attack against Catholicism and Anabaptism is hotly pursued for their presumed overstatement of the agency of man in the business of salvation and their understatement of the sovereignty of God. It is pointed out in the first place that original sin, the root cause of man's whole sinfulness and of his damnation, was established as the ineradicable inheritance of humanity by the freely-willed sin of Adam. "But all and every one received holinesse and happinesse in Adam," Perkins explains, "together with abilitie to persevere . . . in the same holy and happie estate if they had would. But Adam would not but did of his owne accord cast away that grace . . . for which beeing lost, it is a wonder, that all without exception are not damned."[75]

Secondly, all sins performed by sinners, and especially those of the unregenerate, are freely willed by them. God never directly wills a sin; it must therefore be the sinner who does so. To strengthen this argument, appeal is made to the natural reason or the knowledge of natural law which resides in every man, and for the refusal to obey or follow which all men are rightfully condemned even in the total absence of the opportunity to receive the message of grace and to respond to it. Preston writes: "I . . . truly affirme every man hath a free will to do that, for the not doing of which hee is condemned; marke it."[76] Andrewes asserts the same to be established doctrine in the Church of England: "We hold," he states, "that *no man is predestinate to evil.*"[77] The limitation on free will comes at the same point as the limitation on all capacities of human nature: at the point of salvation. Damnation, as it were, is entirely man's doing; but salvation belongs essentially to God. Formal profession of this position is made in the eighth article of the Lambeth Articles: "No man can come unto Christ unless it shall be given unto him,

---

[75] Perkins, *Works*, II, 621.
[76] Preston, *The Saints Qualification* (1634), 225.
[77] Andrewes, *Works*, XI, 30.

and unless the Father shall draw him; and all men are not drawn by the Father, that they may come to the Son."[78]

The English Protestant attack on the Roman Catholic conception of the relationship between man's free will and God's predestination is, therefore, merely another variant on a by-now familiar quarrel: about the relative efficacy or inefficacy of human nature, as human and natural, to provide a basis for or to aid in the realization of man's hope of supernature. "And now since the fall of Adam," Ussher writes, "Wee say further, that freedome of will remayneth still among men; but the abilitie which once it had, to performe spirituall duties and things pertayning to salvation is quite lost: wee denie, therefore, that a naturall man hath any free will unto good."[79] The tenth article of the Thirty-Nine Articles confirms the same as the official teaching of the Church of England: "The condition of man after the fall of Adam is suche, that he can not turne and prepare hym selfe by his owne naturall strength and good workes, to fayth and calling upon God: wherefore we have no power to do good workes pleas-aunt and acceptable to God, without the grace of God. . . ."[80]

At first glance, a simple argument and a straightforward dualism seem to be apparent: man wills the evil that he does and hence his own damnation; but God alone, who only is all good, wills all the good that exists or is done in the universe, including man's ultimate good, his salvation from sin and death. But, of course, no orthodox Christian can approach so near to splitting God's realm in half. On the one side, God is the creator of the entire universe and hence must finally be responsible for everything that is in it, the evil as well as the good and damnation as well as salvation. On the other side, no creature made by God can be so hopelessly lost in evil that it is incapable of at least concurring or cooperating with God's will for its good. Man's will must be free enough, even in the performance of good, to be able at least to affirm God's will to confer salvation. The sort of verbal legerdemain involved is indicated in a discussion by Per-

---

[78] Thomas Fuller, *The Church History of Britain* (6 vols.; Oxford, 1845), v, 221. This is probably the best piece of historical writing in the seventeenth century.
[79] Ussher, *An Answer to a Challenge* (1631), 515-16.
[80] *The Creeds of Christendom* (ed. P. Schaff, 3 vols.; N. Y., 1877), III, 493-94.

kins. He asks first "whether the child of God in his conversion have a libertie and power to resist the inward calling of God?" He answers this question in the negative, since the absolute will of God cannot be resisted. But he insists that the freedom of man's will is not thereby abolished. "It sufficeth to the libertie of the will," he declares, that it be free from compulsion: for constraint takes away the libertie of the will, and not necessitie. Secondly, the determination of man's will, by the will of God, is the libertie of the will, and not the bondage thereof: for this is perfect libertie, when man's will is conformable to the will of God."[81]

However emphatically the concept is presented—that God and not man is the only effective agent in man's salvation—the very activities of an intensely proselytizing and evangelical church, as early Protestantism was, are directly contradictory, in terms of simple logic, to strict predestinarian doctrine. Indeed, the whole literature of English Protestantism is a product of a ministerial enthusiasm which seems constantly to be overstepping the limits which logically it has set for itself—bringing to the listeners a mere awareness of their eternal destiny, whatever that might be. It certainly does not merely inform of salvation; it exhorts to it.

The great majority of English Protestant divines in this period accepted the general formulation of predestinarian doctrine which has been presented here. But around two points of sensitivity in the doctrine there was considerable discussion, if not precisely dispute: the question of the exact quality of the permanence of election or reprobation; and the question of the kind or degree of knowledge of his spiritual estate which the Christian could possess. Despite such controversy, however, generalization still remains possible. The bulk of English Protestant opinion, for example, even in its more Augustinian manifestations, ventured a much stronger positive statement regarding the permanence of election or reprobation than did Roman Catholicism. There was never any doubt, of course, concerning the complete decisiveness of God's choice of His elect, but it was also fairly consistently acknowledged by English Protestant divines that once the Christian individual was truly justified, he could never

[81] Perkins, *Works*, II, 4.

again fall from that condition. Some difficulty was encountered in the definition of true justification or sound justifying faith. The English Protestant does speak occasionally of temporary or partial faith, but he never accepts this as true faith or as the product of God's grace truly given. In the long run, indeed, he presents a circular definition of true or justifying faith, as simply the faith that saves. Therefore, this faith must be permanent and ineradicable, since its very nature depends on the achievement of the end toward which it is directed. The general English viewpoint on the subject is stated in the fifth article of the Lambeth Articles: "A true, living, and justifying faith, and the Spirit of God justifying, is not extinguished, falleth not away; it vanisheth not away in the elect, either finally or totally."[82] "The grace of God in the adoption of the elect," Perkins declares, "is unchangeable, and he that is the child of God can never fall away wholly or finally. On the contrarie, that is a bad and comfortlesse opinion of the church of Rome; which holdeth that a man may be justified before God, and yet afterward by a mortall sinne, finally fall from grace and bee condemned."[83]

It would appear, from occasional procedures in the argumentation in this literature, that no outward difference, that is, difference in behavior, was assumed to separate the reprobate from the saved. But we have seen that by far the heavier weight of emphasis falls on the absolute essentiality of the connection between justification and sanctification. Nonetheless, the Protestant and even more the Calvinistic concept of the profound sinfulness of human nature made impossible the existence of any completely sin-free individual. Just as the hypocrite, though reprobate, might participate in the virtues of the saved, so the true Christian, though justified, sanctified, and salvation-bound, might—indeed, must—participate in the sinfulness of the damned. From this situation, the immediate practical problem for the Christian moralist is how much or what type of sin might be considered compatible with the continuance of a permanent justification. Occasional critics of the predestinarian tenor of Church of England doctrine fastened with particular vehemence on this point

[82] Fuller, *Church History*, 220.
[83] Perkins, *Works*, I, 135.

of tension and brought into question the whole assumption of permanent justification; but again, the majority of English divines dealt with the problem merely by reiterating that the truly justified man would not sin as often or as grievously as the reprobate and/or that the quality of sin would be quite different in the reprobate than in the justified, since sin and repentance would be so intimately interwoven in the justified that the sin could scarcely be committed before repentance took its place.

The nature of the discussion which concerned itself with this problem and still remained comfortably within the confines of a predestinarian viewpoint is well illustrated by certain comments made at the Hampton Court Conference. The Barlow account of this conference notes that on the subject of the problem of falling from grace, the Bishop of London "took occasion to signifie to his majesty how very many in these daies, neglecting holinesse of life, presumed too much of persisting of grace, laying all their religion upon predestination, if I shall be saved, I shall be saved; which he termed a desperate doctrine, shewing it to be contrary to good divinity, and the true doctrine of predestination, wherein we should reason rather *ascendendo* than *descendendo*, thus; 'I live in obedience to God, in love with my neighbour, I follow my vocation, etc.; therefore I trust that God have elected me, and predestinated me to salvation'; not thus, which is the usual course of argument, 'God hath predestinated and chosen me to life, therefore though I sin never so grievously, yet I shall not be damned: for whom he once loveth, he loveth to the end.' "[84] The king, Barlow further comments, responded to the Bishop of London by stating that "he wished that the doctrine of predestination might be very tenderly handled, and with great discretion, lest on the one side, God's omnipotency might be called in question, by impeaching the doctrine of his eternal predestination, or on the other, a desperate presumption might be arreared, by inferring the necessary certainty of standing and presisting in grace."[85] It should be clearly understood that the

[84] *A History of the Conferences . . . Concerned with the Revision of the book of Common Prayer from . . . 1558 to . . . 1690* (ed. E. Cardwell; Oxford, 1840), 180-81.

[85] *Ibid.*, 181. An additional inadequacy of previous over-simple definitions of the theological alignments of the various Protestant professions becomes evident

"desperate doctrine" attacked here is not that of predestination as such, but the "desperate presumption" of salvation which certain English divines, for what reasons the existent sermon literature gives one little basis for discerning, felt to be a prevalent abuse of the predestinarian viewpoint.

The problem of presumption in the permanence of salvation leads directly to the second point of sensitivity in the Church of England's doctrine of salvation: the kind or degree of knowledge of his eternal destiny which the Christian might expect to obtain and hold. The matter of moment to English Protestant divines, of course, was the extent to which it was possible for an individual who was actually of the elect to achieve in this life knowledge of his election and assurance in it. The Roman Catholic position, which tends relatively to underplay the role of predestination in general, limits knowledge of election, where election exists, to extraordinary circumstances and miraculous revelation, and allows under ordinary circumstances only a hope and not an assurance of salvation. English Protestant opinion, on the contrary, probably in part merely by its antagonism to Roman Catholicism, tends to emphasize instead the certainty of knowledge of salvation in the elect and the accomplishment of that certainty through the intellective and spiritual processes ordinarily associated with the presence of true faith. From true faith, says Morton, "ariseth the assurance of salvation, which is the undoubted persuasion, and certaine knowledge of a faithfull man, that he is one of those who shall be made partakers of eternall glorie. . . . Every faithfull man may be and ought to be assured of his owne salvation and that by the wonderfull worke of regeneration wrought in him by the holy spirite."[86] Andrewes also asserts the probability at least of the Christian's possessing

---

through careful consideration of the issues in dispute and the processes of argument at the Hampton Court Conference. It is commonly urged (see, for example, Kemper Fullerton, "Calvinism and Capitalism," *The Harvard Theological Review*, XXI, 1928) that Calvinism is activist and Lutheranism quietistic in its bent, and that the salvation of the individual is in the former displayed more by how he lives or behaves and in the latter more by how he feels. Yet at the Hampton Court Conference it is the more conservative (i.e. less Calvinist) divines who take the activist position, while the so-called "puritans" would appear from the nature of the charges brought against them to be moving closer to the quietistic position.

[86] Morton, *op.cit.*, pp. 266-67.

assurance of his salvation. "Of the Spirit of grace, which is the inner mark of election," he writes, "the signs are familiar. For if it be in us . . . at the heart it will beat, at the mouth it will breathe, at the pulse it will be felt. Some one of these may, but all these will not deceive us."[87] Taking a bolder line, Dent maintains that "he who knoweth not in this life that he shall be saved, shall never be saved after this life."[88]

But no English Protestant asserts or implies that all confidence of election is necessarily equivalent to election. The knowledge of election, obtainable though it be, is almost always hedged around with a variety of cautions and conditions. While Hildersam speaks of the uncertainty in reaching salvation, the elect being often full of "doubts and feares,"[89] Sibbes writes that "many . . . have the seeds, and the worke of grace in them; but the times are so secure, that they know it not."[90] Perkins points out that "many professing service to Christ shall conceive in their minds a persuasion that they are the true servants . . . of God: they shall live and die in this persuasion; and yet for all this at the last judgment they shall receive the sentence of condemnation."[91] The statements of Hall and Rogers carry a tone of caution that is particularly strong. Richard Rogers observes that "in this long and gracious time of peace and libertie . . . he is a rare private man . . . who is able plainly and soundly to set downe, how a sinner may know himselfe to be in the state of salvation, and assured that he is the childe of God. . . . And though I doubt not that some conceive it, yet if they did that well, they could in some sort utter it also."[92] Hall exclaims: "What have we to doe to be rifling the hidden counsells of the Highest? Let us look to our own wayes. We have his word for this; that if we doe truly believe, repent, obey, persevere, we shall be saved. . . . What need we to look any further, than consciously and cheerfully to do what we are injoyned, and faithfully and comfortably to expect what he hath promised? . . . But if

87 Andrewes, *Works*, VI, 192.
88 Dent, *Pathway*, p. 261.
89 Hildersam, *CLII Lectures Upon Psalme LI* (1635), pp. 620-25.
90 Sibbes, *The Churches Riches* (1638), p. 57.
91 Perkins, *Works*, III, 248.
92 Richard Rogers, *Seven Treatises* (1630), p. 114.

we, in a groundlesse conceit of our election, shall let loose the reins to our sinfull desires and vicious practices, thereupon growing idle or unprofitable, we make divine mercy a Pander to our uncleannesse, and justly perish in our wicked presumption."[93]

Summing up the discussion as it has been developed thus far, one can safely say that relative to contemporary Roman Catholicism, English Protestantism in the period under survey is generally and consistently predestinarian in doctrine. For the most part, the pattern which is followed is fundamentally that which Calvin set. Yet, since we are dealing not with the single, unifying, and for the most part brilliantly logical mind of Calvin, but with the thoughts and pronouncements of many divines, we must expect to find deviations, qualifications, and certain differences of emphasis. Moreover, since Calvin represents in the development of Christian theology an extreme of predestinarian doctrine, any deviation from him is bound to be in the direction of the opposition pole to predestination, in the direction of free will.

Yet on the basis of the evidence drawn from the pulpit literature, one cannot locate what may be called English Protestant orthodoxy on the predestinarian issue at any farther remove from Calvin than the Lambeth Articles and Andrewes's comments upon them. The Articles themselves are certainly strongly predestinarian with few and very minor revisions of the language used by the strict Calvinist who originally wrote them. Fuller, it should be noted, who wrote in a later and more contentious epoch, says of these Articles and of that group of Elizabethan churchmen who approved them: "And though those learned divines be not acknowledged as competent judges to pass definitive sentence in those points, yet they will be taken as witnesses beyond exception, whose testimony is an infallible evidence what was the general and received doctrine of England in that age about the forenamed controversies."[94]

Andrewes was one of those who approved the Articles, but his

---

[93] Hall, *Works*, IV, 89.
[94] Fuller, *Church History*, V, 227.

comments on four of them at least indicate that he had certain anxieties about the predestinarian argument; the significance of his anxieties is all the greater since the majority of his contemporaries and successors tended to share them to some extent. In commenting, for instance, on Article v, which establishes the permanence of election in the elect, he takes care to observe that this permanence of election is dependent not upon the quality of election itself, but upon the nature of the person who has been elected and who has been regenerated by his election and hence cannot be associated with behavior other than that proper to the regenerated.[95]

In commenting on Article vi, which is concerned with the knowledge of election in the elect, he cautions that the same degree of certitude that pertains to the knowledge of other types of religious truths cannot apply to this knowledge.[96] In commenting upon Article vii, which states that saving grace is not communicated to every man nor in accordance with the will of man, Andrewes remarks that though he accepts this formulation of the limitations of grace, there is an ultimate sense in which God's grace is in fact offered to all and is consciously rejected by the reprobate. *"Et haec Augustini et Prosperi fuit sententia, qui gratiam saltem parciorem occultioremque omnibus datam aiunt, et talem quidam quae ad remedium sufficeret. Unde Fulgent, 'Quod non adjuvantur quidam a gratia Dei, in ipsis causa est, non a Deo.' "*[97]

Finally, in commenting on Article ix, which simply asserts, "It is not in the will or power of every one to be saved," Andrewes emphasizes—and again he refers to Augustine as his authority—that "despite the fact that man cannot will himself

[95] Andrewes, *Works*, ii, 292, 299.

[96] *Ibid.*, p. 299.

[97] *Ibid.*, 293. A free translation of this passage reads: "And this was the opinion of Augustine and of Prosper of Aquitaine, who say that at least a small and secret grace has been given to all men and of such a kind, indeed, that it would have sufficed for a remedy. Therefore St. Fulgentius has said: 'When men are not helped by the grace of God, the cause is in themselves and not in God.'" Note that though this is close to Paul and to Augustine, it is far removed from St. Thomas Aquinas and the Catholic proliferation of graces into a word-science separating "sanctifying" from "actual" grace, "sufficient" from "efficacious" grace, and arguing the primacy of sacramental restoration of the "sanctifying" grace lost by original sin and subsequent mortal sin, and the free will operation of "efficacious" grace.

into salvation, nonetheless he does possess the capacity to co-operate with and consent to God's will to save him."[98] These commentaries show, incidentally, that Andrewes thinks of himself in his approach to the doctrine of predestination primarily as an Augustinian rather than a Calvinist, though at one point at least he dismisses all such implied disputes as to affiliation and authority by indicating that Calvin too was essentially an Augustinian.[99]

Predestinarian, then, and essentially Calvinist though this literature is on the whole, it also shows a good deal of concern about what are conceived to be possible extremes of predestinarian doctrine. There is concern, on the one hand, lest the individual Christian be allowed to become too easily and too presumptuously assured of his election (or, conversely, too hopelessly confirmed in his reprobation); and there is concern, on the other hand, lest God be allowed to appear too arbitrary or cruel in meting out salvation to some and damnation to many others, without regard to any motion or response on the part of the recipient. Discussion on these issues, however, can only very vaguely be organized up to this point along party lines. It is possible to argue that the so-called puritans are, on the whole, more confidently and unqualifiedly predestinarian, and less troubled by these problems, than the non-puritans. Yet Ussher is as strict a predestinarian and as free of hesitations and doubts as any other English divine that one might name, while Perkins, as we have seen, is generous with warnings about overconfidence in the knowledge of election. Sibbes, moreover, a "puritan" on many lists, is also among the most ardent and eloquent occupants of the English pulpit in urging the mercy rather than the majesty of God—which is generally assumed to be a non-Calvinist emphasis—and in counselling the frailest Christian to unfailing hope in his salvation.[100] "Did Christ," he asks, "ever turne back any that came unto him, if they came out of a true sense of their wants?"[101] God, he further insists, calls all to salvation and offers

98 *Ibid.*, p. 294.
99 *Ibid.*, pp. 291-92.
100 See Sibbes, *The Bruised Reede and Smoaking Flax* (1630).
101 Sibbes, *Bowels Opened* (1639), p. 78.

in some sense sufficient means to all to achieve salvation. Those who are not saved, therefore, have only themselves to blame.[102]

The weakness of the effort to establish a consistent and long-standing difference between Anglican and "puritan" on the subject of predestination is perhaps most dramatically illustrated by the single reference to the issue as a matter of dispute in the Whitgift-Cartwright controversy. Here it is the Anglican John Whitgift who chides the "puritan" Thomas Cartwright as being insufficiently conscious of the crucial nature of predestinarian doctrine. In "A note of such dangerous points of doctrine as are avouched by T. C. in his Reply," Whitgift includes the following as the fourth in Cartwright's list of errors: "He [Cartwright] holdeth that 'the doctrine of free-will is not repugnant to salvation'; and yet is it a doctrine clean contrary to free justification by Christ. . . ."[103] In the fuller discussion to which this point refers, Whitgift states: "The doctrine of free will, because it is an enemy to the grace of God must needs be of itself a damnable doctrine. . . . And full well do you know that he cannot hold the foundation of faith (that is Christ) perfectly which is a maintainer of free-will."[104]

The inadequacy of the predestinarian issue as a point of distinction between Anglican and "puritan" in the late sixteenth and early seventeenth centuries is further indicated by Archbishop Hutton's summary of King James's opinion of the "puritans" after the Hampton Court Conference: "The Puritans," Hutton writes, "whose fantastical zeal he [King James] misliked, though they differed in ceremonies and accidents, yet they agreed with us in substance of religion."[105] Both James and the "puritans" recognized the doctrine of predestination as part of "the substance of religion."

From any generalization on the relative agreement on the issue of predestination of English Protestant divines among them-

---

[102] *Ibid.*, pp. 162-63. Cf. Wilbur K. Jordan, *Development of Religious Toleration in England* (4 vols.; Cambridge, 1932-1940), II, 358.

[103] *The Works of John Whitgift* (ed. John Ayre; 3 vols.; Cambridge, 1851-53), III, 552.

[104] *Ibid.*, I, 189.

[105] John Strype, *Life of John Whitgift* (3 vols.; Oxford, 1822), III, Appendix No. 50.

selves, one group of active controversialists, however, must be excepted. These are those few but extremely vocal individuals who were known, to their opponents at least, as Arminians.[106] The agitation which they represented had taken its name from the Dutch theologian, Arminius, and had arisen in the late sixteenth century as a conscious and relatively wholesale reaction in Protestant circles to the rigidities of Calvinist predestinarianism. It is by no means an easy position to define: like all Christian ideas which endeavor, on the basis of an accepted division between the few who are saved and the many who are damned, to maintain the complete sovereignty of God together with the freedom of the human will to choose between alternatives, the Arminian view is torn by a basic illogic which makes of it a continual dispute rather than a simple affirmative statement. This much can be said of Arminianism, however: relative to Calvinism, it stressed the universality of Christ's atonement and the efficacy of man's will to seek and achieve salvation. Relative to Catholicism, it stressed the achievement of this salvation by a surge of faith in a single act of belief rather than by a long and never completed process of expiatory works. Thus it moved fully as much forward toward the more generous and evangelical concepts of the left-wing Protestant sects as backward toward the penitential formalities of Catholicism.

Thought sufficiently divergent from Calvinist predestinarianism to be called Arminian was evident in England in the late sixteenth century. Particularly associated with this type of thought in this period are William Barret, a Cambridge fellow, and Peter Baro, a French-born theologian who was Lady Margaret Professor of Divinity at the same university. The summary suppression to which both men were subjected (Barret was forced to retract those of his arguments which differed from Archbishop Whitgift's understanding of sound predestinarian doctrine, and Baro lost his position essentially on the basis of his participation in the contention) is sufficient to indicate the dominant tenor of Church of England opinion in the time.[107]

In the third and fourth decades of the seventeenth century,

---

[106] See Clarendon, *History of the Rebellion*, I, 152-55.
[107] Strype, *op.cit.*, III, 228-319.

however, another and more significant Arminian group emerged in the Church of England, whose distinguishing characteristic is rejection of the Lambeth Articles and/or active criticism of the Synod of Dort and denial of its authority. Richard Montagu is the principal representative of this group, but John Cosin may also be included in it, and, again to confound the strict application of party labels to this difference, John Goodwin as well (than whom, Fuller remarks, none fell harder upon the Synod of Dort).[108] The Montagu affair is important because, though his was a decidedly minority viewpoint within the Church of England, he and his ideas, for a variety of extremely complicated reasons, principally political and ecclesiastical rather than theological, acquired official backing from the king and from the king's party in the Church—the party headed by Archbishop Laud. Hence the Archbishop, because of his support for Montagu as well as his specific rejection of the Lambeth Articles,[109] can also be numbered among the Arminians, though, fully viewed, he does constitute a somewhat special case. His interests were institutional rather than doctrinal, and he shared with the monarchs of the period (Elizabeth I, James I, and Charles I) a primary concern with maintaining that latitudinarianism of doctrine in all regards which would best guarantee institutional unity. What he really wanted was that, in the phraseology of James I, "the doctrine of predestination might be very tenderly handled," and that English Protestant orthodoxy on the matter might be defined with sufficient generality and breadth to remove the problem altogether from the arena of dispute. By his techniques, however, and the context of time and circumstance in which he operated he achieved, rather than the compromise he sought, a further division in the differences.

There is one more individual whose departures from the predestinarian majority of English divines warrant special mention, but the peculiar qualities of whose thought preclude, we feel, his rightful inclusion in the Arminian group. This individual is John Donne. Donne is uniquely his own man among the churchmen of England in this period. More than any among

108 Fuller, *Church History*, v, 479.
109 Laud, *Works*, I, 130-31.

them he possesses literary genius, and he exhibits in his theological writings, as elsewhere, much of the capacity of this genius to exalt itself above the limitations of creed and party and to grasp at universals. We are convinced that he was in a general sense unqualifiedly Protestant, but his Protestantism was of his own design and brand. His affiliation with the spirit and outlook of Christian mysticism is much closer than that of most other Protestants; and his humanitarianism and relative lack of interest in dogmatic issues link him both to the Christian humanism of the sixteenth century and to the tolerance and rationalism of the eighteenth. He accepted a conventionally Protestant doctrine of original sin, and yet he departed from this Protestant orthodoxy and from Catholic orthodoxy as well (or, for that matter, from Arminian orthodoxy, if one can speak of such a thing) in his basic questioning, his very near rejection, of the whole concept of predestination. He finds himself incapable of basing the vast distinction between salvation and damnation, in the Catholic fashion, on the small differences in the merit of man's works; nor can he, as the Arminians do, base it altogether on belief or nonbelief in the redeeming power of Christ. Whatever men are, sinful or good, he contends they are that fairly uniformly. "All men were in Adam . . . and then can any be without sin? All men were in Christ too . . . and then can any man be excluded from a possibility of mercy?"[110] The

110 Donne, *Works*, II, 71. Many books, most of them not very enlightening, have been written about Donne's religious views. On the one hand, there are those like M. P. Ramsay, *Les Doctrines médiévales chez Donne* (Paris, 1924), and M. F. Moloney, *John Donne: His Flight from Mediaevalism* (Urbana, 1944). These argue that Donne was essentially "Catholic" and spiritually lost in Protestant England; on the other hand, there is such a book as I. Husain, *Dogmatic and Mystical Theology of John Donne* (1938), which emphasizes Donne's lack of "originality" and his spiritual derivativeness. Donne is, of course, intensely original in his religious thought; so much so, that he is hard to put in any firm theological category. Above all, however, he is not Catholic; for his revolt from the Church of Aquinas is in some ways the most absolute of that of any English divine: none is as impatient as Donne with synthetic theological science and facile rationality.

There is no adequate biography of Donne, and no balanced, detailed study of his religious genius. It is somewhat odd that so much attention has been lavished on putting the poetry of Milton in the context of "puritanism," and so little on understanding Donne as a Protestant poet and preacher, in the context, that is, of contemporary English religiosity. Too much has been made of Donne's "humanism," Elizabethan rakishness, opportunism, and thwarted ambitions. In fact, the theme of God's overflowing, not-to-be limited mercy is a constant one with him. He declares those theologians to be: "... too ... thrifty of God's grace, too sparing of the Holy Ghost that restrain God's general propitious, *venite omnes,* let all come, and *vult omnes salvas,* God would have all men saved. ... Yes, God does mean simply all, so as that no man can say to another, God means not thee; no man can say to himself ... God means not me. *Nefas est dicere, Deum aliquid nisi bonum praedestinare*; it is modestly said by St. Augustine, and more were immodesty; there is no predestination in God, but to good. ... Tears are the blood of a wounded soul, and would Christ bleed out of a wounded soul, and weep out of a sad heart, for that which himself, and only himself by an absolute decree, had made necessary and inevitable?"[111]

He reminds his readers that "by God's grace there may be an infinite number of souls saved more than those of whose salvation we discern the ways and the means,"[112] and he says at another point: "Truly Origin was more excusable ... if he did believe that the devil might possibly be saved than that man that believes himself must necessarily be damned."[113] In short, John Donne ventured nearer than any other spokesman of English Protestantism in the period to that ultimate radicalism in the predestinarian argument by means of which, indeed, the entire problem with its inevitable contradictions and logical obscurities disappears: the assertion of the literal boundlessness of God's mercy and the consequent salvation of all men.

## V. Conclusion

In the basic Christian doctrines which have been discussed in this chapter, the significance of sin in human nature and of man's faith and God's will in salvation, the English pulpit has on the whole exhibited remarkable consistency. It has shown itself to be indubitably Protestant and, except for some tendency to retreat from the extremes of predestinarian ideology, essen-

---

level of Protestant religious intensity in Donne's thought is far above anything to be found in the "puritan" Milton.

[111] *Ibid.,* pp. 38-39.   [112] *Works,* IV, 584.
[113] *Works,* V, 136.

tially Calvinist in viewpoint. It is true that certain individual divines appear to have been more interested or more active in defining these doctrines than others. Perkins, for example, is by all odds the most voluminous and the most precise writer on the particular scope of subjects we have covered here. If a special fervor of approach is sought, one turns first of all to Bolton, or to Downame perhaps. In short, one could argue that the English divines of this period who have come to be known to history as puritans have a somewhat greater intensity of concern for these matters and possibly, since there are proportionally fewer or slighter deviations among them from the line of Calvinist orthodoxy, a somewhat greater cohesiveness of outlook as well. And yet, Ussher is certainly an equally orthodox Calvinist, and Hall and Andrewes do not wander so very far afield—no farther, at any rate, than one or two "puritans" one could name.

The really important point is that until the very end of this period, the pulpit literature gives almost no impression of any internal strain or conflict in this area of doctrine. The energy of antagonistic argument about sin, faith, and predestination— about the very core of the creed—is entirely, or almost entirely, directed outward: against Roman Catholicism first of all, against the radical sects secondarily, and, to a still lesser extent, against Arminianism of unspecified locale. Donne, in pursuing his private genius, actually departed more decisively from Calvinist predestinarianism than any other English divine. And yet, he appears to have done this with no discernible feeling of belligerence on his part and without arousing the belligerence of those who presumably disagreed with him.

The situation is wholly otherwise, however, when Laud and the two English Arminians we have named, Montagu and Cosin, begin to speak on the subject. Laud is obviously exerting pressure against counterpressure, and combativeness is of the essence of the assertions of Montagu and Cosin. Thus on this single issue of predestination a doctrinal quarrel had indeed developed *within* the Church of England, though as far as the literature alone could lead one to surmise, it seems to have been a one-sided quarrel, begun and maintained by an extreme minority for reasons of indecipherable ill-humor. The sermon literature as such provides the reader with no basis for assuming that the great bulk of English divines and their followers were, even at that time, to be found in any doctrinal position other than where Ussher, Perkins, Andrewes, and Hall had placed them.

One emerges from this analysis, then, with what may be called an English Protestant creed for the period. Robert Sanderson, that quintessential Anglican, sums it up: "Sundry of the Doctors of our Church teach truly, and agreeably to Scripture the *effectual* concurrence of God's *will* and *Power* with subordinate Agents in *every*, and therefore even in *sinful* actions; God's *free Election* of those whom he purposeth to save of his own grace, without any *motives* in, or from themselves; the *immutability* of God's *Love* and *Grace* towards the *Saints* Elect, and their *certain perseverance* therein unto *Salvation*; the Justification of sinners by the *imputed* righteousness of Christ, apprehended are applyed unto them by a lively faith, without the *works* of the Law. These are sound, and true, and (if rightly understood) comfortable, and right profitable Doctrines."[114]

As stated by Sanderson, this is no more and no less than the creed of Calvinism.

[114] Robert Sanderson, *XXXVI Sermons* (1689), p. 282.

# CHAPTER 2

## THE ENGLISH PROTESTANT

## AND SOCIETY

$$\dagger \; \dagger \; \dagger$$

"... the Lord when hee commeth in visitation will not respect the mightie more than the weake and impotent; yea rather taking delight to over-master and confound their provd greatness. . . . He draweth them first to punishment and maketh their condemnation more heavie . . . these weake stores of violence and tyrannie are neere unto confusion when the least breath of Gods wrath doth blow upon them."
— JOHN DOWNAME, *The Christian Warfare*, 489

"Oh, I say this is a most excellent, and glorious thing, when every man keepeth his standing, his raunge, and his rancke. When all men with care and conscience performe the dueties of their places. . . . For herein consisteth the honor of God, the glory of the Prince, the crowne of the Church, the fortresse of the Commonwealth, the safetie of Cities, the Strength of kingdomes, and the very preservation of all things."
— ARTHUR DENT, *The Plaine Mans Path-way to Heaven*, 178-179

$$\dagger \; \dagger \; \dagger$$

## I. The Problem of a Christian Society

THOUGH THE PRIMARY FUNCTION of Christianity may be said to be the provision of hope and guidance to the individual who strives to attain an individual salvation, it has nonetheless inevitably been drawn into intimate involvement with social groups and policies. This involvement occurs for a variety of reasons. Christianity, first of all, has been a notably proselytizing faith. The typical ardent Christian has not been content to follow by himself the path to salvation he has discovered, but, in part perhaps to establish more firmly in his own confidence the validity of his find, he has sought to persuade others to join him as companions in the venture. Thus individual though salvation may be in its actual possession and enjoyment, the pursuit of it in Christianity has usually been a group endeavor.

Another factor has tied to social requirements and limitations what at first glance might appear to be the purely free and individual flight to heaven: this has been the tendency, as evident in Christianity as in the other major religions of history, for the religious idea and the group which has clustered around it to solidify into an institutionalized form, a church, which has in turn been eventually integrated into the institutionalized structure of the whole society. Moreover, as such institutionalization and integration of the church proceeds, adherence to all established conventions of behavior becomes, with increasing distinctness and urgency, a necessary condition of the virtuous Christian life. From its earliest Gospel origins, Christianity has been committed to an extremely demanding program of moral conduct, and since moral norms are always social in their reference, there is no aspect of the Christian outlook which is not as necessarily, though not always as fully or immediately, concerned with the problems of man's relations to his fellows as with the problems of man's relations to his God.[1]

[1] At the very beginning of this analysis of the nature of the linkages between Protestant thought and the surrounding climate of social attitudes and practices, the matter of our general viewpoint in the field should be made clear. Max Weber and Emile Durkheim are principal representatives of a school of sociologists and historians who emphasize the significance and vitality of religion as a force in society and history. Durkheim particularly provides a broad theoretical base for the school, and in *The Elementary Forms of the Religious Life* (trans. J. W. Swain; Glencoe, Illinois, 1947) he indicates that he finds in religion the entire cement and ultimate substance, as it were, of all societies. Though some of this emphasis is undoubtedly understandable in terms of reaction to the excesses of eighteenth- and nineteenth-century materialistic thought, we feel that another excess has been perpetrated which also demands balancing. Religious beliefs and practices have been present in all societies known to anthropologists and historians, to be sure; but their causative importance in the static structuring of societies and in the dynamic processes of change occurring within societies appears to us to be brought into serious question, first, by the very universality of the core elements of such beliefs and practices and, secondly, by the quixotic variety of their peripheral expressions. Religions have not always or even primarily exhibited a positive, supportive, binding relationship to their affiliated cultures, as Durkheim claims they have; nor have they consistently tended to check individual deviance or aggression and the disintegrating work of other social solvents. Religious beliefs and practices in and of themselves, after all, involve no more

Once again, therefore, we encounter a conflict of ideas in Christianity, whose similitude may be found in many, if not all, religions, but which in this creed of Western civilization seems to have achieved a unique intensity. From one standpoint the entire faith might appear to be embraced by the full unfolding of the doctrine of Christian individualism or personalism—so significant to Christianity is the individual and wholly personal relationship between the deity and the particular human soul. An individual expression of life meets the source of life face to face, as it were, in the complete absence of any intermediate or companion influence. It is to bring this meeting about that Christianity exists.

Yet one moves out from here to an entirely opposite pole— an unlimited and unqualified sociality which seeks to embrace the whole of mankind in an ethic of brotherly love. On the one hand, there is the commandment to love God with all one's heart and soul; and, on the other, to love one's neighbor as oneself and to conceive one's neighbor as being potentially every other individual in the world. One can hardly imagine a more emphatic statement of either proposition.

The contradictions of these two opposing ideological poles achieve a kind, though an unstable kind, of rest and compromise in the vision of ideal Christian society. To discover the nature of this society one does not have to seek far, since theologian after theologian has lovingly and carefully portrayed it either as it once existed in the Garden of Eden or as it will again exist when the Kingdom of God shall come on earth or in heaven. Two qualities dominantly characterize it. First, it is a like-minded, like-conditioned, or, one might say, a relatively equalitarian society: it lacks any distinction between person and person that is based merely upon a difference of power or

---

than man's presumed access to another source of power in the universe, the power of the supernatural. The orientation and purpose of placation, worship, and sacrifice, and the uses to which this power is applied, whether social or antisocial, widely ethical or narrowly opportunistic, confirming or undermining of institutional stabilities, depend upon time, place, and specific circumstances. We choose therefore to see religion in any social or historical situation as simply one among many conditioning factors and itself conditioned far more than it conditions.

wealth—it is, in short, a society without class in the usual historical meaning of the term.

Second, but perhaps more importantly, it is an intimate or, one might say, a folk or kinship society, whose sense of community is founded in the equivalent of ties of blood and in the natural affections which are assumed to belong to such. Brotherly love is the love, indeed, of brothers.

In a sense, the entire social ethic of Christianity is best adjusted to the most possible practical approximation to this type of society: a small persecuted sect, a religious tribe, the members of which are bound together positively by presumptive bonds of kinship and necessary mutual dependence and negatively by the antagonism to and the antagonism of all outsiders. Those within the circle can then be readily seen and loved as brothers who are all the children of one protective God and share equally in both the perils of this world and the rewards of the next, while those without the circle are readily dismissed as children of the Devil and destined to destruction. The ethical—and many of the theological—tensions in Christianity are lessened or eliminated in such a situation, and it is no doubt in part because of pressures toward this kind of resolution of its internal contradictions that Christianity has shown so strong and continuous a tendency to exfoliate into sectarian groupings.

One gains a feeling for the history of this ethic from observations of its development in the Old Testament. Revealed here are its basic tribal character and the greater vigor which it gains from its primary applicability to a confined and chosen people, a people which can maintain as plausible the myth of kinship community, and which is also sharply distinguished from the surrounding mass of those "outside the law." Yet what is at once the chief triumph and the chief tragedy of the Judaistic ethic is achieved in its prophetic phase. The prophets at once proclaim the universal validity of the ethic, its rightful extension to all humankind, and at the same time, in a torrent of bitter reproach, they assert that it has ceased to be effective even within the limits of the tribe.

Christianity is a continuation and a culmination of the prophetic movement in Judaism. Inheriting the problems and contradictions of this movement, it intensifies them beyond the previous point of strain. The Christian creed takes the social ethic of the prophets, originating in and adapted to an intimate tribal group, and endeavors to apply it to a much vaster and more complicated society than the prophets had ever known, to the society of the Roman Empire which had discarded even the remotest or most theoretical of connections with tribal communion or equalitarianism. The ethic of love in the midst of the practices of the Roman Empire! It is simply ludicrous, a cry in the wilderness without any hope of rescue. And that is the particularly troublesome, the particularly haunting thing about this ethic. It expects, it even invites, failure. Indeed, it glories in failure, as if the very impossibility of its realization in the natural world were the real proof of its supernatural truth.

Just as it is generally assumed in orthodox Christianity that men are wicked, so it is generally assumed that men do not and cannot love one another. *Homo lupus homini.* This is basic Christian doctrine concerning the *facts* of human relations. What actually happens to virtue and to love in such an ideological situation? Since they cannot be found in nature, they are located in supernature. Removed from simply human capacity, they become the mark of God's grace in man, the mark of salvation and of the salvation-bound. For the very reason that so much is asked, it comes in actual practice to be expected of extremely few. Men typically are enemies to other men; not to be an enemy in turn—to follow the ethics of universal love and to love one's enemies—this is the exceptional achievement of that exceptional individual, the true Christian, the brand plucked from the burning by the hand of God.

Within its social ethic, then, Christianity contains much evidence of the tensions and the tragedies of social history. Two themes, or two complexes of problems, may be distinguished. The first problem-complex is the one we have already to some extent considered: the rooting of the Christian ethic in the small kinship group and its tendency always to hark back to this type of group and its intimacies at the same time that it inevitably encounters and tries to deal with the facts of a vast and nonkinship society.

The second problem-complex emerges from the conflict between the relative equalitarianism of the ideal society of Christian love and the enormous inequalitarianism of the actually existent societies of the world. Christian social theory is by no means equalitarian in an absolute sense. No greater inequality between man and man can be conceived than that on which New Testament Christianity is based: the inequality between the damned and the saved. Even where only the community of the faithful is concerned and an ideal society is pictured— either the society of the Garden of Eden in the past or the society of the kingdom of heaven in the future—the pattern used is still authoritarian and patriarchal rather than democratic or equalitarian. Relative to the class societies of history, to be sure, this patriarchal society can well be called equalitarian, but, more precisely stated, its spirit is really that of strict subversion. When Christ assures his humble followers that in the society of eternity those last in the world shall be the first and those first shall be the last, he is not evoking an image of equalitarianism but of subversion in the most literal sense. The society of God's realm will presumably not eliminate hierarchy but will simply reverse the hierarchy of the world. It appears most accurate merely to declare that Christianity establishes a set of standards for the measurement of the excellencies it recognizes—a standard which is different from, even opposite to, those accepted in the world.[2]

Why does Christianity, at least in one aspect of its social theory, so persistently reject the standards of the world? This is not an easy question to answer. One thinks first, perhaps,

2 The most specific and decisive statement in the Gospels of Christian antagonism to the hierarchies of the world is to be found in *Mark* 10: 42-45. Here Jesus reminds his disciples that "they which are accounted to rule over the Gentiles, exercise lordship over them; and . . . authority upon them" and then admonishes that "so shall it not be among you. . . ." With true Christians, rather, "whosoever shall be great among you, shall be your minister and whosoever of you will be the chiefest, shall be servant of all." This is indeed a striking declaration, but even it is placed in the context of a concept of holy society which continues to admit differences of degrees. Degrees of humility and service in the world are rewarded by proportionate degrees of preferment and glory in heaven.

of the fundamental nonnaturalistic or antinaturalistic bias characteristic of sophisticated religions—those religions which have come to dominate in the civilized culture of the world. These religions deal not in life and death but in immortality, not in nature but in supernature, not in what is seen but in what is hoped for. The very fact that a thing exists and is observable militates to some extent in such a system against its being accepted as the true embodiment of divine reality. Thus, as a product of man's discontent with his natural limitations, the religious viewpoint comes to have an affinity with all manner of trouble, sorrow, and frustration. What earth has not given, heaven will provide. It is altogether a fertile soil for the cultivation of dreams.

So much can be said in a general way, but there are more specific and concrete factors which encourage in Christianity in particular a tendency to reject the values of the world, especially as they are expressed in the standards and practices of social caste and class. Among the religions of the world whose historical origins are known, Christianity is the humblest in its primary source of inspiration and leadership. There is no need lingering on this point; it is too well known to require elaboration. But one should consider well the impact which this fact of Christianity's humble social origins would inevitably have upon the Christian social ethic: that is the strengthening of any already-present tendency to bring into question or reject the hierarchy of the world as it existed and to assert the establishment of God's hierarchy of grace (ultimately to be the hierarchy of heaven) upon totally different foundations.

This theoretical denial of the hierarchies of the Roman world was all the easier because they ran so patently counter to all the principles of human relationship which the Christian ideal of kinship society embodied. Insofar as the Christian ideal accepted or defended hierarchy, it was the mutually sustaining hierarchy of the kinship community where greater prestige was presumably the badge of greater capacity for service to the group as a whole. But Roman society, at least as viewed by inferior groups within it, exhibited little if any concern for such kinship moralism. It was basically a military society and its hierarchies were therefore originally ones of conquest and derivatively ones of the difference in wealth and power which are the heritage of conquest. It was, moreover, a slave society and great masses of human beings were held in the social group simply as captives without any substantial claims upon it for regard or protection. It was a society which the social theory of Christianity, as that theory has been here defined, could do nothing but reject in whole or in large part.

Thus a number of factors in the development of early Christianity pressed toward an identification between the way of the socially humble, oppressed, and deprived and the way of godliness or salvation; the socially powerful and affluent, on the other hand, were seen as running a risk, by virtue of their very power and wealth, of damnation in eternity. Here, then, is that Christian transvaluation of values, to which Nietzsche pays the tribute of his animosity, by means of which the multitude of the weak in the world could achieve in the weak man's feminine way (by words instead of deeds) a satisfying revenge against the few who were strong.

These ideas we have been analyzing constitute the substance of Christian radicalism, and there is no radicalism in history which, as pure concept, is more thoroughly disruptive of the usual patterns of civilized society. Yet, despite this essential substratum of subversion within it, Christianity, in itself at least, has never become the basis for a program of social revolution or even of social reform. The acid which might dissolve the social fabric has been neutralized, the force which might disintegrate it has been harmlessly diverted by other factors in the Christian complex. Christianity is a religion, first of all, whose principal concern has been not with justice in this world but with salvation in the next. A positive correlation has been established in Christianity, moreover, between suffering and deprivation here and reward hereafter. This ascetic inclination, rather than endeavoring to avoid or ameliorate worldly suffering, has actually pursued it. Even when so complete a reversal of nature's impulses has not been attempted and the believer has not been led to seek for suffering, the Christian faith has at least assured him of heavenly compensation for the afflictions which come to him. Because of the nature of Christianity's subversiveness, therefore, the worldly status quo has been more often sustained than undermined. Rather than stimulating policies to remedy what are viewed as social injustices, Christianity has served as an effective safety valve to draw off from the social body discontent and potential protest and disturbance. The "opiate of the people," Marx has called it.

In addition, Christianity was at first and to some extent has always been a force without a force, as it were—a collection of ideas essentially, whose only chance for survival as an entity was adjustment to and acceptance by the real agencies of power, the military, political, and economic elite, the ruling classes of the world. How quickly this effort at placation and adjustment was made is evident even in the pronouncements of Christ Himself and, with especial emphasis, in the epistles of St. Paul. The pressure within Christianity toward church building or institutionalization did clothe the ideology, to be sure, in a certain concrete power, but it tended to confirm it also in a taste for the dun raiment of social conservatism. For it is the mutual and cooperative interworking of institution with institution which, by maintaining the security and stability of all, best assures the security and stability of each. In order to achieve their central purpose, the right peaceably to direct their followers toward salvation, Christian churches have understandably endeavored for the most part, on the minimum terms of tolerance of doctrinal tenets, to become established parts of the societies in which they have existed, whatever their form or type, and have in turn afforded loyal support to these societies.

At the time of Protestantism's emergence, Roman Catholicism had been the established faith of Western Europe for a millennium. A massive institutionalism had grown up around this faith, moreover, and the Roman Catholic Church had come to claim and exercise powers which few if any other churches in history could match. This powerful church, having withstood not only the predations of the barons of feudal Europe but also the upthrusting popular heresies of the later middle ages, had moved into a role of leadership which far transcended the basic and originally exclusive obligation to preach the Gospels.

Thus the nature of church authority in the middle ages—the fundamental institutional character of that authority—decisively shifted the focus of professional Christianity from invisible to visible church, from chiliastic expectation to the defense of status quo realities, from preaching to sacramental science, from the mystical, visionary, and persecuted community of saints to the worldly, manipulating, and persecuting partner in the rulership of Europe.

For all practical purposes the social theory of Roman Catholicism became so thoroughly a declaration and defense of the shape of society in medieval Western Europe—so thoroughly entrenched in the Thomistic idealization of the feudal structuring of human relationships—that to this day it can be said to include a determined bias in the direction of such a system.[3] What precisely this medieval system was it is not within the scope of our study to define (though a number of specific issues will be dealt with in later chapters), but its watchwords in general were hierarchy and stability. The hierarchy of the church imposed upon but also giving strength and permanence to the hierarchy of secular society—this is the plan of social organization which Catholic concepts exhibit and champion; and what adjustments have been made to the greater mobility and equalitarianism of the modern world have, for the most part, been made reluctantly and with many a regretful backward glance to a time when a single church's religious authority stood relatively unchallenged in the West and society moved more nearly in the ways which this church had found and declared to be Christian.

It is an historical truism that Protestantism came into existence when the social and cultural synthesis of medieval Europe had been for some time in a process of disintegration. Protestantism is itself a symptom in part of this disintegration, if for no other reason than because it spelled the break-up of the

---

[3] The big book on Christianity and its social theory is still Ernst Troeltsch, *The Social Teaching of the Christian Churches* (2 vols.; N. Y., 1931), always stimulating, a genuinely seminal work. For his discussion of the Thomistic Ethic, see Volume I, 257-328. See also Katherine Archibald, "The Concept of Social Hierarchy in the Writings of St. Thomas Aquinas," *Historian* (XII, 1949), 28-54.

monolithic religious institution which had dominated Western Europe for so long. Protestantism emerged, in sum, into a world in process of rapid and profound change. To what extent and in what manner does the Protestant social theory of the sixteenth and seventeenth centuries reflect these changes? To what extent and in what manner does it differ from Catholic social theory?

One must note first—and one cannot emphasize too much—that Protestantism is primarily a religious movement. Its social theory is entirely secondary and coincidental to its religious theory. This is perhaps especially true in the earlier decades of its struggles to exist when it had made no commitments to any particular type of society and was really conscious of only one mission: to save souls from the weltering sea of Catholic error and indifference and bring them safe to the rock of faith and the Gospel. But inevitably, of course, religious discontent ties up with other kinds of discontent and a variety of groups choose to embrace Protestantism for a variety of reasons, not all of them religious. Thus alliances between ideas are made, so many alliances, in fact, that it is virtually impossible to speak of a Protestant social theory as such at any stage of Protestant development. Without implying crass opportunism, one is still compelled to say that to a large extent the social philosophy of a given brand of Protestantism, where such a philosophy can be defined as a specific entity, depended largely for its character on the interests and problems of the group in society or the power-complex on which the form of Protestantism was itself dependent.

Having acknowledged its great variety, one can still assert of Protestant social theory that it did in general represent a moving away from the type of social theory embraced by Roman Catholicism—that theory which, on the one hand, glorified a saint's society completely separate from and antagonistic to the standards of the world and, on the other, confirmed as acceptably Christian a class society in the rigid feudal pattern. Some of the rejection of this Catholic social theory comes about because of Protestantism's tendency to deny totally the validity of a double standard of morality. No doubt some of it comes

about as well because, as we have seen, Protestantism first began
and was accepted in a period when certain segments of society
were more or less consciously in rebellion against some aspect
of the feudal structure which Catholicism had sponsored or protected; they sought in the new religion those elements by which
new social practices would be adequately sanctioned and the
growth in Protestantism of an accommodating anti-Catholic
social theory was thereby encouraged.

How much can we balance this minimal and largely negative
statement of the anti-Catholic cast of Protestant social theory
by asserting some of Protestant theory's positive qualities? Can
any positive connection be posited, for example, between Protestant social theory and the attitudes of Christian radicalism?
To a certain extent we feel that it can.

Early Protestantism does represent, first of all, a movement
of Christian revival and as such it harks back, more immediately
than Roman Catholicism, at least, to the temper of early Christianity and to Christianity's Old Testament origins. Thus it
comes closer to the spirit of tribal community which is the essence of Christian radicalism. Then too, the breakdown of the
Roman Catholic double standard releases into the general religious body the impulses toward Christian radicalism which had
previously been confined within monastic boundaries. The
Christian saint, with all that he implies of an effort to shape
the existence of today after the pattern of eternity, is a man
among men, living in all institutional or occupational regards
the ordinary life of men. He is capable of making noisy criticisms of what he considers to be worldly improprieties or injustice, or even of engaging in troublesome activities of reform.

The institutional weakness or inefficiency of Protestantism, as
compared with Catholicism, and its consequent efflorescence into
a variety of sects is a further factor encouraging the relatively
luxuriant growth of radical mentality. Protestant sects, unrespectable by their very institutional nature, tend to attract as
members those who are also unrespectable or whose ties to their
societies are for some reason frail or frayed. The voice of social
as well as religious protest comes readily to such people, particularly in the period of active persecution by established

authority. Yet, insofar as such protest remains only a statement of Christian radicalism, it is likely to have little practical content or effect, for the concept of Christian radicalism, with its emphasis on brotherly love and kinship equalitarianism, has its real roots, after all, in the dream of a primitive and tribal past. It makes extremely tenuous contact with civilized society, whether with the imperial society of Rome, the feudal society of the middle ages, or the capitalistic society of the modern world.

In one respect, indeed, the existence of Protestant sectarianism has a negative effect upon the content of Christian radicalism in Protestantism as a whole. The strictures of St. Paul enjoining the good Christian to an entirely obedient acceptance of worldly institutions and authority (except as they directly conflicted with the proper performance of religious duties) were undoubtedly prompted, at least in part, by the understandable eagerness of certain Christians to put into practice on earth some of the provisions of mutual service and community sharing which were presumed to apply to the society of heaven. The very social radicalism of some Christians further insured the conservatism of the main body of Christianity. The same story was repeated in Protestantism, for the suggestions which the sects provided—that Protestant doctrine might be used as an argument to stimulate social change and reconstruction—made all the more conscious and concerted the effort of the leading lights among the major Protestant denominations to assure their princely, aristocratic, and respectable burgher followings that in truth the doctrine contained no such dangerous potential.

Though one can say, therefore, that the total content of Christian radicalism is larger in Protestantism as a whole than in Roman Catholicism as a whole, and that a way is more readily available in the former than in the latter body of Christian belief to the occasional undisciplined upsurge of such radicalism into the realm of practical policy, still it would be extremely rash to make any precise or emphatic statement on the greater susceptibility of Protestant social theory to the influence of the equalitarian and communalistic thought of early Christianity.

It has been much more common among the historians of ideas to link the greater Christian personalism of Protestantism to the political and social concepts of modern liberalism. Numerous students of the subject have presumed to discover a carryover between the widespread Protestant recognition of the religious autonomy of the individual and a corresponding recognition of his political and economic autonomy. Thus it has been alleged that there existed an early ideological sponsorship by Protestantism for the capitalistic and democratic institutions of the modern world.[4] But again, we wish first to introduce a note of caution. We must remind ourselves that Protestantism is primarily a religious movement and Protestant individualism, though it may be tied to the general impulses which make for Christian radicalism, is primarily a religious individualism with no line to any particular form of civilized society. The intensity of early Christian individualism was certainly equal to that of the strongest Protestant expression of the idea, but nonetheless these early Christians found it altogether possible to accept and settle into the slave society of the Roman Empire.

It should be noted further that the autonomy of the individual in Protestantism, even in religious matters, is wholly relative. The entire concept of Protestant personalism acquires its validity only in comparison between the Protestant and the Roman Catholic layman. Certain institutional obstructions and limitations which confront the latter individual in his contacts with his God do not confront the former. Yet if one considers the Roman Catholic cleric and, above all, the Roman Catholic saint, the contrast is far less evident. Indeed, a sound argument could be made that, insofar as there is a contrast, it is the Roman Catholic who has before him the freer and more personal pathway to the deity. Mysticism represents an ultimate development of religious individualism, and mysticism has surely flourished more luxuriantly in Roman Catholic than in Protestant circles. It is a gross distortion of the facts, therefore, to conceive of the Protestant, saint though he be, as standing alone in the world

[4] Cf. A. S. P. Woodhouse, *Puritanism and Liberty* (1938); William Haller, *The Rise of Puritanism* (N. Y., 1938); B. N. Nelson, *The Idea of Usury* (Princeton, 1949) for a sampling of recent opinion all tending to elaborate the connections first suggested by Troeltsch, *op.cit.*, and Weber, *The Protestant Ethic and the Spirit of Capitalism* (1930).

and seeking within himself for the true course of salvation. The Protestant belongs to a church; he is guided and even commanded by ministers; he is surrounded by a creed. There is sufficiently greater flexibility and openness in Protestantism, to be sure, so that creeds multiply much more readily within it than in the older faith, but each creed in its turn can become an intellectual strait-jacket for its adherents.[5]

The individualism of the Protestant is confined still further. Like all Christians, the Protestant founds and builds his doctrine not on a discovery of new truth but on an uncovering of old. His glance is always directed backward toward a source of revelation in the past, and genuine invention is anathema to him. In this regard, too, the individual whom the liberal celebrates as the triumphant representative of modernity has far more to do with the rakes, explorers, scientists, scholars, artists, and commercial speculators of the sixteenth and seventeenth centuries than with the Protestant saints of that epoch.

The really definitive and general quality of Protestant, as compared with Roman Catholic, social theory appears to us to be primarily the greater pliability of the Protestant temper and its greater responsiveness to the pressures of time and circumstance. Born into an age of rapid change, splitting itself almost at once into a number of creeds and sects, each with its own particular national locale and social affiliations, Protestantism never possessed a base of stability or an island of isolation on which to establish a single, consistent, and long-lasting dogma for social issues. One can only speak specifically or fully of the social theory of a given form of Protestantism in a given time and place. Hence this survey of the nature of Protestant social theory must be concluded at the very point where it was begun—with a statement of its variety and with an acknowledgment that it can best be studied in terms of particulars rather than in a wide or universal way.

## II. Christian Brotherhood

In regard to the basic concepts of man and his relationship to other men, the viewpoint of English Protestantism does not

[5] See Troeltsch, *op.cit.*, I.

differ from that of any other form of Christianity. In terms of their original God-created qualities, men are believed to be by nature social rather than solitary, and fitted for friendship with one another rather than antagonism. "Civil society," Hooker asserts, "doth more content the nature of man than any private kind of solitary living. . . ."[6] "Man and man are not contrarie in nature, or naturall properties," Perkins writes, "but are all one flesh. The contrarietie that is, is by reason of the corruption of nature."[7]

By virtue of their original nature or of their rational qualities in their present nature, men are social; but by virtue of their fallen nature, they are often enemies of one another. "In respect of ourselves," Andrewes observes, "this is our estate before we become true Christians, To be 'hateful, and to hate one another.' . . ."[8] It becomes the function of Christianity, or of the saving grace which Christianity bespeaks, to lift man out of his fallen state and to restore to him his original sociability and capacity to love and be loved. But all men cannot be restored to their original condition, for all men cannot be saved. Thus the world is destined to be principally inhabited by hating and hateful men. This is the structure of English Protestant thinking, as it is of all Christian thinking on the subject.

The Christian social ethic demands, in its extremest statement, that the true follower love his neighbor as himself and see his neighbor as every other human being in the world. "Our neighbour is every one," Perkins insists, "which is of our owne flesh."[9] Andrewes comments that "Christ . . . sheweth that 'mercy and not difference of country, makes one our neighbour, and if he be a neighbour that sheweth mercy . . . then he must be also a neighbour that standeth in need of mercy, though he be our enemy.' "[10] The occasional English Protestant, accepting Calvin's lead,[11] conceives of himself as maintaining for his faith more rigorous demands in this direction than those accepted

---

[6] Hooker, *Polity*, I, x, 12.     [7] Perkins, *Works*, II, 334.
[8] Andrewes, *Works*, VIII, 432.     [9] Perkins, *Works*, I, 49.
[10] Andrewes, *Works*, II, 171.
[11] See C. H. George, "English Calvinist Opinion on Usury, 1600-1640," *Journal of the History of Ideas* (October, 1957), pp. 458-460, for a discussion of Calvin's concept of brotherhood.

as sufficient by the faith of Rome. Thus Perkins attacks the Roman church for making of the injunction to love one's enemies almost exclusively a counsel of perfection rather than a precept for expected Christian action. "But this doctrine is damnable," he asserts, "and therefore we must renounce it and acknowledge that we are bound in conscience on every occasion, to shew our love in word and deed unto our private enemies. . . . It is true, indeed, this is hard for flesh and blood to doe; but if we be but flesh, that is, naturall men, why doe we professe ourselves to be Christians?"[12]

Such pronouncements on the requirement of universal brotherhood and love as one finds in this literature, however, are generally characterized by abstractness of expression and aridity of tone. The theme exists only as a restrained reflection of its form and quantity in the New Testament, where also, it must be admitted, it lacks substance beside the far more strenuous emphasis on the essential and intimate community of believers. English Protestant divines, moreover, following the long-established traditions of social practicality, tend to qualify this doctrine of unlimited love by parcelling out differing degrees of required affection on the basis of differing kinds and degrees of worldly relationship. By means of such a rationing system, Andrewes, for example, immediately circumscribes and weakens his statement, cited above, of the necessary universality of Christian love. "Now where there is a greater duty," he enjoins, "there must be a greater affection, and so greater love; and the order of our love must be thus, a. To God . . . b. Our own souls . . . c. The souls of our brethren before our own bodies . . . d. Our own bodies before other men's . . . e. The bodies of our neighbours: and among them first to them that have need; and of those first to the household of faith . . . and of them first to our countrymen . . . and of these first them which are our friends and acquaintance; and of them first to our own, and namely, them of our household."[13]

The universal brotherhood of man is a corollary in Christianity of the assumption of the universal fatherhood of God. It is

---

[12] Perkins, *Works*, III, 97-98.
[13] Andrewes, *Works*, II, 171-73.

from this point too, the all-embracing creativity of God, that the Christian argument moves out to assert the requirement of universal love among men. Yet this nexus of ideas, positive, optimistic, love-laden as it is, inevitably encounters in Christianity the opposite nexus of ideas which is negative, despairing, and burdened with judgments of doom and hate. For God, though he has created all men, will save only a few; the majority are destined for destruction. Through the mass of humanity runs this line of profoundest separation between the saved and the damned.

This is universal Christian doctrine. Does English Protestantism bring anything special to its exposition? Only, relative to Roman Catholicism, a certain intensification of the common theme. Just as the requirement of love for one's fellows is somewhat more strictly and broadly stated in English Protestantism than in Roman Catholicism (what in Roman Catholicism is a counsel for the peculiarly dedicated soul becomes in English Protestantism a precept for all Christians) so, as we observed in the previous chapter, there is in English Protestantism a greater general awareness of the nature and the prevalence of damnation. Yet lest this contradiction should produce too patently schizoid a mentality, a moderating influence is introduced. We have seen that English Protestantism encourages on the whole, and quite specifically, a certain confidence in the believing Christian in his own salvation. But it does not, directly or doctrinally at least, encourage any similar confidence regarding the spiritual state, be it saved or reprobate, of anyone else. Indeed, the English Protestant is repeatedly enjoined to maintain a condition of suspended judgment on this subject or even to assume, for charity's sake, the probable eventual salvation of other men, whoever or whatever they may be. "It may be demanded," Perkins inquires, "what we are to judge of them that as yet are enemies of God." And he answers his own question by remarking that our duty is "to suspend our judgment concerning their finall estate; for we know not whether God will call them or no; and therefore we must rather pray for their conversion, then for their confusion."[14] He makes particularly emphatic this pro-

14 Perkins, *Works*, I, 290.

nouncement as it applies to those who are nominally Christians or members of one's own church. "Now the judgement of charitie," he writes, "belongs unto all men; and by it leaving all secret judgements unto God, we are charitably to thinke, that all those, that live in the Church of God, professing themselves to be members of Christ, are indeede elect to salvation, till God make manifest otherwise."[15]

Gouge, in discussing the question of the extent of the Christian's social responsibility in prayer, sums up this judgment of charity. "All men living on earth," he asserts, "are to bee prayed for . . . whether they be in the Church or out of it, called or not called, friends or foes." He gives two reasons for this injunction. First, he explains, all men "are made after the same Image of God that wee are . . . all [are] our neighbours." He notes secondly that "for ought we know, all may belong to the election of God and so have a right to priviledges of Gods Elect . . . we [can] not say of any particular man, that he belongeth not to Gods election. If he be not now called, he may be hereafter."[16]

Thanks in part to the contradictions inherent in Christianity itself, thanks, too, no doubt to the very excessiveness of the demand of the basic Christian ethic that all men are to be viewed as members of a single family and loved with the love of kinship, the actual doctrinal product of the preachment of Christian love, even as it appears in English Protestantism with its revivalistic recall of early Christian enthusiasms, is a rather pale and unsubstantial affair. The only practical effect of the social ethic of English Protestantism, when viewed from this initial standpoint, would seem to be a somewhat greater capacity for tolerance of other Christian sects and creeds than the social ethic of Roman Catholicism afforded. And even this capacity was only a potential, dependent for realization on external circumstances. The ethic of love in English Protestantism, like the ethic of love in Christianity as a whole, was in and of itself incapable of withstanding the pressure of any worldly hostility whether of sectarian, political, racial, or class origin. It was a pious wish, rather than an effective stimulant of attitude or action.

[15] Ibid., p. 282.
[16] Gouge, The Whole Armour of God (1627), p. 187.

## III. Christian Equalitarianism

With one aspect of Christian radicalism so readily disposed of, what can be said of the significance in the writings of English Protestantism of that other ingredient of the early Christian social outlook: the tendency to reject the social hierarchies of the world in favor of a relative equalitarianism or at least a restatement of what is worldly in terms of what were conceived to be heavenly evaluations? Were pronouncements from the English Protestant pulpit critical of or disturbing to the general hierarchical structuring of contemporary society?

The reader who pursues an overtly equalitarian doctrine in these sermons will find little to encourage or reward his search. Viewed from any time later than their own but viewed, too, from the standpoint of Christianity's earliest centuries, these English Protestant divines appear strongly conservative in their organized and conscious social teachings. They are, indeed, seemingly inexhaustible fountains of comment and counsel supportive of both the principle and the particular facts of a graded social structure. The natural necessity of social hierarchy is consistently upheld by them and firmly buttressed with a variety of argument. Perkins, for one, presents a classic statement of the organic basis and purpose of social distinctions of an hierarchical type: as there are in the human body differentiations in the nature and function of parts, so "God hath appointed that in every societie one person should be above or under another; not making all equall, as though the bodie should be all head and nothing else: but even in degree and order, he hath set a distinction, that one should be above another."[17]

Turning to a more architectonic image to provide a framework for his thought, Adams draws a picture of the upward thrust of dominions from the individual to God in which each man "hath . . . a kingdome over reasonlesse creatures . . . the householder in his familie, the Magistrate over the communaltie, the king over all."[18] God, of course, is "onely and solely an absolute king," but even while God's infinite supremacy over

[17] Perkins, *Works*, I, 755.
[18] Adams, *Works*, pp. 431-32.

all interhuman differences is seen to limit their significance and control their exercise, the fact that God has decreed the existence of such differences in the first place assures them of validity and permanence in society. Adams comments further: ". . . if God gives to some men Honour, it is then manifest that God allowes difference of persons. Hee ordaines some to rule and others to obey . . . hee setteth some up on high, and placeth others in a low degree. To repine at others greatnesse and our owne meannesse, is to cavill with God. . . . It is a savage and popular humour, to maligne and inveigh against men in eminent places. That rhyme, when Adam delved, and Eve span: Who was then a Gentleman? seemes to bee made among Jack Strawes followers, and to savour of rebellious discontent. . . . Where the Lord conferres and confirmes Honour, woe to the tongue that shall traduce it."[19]

As the passage from Adams's sermons shows, the dynamics of contention on this subject involve not only general support for the inequalitarian structure of society, but specific attack upon equalitarian ideas; indeed, the existence of such ideas in the world is acknowledged in this literature only by means of such opposition. "There be some," Andrewes notes, "that would make us believe, it is a sin to stand upon a pinnacle; but then, if that had been so, Christ would never have stood there. And since Christ stood there, it is no . . . sin for any man else to stand there . . . for it is lawful for us to follow His footsteps, and to tread wheresoever He hath trod before us. . . ."[20]

Gouge assails the Anabaptists, "who teach that all are alike, and that there is no difference betwixt masters and servants." He then proceeds to demolish what he asserts to be the Anabaptist claim that Christians, since they are bound by brotherly love, cannot therefore be separated by sharp distinctions of social status. "Rule and subjection are matters of outward policy," he explains, "they tend to the outward preservation of Church, Commonwealth, and family, in the world: but faith, piety, and such graces are inward matters of the soule, tending to a better life."[21]

[19] *Ibid.*, p. 872.    [20] Andrewes, *Works*, VIII, 517.
[21] Gouge, *Domesticall Duties* (1627), p. 4.

Confronting this same "Anabaptist" contention that because "all believers are one in Christ: therefore there is no subjection among them," Perkins gives the same type of reply; it is, to be sure, little other than the reply of St. Paul to what must have been a very similar proposition arising long before out of certain aspects of the Christian viewpoint. "Believers are under a two-fold estate or regiment," he writes, "the first is, the regiment of this world, in civil societtie: the second is, the regiment of the kingdom of heaven. . . . In the first estate, there are sundry differences of persons that believe: some fathers and mothers, some children, some masters and servants, some magistrates and some subjects. In the second estate, there are not outward differences of men, but all are members of Christ, and all one in him."[22]

In accordance with the moral preoccupations of Christianity, the appurtenances of status, whether high or low, tend to be defined in this literature in terms of duties instead of rights. Gouge introduces a long discussion of the function and purpose of differentiations in class and rank with the primary injuction: *"It is a generall mutuall duty appertaining to all Christians to submit themselves one to another*: For this precept is . . . generall . . . belonging to all sorts and degrees whatsoever." He further elucidates this general rule of submission by distinguishing between two types of subjection: the "subjection of reverence," which is owed only by inferiors to superiors, and the "subjection of service," which is owed by every Christian to every other Christian. "Subjection of service," he explains, "is that whereby one in his place is ready to doe what good he can to another. This is common to all Christians, a duty which even superiours owe to inferiours . . . in which respect even the highest governour on earth is called a minister for the good of such as are under him."[23] The moral nature of the whole network of social relationships is affirmed again in the statement: "The reason why all are bound to submit themselves one to another is because every one is set in his place by God not so much for himselfe, as for the good of others: whereupon the Apostle exhorteth, *that none seeke his owne but every man anothers wealth.*"[24]

[22] Perkins, *Works*, II, 266.     [23] Gouge, *op.cit.*, p. 3.     [24] *Ibid.*, p. 4.

The traditional concern of Christian moralism with both the guidance and the support of the hierarchies of society is also exhibited in the many references in this literature to the duties of superiors and inferiors to each other, but especially of inferiors to superiors, in specific institutional categories of interclass relationship. Such a duty-centered interpretation of social hierarchies serves to make all the easier their defense as necessary, righteous, and godly, and further assures that something of the same universalization of the status quo that was once so singularly achieved by Thomistic social theory will eventuate from the arguments of English Protestantism in this area.

## IV. The Protestant Saint

By the compromising and compliant tone of the English Protestant social theory we have been considering, we are reminded with what facile sophistry in established Christian creeds Christian radicalism is tamed and transmuted into Christian conservatism. We have looked on and without astonishment at what is an old story in the long and circuitous history of Christianity: certain of the human discontents and hungers basic to the initial Christian vision of a good society and clearly critical and rebellious in one context have, in another context, been drained of all their troublesome potential and fitted smoothly into an ideology of conformity.

But this old story, repeated here with little variation on traditional themes, is not all that English Protestantism has to tell. For Christian radicalism also exists in these sermons as a bold and aggressive force and with much of its ancient penchant for questioning the ways of worldly power. One must look for it, however, not so much in terms of general definitions of and formuli for the good society, as in specific recommendations for the conduct of an individual Christian life. One must look for it, in short, in the English Protestant doctrine of the saint.

Essential to understanding the English Protestant saint's special qualities is a preliminary consideration of the nature of the saint of medieval Roman Catholicism. This saint is, to begin with, a representative of that double standard of morality in

Roman Catholicism to which we have made so much reference; indeed, concerning the actual fulfillment of the requirements, the Roman Catholic saint *is* the upper level of that double standard. But this means that typically (though not without exception) he is institutionally segregated from the rest of mankind—a special brand of man, living a special brand of life.

On the other hand, the purpose of the Protestant was, as we have seen, to bring to every kind of life the opportunity of achieving the utmost pinnacles of religious experience possible in this world. Thus in comparison with the Catholic "saint," the term as used by the Protestant—or specifically by the English Protestant—is far more broadly applicable. In the last analysis, every truly faithful Christian, every man who possesses and who lives by God's grace is, in the English Protestant view, as much of a saint as it is given to any man to be.

English Protestantism generally rejects all Roman Catholic doctrines and practices based on the assumption of the intercession of the saints. Andrewes does exhibit some tendency to compromise in this regard. Though God has no need of any mediator between Himself and men other than Christ, still it is possible, he suggests, that saints may occasionally intercede. But even if this is true, saints may still not be properly invoked by men to offer intercession. "And we will hope well," Andrewes comments, "that Theodosius might intercede with God for his children; we see no cause to the contrary. But that Theodosius should be called on by his children, that is the question. And that will not stand with *Tu, Domine, solus invocandus es.*"[25]

The more usual English Protestant position, however, is stated by Perkins: "They [the Roman Catholics] hold . . . that the Saints in heaven . . . doe make intercession to God for particular men . . . but this doctrine we flatly renounce . . . the Saints departed see not the state of the church on earth, much lesse do they know the thoughts and praiers of men. . . . No creature . . . can bee a Mediatour for us to God, saving Christ alone, who is . . . the onely Advocate of his Church."[26]

The goodness of the saint, this argument continues, is, after

[25] Andrewes, *Works*, XI, 58-59.
[26] Perkins, *Works*, I, 603-04.

all, only a reflection of the goodness of God, a gift of God's grace; it has, therefore, no merit in itself. Perkins concludes the matter by contending that, even if man were granted the capacity to earn spiritual merit through human deeds, "yet should his merits be for himselfe alone and for none other: for everie man in regard of salvatie is a private man, and the reward of his workes can only redound unto himselfe, only Christ Jesus . . . who was by God himselfe made a publike person for this end, can merit for others."[27] Yet Perkins, too, speaks for a kind of honor to be rendered unto saints: "such as are Saints indeed," he writes, "are to be honoured by an approbation of Gods gifts in them, and by an honourable mention of them, and also by imitation of their manners and lives, being as patterns for us to walke after."[28]

The saint for English Protestantism is, in summary, anyone in any profession, calling, or station who lives a fully Christian life. *"Why are all Believers called Saints?"* Ussher asks. "Because they are partakers of Christ's holinesse," he answers, "dayly growing and increasing in the same; and to let us know that none shall ever be Saints in heaven, but such as are first Saints on earth."[29]

"The Christian," Hall declares, "is a man and more; an earthly Saint, an Angell cloathed in flesh . . . the abstract of Gods church on earth; a modell of heaven made up in clay; the living Temple of the holy Ghost."[30]

If one seeks a more precise definition of the saint in the sermons of English Protestantism, one must turn to all those discussions of the inner qualities and outer practices which are presumed to be essential to the virtuous Christian. The core of the matter is, as we have seen in the previous chapter, wholly interior, since it consists of the ingrafting of God's grace, inwardly felt as faith, into a man. There are outer signs too, of course—signs in behavior which are signified by the term of sanctification. Preston, after discoursing at some length on the transformation of conduct which will occur in the regenerate man—the giving up of drinking, gaming, "uncleannesse," Sab-

27 *Works*, III, 164-66.  28 *Works*, I, 39.
29 Ussher, *Divinitie*, p. 191.  30 Hall, *Works*, IV, 626.

bath-breaking, the acquiring of a new manner of speech and a taste for new company, and so on—observes: "Therefore, it is no strange marke that I give, that examining your selves by the out-side should bee a meanes to know if you bee New Creatures; for, though we cannot say that because the out-side is good, the in-side is so too; yet wee may conclude if the out-side bee not good, certainly thou art not a New Creature yet."[31]

As for Roman Catholicism, the saint for English Protestantism is the perfect man, but because of English Protestantism's profound conviction of the ineradicable sinfulness of all men, there is always this element of contradiction in the concept of the saint: the most nearly perfect man is he who is most aware of his imperfections. Thus Hall declares that a recognition of the "weakness of Grace" is the mark of the saint.[32] And Perkins points out that though "there is a perfection in the child of God," it is "joyned with much weaknesse . . . in this life," and though "his actions are perfect in God's acceptance through Christ," they are so only because "he bewailes his imperfections, and endeavours sincerely to please God in all things."[33] As consciousness of sinfulness and weakness is a necessary ingredient of the English Protestant saint, any departure from a suitable humility is in the direction of spiritual pride. Perkins observes that "many other sinnes prevaile in the wicked, but pride is the sin that troubleth the children of God, and when other sinnes die, then will pride revive, yea it will arise out of grace itselfe: for the child of God will be proud because he is not proud."[34]

Hence the English Protestant saint possesses a double nature. He must be humble, since humility is an indication of sanctity; yet, since he is allowed an awareness of his sanctity, he cannot but feel set apart and especially privileged. It is indeed a duty which he must fulfill that he should militantly assert his virtue and the power of his faith in the world. Perkins, for example, while discoursing on the scriptural dictum that the meek shall inherit the earth, cautions the believer that his meekness must be displayed "not in the matters of God, when his glorie is

---

[31] Preston, *The Saints Qualification* (1634), p. 365.
[32] Hall, *Works*, IV, 548.      [33] Perkins, *Works*, III, 102.
[34] *Ibid.*, p. 105.

impeached: for therein we must have zeale as hot as fire: but in the wrongs and injuries that concerne our selves."[35] And Bolton briefly sums up these two opposing aspects of the saint by declaring that the "inhabitants of Heaven Elect, are (1) Humble Soules thirsting after grace and God's favour . . . and (2) Christ's champions here upon earth against the power of darkenesse, and conquerors of their own corruptions."[36]

Viewed from the standpoint of the devout Christian, no earthly honor or position can match in importance or privilege the status of the saint. "Here note a singular fruit of true faith," Perkins remarks, "it brings a man to that estate . . . that he is more worth than the whole world. . . . If then a man would have true and stable dignitie, let him labour for true faith."[37] True believers, he observes, have the dignity both of kings and priests. "They are called kings," he writes, "not in regard of an earthly kingdom . . . but in regard of a spiritual kingdom, the kingdom of heaven, whereto the Lord gives them . . . title. . . . They be priests consecrated and set apart by Christ to the worship and service of God . . . in this life, and in the life to come. . . ."[38]

"A Christian is above all," Sibbes contends. "He is over sin and Satan and the Law, he is free and supreame and independent; all are under him. . . . The spirituall man judgeth all things, yet hee himselfe is judged of no man. . . . All earthly things he commands . . . by the Spirit of Christ in him he rules over all."[39]

For Bolton, the saint not only properly rules over all the world but he properly possesses it as well: ". . . a godly man, by the great worke of regeneration is become *more excellent, than his neighbour*; as indeed he incomparably is, howsoever the worlds estimation be otherwise . . . the worldling is a wrongful usurper of the riches, honors, and preferments of this life; for which hereafter he must be condemned to chaines of eternall darkenesse . . . the saint, whiles hee continues in this world, is a right-

[35] *Ibid.*, p. 8.

[36] Bolton, *Instructions for a Right Comforting Afflicted Consciences* (1631), Dedicatory Epistle.

[37] Perkins, *Works*, III, 194.

[38] *Ibid.*, pp. 225-26.

[39] Sibbes, *Beames of Divine Light* (1639), pp. 231-33.

full owner and possessor of the earth, and all the creatures and blessings of God; and when he departs hence, he shall be made a glorious inhabitant of those sacred mansions. . . ."[40]

The saints are priests, kings, judges, currently possessors of all the world in the true spiritual sense of ownership and ultimately its inheritors in full fact. In the last analysis, it is for them alone that the world is permitted by God to continue its existence. "The world stands for the Elect," Sibbes asserts. "If all the Elect were gathered out of the world, there would be an end of all things."[41] Perkins observes that "the Lord stayes the execution of his Judgements for a time, that his elect may be gathered and converted. . . . So that every nation and people in the world have benefit by Gods children; because for their sakes doth the Lord stay his wrath, and deferre his judgments."[42]

Even Sanderson, the conservative Anglican, supports this thesis and extracts from it this admonition to the wicked: ". . . here is Instruction for Worldlings, to make much of those few godly ones that live among them; for they are the very Pawns of their Peace, and Pledges of their security. Think not, ye filthy Sodomites, it is for your own sakes, that ye have been spared so long; know to whom you are beholden. This Fellow that came in to sojourn among you, this Stranger, this Lot . . . he it is that have bailed you hitherto, and given you Protection. . . . Learn, O ye Despisers, that if God thus forbear you, it is not at all for your own sakes, or because he careth not to punish evil doers; no, he hath a little remnant, a little flock, a little handful of his own among you; a few names that have given themselves unto him, and call upon him daily for mercy upon the Land, and that weep and mourn in secret . . . for your Abominations. . . ."[43]

The "little remnant," the "few godly"—these are phrases which come readily from the pen of the English divine who writes about the saints, and they convey the general existing sense that the saints are a proportionately small number among

[40] Bolton, *Works*, IV, 25.
[41] Sibbes, *The Christians Portion* (1638), p. 11.
[42] Perkins, *Works*, III, 195.
[43] Sanderson, *XXXVI Sermons*, pp. 182-83.

men. Bolton makes a detailed accounting of the matter: "That they [the godly] are but few . . . may thus plainely appeare . . .

"1. First, let there be taken from amongst us, all Papists, Atheists and scourners of godlinesse and Religion.

"2. Secondly, let there be removed all notorious . . . evill livers: as Swearers, Drunkards, Whoremongers, Usurers, Worldlings, Deceivers, proud persons, prophaners of the Sabbath, Gamesters, and all the prophane and ignorant multitude.

"3. Thirdly . . . those . . . that are but onely civill honest men. . . .

"4. Fourthly . . . all grosse hypocrites.

"5. Fifthly . . . all carnall Protestants, formall Professors . . . and unzealous Christians. . . .

"Let all these . . . men be separated out; and how many doe you thinke will remaine amongst us, sound professors, and practisers of saving Truth. . . . For such onely are Gods servants, and in the state of Grace."[44]

Being few, Bolton further remarks, the saints are "singular"; they are "odde fellowes" and cannot be otherwise. "Singularitie . . . of sanctification," he explains, "is no fruit of Pride but an inseparable marke and necessarie state of true Christianity."[45]

Insofar as its social tone or tendency is concerned, the primary emphasis in this Protestant doctrine of the saint is isolating rather than integrating. The Protestant saint is primarily conceived as an individual plucked out by the grace of God from the great mass of damned humanity and set straight and infallibly on the road to salvation. He is set apart by his spiritual endowment—God's child who sojourns, but only for a while, in the devil's world. "I am a stranger even at home," Hall confides, "therefore, if the dogs of the world barke at me, I neither care nor wonder."[46] "Most men," Airay observes, "had rather go to hell with company, than go to heaven alone." But the truly God-dedicated soul will realize that he must go on alone and will avoid even the entanglement of concern for the inevitable doom of the majority of men. Airay concludes his counsel with the statement that "if there were any possibility to do good for the

44 Bolton, *Works*, II, 130-31.   45 *Ibid.*, p. 131.
46 Hall, *Works*, I, 3.

majority of men we would bestow our voice as we should, but being none, we may not lose our voice that way."[47]

Thus the true Christian is not only seen as one whose peculiar virtues will automatically assure him a certain isolation in the world; he is also cautioned that he must positively avoid the company of the ungodly. "Let not any man then," Sanderson warns, "that hath either Religion or Honesty, have anything to do with that man; at least, let him not trust him more than needs he must, that is an enemy either to Religion or Honesty."[48] Even Andrewes, who usually displays little interest in these issues of Protestant sanctity, commands the faithful "to avoid and shun" association with worldlings, "not only such as are lewd of life . . . but even such also as are unsound in matter of religion." "Evil doctrine is against truth," he explains, "evil life against walking in the truth, evil company will bring us to both."[49] "Multitudes conspiring in evill must be left," Gouge advises, and he repeats the classic Christian dictum: "The way wherein multitudes run, is the broad way that leadeth to destruction. But strait is the gate, and narrow the way that leadeth to life; and few there be that find it."[50]

Admonished to avoid the company of the ungodly, the English Protestant saint is enjoined with equal vigor to seek out and cherish the company of his fellow saints. The life of the true isolate, the life of the hermit, is not upheld in this literature as an ideal for him. A problem in logic confronts us here, however. While the saint is, on the whole, specifically encouraged by English Protestantism to be confident in the knowledge of his own sanctity, he is specifically not encouraged to have the same sort of confidence in the knowledge of another's sanctity or lack of it. Doctrinally the English Protestant was urged, as we have seen, to make a judgment of charity in regard to other English Protestants: to assume that those who for reasons of outrageous behavior were not patently reprobate were probably destined for salvation with oneself. One needs to spend no great amount of

[47] Henry Airay, *Lectures Upon the Whole Epistle of St. Paul to the Philippians* (1618), p. 906.
[48] Sanderson, *XXXVI Sermons*, p. 292.
[49] Andrewes, *Works*, v, 305-06.
[50] Gouge, *Gods Three Arrowes*, pp. 25-26.

time with English Protestant sermons, however, to be aware that this dictum, though piously recited, was not always operative within them. For a number of English Protestant divines worked to some extent on the assumption that, by knowing himself and by having a standard of sanctity in himself which he could apply to the beliefs and actions of others, the saint would be able to know who among the lost multitudes of the world were vessels of grace with him. From this point, logic presses toward some sense of, some confidence in, the existence on this earth of a community of saints.

The idea of a community of saints is not developed very precisely or intensively in this body of literature, which is, we note here especially, almost entirely the literature of nonseparatist English Protestantism. The importance of such an idea has probably been over- rather than under-stated in previous analyses of the material. It does, however, indubitably exist. Ussher provides us with this brief but specific reference to the concept: "What duty doth this communion of the Saints require of him [the true Christian]? To renounce all fellowship with sin and sinners . . . to edifie one another in faith and love . . . to delight in the society of the Saints . . . and to keep the unity of the Spirit in the bond of peace."[51]

"This love of the saints," Morton maintains, "is an infallible signe of true regeneration and of the true love of God. . . ."[52] For Preston, too, the "love of the saints" becomes a necessary test of a Christian's state of spiritual health: "To love all holinesse in all the Saints, wheresoever it is found, it is an infallible signe that thou lovest the Lord Jesus."[53]

Demanding of the saint a close association with the godly is only the reverse of prohibiting him a close association with the ungodly; it is always a double requirement that is involved. Into this simple query which he puts before the faithful, Preston concentrates the whole matter: "Consider whether you love all those that feare the Lord, and hate all those that are enemies to the Lord."[54] Thus in a phrase he evokes the primitive pattern of

---

[51] Ussher, *Divinitie*, p. 191.
[52] Thomas Morton, *A Treatise of the Threefolde State of Man* (1596), p. 334.
[53] Preston, *Breast Plate*, pp. 101-02.
[54] *Ibid.*, p. 120.

sociality which appears to us to lie at the root of the Christian social ethic: the kinship group whose members, commonly recognizing the fatherhood and authority of a single deity, are commonly bound to one another by ties of love and commonly confront with antagonism the circling mass of enemies. How much more meaningful the theme of Christian love becomes when it is so delimited and how much closer we feel we are to the living heart of a faith!

In Bolton, too, one can watch the cool abstractions of Christian brotherly love acquire substance from being circumscribed, catch light from the ardor of intimacy, and burn the more intensely from the very heat of hostility which it directs toward the outside world. In this, the most emphatic statement about the community of saints which we have found in the literature of conformist English Protestantism, Bolton reaches a peak of emotional intensity—a peak approximating that achieved by the many passionate and urgent passages in the Gospels which bespeak the kind of society of the first followers of Christ. Bolton is considering some of the manifestations in an individual's behavior which necessarily follow from true conversion: "And being thus incorporated into Christ, he presently associates himself to the *brotherhood*, to the *Sect that is everywhere spoken against*. . . . He now beginnes to delight himselfe in them, whom he heartily hated before, I meane the people of God, Professours of truth and power of religion; and that, as the most *excellent of the earth*; the only true noble worthies of the world: worthy forever. . . . And hee labours also might and maine, to ingratiate himselfe into their blessed communion, by all ingagements and obligations of a comfortable, fruitfull, and constant *fellowship in the Gospell* . . . resolved to live and die with these neglected happy ones . . . and assured to raigne with them hereafter everlastingly in fullnesse and height of all glory. . . . If thou hast this fellow-feeling thou art of that blessed body and brotherhood; if not thou art not."[55]

The element of social subversion in the English Protestant concept of the saint is so apparent that it scarcely requires ex-

[55] Bolton, *Instructions for a Right Comforting Afflicted Consciences* (1631), pp. 331-32.

traction from the commentary we have been considering. It is bone-deep doctrine in Protestantism as a whole that the spiritual king may be, not only in origin but in current functioning, a worldly carpenter. We become more conscious of how much this viewpoint breaks from medieval Roman Catholic theory and practice when we note that of the medieval saints listed in the Roman Catholic calendar and whose social origins are known or reported to be known, the vast majority are of noble or royal birth and heritage.[56] Moreover, Thomistic argument on this matter tends to equate in a tentative and general way God's hierarchy with the ecclesiastical, intellectual, and even social and political hierarchies known to man. In neither of his *Summae*, at any rate, is there a passage which concretely and generically opposes—and a considerable amount of discussion incidentally encourages, if it does not directly propound—such a relative linkage between the rankings recognized in human and heavenly society.[57]

To the literature of English Protestantism, whether the whole body or the products of particular divines, this type of interpretation cannot even remotely be applied, for it embodies and is dominated by two altogether contrary principles. The first more moderate and absolutely universal principle maintains that there is absolutely no correlation between the hierarchies of God and man. This position is represented by frequent reiterations of the usual Christian assurance to believers that God, in His choice of the saved, is no respecter of persons, and by the peculiarly Protestant emphasis upon the common degradation before the majesty of the Lord of all men in all ways and conditions of life. The second more radical principle, not universally but still commonly asserted, maintains that there does tend to be a correlation between the hierarchies, but that insofar as it exists, it is, in the ancient Gospel pattern, directly negative.

The English Protestant saint, furthermore, is assigned a more restless and troubled role in the world than that which the Roman Catholic saint has usually occupied. He is placed in the

[56] See the authors' "Roman Catholic Sainthood and Social Status: A Statistical and Analytical Study," *The Journal of Religion* (April, 1955).

[57] See Katherine Archibald, "The Concept of Social Hierarchy in the Writings of St. Thomas Aquinas," *Historian* (XII, 1949).

world, rather than being institutionally abstracted from it, and he is expected in a fundamental sense to be continually at odds with it. He is by definition an "odd fellow" who, being in the stream of worldly life, still swims against it. There is a reminder here once more of the Protestant tendency—inherent in the surge of its revivalism—to emphasize and magnify the gulf between all things natural and all things spiritual. Protestantism deals in tensions. Where Roman Catholicism works to obscure the contradictions in the Christian universe by settling them into ordered hierarchies, Protestantism, or early Protestantism at least, places them side by side and forces them constantly to contend with one another.

It is a broad and general drama in which the English Protestant saint plays his part when he is given to the world or to society to do battle with and to be contemned by it. The harshness of his life and situation will often be founded first, in the view of English Protestant divines, upon the actual humbleness and restrictions of his social status. The argument which positively ties God's grace and choice to relative meanness of social estate is presented frequently in these sermons.[58] "It commeth to passe commonly," observes Dod, "as is dayly to be seene in many places, that the most gracious are least prosperous. . . . Many of them are poore, many of them are despised, many of them are oppressed, and all of them are afflicted."[59] The obverse of this argument—the negative joining of vice with exaltation of position in the world—is also not difficult to discover when consciously sought among the variety of its manifestations. One repeatedly hears the Pauline warning that not many noble, wise, rich, or great men are called. Great and rich men, Bolton explains, are "beset with such variety, and strength of temptations," that they are "rarelier, and hardlier wrought upon by the word, and wonne out of Satans ensnarements. High roomes, temporary happiness, and abilities above ordinary, so puffe them up . . . with such a deale of Selfe-love . . . that their proud spirits will

---

58 See Preston, *Sermons* (1630), p. 46; Perkins, *Works*, III, 225; Hildersam, *op.cit.*, pp. 221-22; Benefield, *Commentarie . . . on Amos*, pp. 9-10; Sibbes, *The Saints Cordials* (1637), p. 248.
59 Dod, *Proverbs*, p. 42.

by no means stoope to the simplicity of the Gospell, singularitie of the Saints, and the foolishnesse of preaching."[60]

Clearly, the consensus of the English Protestant pulpit is that many saints, in fact, most of them, will occupy a status in the world low enough to guarantee contempt of them by the majority of the members of society. But this is only a partial and derivative element in the complex of difficulties which surrounds the saint. The true and basic source of his afflictions—and all saints are afflicted—is to be found, the English Protestant maintains, in the enmity which inevitably exists between good and evil in the world of time and in the fact that while this world lasts it is evil which dominates and good which goes a-begging. The saint, who is a singular child of God and whose proper home is heaven, can only expect to suffer and endure in such a world. In the pattern of his life, therefore, the Protestant saint comes typically to exemplify the traditional Christian balance between temporal abasement and eternal glory. Such a view of the destiny of the saint obviously inspires, for example, this statement by Preston; here he seeks to console the Christian for present deprivations by reminding him of the future brilliance of his prospects: ". . . be not discouraged, because you have not such outward contentments, because you are not above, but below, for the present life, the time is not yet come; for God doth not yet rule the world . . . he hath, as it were, left the world to be ruled by others, he hath left men to rule: now *errour comes from the face of the Ruler* (Eccles. 10.5) . . . those that are in place of government generally permit That *Servants ride on Horse-backe, and Princes and wise-men goe as Servants on foot* . . . the time is not yet come that thou shouldest be on Horse-backe, thou must be content to goe on foot yet."[61]

Adams draws the same contrast between the saint's earthly and heavenly state and hence between man's and God's estimate of him: "A great Gallant . . . thinkes himselfe disparaged by thy company; bee content, the God of heaven and earth thinkes

[60] Bolton, *Instructions for a Right Comforting Afflicted Consciences* (1631).
[61] Preston, *The Saints Qualification* (1634), pp. 348-49. See the interesting skepticism of Fuller regarding the "numerosity of saints . . . of royal or noble extraction" in the eighth century, which he contrasts with Paul's "not many noble are called," *Church History*, I, 257-58.

himselfe not perfect without thee. Hee that can brake thy contemners to pieces, respects thee. . . . What a terror shall this bee to the wicked to see those men crowned Kings with Christ, to whom they disdained to give notice in the world. . . . It shall bee no small aggravation to the ungodly torments to say of the Saint, this was hee whom we had sometimes in derision, and a proverbe of reproach; wee fooles accounted his life madnesse, and his end without honour. Now hee is numbered among the children of God, and his lot is among the Saints."[62]

At least in occasional and general comment, the theme of the true Christian's inevitable tribulations in the world through the scorn and even active persecution he will encounter from the ungodly is nearly universal in the literature. "The promises of our religion," remarks Andrewes, "are not worldly pleasures, as other religions do promise; but contrary; 'they shall whip and scourge you; they shall bind and lead you whither you would not' . . . let each man take up his cross and leave all."[63] Sanderson observes that "the Church, and Children, and servants of God . . . live among Scorpions, and as sheep in the midst of wolves; and they that hate us without a cause, and are mad against us, are more in number than the hairs of our heads. The seed of the Serpent beareth a natural and an unmortal hatred against . . . all good men."[64] The same author speaks in another sermon of the children of God whom the worldly "hate and despise, and persecute, and defame and account as the very Scum of the People, the refuse and off-scouring of all things."[65]

Common to all English Protestant writings though this image of the persecuted saint may be, it achieves its fullest and most intense development—as does indeed the whole concept of Protestant sanctity—in the sermons of those most intense of English Protestants who have come to be labelled "puritans." "There is an implacable and everlasting enmity between the children of light and the children of darknesse," Bolton insists. "All worldlings are kind one to another, but of a world of goodfellows, not one of them is kind to a Christian, but would do him a displeasure if he could."[66]

[62] Adams, *Works*, p. 749.     [63] Andrewes, *Works*, II, 55.
[64] Sanderson, *op.cit.*, p. 290.     [65] *Ibid.*, pp. 182-83.
[66] Bolton, *A Cordiall for Christians* (1640), pp. 16, 21.

"And look as then it was with Christ," writes Perkins, "so hath it beene with all his members and will bee to the end of the world. They are all accounted as the off-scouring of the world, men not worthie to live on the face of the earth; as Christ told his Disciples, saying: 'Ye shall be hated of all nations for my names sake.' "[67] "Christ's militant church," he further states, "is in this world as in a wilderness and desert of wild beasts: for during their aboad on earth, God's children live with men, who in disposition and affection are like woolves, Beares, Tygers, Lyons, and Cockatrices."[68]

"Who is not against a Christian!" Sibbes exclaims. "There are two grand sides in the world, to which all belong: there is God's side and those that are his; and there is another side that is Satan's, and those that are his; two Kingdomes, two sides, two contrary dispositions, that pursue one another, till all the one be in hell . . . and the other be in heaven."[69]

The saint is expected in the very broadest sense to suffer in society and the world, and thus to follow in the thorny way long-since marked out by Christ. However truly and directly one may attribute much of the saints' sufferings to the Satanic character of the world and of most of its inhabitants, moreover, it is ulti-mately God Himself, who, in determining all things, determines too the afflictions which His children must endure. Consider-able effort is devoted in these English Protestant sermons to the exposition and the explanation of this fairly startling aspect of God's will. God, we are told, permits afflictions to beset His children and even brings afflictions upon them with a definite and steady purpose in His view, a purpose which, while single in direction and goal, is manifold in application and particular effect. God endeavors through the affliction of the godly to ac-complish these several objectives: to punish the godly for the sins which continue to subsist in them; to test them for the soundness of their vocation; to display their constancy in faith before the world; to instill in them a distaste for earth and a love of heaven; and, finally and supremely, to purify and prepare them while they live in time for the glory destined to be theirs

[67] Perkins, *Works*, I, 192.
[68] Perkins, *Works*, III, 378.
[69] Sibbes, *Beames of Divine Light*, pp. 73-74.

in eternity. Gouge assures the godly that "The afflictions which befall the righteous are . . . chastisements, and corrections, even such as tender Parents lay upon their deare children . . . they are not vindictive for revenge, but medicinable for Physicke. . . ."[70]

The afflictions of the godly become, in the course of this argument, not indications to him of God's anger or disfavor, but, "a most comfortable assurance . . . that the kingdom of heaven belongs unto him."[71] "It is so far from being an ill signe that Christ is at cost with us in following us with afflictions," argues Sibbes, "that it is rather a sure signe of his love. For the care of this blessed Husbandman is to prune us so, as to make us fruitful. . . . So when God prunes us by crosses and afflictions . . . it is a signe, he meanes to dwell with us, and delight in us."[72]

Downame contends that "our momentary crosses doe not only further our everlasting happiness, but also doe much increase it; for the more painful our labours are in God's service, the more rich will be our wages."[73] Andrewes maintains similarly that, "If they be in the state of those that come 'into no misfortune like others' it is an evil sign, and they little differ from the world 'which have their portion in this life,' whereas the troubles and miseries of this world are to the godly a pledge of joys that are to come."[74]

In this system which sees in suffering both a proof and a test of grace, the patient and uncomplaining tolerance of affliction is crucial. "Labour therefore to carry thy selfe well in suffering evill," Sibbes admonishes.[75] "Let every godly man then with comfort and benefit undergoe those crosses which the Lord layeth upon him," urges Bolton, "for they are unto him as looking glasses, wherein God sees his faith and dependence upon His providence; the world his patience and constancy; himselfe the spots of his soul. . . ."[76]

Indeed, since afflictions come in some measure to all men, the rejected as well as the chosen, it is not the affliction as such but the manner of bearing it which really differentiates the two

70 Gouge, The Workes (2 vols.; 1627), p. 95.
71 Perkins, Works, III, 6    72 Sibbes, Bowels Opened, p. 16.
73 Downame, Warfare, p. 958.    74 Andrewes, Works, VIII, 454.
75 Sibbes, Saints Cordials, p. 252.    76 Bolton, Works, IV, 57.

groups and distinguishes the chastisement that compounds sin with despair from that which corrects and purifies. Says Perkins, ". . . a notable difference, between the godly and wicked is apparent in the suffering of afflictions. A reprobate the more the Lord laieth his hand on him, the more he rebelleth against God: it is contrary with the true Christian . . . none is more assaulted by Satan than he, and oftentimes God withdraweth the signe of his favour from him, and lets him feele his wrath. . . . Yet the true Christian when the world, the flesh, and the divell and God himselfe too are against him, doth even then most of all rest in the Lord, and by faith cleave to him."[77]

The Christian is advised again and again that, as the very badge of his election and sanctity, he must expect and must patiently endure suffering throughout his life in the world; but as firmly and as frequently he is also admonished that he must not seek or invite suffering. For the English Protestant doctrine of the saint and the saint's life in society almost entirely repudiates the principles and practices of asceticism which had developed within Roman Catholicism. The total English Protestant viewpoint on afflictions is presented in one succinct sentence by Robinson: "We are never simply to desire crosses because they are natural evils, nor to abhor them, because we know they work together with our election . . . for our good."[78]

Downame, peculiarly the theologian of the suffering Protestant saint, establishes as a necessary caution in this area of Christian living "the rule . . . that wee doe not wilfully run into afflictions, nor put the crosse upon our sholders; but that wee diligently use all good means, either to escape them before they come, or to be freed from them when they are inflicted on us . . . as wee ought not to flee those enemies through cowardly fear in the use of unlawfull meanes: so must wee not provoke them to assault us when wee might live in peace. . . ."[79]

---

[77] Perkins, *Works*, I, 377.     [78] Robinson, *Works*, I, 142-43.

[79] Downame, *Warfare*, p. 784. Donne declared ". . . he that retires into a monastery upon pretence of avoiding temptations and offences in this world, he brings them thither and he meets them there." (*Works*, IV, 290.) In another place he insists that "the affliction only is mine which God hath appointed for me." (*Ibid.*, p. 273.) Donne also disliked the way "those retired and cloistered men" avoided "that part of the world that sweats in continual labor in serveral vocations" to "anoint themselves with other men's sweat." (*Ibid.*, p. 291.)

The full depth and emphasis of English Protestant feeling on this issue are most evident in the censure and invective which almost every writer of the sermons sees fit at some point to direct against one or another aspect of Roman Catholic asceticism. The practices of physical asceticism are vehemently denounced. "Many blinded with superstition, and besotted with idolatry, spare not their flesh," Gouge comments. "Papists beare their flesh with whips, and sundry other wayes macerate their bodies; whereof it may be said, Who required this?"[80]

Downame attacks Roman Catholic acts of bodily penance as acts of pride in which the participant makes a spectacle of himself to attract the approbation of his fellows; by these acts he presumptuously endeavors to claim for himself and his own merits a share in what is really God's altogether voluntary gift of salvation. He charges against Catholic ascetics that "the leaner they make their bodies with penance and punishment, the more their hearts are fatned with pride."[81] The whole structure of Roman Catholic monasticism is subjected to repeated verbal assault, and each of the three monastic vows of poverty, chastity, and obedience is systematically demolished and discarded.[82] By the very nature of the Protestant concept of the saint, the traditions of eremitism and monastic segregation are shattered without logical hope of reestablishment.

The nonascetic bias of English Protestantism is further entrenched and strengthened by the predestinarian tenor of the viewpoint and more specifically by the emphasis upon God's providence which is characteristic of the school. Providence is God's "generall government of all things in the world," asserts Sibbes; with respect to the individual Christian, this providence is invariably "serviceable to predestination and election," since "whom God purposeth to save . . . he directs providence, so that all things shall serve for that end."[83] Through election, in short, God draws out of the world whom He will to be saved and these, through providence and by ways of His solitary choice, He directs, while they are still in the world, to their heavenly goal. Man lacks the right even to investigate, let alone to question or

---

[80] Gouge, *A Guide to Goe to God*, p. 122.
[81] Downame, *Warfare*, pp. 1023, 1027.
[82] Perkins, *Works*, II, 99; I, 38, 585.
[83] Sibbes, *The Rich Poverty*, p. 105.

to tamper with, such a system of absolute design. English Protestant revulsion to asceticism is an obvious consequent of this concept of the significance and power of providence. For he clearly flies in the face of providence and thereby flouts God's will who, having been placed in the world, endeavors in any manner or direction to flee from it, or, having had no cross bestowed upon him, endeavors for any reason to find and to assume one.

Since, moreover, all things that happen in the world are part of God's providence and since God's providence is bound to serve the end of salvation in the elect, it is the evident duty of the godly to accept in contentment and with gratitude whatever condition, afflicted or comfortable, God may afford him. "If there be a providence of God over every thing," Perkins remarks, "then we must learne contentation of minde in every estate; yea, in adversitie under the crosse [and] when outward meanes of preservation in this life doe abound, as health, honour, riches, peace, and pleasure, then we must remember to bee thankful, because these things alwaies come by the providence of God."[84]

Fuller likewise recommends contentment to the Christian, which "is an humble and willing submitting ourselves to God's pleasure in all conditions." Contentment, he continues, "makes men carry themselves gracefully in wealth, want, in health, sickness, freedom, feeters, yea, what condition soever God allots them."[85] The Christian is reminded further that, in the single fact that he possesses Christ, he possesses all a man requires to make him happy. Thus Sibbes declares: "And this should be a ground likewise of contention in our condition and state whatsoever. Christ himselfe is ours. In the dividing of all things, some men have wealth, honours, friends and greatnesse, but not Christ . . . and therefore they have nothing in mercy: but a Christian he hath Christ himselfe . . . therefore what if he wants those appendencies, the lesser things, he hath the maine, what if he want a riveret, a streame, he hath the spring, the ocean, him in whom all things are, and shall he not be content."[86]

84 Perkins, *Works*, I, 157-58.
85 Fuller, *The Holy and Profane States*, pp. 240-44.
86 Sibbes, *Bowels Opened*, pp. 454-56.

"Joy is the habitation of the Righteous," Sibbes even more enthusiastically proclaims. "How ever outwardly it seems yet there is a Paradise within. Many such objections the flesh makes, some take scandall at the prosperity of the wicked, and affliction of the Saints . . . but what saith Christ *Happy is the man who is not offended in me.*"[87]

Coming to the close of this discussion of the English Protestant concept of the saint, we find ourselves entangled once more in complexities and contradictions of argument. This doctrine of saintly life and privilege undoubtedly constitutes the cutting edge of the faith where social criticism or the advocacy of social change is concerned. Viewed from one standpoint it is a doctrine which undoubtedly possesses enormous strength; by means of it, certain individuals who are neither ecclesiastically nor socially distinguished are encouraged to see themselves as principal representatives of the Christian ethic in the world, as judges of society and other men, and as rightful spokesmen of God.

Yet no sooner do we note the self-righteousness, the courage, the virtual spiritual invulnerability which the Protestant idea of the saint can afford to dedicated and believing individuals than we must also acknowledge the elements within it which weaken and neutralize it—as all Christian radicalism is ultimately weakened and neutralized in the established creeds of Christendom. Protestant saints may judge; they may even speak; but, without the intervention of other stimuli and supports, what may they really do? Their avowed model, after all, is not even that of the militant, if despairing, prophets of the Old Testament, but that of the gentle Christ who spoke merely to be mocked and who protested merely to be crucified. Humility is their watchword, and suffering the injustices of the world rather than triumphing over them is the mark of their sanctity. The doctrine of the Protestant saint is an important and necessary ingredient in the nature and achievements of a Cromwell, but much more than this doctrine is required to make that nature and those achievements an historical reality.

[87] *Ibid.*, p. 211.

114

*PART II*

THE SOCIAL AND INSTITUTIONAL
STRUCTURE OF THE ENGLISH
PROTESTANT MIND

"The world is a sea. . . . It is a sea as it is subject to storms and tempests; every man (and every man is a world) feels that. And then it is never the shallower for the calmness, the sea is as deep, there is as much water in the sea in a calm as in a storm; we may be drowned in a calm and flattering fortune, in prosperity, as irrecoverably as in a wrought sea, in adversity; so the world is a sea. It is a sea as it is bottomless to any line which we can sound it with, and endless to any discovery that we can make of it. The purposes of the world, the ways of the world, exceed our consideration; but yet we are sure the sea hath a bottom . . . so the world is a sea. It is a sea as it hath ebbs and floods and no man knows the true reason of those floods and those ebbs. . . . It is a sea as the sea affords water enough for all the world to drink, but such water as will not quench the thirst. . . . It is a sea, if we consider the inhabitants. In the sea the greater fish devour the less, and so do the men of this world too.

"All these ways the world is a sea, but especially it is a sea in this respect, that the sea is no place of habitation, but a passage to our habitations. So the apostle expresses the world, 'Here we have no continuing city, but we seek one to come'; we seek it not here, but we seek it whilst we are here, else we shall never find it. Those are the two great works which we are to do in this world: first to know this world is not our home, and then to provide us another home whilst we are in this world. . . .

"Now in this sea, every ship that sails must necessarily have some part of the ship under water; every man that lives in this world must necessarily have some of his life, some of his thoughts, some of his labors, spent upon this world, but that part of the ship by which he sails is above the water . . . And in this sea are we made fishers of men. . . . And for this fishing in this sea, this Gospel is our net.

"Eloquence is not our net; traditions of men are not our nets; only the Gospel is."

—JOHN DONNE, *Works*, III, 300-301

## CHAPTER 3

# ENGLISH PROTESTANT ECONOMIC THEORY: THE WORLD AND ITS CALLINGS

————————— ✠ ✠ ✠ —————————

"What hath the minister to doe with our Callings, with Lawyers, with Trades-men or States-men? What hath the minister to doe with these things? . . . Religion is a skill that fits man for . . . his last end, that fits him for heaven.

"Now being such a skill it must direct everything so farre as it helps or hinders that . . . so all trades wee must tell them of their faults, as they are blemishes to Religion, for wee must not bee so in this or that trade, as that we forget we are Christians, and therefore we must heare meekly the word of God, when it meets with our particular callings. . . ."

—RICHARD SIBBES, *The Spirituall Man's Aime*, 6-8

————————— ✠ ✠ ✠ —————————

### I. In the Sweat of Thy Face
### Shalt Thou Eat Bread

THE ECONOMIC FACTS OF LIFE AND SOCIETY had always been an embarrassment to Christianity, a source of ambivalence, tension, and ultimate frustration. Most basically, there was the nuisance of man's organic and social structure which demanded a major concentration of effort to sustain life itself. The earliest temples of civilization had served as granaries. Man might not live by bread alone, but the sweat of the brow was for the majority the inevitable price of a soul. Then to worsen the biological and social fiats of creation, there was the problem of class and caste exploitation, the problem of history, the cruel certainties of inequality, of palpable injustice everywhere in a world committed to God, of the minorities of privilege and power before whom all religions had eventually to abase themselves or perish as churches.

*117*

Thus economic life was the first necessity and the utmost tyranny. Christianity began its church existence in one of the advanced economic regimens of civilization, and throughout the decline of that polity and the rise of the new European economy, Christian theorists were called upon to explain and justify the economic ways of God to man, and to provide solace for the victims of the economic ways of man to man. The task was formidable, especially because New Testament texts contained endemic and stubborn traces of social protest and an even more militant bias against the concerns of the flesh. For these reasons Christian economic theory, even more than Christian political theory, was halting, contradictory, and dishonest. The way out of consistency and a genuinely moral economics was found in the ancient myth of a Golden Age: the Garden of Eden in the Old Testament version. The idea, of course, was to say that originally man lived in economic plenty and with communal justice; then the Fall swept away the plenty and the justice, leaving all consequent economic and social arrangements tainted by sweat and greed and gross exploitation. Thereafter, only chiliastic radicalism dared hope for a return of the good life lost in Eden.

The great Catholic orthodoxy emerged with an explanation of slavery and a defense of private property. Slavery was not so much "natural" in the Aristotelian sense as it was the wage of sin and the concomitant of civilization. Private property was morally inferior to the communism of Adam's progeny, but it must now be defended because it was positive law and suited to the nature of fallen man. Then gradually, as the centuries wore on and the Church fashioned its own economic being into an identity with the manorialism of lay society (producing on monastic estates some of the most intensive economic activity and innovation in Europe, and an increasingly vast accumulation of wealth in manors and chattels), there developed an interest in defending more than negatively the whole complex of medieval landlordism. Ecclesiastical lawyers interested themselves in contract, testamentary law, marriage settlements, and a more vigor-

SHALT THOU EAT BREAD

ous statement of the positive, natural rights of property control or ownership.[1]

The economic life of the towns was harder to adjust to. The complexities of industrial and trading operations baffled and alarmed the clergy into occasional worries over "just price" and "usury," and indeed over the ethical propriety of most competitive commercial operations. But eventually, and particularly in the cities themselves, even the merchant classes won from the Church the respect of pulpit silence on the issues of economic abuse—a grudging and ungracious acquiescence due the undeniable power behind the town walls.[2]

The coming of the Reformation in England coincided with an acceleration of economic activity in the towns and significant changes in the nature of estate management in the counties.[3] The new coal mining industry, new financial and monetary techniques, vastly expanded investment and profit in various sea trading and piratical enterprises—these and many other complicated, interrelated, and often crucial developments strained the already-weak fabric of Christian economic theory.

Economic theory is usually even slower than political theory in reacting to changes in practice and fact. In addition to and associated with the problems involved in the growth of capitalism, the new national Church of England inherited a whirlwind of institutional economic problems.[4] To begin with, the hundreds of thousands of pounds in land revenue, bullion, and plate confiscated with the dissolution of the monasteries was an almost

[1] See William Holdsworth, *A History of English Law, passim,* for information about these complex developments. Also Richard Schlatter, *Private Property: The History of an Idea* (New Brunswick, 1951) is a useful essay.

[2] See Sylvia Thrupp, *The Merchant Class of Medieval London* (Chicago, 1948). For the "laissez-faire" theory of the scholastics, see Raymond de Roover, "The Concept of the Just Price: Theory and Economic Policy," *The Journal of Economic History* (December, 1958), pp. 418-34, with a discussion, pp. 435-38. Werner Sombart, *The Quintessence of Capitalism* (New York, 1915) has interesting views of the effects of Catholic theory in promoting capital accumulation.

[3] On this vastly important, complicated, and disputed development, see the last twenty years (!) of the brilliantly edited *Economic History Review*. Two recent and unusually interesting contributions are E. E. Rich, "The Population of Elizabethan England" (1950), and D. C. Coleman, "Labour in the English Economy of the Seventeenth Century" (1956).

[4] Christopher Hill, *The Economic Problems of the Church,* is the definitive work.

total economic loss to the Church. Further, estate management by the Church was seriously handicapped by the psychology of clerical life (especially by the Protestant psychology of intense religiosity, as we have elsewhere argued) which led to casual and disastrous leasing of church manors and an almost total failure to adopt the "improving" techniques of the progressive landlords. More crucial still, the condition of parish economics, based on tithes, was worsened intolerably by the aggressive legal chicanery of lay patrons. Finally, the economic relations of the Church to the monarchy were also changing rapidly: ecclesiastical taxation became increasingly a burden and a political liability. The clergy were far less than one per cent of the population, yet in the subsidies voted by Convocation they paid 25 per cent of the principal direct tax.[5] And of course they continued to be the major source of arbitrary taxation by the Crown in the form of the "benevolence."[6]

The consequences of this deteriorating economic situation were extremely serious. Pluralism and nonresidency; the dwindling opportunities for recruiting capable parish clergy; the subservience of the bishops to the Crown for protection from the plundering gentry; and the continual temptations to simony and nepotism; these and the inevitable psychological scarring which resulted from such problems led the Church into disaster.

At no point, then, is the this-worldly failure of Protestant clerical theory more tragic than in economics, partly because the success of the whole Church as an institution depended upon economics; and, more important, because the direct confrontation of Protestantism with the society of man's work and home—the emphasis upon *vocatio*, the identification of the Church with calling—revolutionized the role in Christian thought of economic morality. This is not to say the Church could have saved itself or Protestantism by a realistic or courageous economic theory; indeed, it may well be that the theology and psychology of English Protestantism were too fundamentally at odds with the emerging modernism of capitalist enterprise to allow ethical integration of the Christian precepts of love, brotherhood, and charity with the economics of capitalism. But there is historical

[5] *Ibid.*, pp. 192-93.　　　　　　　　[6] *Ibid.*, p. 196.

tragedy in the helplessness of the Protestant clergy before the accelerating triumph of modern capitalist institutions and the acquisitive rationale that sprang up, weed-like, in the garden of their carefully-nurtured Christian sentiments about economics as a moral science. The intense Protestant divines tried to kill the weeds when they recognized them; but they were overwhelmed by the cancerous rate and subtlety of growth; they generally saw only the grossest injustice, the most shocking cruelty; and soon the garden was beyond saving. Moreover, the bourgeois world, the chief supporters of Protestantism, proclaimed the new garden splendidly beautiful and impeccably Christian! Certain cherished Protestant blossoms, the work ethic and "individualism," were pointed out as evidences of a sanctified tradition. But the central and critical genius of Protestantism—its insistence upon a single standard of morality in society as in the individual—had been violated, and the garden was utterly transformed.

The ultimate historical test of Protestantism, perhaps of Christianity itself, centered in the ethical challenge of capitalist economics. Protestantism made the last great effort in the history of Christianity to identify the moral goals and to direct the moral actions of the ruling classes in the West. That Protestantism, particularly English Protestantism, failed to understand the necessity of concentrating upon a positive Christian economics as the starting point of a Christian Society explains, in part, the breath-taking collapse of the Protestant ethos before the seventeenth century had run its course. The tremendous religious gamble of giving up institutional power, dualism in ethics, and sacramental magic for the high stakes of an individual, social, and total Christianity was lost, decisively, probably irretrievably. This may well prove to have been the last compromise, the failure of luck and imagination, that would leave Protestant Christianity forever out of the historical mainstream of cultural creativity. For the world that Protestant Christianity failed to lead carried within its social structure a dynamism that would not wait for decisions and no longer required the façade of religious magic. Protestantism had either to conquer its world whole or lose it absolutely. When Protestantism found itself simply ignoring or justifying the bourgeois ethos of economic liberalism, as

Roman Catholicism had ignored or justified medieval predatory landlordism, it was left with no moral initiative in its own chosen church: the workshop. It was left with a receding heaven and mere apologies for a world outrunning its tutelage. But though as an ideology Protestantism floundered on the shoals of economics, the service of Protestantism to the evolution of the modern mind is no less great than we have repeatedly asserted it to be: the focusing of moral concern, indeed of sanctity, in the vocations of man, the hallowing of work in the world; these monuments stand proudly still, regardless of their isolation in positive moral content from the Christian ethic of brotherhood and charity.

## II. The Protestant Concept of Wealth

Few attitudes characterizing the Protestant mind are more difficult to state than that concerning the proper approach to the City of Man. We have already discussed basic aspects of the Protestant theologians' rejection of the Catholic double standard which allowed major concessions to the laity—especially to those of the ruling classes—in sanctioning their pursuit of wealth and power and the enjoyment of privilege. So long as the institutional supremacy and spiritual primacy of the Church were acknowledged, so long as the hierarchy of values explicit in the theory of ordination and of sainthood went unchallenged, the Catholic layman was granted a secure enough place in God's master plan. The Lutheran revolution in theology, reaching a climax in English Protestantism, overthrew all the implications of this moral structuring of the City of Man. For the Protestant, sainthood is the vocation of everyman. There are not two ways to go to God; there is only one and that one must lead directly from earth to heaven. Religious experience is unified in ordinary life experience; sanctity is no longer the business of priests and monks. And the world is neutral. The world is the means of salvation: it can be neither fled nor embraced. The true Protestant works in the world for a destiny transcending the world.

Yet the Protestant position is rent by contradiction and new forms of tension. Success in the world is quite compatible with godliness, but God's saints must accept the hard fare of worldly suffering; the patient bearing of afflictions is a distinction of the saint, yet afflictions must not be sought out for the testing of one's soul; it is the duty of the Christian to be happy in the world where God's providence has placed him, yet his happiness is essentially the condition of being lifted out of the world by election. Perkins provides an excellent introduction to this complicated English Protestant psychology. He first inquires: ". . . if every man . . . must shewe himselfe to be a pilgrime and stranger in this world . . . is it not a good state of life, for a man to condemne the world, and all things in it, and to betake himselfe to perpetuall beggarie, and voluntarie povertie?" He answers his own question by explaining: "The world in Scripture is taken divers wayes: first, for the corruptions and sinnes in the world: and these must be condemned by all meanes possible. . . . Secondly, for temporall blessings, as mony, lands, wealth, sustenance, and such like outward things, as concerne the necessarie or convenient maintenance of this naturall life. And in this sense, the world is not to be condemned, for, in themselves, these earthly things are the good gifts of God, which no man can simply condemne, without injurie to Gods disposing hand and providence, who hath ordained them for naturall life."[7]

There are many similar and some even more emphatic passages in this literature in which the Christian is enjoined to look upon the world in terms of its temporal blessings as essentially good and apt for the service of the most religiously dedicated man, provided, of course, that he uses it aright. Dod remarks that "all manner of goods and possessions are for the service of life, either to be for the necessary use, and reliefe thereof, or as ornaments and delights unto it, to make it the more comfortable."[8] Andrewes points out that though certain heathen philosophers doubted whether temporal gifts were good, "Christians are resolved that they are good." So our Savior teacheth us to esteem them," he continues, "when speaking of fish and bread. . . . 'That is not only good that makes good, but whereof is made good': so albeit riches do not make a man good always, yet be-

[7] Perkins, *Works*, III, 102-03.
[8] Dod and Cleaver, *A Plaine . . . Exposition of the . . . Proverbs of Soloman* (1609), p. 20.

cause he may do good with them they are good."[9] In the course
of a discussion of the Lord's Prayer (specifically of the petition
for "our daily bread") Andrewes further affirms the spiritual
worthiness of temporal goods by defending the propriety of en-
treaty to God for them. "This," he concedes, "is nature's prayer."
Yet he also insists that "the prayer that we make for outward
things is not without respect to things spiritual," since "we shall
be unfit to seek God's Kingdom, and to do His will, unless we
have the help of this life." "Therefore we desire," he concludes,
"that God will give us the things of this life, those things without
which we cannot serve Him; that as we desire the glory of His
Kingdome, and the grace of His Spirit whereby we may be enabled to do His will, so He will minister to us all things for the
supply of our outward wants in this life, the want whereof hath
been so great a disturbance to the saints of God in all times,
that they could not go forward in godliness as they would."[10]

Even Bolton, the "puritan" firebrand, grants to Christians a
rightful affection for the world when their purposes are right.
He observes that "true Christians . . . love riches, honours,
knowledge . . . and the like; not that they may . . . domineere
in the world, oppresse and proudly overlooke their brethren;
but that they may be the stronger to withstand ungodly oppositions . . . give the more enlargement to Gods glory, and further-
ance to good causes . . . performe more good works, doe more
good unto good men, and more honourable service to the Majestie of Heaven."[11]

The world, as Perkins said, then, is not simply to be condemned since it is not simply evil in itself. It is evil only as it
is put to evil use. "All evil," Robinson informs the Christian,
"stands in the abuse of good. And good things are abused commonly, either when they are unmeasurably used . . . as by applying them unaptly, or to wrong ends, or persons . . . or in regard
of their super-natural use, when we refer not all to the glory of
God, and our own, and other's eternal good, and welfare. . . ."[12]
"Yet wee must know it is not the *World* simply that draws our
heart from God and goodnesse," Sibbes similarly comments,

[9] Andrewes, *Works*, VIII, 314-15.   [10] *Ibid.*, pp. 413-14.
[11] Bolton, *Works*, II, 141-42.   [12] Robinson, *Works*, I, 121-22.

"but the *love* of the world; Worldly things are good in themselves and given to sweeten our passage to Heaven; they sweeten
the profession of Religion; therefore bring not a false report
upon the world, it is thy falseness that makes it hurtfull, in loving
it so much. Use it as a servant all thy dayes, and not as a Master,
and thou maiest have comfort therein."[13]

Though it is not the world but immoderate love of the world
which is the evil, the typical English Protestant divine clearly
indicates a conception of men in the world as almost irresistibly
prone to such immoderate love. It follows that in this literature
the initial presumption of the goodness of the world—good in
that it is, after all, the creation of a good God—becomes the
basis for a far greater proportional emphasis on the danger of
too much involvement with or dependence on the world. Sibbes
develops this line of argument with particular explicitness and
detail. "There must be buying where there is wife and children,"
he explains, "there must be looking to posteritie: and then all
this enforceth, using of the world. . . . You may use the World;
but as there is a libertie, so there is a danger, you may, but you
may goe too farre . . . it is in vaine for you to be overmuch in
those things, that are passing things."[14] Even more pointedly he
warns his readers that "where the world hath got possession in
the heart, it makes us false to God, and false to man, it makes us
unfaithfull in our callings, and false to Religion it selfe. Labour
therefore to have the world in its owne place, under thy feet. . . .
Labour . . . to know the world that thou maiest detest it . . . for
the more we know the vanities of the world, and the excellencies
of grace, the more we will love the one, and hate the other."[15]

With the world viewed in this negative light—with the world
defined as inordinate love of worldly things—the Christian must
consider himself to be in mortal and eternal combat. Downame
devotes one long section of his *Christian Warfare* to "the contempt of the world"; in this section he attempts, as he states on
his title page, to preserve the reader "from the immoderate love
of earthly things; by proving unto him, that both the world and

[13] Sibbes, *The Saints Cordials* (1637), pp. 187-88.
[14] *The Spirituall Mans Aime* (1637), pp. 22-24.
[15] *Saints Cordials*, pp. 188-89.

worldly vanities are so base and worthless, that they deserve not to be esteemed and loved of a Christian, in comparison of Gods spirituall graces and heavenly Joyes." Downame's attack against the evils of the world is wholesale and vehement. In considering "Reasons to move us to resist and fight against our enemie the world," he lists, among others, the following general arguments: that "it is necessarie that wee fight against the world, or else we shall fight against God," that "of necessitie we must renounce the world . . . or else we cannot be received in the number of the faithful," and that "of necessitie wee must undertake this combat against the world and worldly vanities, because our religion in a great part doth consist in abandoning of them."[16]

This exhaustive analysis of the problem of the world, proceeding through hundreds of pages of exhortation and example, provides the fullest statement in the sermon literature of the English Protestant view of temporal man closed within the arena of life: though good in themselves and good when properly pursued and employed or when possessed and used by the good, worldly things are evil when improperly pursued and employed or when possessed and used by the evil. For two reasons they are evil in such circumstances: because they are vain and transitory and thus negatively productive of no true good; and because they conceal the gifts of the spirit and are thus positively productive of sin.

### III. The Protestant Concept of "Calling"

If one seeks a single concentrate of the English Protestant abandonment of Roman Catholic asceticism for an attitude which regards the world as a worthy place of Christian trial and sojourn, one finds it best in the doctrine of the calling. English divines were obsessed with the urge to penetrate to the marrow of this peculiarly Calvinist concern. The issue in question is, of course, the "particular" rather than the "general" calling. The "general" calling, as Sanderson explains, "is that wherewith God calleth us . . . to the faith and obedience of the Gospel, and to the embracing of the Covenant of grace," and it appertains only

16 Downame, *Warfare*, pp. 365-66.

to the elect. The "particular" calling, on the other hand, "is that wherewith God enableth us, and directeth us . . . on to some special course and condition of life, wherein to employ our selves, and to exercise the gifts he hath bestowed upon us," and it appertains to the elect and the reprobate alike.[17]

Perkins, who devotes an entire treatise to vocations or callings,[18] makes a further two-fold distinction within the category of particular callings. He marks out, first, a category of personal callings, "such as be of the essence and foundation of any societie, without which the societie cannot be"; in a family, these are the callings of husband and wife, parent and child, master and servant; in a commonwealth, the callings of magistrate and subject; and in the church, the calling of the minister. In the second category are those callings "such as serve onely for the good . . . estate of a society": the callings of husbandman, for instance, merchant, physician, lawyer, carpenter or mason.[19] Most of the commentary by Perkins and by other English Protestant writers on the subject has more direct and specific reference to the second type of "particular callings" than to the first.

A man's proper calling is determined by the providence of God and is matched by the possession of natural gifts appropriate to the tasks involved. Sanderson declares that "that is every man's Proper and right calling, whereunto God calleth him. . . . When therefore we speak of the Choice of a Calling, you are not so to understand it, as if it were left free for us ever, to make our Choice where and as we list. The Choice that is left to us, is nothing but a conscionable Enquiry which way God calleth us, and a conscionable Care to take that way."[20] As "graces of edification" he designates those gifts "whereby men are enabled in their several Callings according to the quality and measure of the grace they have received, to be profitable members of the publick body, either in Church or Commonwealth. Under which appelation . . . I comprehend all other secondary endowments, and abilities whatsoever of the reasonable Soul, which are capa-

17 Sanderson, *XXXVI Sermons*, pp. 205-15.
18 Perkins, "A Treatise of Vocations," *Works*, I.
19 *Ibid.*, Preface.
20 *XXXVI Sermons*, p. 215.

ble of the degrees of more and less, and of better and worse; together with all subsidiary helps anyway conducing to the excercise of any of them."[21]

Perkins offers a brief formula for Christian assurance in the assumption of a calling: "that every man may certanly know himselfe to be called of God, to this or that calling," he writes, "he must have two things: Gifts for the calling from God, and allowance from men."[22]

A calling to be suitable for an individual, then, must correspond first to the individual's gifts, but it must also be socially approved and useful. "A vocation of calling," Perkins asserts, "is a certaine kind of life, ordained and imposed on man by God, for the common good."[23] He further explains: "Now all societies of men, are bodies . . . the common wealth also, and in these bodies there be several members, which are men walking in severall callings and offices, the execution whereof, must tend to the happy and good estate of the rest; yea of all men every where, as much as possible is. . . . Here then we must in generall know, that he abuseth his calling, whosoever he be that against the end thereof, imployes it for himselfe, seeking wholly his owne and not the common good. And that common saying, *Every man for himselfe, and God for us all*, is wicked, and is directed against the end of every calling, or honest kinde of life."[24]

Sanderson similarly affirms the necessary social utility of the calling and joins Perkins in employing the organic analogy to exhibit both the omnipresence and propriety of relationships of superiority and subordination in society and the nonetheless-encompassing dependence of all members of the social group upon each other. "God so distributed the variety of his gifts with singular wisdom," he observes, "that there is no man so mean, but his service may be useful to the greatest: nor any man so

21 *Ibid.*, pp. 44-45.

22 *Works*, I, 760.

23 *Ibid.*, p. 750. Cf. Donne, *Works*, IV, 507: ". . . a man will no more get to heaven without discharging his duties to other men, than without doing them to God himself. Man liveth not by bread only, says Christ; but yet he liveth by bread too"; and *Works*, III, 253: "Direct the labours of thy calling to the good of the public . . ."

24 *Ibid.*, p. 751.

eminent but he may sometimes stand in need of the meanest of his brethren. . . ."[25]

With some emotion Sibbes invokes the fruitful quality of the calling: "Let us then strive and labour to be fruitfull in our Places and Calling: for it is the greatest honour in this world, for God to dignifie us with such a condition, as to make us fruitfull. We must not bring forth fruit to our selves . . . Honour, Riches, and the like, are but secondary things, arbitrary at Gods pleasure to cast in: but, to have an active heart fruitfull from this ground, that God hath planted us for this purpose, that we may doe good to mankind, this is an excellent consideration not to profane our calling."[26]

All this discussion has assumed and proclaimed the necessity of a particular calling for every particular man. Such necessity applies, of course, not only to the saint but also to the reprobate and it is a basic premise of natural as well as Christian law. The principal interest of these Christian writers, however, was to develop the calling as an aspect of Christian life and to assert its function as the Christian's primary worldly duty—indeed, as almost the whole embodiment of a Christian's worldly, as distinct from his directly religious, duty. The religious duty and the duty of the calling were seen to be, in fact, inextricably intertwined. The calling thus becomes a kind, and an absolutely essential kind, of Christian worship. Perkins writes that "if a man be zealous for Christ, he must be zealous within the compasse of his calling; and not be zealous first, and then looke for a calling, but first looke for a calling, and then be zealous."[27] Hildersam, feeling that some Christians tend to sacrifice the responsibilities of their callings to excessive involvement in religious duties, warns that, "It is indeed a great sinne in any professor to neglect his calling, upon pretence of following sermons,

---

[25] *XXXVI Sermons*, p. 56.

[26] Sibbes, *Bowels Opened*, pp. 17-18. Donne proclaimed that temporal blessings without spiritual sanctification would "not purchase a minute's peace of conscience here nor a minute's refreshing of the soul hereafter" (*Works*, III, 334-35). But he emphasized that religion was an insistently immediate fact of the Protestant vocation, for "we look upon God in history, in matter of fact, upon things done and set before our eyes . . ." (*ibid.*, p. 215).

[27] *Works*, I, 194.

and serving God . . . and . . . many of the better sort of Christians are too much inclined to this sinne. . . ."[28]

In listing the good things which a Christian must do, Bolton notes first that he must "before all other things, have a speciall eye . . . to a sincere, constant, and fruitfull performance of holy duties, God's services." But there follows shortly after the Christian's second duty: he must "decline idlenesse, the very rust and and canker of the soule. . . . And be diligent with conscience and faithfulnesse, in some lawfull, honest, particular Calling (a good testimonie, if other saving marks concurre, of truth . . . in thy generall Calling of Christiantie) not so much to gather gold . . . as for necessary and moderate provision for family and posteritie: and in conscience and obedience to that common charge, laid upon all the sonnes and daughters of Adam to the worlds end."[29]

Dod even more emphatically asserts the God-directed quality of the calling: "Would wee be Christs scholars? then the first letter and lesson that wee must learne is, to doe well in our places . . . whatsoever our callings be, we serve the Lord Christ in them. . . . Though your worke be base, yet it is not a base thing to serve such a master in it. They are the most worthy servants, whatsoever their imploiment bee, that do with most conscionable, and dutifull hearts and minds, serve the Lord, where hee hath placed them, in those works, which hee hath allotted unto them."[30]

Sanderson makes again the point that the gifts which an individual possesses are given of God and are the manifestations, therefore, of the spirit of God in him. He then proceeds to argue: ". . . this manifestation of the Spirit . . . imposeth upon every man the necessity of a Calling . . . where the end of a thing is the use, there the difference cannot be great, whether we abuse it, or but conceal it . . . O then up and be doing: Why stand ye all the day Idle? . . . in the Church, he that cannot style himself by any other name than a Christian, doth indeed but usurp that too. If thou sayest thou art of the body: I demand then, what

---

[28] Hildersam, *CVIII Lectures Upon the Fourth of John* (1632), p. 240.
[29] *Works*, IV, 66-67.
[30] Dod and Cleaver, *Ten Sermons . . . of the Lords Supper* (1609), p. 82.

is thy office in the Body? . . . If thou hast a Gift get a Calling."[31]

It is extremely significant that in this literature the particular calling is linked so frequently to labor with the hands; perhaps more accurately, that mental and manual toil are so frequently, indeed, so consistently, equated in the dignity of the calling. For we find here a very real break from the Roman Catholic tradition as represented by St. Thomas Aquinas which made a sharp and invidious distinction between mental and manual toil or the liberal and servile arts.[32] The metaphors, the examples, the images in English Protestant discussion of the necessity of work are drawn almost entirely from the terms and tasks associated with labor with the hands. The sheep to be watched, the vineyard or the garden to be cared for, the sweat that drops from the diligent worker's brow—these are the references one meets repeatedly. "We must then," Robinson typically declares, "mingle our own sweat with faith to make a sweet odour withal to God."[33] "The labour of a Christian," Adams remarks, "is like the labour of an husbandman . . . it is endlesse; they have perpetually somewhat to doe, either plowing, or sowing, or reaping."[34] It is Adams who, starting again from a metaphor of the husbandman, states precisely and emphatically the essential equality of all Christian toil: "Every one thinkes himselfe Gods sonne: then heare this voyce, Goe my sonne. You have all your vineyards to goe to. Magistrates Goe to the bench to execute judgement and justice. Ministers Goe to the Temple, to preach, to pray, to doe the workes of Evangelists. People Goe to your callings, that you may eate the labours of your owne hands: Eye to thy seeing, eare to thy hearing, foote to thy walking, hand to thy working . . . every man to his profession, according to that station, where-

---

[31] XXXVI Sermons, p. 46. Sibbes's pronouncement on the subject is similar: ". . . God hath placed us in the world to do him some work. This is Gods working place, he hath houses of work for us: now, our lot here is to do work; to be in some calling . . . to work for God. We are not sent here into the world to play, or to live idly. Religion is no vocall profession: every man must have some calling or other, and in his generation he must doo good . . . We must serve God . . . in our life" (Beames of Divine Light, p. 184).

[32] Aquinas, Sum. Theol., II-II, q. 57, a. 3, ad. 3. (Though the Judaic, as opposed to the Aristotelian, tradition could be found in the Rule of St. Benedict [XLVIII] and in the precepts of St. Francis.)

[33] Works, I, 116.

[34] Adams, Works, p. 420.

in God hath disposed us. . . . The Incitation gives way to the Injunction, worke."[35]

Hall brings the lesson home with a warning against the scorn of any honest labor: "Forty years was Moses a Courtier, and forty years (after that) a Shepheard. That great men may not bee ashamed of honest vocations, the greatest that ever were have beene content to take up with meane trades. The contempt of honest callings in those which are well borne, argues pride without wit."[36] Still another important departure from Roman Catholic tradition is encountered in the shift in this literature from the Thomistic emphasis on the penal quality of labor, and particularly of manual labor, to a contrary emphasis on the positive, creative, and even enjoyable aspects of work. Occasional references to the older view of labor may be found in this literature, to be sure, and none of the ministers specifically or entirely deny the expiatory function of arduous toil. They speak far more often and more fully, however, of the positive, self- and God-satisfying, creative, and useful character of work than of its painfulness. While God's judgment on Adam in his fall is seen to provide the scriptural basis for that painfulness which does in fact adhere to toil, the primary sanction for human labor as such is discovered not in the primal tragedy of man's existence, but in the even more fundamental and wholly happy fact that Adam tended a garden in Paradise. Herbert points out that "even in Paradise man had a calling."[37] Although "Adam in his innocence had all things at his will," Perkins observes, ". . . yet then God employed him in a calling": the tending of his garden.[38]

Hall similarly declares: "Paradise served not onely to feed his [Adam's] senses, but to exercise his hands. If happinesse consisted in doing nothing, man had not beene employed; all his delights could not have made him happy in an idle life. Man therefore is no sooner made, then he is set to worke: neither

---

[35] *Ibid.*, p. 419.

[36] Hall, *Works*, II, 889.

[37] Herbert, *The Works* (Oxford, 1941), p. 274. See Troeltsch, *op.cit.*, I, 118-27, for early Catholic views of work and the calling which tended to "dignify labor," but which from Augustine to Aquinas were supplanted by a "cosmos of callings" which reflected "the actual form which medieval Society had assumed" (*ibid.*, p. 295).

[38] *Works*, I, 152.

greatnesse, nor perfection can priviledge a folded hand; he must labor, because he was happy; how much more wee, that wee may bee? . . . How much more cheerfully we goe about our businesses, so much nearer we come to our Paradise."[39]

To praise labor is to censure idleness, but English Protestant sermon writers are not content with derivatory logic alone. They attack idleness itself directly and voluminously. "Idlenesse is of it selfe," Adams indicates, "against the law of Scripture, against the law of nature. . . . God the greatest of invisible, the world the greatest of visible creatures; neither of them is idle."[40] Again Adams maintains that "to be idle, is to be barren of good; and to be barren of good, is to be pregnant of al evil."[41] "The very word work," Andrewes counsels, "at once condemns . . . idle-bodies who do no work at all. . . . Who is not Himself would not have us idle."[42]

Idleness, of course, is sinful not only in itself but also in its consequences. The devil finds work for idle hands to do. Thus Herbert, speaking on behalf of the wise and conscientious Country Parson, defines the gravity of the sin of idleness: "The great and nationall sin of the Land he [the Country Parson] esteems to be Idlenesse; great in itselfe, and great in Consequence: For when men have nothing to do, then they fall to drink, to steal, to whore, to scoffe, to revile, to all sorts of gamings. . . . Wherefore the Parson strongly opposith this sin, whersoever he goes. And because Idleness is two-fold, the one in having no calling, the other in walking carelessly in our calling, he first represents to every body the necessity of a vocation. . . . The Parson . . . sheweth, that ingenious and fit employment is never wanting to those that seek it. . . . All are either to have a Calling, or prepare for it."[43]

The admonition to conserve and make proper use of time is a further corollary of the English Protestant philosophy of the calling. "Time is short," Bolton warns. "Time is precious. If all this great massie body of the whole earth, whereupon we tread, were turned into a lumpe of gold, it were not able to purchase

[39] *Works*, II, 836.   [40] *Works*, p. 420.
[41] *Ibid.*, p. 959.   [42] Andrewes, *Works*, VIII, 391.
[43] *Works*, pp. 274-75.

one minute of time. . . . Shall we then triflingly passe and play away the time that is so precious?"[44] "Wee must bee countable for time," he stresses further. "At the dreadfull Barre of that last Tribunall . . . must wee . . . give up a strict account for the expence of every moment of time."[45]

The same peremptory commandment in regard to the value of time is delivered by Hall to his Christian audience: "Nothing is more precious than time," he declares, "or that shall abide a reckoning more strict and fearfull. . . . God plagues the losse of a short time, with a revenge beyond all times . . . the misspence of every minute is a new record against us in heaven."[46]

All comment on the virtue of the calling assumes the propriety of its choice and the correctness of the manner of its pursuit. The nature of propriety of choice we have observed already: the calling must be appropriate to one's gifts, must actually express these gifts, and must be lawful and serviceable to society.

The manner of its suitable pursuit cannot be so easily summarized. Numerous rules are mentioned in this literature. Diligence in the calling is urged, of course.[47] But a more frequently and emphatically cited rule is the requirement of constancy in or restriction to a particular calling. Perkins, for example, insists that "whatsoever any man interprizeth . . . either in word or deede, he must do it by vertue of his calling, and he must keepe himselfe within the compasse thereof." Moreover, "whatsoever is not done within the compasse of a calling, is not of faith, because a man must first have some warrant . . . of God to assure him of his calling, to do this or that thing, before he can doe it in faith."[48] The constancy which God requires of man in his calling Perkins defines as "nothing else, but a perseverance in good duties. . . . For even as the souldier in the field must not change his place, wherein hee is placed by the Generall, but must abide by it, to the venturing of his life: so must the Christian continue . . . in his calling, without change or alteration."[49]

Since it is assumed that God's providence placed each man in his calling with due regard for his particular abilities and for

[44] Works, IV, 158.
[46] Works, I, 476.
[48] Ibid.

[45] Ibid., p. 166.
[47] Perkins, Works, I, 751-52.
[49] Ibid., p. 773.

society's general need for his services, it is obviously not man's right to question lightly or restlessly rebel against the nature or status of his assignment. "We are compared to a Bodie," explains Smith. "Some men are like the Head, and they must rule; some are like the Tongue, and they must teach; some are like the Hand, and they must work: when this order is confounded, then that cometh to passe which we reade of Eve; when the woman would lead her husband, both fell into the ditch."[50]

Perkins, too, warns against "Ambition, Envie, Impatience" in the calling. "Ambition," he writes, "is a vice whereby any man thinking better of himselfe, then there is cause hee should, becomes malecontent with his particular calling and seekes for himselfe an higher place, and a better estate. . . . Envie, which is a pining away of the heart, when we see others placed in better callings and conditions then ourselves . . . is a common sinne, and the cause of much dissention in the common-wealth."[51]

One hears again the authoritative voice of St. Paul who counsels all Christians to abide in the places and the occupations where they were found by their conversion. Bolton repeats the Pauline moral: "Others there are, who . . . put on a temporary counterfeit profession . . . that thereby they may passe more plausibly, out of one calling into another: from a baser . . . and more toilesome Trade, into some other liberty . . . and ease. . . . Such as these, are ready to pretend . . . that such base employment . . . is disgracefull; and derogatory, to the providence of God, and their Christian liberty. . . . But let them know, that Christianity, if sound and true, doth not nullifie, but sanctifie our particular callings; thou oughtest to continue with conscionablenesse and constancy in that personal calling wherein thy Calling to grace did find thee, if it bee warrantable and lawfull."[52]

These writings repeatedly remind the reader of a further requirement for the proper conduct of the calling: to be truly God's work the calling must be pursued in faith, by faith, and for faith. Every Christian must completely acknowledge and accomplish the integration of his own calling to a worldly task with the general calling to Christianity. ". . . Every particular

[50] Smith, *Sermons*, p. 383.    [51] *Loc.cit.*    [52] Bolton, *Works*, IV, 48.

calling must be practised in, and with the generall calling of a Christian," notes Perkins. ". . . both callings must be joyned, as bodie and soule are joyned in a living man."[53] The Christian, he admonishes further, must always bear in mind that the whole purpose of our lives as we live them in the world is "to serve God in the serving of men in the works of our callings."[54] "They profane their lives and callings that imploy them to get honours, pleasures, profites, worldly commodities etc. for thus we live to another end then God hath appointed, and thus we serve ourselves, and consequently, neither God, nor man."[55]

Hall gives the same advice on the suitable Christian attitude toward the calling. "These businesses of his Calling," he writes, "the Christian follows with a willing and contented industry, not as forced to it by the necessity of humane Laws, or as urged by the law of necessity, out of the . . . fear of want; nor yet contrarily, out of an eager desire of enriching himself in his estate, but in a conscionable obedience to that God who hath made man to labour as the sparks to flie upward. . . ."[56] "Remember to doe all things to God, and not to man in our Callings, both of Religion, and in our particular Callings," Sibbes similarly counsels.[57] And Bolton urges the Christian to "ever go about the affaires of his Calling with a heavenly mind, seasoned, and sanctified with habitual prayer . . . pregnant with heavenly matter and meditation."[58]

Thus, as befits the religious frame of reference of this discussion of the calling, it is always assumed that the general calling of the Christian is superior to any particular calling and that service to God must in all cases supersede service to man. Perkins makes the preference quite explicit when he states: "A particular calling must give place to the generall calling of a Christian, when they cannot both stand together. . . . The particular calling of any man is inferiour to the generall calling of a Christian . . . because we are bound unto God in the first place, and unto man, under God: and so farre onely as we may withall, keepe our bond with God."[59] In following the same theme,

[53] *Works*, I, 756-57.    [54] *Ibid.*
[55] *Ibid.*    [56] *Works*, IV, 628.
[57] *Bowels Opened*, p. 235.    [58] *Works*, IV, 71.
[59] *Works*, I, 757-58.

Hooker advises that "we must . . . never over-charge our spirits with multiplicitie of worldly businesses, but keepe our souls in such a frame that we may be able when ever we goe to converse with God . . . to set aside all worldly occasions, that neither our hearts, nor our thoughts may run out upon them."[60]

Although English Protestant divines, as we have seen, emphasize the iniquity of using the calling to the end of securing material reward, they nonetheless assure the Christian that in connection with, if not as a consequence of, the diligent and God-fearing performance of one's proper work in the world, material reward may be confidently expected. "In every honest vocation," Dod declares, "wherein a man shall diligently and faithfully imploy himselfe there is aboundance. . . ."[61] Downame observes that "it is required, that wee live in a lawfull calling, and therein that we get our riches."[62] While discussing the necessity of every man's having a calling, Herbert remarks that "riches are the blessing of God, and the great Instrument of doing admirable good, therefore all are to procure them honestly and seasonably [that is, in a calling]."[63]

Since God is the ultimate source of all reward, Preston even ventures to suggest that the material reward may well be greater for the person who follows his calling in a godly manner than for him who thereby seeks only to serve himself. He first makes the point that Christians must exercise the duties of particular callings, "not for our owne good, but for the good of others," and on this premise he builds the further argument: "Now, I say, what is the reason that men in the exercise of their callings, have such an eye to their own profit, and not to the profit of others, whom they deale with, that they have such an eye to their owne profit, and not to others good? It is because they thinke they must be carefull to provide for their owne estate. . . . Now let a man be persuaded that God takes care for him, that riches are the shadow that followes the substance of a man's perfect walking with God, that it is God that gives them, it is he that dispenseth them, it is he that gives the reward . . . the

60 Hooker, *The Works* (Oxford, 1890), ii, 169-70.
61 Dod and Cleaver, *Proverbs*, 122.
62 Downame, *Warfare*, p. 448.
63 Herbert, *Works*, p. 275.

care of the worke onely belongs to us. If a man would deny him-selfe, and be a looser many times in his calling and be content to doe many things for the profit of others, to use those talents that God hath given him, not for his owne but for his Masters advan-tage; I say, if he would doe this, he should finde God All-sufficient. . . ."[64]

Whatever the worldly rewards of the conscionable pursuit of the calling, there is no question of the certainty of the spiritual reward and of its approximation to the quantity and quality of work performed. At the Day of Judgment, says Perkins, there will surely be a "giving and rendring to every man according to his workes," and not the least of the works which will be con-sidered and appraised will be those of a man's calling.[65]

But this ultimate evaluation of the work of the calling, the Christian is always assured, will be made completely without regard for the kind of calling involved. It will, instead, depend solely upon the manner in which the duties of the calling, what-ever they may be, are conducted and fulfilled. We are provided here again with an important distinction between the viewpoint of St. Thomas Aquinas and that of the English Protestant, since the Thomistic estimation of the worth of labor is inextricably intertwined with considerations of differing levels of social or in-stitutional status and differing degrees of occupational dignity.[66] Thus Perkins asserts: "Now the works of every calling, when they are performed in an holy manner, are done in faith and obedience, and serve notably for Gods glory, be the calling never so base. . . . The meanenesse of the calling, doth not abase the goodnesse of the worke: for God looketh not at the ex-cellence of the worke, but at the heart of the worker. And the action of a sheepheard in keeping sheep, performed as I have said, in his kind, is as good a worke before God, as is the action of a Judge, in giving sentence or of a Magistrate in ruling, or a Minister in preaching."[67]

Perkins exhibits the vigor of the concept in this almost shock-ing presentation: "Now if we compare worke to worke, there is

[64] Preston, The New Covenant (1630), p. 178.
[65] *Works*, I, 777.
[66] See Katherine Archibald, *op.cit.*
[67] *Works*, I, 758.

a difference betwixt washing of dishes, and preaching the word of God: but as touching to please God none at all. For neither that nor this pleaseth God, but as farre forth as God hath chosen a Man, and hath put his spirit in him, and purified his heart, by faith and trust in Christ. As the scriptures call him carnall which is not renewed by the spirit and borne againe in Christs flesh, and all his workes likewise . . . whatsoever hee doth, though they seem spirituall and after the law of God never so much. So contrariwise he is spirituall which is renewed in Christ, and al his workes which spring from faith seeme they never so grosse . . . yea deedes of matrimonie are pure and spirituall . . . and whatsoever is done within the lawes of God though it bee wrought by the body, as the wipings of shoes and such like, howsoever grosse they appear outwardly, yet are they sanctified."[68]

The more one penetrates this commentary on the calling in the literature of English Protestantism, the less appropriate appears the application to it of any of the central concepts of asceticism. Work is not penal, but an expression of the nature of man; hence it is enjoyable to man. Moreover, though work in this sense constitutes its own reward, it will in all probability bring with it, if conscionably pursued, the additional benefit of adequate or even abundant sustenance. Finally, since the moral or spiritual value of all proper callings is alike, there is no need for the Christian to be concerned for his heavenly destiny in terms of the type of work allotted him on earth. Altogether this is a comfortable doctrine, particularly as compared with the rigors of self-deprivation and unnatural restraint which have constituted the ideals of the monastic tradition.

The relative congeniality of the doctrine is climaxed by the permission, even the encouragement, of a regular interrupting of the regimen of labor with needed rest and lawful recreations. The Sabbath, it should be noted, though it is seen as a day of rest,

[68] *Ibid.*, p. 391. Though less dramatically, Hall says much the same thing: "The homeliest service that we doe in an honest calling, though it be but to plow, or digge, if done in obedience, and conscience of God's Commandement, is crowned with an ample reward; whereas the best workes for their kinde (preaching, praying, offering Evangelicall sacrifices) if without respect of God's injunction and glory, are loaded with curses. God loveth adverbs; and cares not how good, but how well" (*Works*, I, 137).

is never positively asserted in these writings to be part of the recreational allowance. What is meant by recreation are other periods of time in the regular work-day week which are devoted to approved kinds of relaxation of mind and body. Though occasionally some approved kind of relaxation is specifically mentioned, the definition of this category of activities is achieved principally by negative rather than positive means. That is, disapproved recreations are fairly frequently mentioned and censured. The list is actually not a long one, however: when one has indicated gaming, undue drinking or carousing, the mixed dancing of men and women, the attending of plays (sometimes merely the attending of licentious plays, but, for the most part, all plays were deemed to be licentious), and cock-fighting or bear-baiting, one has about named them all.[69]

Moderation is urged, of course, in the indulgence even in lawful recreation, and there is an expected subordination of means to end in the entire formula of conduct: just as the calling is a means subordinated to the end of total, godly living, so recreation is a means subordinated to the end of the calling. "And therefore . . . God admitteth lawful recreation," Perkins writes, "because it is a necessarie meanes to refresh either bodie or minde, that wee may the better doe the duties which pertaine unto us."[70] In another treatise, Perkins refers recreation to the

---

[69] The "Sabbatarian" issue is a complicated one. It is related to the doctrine of the calling: indeed, the industrious man in a vocation is declared to be in particular need of his Sunday concentration because of the dangers of becoming "glued to the world" (Hildersam, *Lectures*, p. 320). Also, the emphasis on Sunday is part of the English Protestant campaign against the Catholic festival holy days—which were regarded as idolatrous (Perkins, *Works*, I, 624; II, 286). Even the "puritans" were not fanatics on the issue, however. Certain work ("things needfull to the life of man"), such as the dressing of meats, was permitted (Greenham, *Works*, p. 162). But the Sabbath was, of course, not to commemorate Jahweh's rest day after creation, but the miracle of Christ's resurrection and the associated assurance of man's redemption from sin; "this redemption," Perkins writes, "is a more glorious work then the creation" (*Works*, III, 239-40); it is therefore most appropriate that this first day of the week should have been chosen by Christianity as its day of particular spiritual dedication in preference to the last day of the week which was the Jewish Sabbath. The activist concept of the Sabbath (it is seen as a day of spiritual work, rather than of rest) only serves to enhance its religious significance and intensity, and concern for its proper conduct is very widespread in English Protestant literature. Andrewes had his churchwardens on the watch for Sabbath violations (*Works*, XI, 119) and felt as strongly about the whole matter (*Works*, II, 160-66; V, 426) as did Perkins.

[70] *Works*, I, 774.

sixth commandment and sees in it a means "to the peculiar preservation of every severall mans life." He continues: "Recreation is an exercise joyned with the feare of God, conversant in things indifferent, for the preservation of bodily strength, and confirmation of the minde in holinesse. . . . To this ende hath the word of God permitted shooting . . . and putting forth of riddles . . . and hunting of wilde beasts. . . . Lastly the searching out, or the contemplation of the workes of God."[71]

"All lawfull recreation," he generalizes, "is onely in the use of things indifferent, which are in themselves neither commanded nor forbidden. For by Christian liberty, the use of such things for lawfull delight . . . is permitted unto us."[72]

Sibbes offers similar advice: "It is a blessed state, when a Christian carries himselfe so in his liberty, that his heart condemns him not for the abuse of that which it alloweth and justly in a moderate use. Recreations are lawfull, who denies it? To refresh a mans selfe, is not onely lawfull, but necessary. God knew it well enough. Therefore hath allotted time for sleepe, and the like. *But we must not turne Recreation into a Calling*, to spend too much time in it."[73]

One must again be reminded that the ministers who are speaking here about the lawfulness of moderate recreation are themselves presumably saints who are addressing other saints to be fully conscious of the sturdily anti-ascetic temper of the doctrine they preach. The ascetic tradition in Christianity cannot be said to encompass the advice to saints on the propriety of enjoying simple pleasures that English Protestant divines feel free to give. That a conscious antiasceticism is central to the English Protestant support of recreation is clearly evident in

[71] *Ibid.*, pp. 57-58.

[72] *Works*, II, 140.

[73] Sibbes, *Bowels Opened*, p. 124. Catholic preachers had long worried about the moral effects of stage plays, and all of the Protestants worried also. The principal crank (in general, "puritans" were no worse than Catholics as cultural kill-joys— the whole question of Protestant esthetics needs analysis) was the lay puritan and paranoid, William Prynne, for whose viewpoint see the amazing *Histrio-Mastix* (1633) which contains over a thousand pages of trivial and fanatical vituperation. For more of the same, see *The Sword of Christian Magistracy Supported* (1653) and *Canterburies Doome* (1646). To balance this, see Perkins, *Works*, I, 141-42, on "the end of our recreation, to refresh our bodies and mindes," with a list of approved recreations. Cf. Fuller, *Holy and Prophane States*, pp. 225-28.

this passage from the works of Adams: "They are too rigid and austere, that forbid lawfull delights: let no Teacher make the way to heaven more thorny, than God himselfe made it, and meant it. . . . I cannot believe, that God will ever give a Papist thankes for whipping himselfe. Our lawfull pleasures are his pleasures. . . . That is a superstitious worship which makes the worshippers miserable. God delights not in our blood, but when the witnesse of his glory calles for it. The world hath wages enough to vex us, we need not be our owne tormentors. It is no credit to a man's holinesse, that he condemns all recreation. Let me looke to please God, and then know that he hath made the world to serve me. Men may eate and drinke, even to honest delight, so withall they worship the giver."[74]

The intricacies of this fine dialectical dance to the tune of the calling reveal certain firm patterns. There is in all this balancing of antagonistic precepts an obvious total preference for the view that the world was created more for the employment than the enjoyment of the saints. So much basis is provided by the literature, therefore, for justification of Max Weber's definition of the Protestant ethic as one of *innerweltliche Askese*. But though enjoyment of the fruits of labor in the world is indeed circumscribed by the Protestant emphasis on vocation as serving transcendent ends, the Weberian thesis must be modified by the Protestant advocacy of proper and godly pleasure in both the world and its rewards. More important, English Protestantism found satisfaction and delight in the particularized ideal of work in the world; the penal and disciplinary functions of work are only incidental to the primary fact that work is at once an expression of salvation and also of the spontaneous relationship of man to the world around him. In the development of the ideal of the calling, there is very little concern with the frailty of man—in no other area of dogma is there such generous treatment of the reprobate; all men are not only capable of a calling, but must follow one. Work in the godly is prayer, but in the ungodly, too, it is regarded as creative, essential to society, and worthy of reward. As English divines focused their attention upon the particular calling as an adjunct of the general calling,

74 Adams, *Works*, p. 1130.

the positive character of work became generalized. By virtue of its own inner logic and psychology the calling cannot be ascetic: it is fulfillment, personal, social, and religious. The doctrine of the calling as it emerges from these sermons incorporates the most outgoing and positive view of work which exists in the Christian tradition.

One final and crucial aspect of the Protestant vocational ethic should be emphasized in this summary of our discussion: this is a tendency to abolish or even to reverse the traditional and hence medieval and Roman Catholic moral hierarchy of vocations. The "lawful" callings in the Protestant view, though still a function of social hierarchy, were measured morally by very different standards from those applied in previous theologies and philosophies. Looking at a sermon such as that of Berthold of Regensburg, "On the Ten Choirs of Angels and of Christendom," in which all industrial and mercantile and farming vocations are grouped as "The Six Lower Orders" and are separated absolutely from "the first three kinds of people [priests, monks, and temporal lords] who are the highest and the most sublime, whom almighty God has chosen and to whom he has ordained that the other . . . orders should be subject and render service," then one begins to appreciate the Protestant doctrine's truly revolutionary nature.[75] For the doctrine insists upon a concrete rejection of such Catholic preference for the vocations of sacrament, asceticism, and status. To the Protestant, the most obviously godly calling is the most obviously economic or productive one: that of the husbandman, the artisan, the tradesman. We have here a genuine transvaluation of values.

[75] *Berthold von Regensburg. Vollständige Ausgabe seiner Predigten* (Vienna, 1862), I, 140-56. We are indebted to Howard Kaminsky of the University of Washington for a translation of this sermon.

# CHAPTER 4

# ENGLISH PROTESTANT ECONOMIC THEORY:
## THE CHALLENGE OF CAPITALISM

"The real significance of Calvinism for the modern economic development which culminates in the all-embracing capitalistic system of the present day . . . has lately been pointed out by Max Weber who . . . raised the question regarding the spiritual, ethical, and philosophical pre-suppositions of this system. Without a definite mental and spiritual background, a system of this kind cannot become dominant. . . . From the capitalistic system we have to distinguish the 'capitalistic spirit' apart from which the former would never have come to exercise such power over men's minds. For this spirit displays an untiring activity, a boundlessness of grasp, quite contrary to the natural impulse to enjoyment and ease . . . it makes work and gain an end in themselves, and makes men the slaves of work for work's sake; it . . . gives to life a clear calculability and abstract exactness. . . . This spirit, Weber said to himself, cannot have simply arisen of itself as a necessary concomitant of industrial inventions, discoveries, and commercial gains. . . . Following this line of thought, Weber was led, by way of conjecture from the fact that capitalism flourishes best on Calvinistic soil, to draw the conclusion that the ethico-religious spirit of Calvinism had a special significance for the arising of this capitalistic spirit. . . .

"Weber has, in my opinion, completely proved his case. . . ."
—Ernst Troeltsch, *Protestantism and Progress*, 132-138

## I. The Weber Thesis

THE MOST INTRIGUING ECONOMIC ASPECT of the Protestant mind remains its relationship to the mind of capitalist enterprise. Few subjects in modern history have attracted such a plethora of polemics. For half a century, leading social scientists in the West—Weber, Troeltsch, Sombart, Tawney, Sée, Brantano, Hauser, and Parsons—have debated the issues involved in an analysis of the causal matrix which envelops at once the origins of modern capitalism and modern Christianity. The principles of this analysis were formulated by Weber, the most important social scientist since Marx: the theory stands in outline, in the words of Troeltsch, at the head of this chapter. It would not be consistent with the intention of our book, which attempts to minimize debate and to work empirically from the sources, to involve ourselves in a reconstruction of the entire controversy or an assessment of the value of the work of its various participants. Almost everything has been said of Weber that can be said: he has "proved" his case to Troeltsch and to Parsons;[1] to H. M. Robertson and Albert Hyma he has disastrously misplaced his evidence;[2] Brentano and Tawney criticize the thesis for isolating the religious phenomena from the broader social and cultural milieu;[3] and among recent studies the range is from Benjamin Nelson's apotheosis of Weber's hypothesis to Fanfani's perversion of it.[4] But in view of the importance of Weber's work as a social scientist and the crucial role which his theory has played in the formulation of the modern sociology of religion (as well as in the contemporary disenchantment with Marxism),[5] we must at least pause to state clearly where we stand with regard to the Weberian thesis.

Weber's historical exercise with the materials available for an understanding of the genesis of the spirits of capitalism and

[1] Ernst Troeltsch, *Protestantism and Progress* (Boston, Mass., 1958), p. 138; Talcott Parsons, *The Structure of Social Action* (New York, 1937), pp. 500-78.

[2] H. M. Robertson, *Aspects of the Rise of Economic Individualism* (Cambridge, 1933); Albert Hyma, *Christianity, Capitalism and Communism* (Ann Arbor, 1937).

[3] Lujo Brentano, *Die Anfänge des Kapitalismus* (München, 1916); R. H. Tawney, *Religion and the Rise of Capitalism* (London, 1926).

[4] B. N. Nelson, *The Idea of Usury* (Princeton, 1949); Amintore Fanfani, *Catholicism, Protestantism and Capitalism* (New York, 1955), argues that predestinarian dogma explains the affinity of Protestantism with capitalism because "Protestantism encouraged capitalism inasmuch as it denied the relation between earthly action and eternal recompense" (p. 205). This is a standard Catholic misunderstanding of the Protestant doctrine. (Fanfani's book was first published in London in 1935.)

[5] See H. Stuart Hughes, *Consciousness and Society* (New York, 1958), 278-335.

Protestantism was in many ways less anti-Marxist than anti-empirical. He was interested in establishing a methodology of ideal types of social being—categories of mind and institution which would be cross-cultural tools of social analysis. These categories he derived intuitively and brilliantly; but as with most such categories (outside mathematics and pure logic), their usefulness is vitiated by the demands of the system of analysis itself. Thus Weber's interest in the growth of rationality and bureaucracy (and the irrational bases of such development) in the modern world of capitalism and socialism (which he regards as essentially the same because of the "rational disciplining of the acquisitive impulse" in each) leads to a definition of the spirit of capitalism which makes his definition of the "Protestant ethic" a distinct corollary to the system and spirit of modern economics. That is, he builds into his system of analysis *a priori* terms which are interlocking and mutually supporting. Weber and his school define the "spirit of capitalism" as an unnatural acquisitiveness seeking an eternally greater profit, an endless profit which becomes an end in itself without any rationale beyond that of blind devotion to discipline. Thus we are given a definition of a system whose facade of rationality conceals a basically irrational mechanism—the profit motive. By means of this definition we are prepared to accept the congruence or, indeed, causal relationship of another irrational psychological mechanism—the "worldly asceticism" of the Protestant ethic.

But what evidence is there of the irrational drive behind the profit system—that is, of the individual irrationality which motivates the pseudo-rationality of the system itself? What evidence is there of any such psychology of endless, selfless devotion to work without the usual rewards of power and pleasure that historic societies have accorded the successful? Is there not, in fact, something bizarre in all of the recent effort to follow Weber in considering the "spirit of capitalism" a perversion of the human spirit so mysterious that only the depths of the irrational can reveal its sources? *Homo bourgeoisiensis* is no such queer fellow: he has grown wealthy by rationally exploiting the resources of the earth, including as many of his fellow creatures as possible; and the fruits of his success have been palpable and enjoyed. Furthermore, the kind of capitalist who could conceivably be a model for Weber's portrait—sour, frugal, untiring, joyless moneygrubber—is not the sort who made the major contribution to the achievement of the Industrial Revolution.[6] Weber and Parsons are unwise to insist on the distinction between their "ascetic" capitalist and the adventurous "Venetian" type who is supposed to have been outmoded by the Calvinist grub: for the financing and organizing of great segments of the Industrial Revolution was the work of men like Thomas Gresham, Horatio Palavicino, Lionel Cranfield, Josiah Child, Josiah Wedgewood, or the Liverpool slave-merchants, or London's eighteenth-century war profiteers—a galaxy of adventurous, risk-taking, and enjoyment-centered individuals. Calvinist shopkeepers brought out their savings to invest after the economic revolution was over; and it required no Calvinist ethic to convince men of the desirability of further profits if the system provided the opportunities. In other words, Weber's particular "spirit of capitalism" may be one of the least essential ingredients in the complicated system of capitalism as a whole. Conscientious and thrifty and hard-working businessmen can be found in all civilized cultures; in the West they made up the vast majority of entrepreneurs in the prosperous towns of the Catholic middle ages. But Weber *has* to insist on the importance of the "calling to profit" as the key to modern capitalist success because it can, he thinks, be accounted for in turn by the new religious factor.

Weber argues that in many other cultures where all "material" factors were as favorable for a great industrial and commercial expansion, the dominant religious traditions were unfavorable, *ergo* it was the need of a proper religious psychology which prevented modern economies from developing elsewhere or earlier.[7] We note again the manner in which he loads the terms of his analysis to get the desired conclusion. We are told that all the "material" factors—indeed, all the nonreligious factors, "material" or otherwise—were the same in various other

6 See the very perceptive Werner Sombart, *The Quintessence of Capitalism* (New York, 1915), especially pp. 236-62.

7 Max Weber, *General Economic History* (trans. Frank H. Knight, Glencoe, Ill., 1927), pp. 352-69. See Parsons' discussion, *loc.cit.*

times and places, that the situation of seventeenth-century Western Europe was unique only in its Protestantism.

The objections to this assertion—an assertion that is one of the major elements in the Weberian analysis—are almost a function of one's knowledge of the seventeenth century: the greater the knowledge, the more numerous the objections. The most significant new factors in the complex of seventeenth-century culture out of which the new industrialization was created were probably, first, such intellectual but clearly non-religious novelties as the mathematics of Descartes, Pascal, Leibnitz, and Newton; the physics of Galileo and Newton; the philosophies of Bacon and Descartes; and the systems of secular social theory associated with the English revolution.

Second, there were those more directly "material" innovations which may be best summed up perhaps in terms of the culmination of the development, centuries-long in its total execution, of the nation-state. In what previous culture or civilization may political and social bodies like the nation-states of seventeenth-century Western Europe be found, vigorous like them in the very initial absence of imperialistic extension, mercantilistically oriented, technologically equipped, militarily ambitious and capable, and possessed of a world-wide stage on which to play out their political and economic destinies? We should thus be inclined to think the major factors in the industrial genius of the West were science, secularism, and the nation-state—"material" factors all in Weber's terminology—and that they were all in unique combination from the seventeenth century on. The "spirit of capitalism," though possibly constituting an influence, albeit a changing and nebulous one, in this complex, is surely of minor importance beside the verifiable and accelerating modes of cultural change which we have indicated.

Yet even if for the purpose of argument one accepts Weber's assertion of the significance to capitalism of the sort of "spirit" he describes, there remains the issue to which our study is immediately addressed: what evidence is there of a causal or at least congruent relationship between the Protestant, specifically the Calvinist, ethic and the ethic of capitalism?[8] Weber insists that the spirits of the Calvinist calling and of capitalism were not the result of common material changes, and that the evolution of theocratic and "socialist" Geneva into the secular and individualistic world of Manchester was not the result of the accommodation of Christianity to the new pressures of a new society; rather, Weber maintains, the Protestant ethic was a dynamic causal factor in giving "capitalistic callings" religious import and character.[9] In other words, the person committed to the Protestant ethic was driven by the religious compulsion of that ethic to direct his actions toward the goal of continuous, unremitting acquisition for the "ascetic" satisfaction of acquisition itself.

Talcott Parsons follows Troeltsch in believing that the key to Weber's theory is not—as we have argued—his method of intuitively-derived assumptions, but that the theory is proved empirically from evidence found in the writings of English Protestantism.[10] Calvinism in seventeenth-century England is seen to evolve directly and dynamically into the "spirit of capitalism." The value of Weber's empirical proof will be challenged by the evidence presented in this chapter, as the value of his interpretation of the Calvinist calling was questioned in the previous chapter.

## II. The Tragedy of Change

The spawning years of the lusty, ruthless English capitalism of the sixteenth and seventeenth centuries constituted a transformation in society which the English ministers—who lived through the epoch of lost villages, mass unemployment, hordes of beggars and vagrants, unprecedented inflation, and the dwindling of parish incomes—protested with vehemence. Troeltsch

[8] See Ephraim Fischoff, "The History of a Controversy," in *Protestantism and Capitalism: The Weber Thesis and Its Critics* (ed. Robert W. Green: Boston, 1959); Charles and Katherine George, "Protestantism and Capitalism in Pre-Revolutionary England," *Church History* (December, 1958).

[9] Weber, *op.cit.*, p. 367.

[10] See Norman Birnbaum, "The Zwinglian Reformation in Zurich," *Past and Present* (April, 1959). From his study of a parallel case he concludes that "if Zwinglianism was the road towards capitalism for Zurich, it was taken because the route in any case led in that direction."

and Weber have argued that in the death throes of the old feudal economies of Europe, it was the Protestants who welcomed the new dispensation and rejected the old. But though it is obviously true, especially for lay Protestants, that the old economic regimes benefited them less than they did the Roman Catholic hierarchy and that much "Protestantism" was essentially economic cupidity, the Protestant pulpit in England lamented bitterly the passing of a merry land under the shadow of the new sort of landlordism and the newly-hatched economic tyrannies of the open market. Arthur Dent made a catalogue of the economic "oppression" of this era which was "so infinite a matter, that I know not where to begin, or where to make an end of it." Indeed, he does go on to a score of itemized abuses, headed by enclosures, usury, rack-renting, "hiring poore men's houses over their heads," and concluding with offenses against ministers, widows, and orphans.[11] Other such angry catalogues of the sins of economic exploitation abound.[12] Some of the preachers complained that, although "people now are more rich then they have been . . . yet they want the desire they have had to become liberal"[13] and that the new wealth, based, as they believed, upon the "infinite summes of gold and silver which are gathered from the Indies, and other countries, and so yearly transported unto these coasts," produced "the degenerations of our gentility" into arrogance and cruelty.[14]

Bishop Hall was perhaps the most eloquent flayer of the economic order, vying with Bolton for the honor. His writing is saturated with indictments against "yee that grinde faces like edge-tooles, and spill bloud like water";[15] the brave, expansive new world of economic adventure, Hall charges, censures not history's social criminals, but rather the victims of the new order: "In the Country they censure not the oppressing gentleman that tyrannizes over his cottagers, incroches upon his neighbors inheritance, incloses commons, depopulates villages, scruges his tenants to death, but the poore soules that when they are

11 Arthur Dent, *The Plaine Mans Path-way to Heaven*, pp. 200-04.
12 E.g., Perkins, *Works*, I, 461-62; Hall, *Works*, p. 416.
13 Henrie Smith, *Sermons*, p. 435.
14 Bolton, *Works*, I, 162; *A Three-Fold Treatise* (1634), p. 82.
15 Hall, *Works*, III, 361.

crushed, yield the juyce of teares, exhibit bits of complaint, throw open the new thornes, maintaine the old wounds; would these men be content to be quietly racked and spoiled, there would be peace."[16]

Though it was usual for the clergy to make a point of the presumed relative equity of the old economic order (that is, before the Spanish silver fleets), one of the hallowed institutions of that order did come in for criticism: the rule of primogeniture in freehold inheritance. Typical is the attack of Dod, who insisted that the best and most godly children should get the greater inheritance and that all, including daughters, have a moral right to inherit.[17] And Adams argued that the economic result of primogeniture was the squandering of the inheritance in London and abroad.[18] William Gouge and Richard Field defended the system because "heirs are made in heaven";[19] but Thomas Fuller worked out a neat rationale (to some extent justified by the facts) by which the disinherited was spurred on by the system to "more wealth if betaking himself to merchandise; whence often he riseth to the greatest annual honor in the kingdom."[20]

But the tide of complaint ran most strongly against the abuses of more recent economic provenance. Enclosures have no defenders among the clergy; with usury, this economic technique was regarded as sin, and the root of the major social evils of the time.[21] In general, the appeals of complaint may be said to be directed to the consciences of the guilty. However, there are occasional demands that "authority knowes how to remedy this evill," and more frequent hints that bribery in high places is the explanation of the failure of the government to act.[22] John Downame maintained, quite typically, that "heretofore men were preferred unto offices for their service, sufficiencie, and desert; but now the usual entrance unto them is by large gifts."[23]

[16] *Ibid.*, p. 542.
[17] Dod and Cleaver, *Ten Commandements*, p. 206; cf. Hall, *op.cit.*, I, 64.
[18] Thomas Adams, *Works*, pp. 417-18.
[19] Gouge, *Works*, I, 323-24; Field, *Of the Church*, p. 441.
[20] Fuller, *The Holy and Prophane States*, pp. 63-67.
[21] E.g., Bolton, *op.cit.*, pp. 184-85; 237-44; Adams, *op.cit.*, p. 1058.
[22] Hall, *Works*, I, 491; Downame, *A Treatise of Swearing* (1609), pp. 207-12.
[23] *Op.cit.*, p. 210.

Therefore, "what wonder is it if these men who entred into their places by bribing, doe in the execution of them live by extorsion?"[24] The money nexus, the whole economic bias of the new economy, was felt to be degenerate and infinitely corrupting.

The church itself, as an institution, was universally known to be in a deplorable economic state. Hall, with the fury of impotence, lashed out at "hee whose sacrilegious throats have swallowed downe whole Churches and Hospitals . . . whose mawes have put over whole Parishes of sold and affamished soules."[25] These bitter terms were spoken out of the deepest self-consciousness of the clerical dilemma in Protestant lands: Beza and Bullinger had insisted upon the critical importance of keeping church livings out of lay hands and of retaining a tight fist upon tithes and other church revenues.[26] Archbishop Whitgift spoke for the hierarchy in declaring, "It is true that covetous patrons of benefices be a great plague to this church, and one of the principal causes of rude and ignorant ministers. God grant some speedy reformation in that point."[27] Archbishop Sandys attacked the "Spoilers of the patrimonie of Christ"; "the pretense is reformation, but the practice is deformation."[28] Bolton cried out against the evil times in which "incrochments upon the Church be like the breaches of the sea. . . ."[29] Adams spoke often of the "good stomacks" of the gentry, which could "devoure (and digest too) three or four plumpe Parsonages . . . and they have fed so liberally, that the poore servitors . . . the Vicars, have scarce enough left to keepe life and soule together . . . your fathers thought many acres of ground well bestowed, you thinke the Tythe of those acres a wast."[30]

There were no parties on this issue. From the Presbyterian Walter Travers to Archbishop Laud, all the clergy agreed a truly godly ministry depended upon what Travers called a "reason-

24 Ibid.
25 Works, III, 361. Cf. Strype, The Life and Arts of John Whitgift, II, 319, for the trouble such arguments could bring on the head of the preacher.
26 Théodore de Bèze, A Briefe and Pithie Sum of the Christian faith (1572), Epistle; Bullinger, Decades, II, 45-46.
27 John Whitgift, Works, III, 456.
28 Edwin Sandys, Sermons, p. 104. Cf. Henry Burton, A Censure of Simonie (1624).
29 Op.cit., I, 160.    30 Works, pp. 38-39.

able maintenance."[31] To this end, Hooker defended tithes by natural and positive law, and inferentially by divine law; and he attacked repeatedly the spoilers.[32] Fuller wrote a fine essay to the effect that the "maintenance of ministers ought to be plentiful, certain, and in some sort proportionable to their deserts."[33] In his treatise on the *Calling of the Ministerie*, William Perkins demonstrated again his sensible interpretation of the economic basis even of the highest calling; he asked why good ministers are so rare, and concluded that in addition to the eternal opposition of the "wicked and prophane men" and the inherent difficulties of the rhetoric of the spirit, "the last reason is more peculiar to this age of the new Testament, namely *want of maintenance and preferment* for them that labour in this calling . . . especially now under the gospel, this calling is unprovided for when it deserves lest of all to be rewarded . . . the want thereof is the cause why so many young men of . . . greatest hope turne to other vocations, and especially to the Law, wherein at this day the greatest parts of the *finest wits of our kingdome* are imployed, and why? But because they have all the meanes to rise, whereas the ministerie for the most part yieldeth nothing but a plain *way to beggerie.* . . ."[34]

It is interesting to note in Perkins, and more explicitly in Fuller,[35] the unfavorable comparison of the financing of the Protestant ministry with that of the Roman Catholic priesthood. Of course, all the divines also saw that the economic problems of the church were the basic cause of the other moral abuses so widely complained of: simony, pluralism, absenteeism, and the like.[36] Finally, there remains to be observed the very general fatalism and hopelessness, the resignation of saints, before the magnitude of the task of economic salvation for the church. Projects like those of Preston and the Feoffees for Impropriations, or like the great effort of Laud as archbishop, were ameli-

[31] Cf. Walter Travers, *A Full . . . declaration of Ecclesiastical Discipline* (Zurich, 1574), pp. 113-24.

[32] Hooker, *Ecclesiastical Polity*, Book v, Chapter 79; vii, 21-24.

[33] *Op.cit.*, p. 272.

[34] *Works*, iii, 432-33.

[35] *Ibid.*, p. 275: ". . . the Papists in time of Popery gave their priests plentiful means."

[36] Cf. Henry Burton, *A Censure of Simonie* (1624); Dering, *Works*, pp. 177-78.

orative and ephemeral. Bishop Thomas Cooper put the case in its true perspective: "Those laws likewise must be taken away whereby Impropriations and Patronages stand as men's lawfull possession and heritage. In these Impropriations and Patronage, as I doe confesse, there is lamentable abuse, and wish the same by some good Statute to bee remedied: so how the thing itselfe can without great difficultie and danger be taken away, being so general as it is in the state of this Realme, I leave to the judgment of the wise and godly."[37]

In looking upon the sorry panorama of economic abuse, an abuse rooted in institutions and social classes which had shaped and were still the bulwark of Protestantism itself, the divines were left with no critical ground to stand upon, save the lonely, radical islands of the sectaries. In some desperation, then, they turned to the oldest concept of justice in the Christian vocabulary: the concept of charity. Standing upon charity had for a millennium been a permitted posture amid the predatory economic and social operations of European elites. Injunctions to succor the poor and dispossessed were common moral coin, expected of the clerical profession; and charitable bequests were the mark of lay sanctity and the salve to whatever conscience might lurk in the psychological recesses of the successful and powerful.

But the Protestant divines refused to accept the Roman Catholic definition of Christian charity. Indeed, their redefinition of charity is one of the more arresting manifestations of the Protestant spirit.[38] Above all, as was true of the Protestants'

---

[37] Cooper, An Admonition, p. 170.

[38] See W. K. Jordan, Philanthropy in England, 1480-1660 (1959) for a most important treatment of a subject pivotal to the nature of the Protestant ethic and to the ethos of emerging capitalism. In general, Professor Jordan is impressed with the "incredible" and "immense" altruism of the "great and generous merchant class" who were laying the foundations of the liberal state in England. His picture of the morality of the bourgeoisie is the antithesis of Tawney's—his merchant oligarchy is bountiful, socially responsible, and effectively compassionate. We feel he has made one major error in reading the wills and the literature exhorting to charity: he concludes that the idea of philanthropy is "secular" in this period, that the older religious concept of charity is abandoned for a concept that in its "intense secularism" reflects the revolutionary character of a new age. We feel his own evidence contradicts such a conclusion and that "secular" can mean only "nonecclesiastical" or "lay" as it applies to the Protestant attitude toward responsibility for charity and the poor. Professor Jordan admits most of his donors were

vision of sainthood, there is in their view of charity an assertion of equality, of brotherhood, quite distinct in emphasis from that of Catholic theory. To Thomistic and Dantean Christianity, charity was the obligation of superior human essence to inferior human essence in need. To the idealist tradition, whether in Platonic or Christian garb, inequality was an essence, and was identified with the social hierarchies of the world. It is no parody of the typical medieval view to say the poor were regarded as furniture in the moral gymnasium of superior beings: without them the exercise of the prime virtue of *caritas* would be impossible. How could the treasures of this world be laid up in heaven? Only by the agency of charity, of bountiful giving out of munificence, could the magic transmutation take place, and then very nearly *ex opere operato*.

Lutheran theology, with its insistence upon total and universal depravity of the will, supplemented by the later Protestant concept of election as invisible and likely an inversion of the worldly mirror of graces, made it increasingly difficult to look upon charity as moral exercise for a rich elite. The English divines stressed the doctrine that all earthly inequalities are accidents, that such inequalities are no reflection of essences. Thus charity becomes an assertion of brotherhood—of the love that spontaneously seeks out a brother's misfortune and acts to relieve on a principle of equal regard. Charity is not condescension or the obligation of superiority; it is an imperative of common humanity under God. "To profit or benefit others, is a duty belonging to all men," said William Ames. "Not onely the will of God revealed in the Scriptures doth require this, but also the law of humane nature. For nothing is more naturall than that wee should doe so to another, as wee would bee done to ourselves. And nothing is more humane then to helpe the necessity of man. . . . In pitty, and its workes, wee doe especially

"deeply pious men" (p. 20), that wills to 1640 are prefaced with the phrase "In Dei nomine Amen" and are "completely honest documents . . . drawn with searching of soul and in the sight of God" (p. 16); but he unwisely insists that this activity is nonreligious! See also Christopher Hill, "Puritans and the Poor," *Past and Present* (November, 1952); V. Kiernan and Hill continue the argument, *op.cit.* (February, 1953), pp. 45-54.

put on the image and likenesse of God . . . Love towards God cannot consist without this charity towards our neighbour . . . neither can any true religion."[39]

Richard Bernard, in *The Ready way to Good Works*, argued that "the Sweet Harmony of the body naturall" counselled charity as a principle of cooperation and fellowship; for we are all "hewed out of the same rocke," so that though "perhaps thy poore neighbour may be, or hath been, a careless loose-liver, an idle droane . . . . Notwithstanding if need so require, thou must succour him, *non quia peccator, sed quia homo*, because he is a man . . . for herein thou art but a supporter of the common state of humanity."[40]

In fact, Bernard continued, "one maine end of all our civill actions, politicall imployments, or corporeall endeavours in our particular callings, must be to give to the poore."[41]

Thus the Protestants have a kind of welfare-state approach to charity, completely rejecting the treasure of merits theory of Catholic persuasion. "Heaven is not to be had in exchange for an Hospital, or a Chantry, or a Colledge erected in thy last will . . . the giving of all that we have to the poor, at our death, will not do it. . . ." So preached John Donne.[42] Downame's *The Plea of the Poore* and Perkins in his *Cases of Conscience* strongly urged that charity is the fruit of righteousness rather than a payment for Grace.[43] Henry Smith warned against using charity as a bridge to serve two masters, God and Mammon: "It is said of this City, that many citizens of London have good wills, but bad deeds . . . First, ye are ungodly that you may be rich; and then you part from some of your riches to excuse for some of your ungodliness."[44]

Instead of such individual treasures of merit, the Protestant pulpit urged charity as a social obligation. Smith vehemently indicted the commonwealth for its failure to see to basic wel-

39 William Ames, *Conscience with the Power and Cases Thereof* (1639), pp. 255, 258.
40 Richard Bernard, *The Ready Way to Good Works* (1635), pp. 160-64.
41 *Ibid.*, pp. 294-95.
42 *The Sermons* (Berkeley, 1953), p. 156.
43 Downame, *The Plea of the Poore* (1616), 153; Perkins, *Works*, II, 146.
44 Smith, *Sermons*, p. 15.

fare (that is, prevent starvation).[45] "The people of this world can very easily find a staff to beat a dog," he wrote, but they seem disinclined to share their wealth with the needy.[46] Dod complained that the inadequacy of the magistrates offended the sensibilities of those who must "see men stand crying at the doore, like dogs for bread."[47]

Related to this social welfare tendency in Protestantism was an emphasis on what might be called "preventive charity": "large expenses in building and enlarging colledges, and erecting Hospital, libraries, Free-Schooles."[48] Boasted Hildersam, "more hath bin given in this land within these three score yeeres to the building and increase of hospitals, of colledges, and other schooles of good learning, and to such like works as are truly charitable, then were in any one hundred yeeres, during all the time and reigne of popery."[49]

Richard Bernard put the case in terms which have a striking, really quite revolutionary tone of enlightenment: ". . . it were to be wished that publike Schools might be more frequently erected in every great Countrie parish, though no Market towne, where the inhabitants are of sufficient wealth and abilitie. This were indeede a noble worke, farre more worthie mens cost and expenses than the foundation of some kinde of Hospitalls and Almes-houses, who wee filled too often with swarmes of idle, lazie, unworthy Drones, and perhaps with some truely poore, aged, impotent creeples among them, the one whereof might bee better imployed, and the other otherwise, as well, if not better relieved. . . . You shall finde that erection of Grammar Schooles is a worke as farre transcending and surpassing the foundation and building of Almes-houses, as the instruction of the minde doth excell the outward relieving and sustentation of the bodie."[50]

Protestant charity made another distinction which changed the older Catholic charity quite profoundly. This was with regard to the "objects of charity," the definition of morally proper giving. It was consistently argued not only that the donor of

[45] *Ibid.*, p. 433.   [46] *Ibid.*, p. 435.   [47] Dod, *op.cit.*, p. 244.
[48] Bolton, *A Three-Fold Treatise* (1634), p. 81.
[49] Arthur Hildersam, *CLII Lectures upon Psalme LI* (1635), p. 479.
[50] Bernard, *op.cit.*, pp. 344-45.

charity be clean-handed (that his "charity" be not "conscience money," wrung initially from people by usury, extortion, and bad practice), but also that the recipient be truly benefited by the charity. For idleness is a sin, and "beggars commit sacrilege who abuse the name of Christ, and make their poverty a cloak to keep them idle still."[51] There are, said Andrewes, two sorts of poor: the orphans, widowes, "strangers," and "poor scholars" who "shalbe with us alwayes" and all of whom "must be suffered and succoured" to the limits of charity; then there are the "beggers and vagabonds able to work; to whom good must be done by not suffering them to be as they are, but to employ them in such sort as they may do good."[52] This latter group can be salvaged physically and spiritually and restored to citizenship and service in the Commonwealth.[53]

A most interesting and progressive-tending distinction, this, between charity and human waste; yet one in which lurked the dangers of the later bourgeois viciousness described by Tawney.[54] On the one hand, it was important to look upon poverty neither as a holy state in the monastic tradition, nor as a necessity for relieving the consciences of the rich in the broadly Catholic tradition, but as an individual degradation and perhaps even a social crime. Robert Allen spoke of the possibility of a public treasury for the poor,[55] and Henry Smith declared, "A good Commonwealth . . . looketh to every member in the Commonwealth."[56]

On the other hand, as many preachers saw, the process of separating the sheep from the goats (". . . the other extreme is too much care and scrupulosity when men . . . are so busie in examining the poore about their estate and desert that they can finde no leasure to open their purse or relieve their wants . . ."[57]) might become cruelly unjust. So Hildersam: ". . . true it is that the poore in all places are for the most part the most

[51] Bullinger, *Decades*, II.
[52] Andrewes, *XCVI Sermons*, p. 21.
[53] *Ibid*. See Donne, *Works*, v, 247, for a passionate statement of concern.
[54] Tawney, *Religion and the Rise of Capitalism*, pp. 210-26.
[55] Robert Allen, *The Oderifferous Garden of Charitie* (1603), p. 37.
[56] *Op.cit.*, p. 431.     [57] *Op.cit.*, p. 40.

void of grace, and not so miserable in their corporall as in their spirituall estate";[58] Perkins' asking why in a country blessed by God with the Gospel there are so many beggars, and answering, "They are (for the most part) a cursed generation . . .";[59] Dod counselling that beggars "be severely punished and set to worke . . . these filthy persons and unprofitable generation, this refuse and off-scouring of the world, must be purged away by the hand of the magistrate";[60] and Sanderson urging solid citizen and magistrate, "harden our hearts against them, and not give them; do you execute the severity of the Law upon them and not spare them . . . These ulcers and Drones of the Commonwealth are ill worthy of any honest man's alms, of any good magistrates protection."[61]

Finally, on the grimly bourgeois side of this new-coined concept of charity, should be mentioned the invariable "order of preference" in approved charity which Downame trots out, and which is endlessly copied thereafter: first, "church and commonwealth; second, our own necessities, for charetie and mercie beginne at home, and to whom then he bee pittiful and compassionate, that is cruell to his own bowels?"; then parents (man and wife are treated as "one flesh" and the Catholic view that parents should precede the wife in consideration is rejected); then children; then benefactors (!), kindred, and friends; and only after all these claims to "charity" have been satisfied, is one to look to the needs of the parish poor![62]

In balance, however, for all the horrors of (bourgeois) sanctimoniousness and hypocrisy about the poor, there was real advance in looking upon charity with suspicion; it was a moral suspicion founded basically upon the ethic of work, an ethic which quite properly insisted upon the awful degradation, spiritual and physical, of idle minds and begging hands.

[58] Hildersam, *op.cit.*, p. 118. On the next page he declares the same poor "may belong to Gods election for ought thou knowest"!

[59] *Works*, III, 191; cf. Donne, *Works*, II, 211.

[60] *Op.cit.*, p. 243.

[61] Sanderson, *Sermons*, pp. 103-04.

[62] *Op.cit.*, pp. 130-38. But see Jordan, *Philanthropy in England*, for the evidence of a liberal bourgeois response in bequests to the poor, but a disinclination to follow the clerical preference for church donations.

### III. Calvinism to Capitalism?

Our evidence has so far led us to observe the essentially con-servative, angry, and frightened tone of Calvinist opinion re-garding the social and psychological realities of early English capitalism.[63] In the previous chapter we analyzed in some detail the nature of the Calvinist concepts of wealth and of the calling. It will now be appropriate to our task of evaluating the Webe-rian thesis to examine further and by way of summary the whole range of English Protestant religious attitudes as they were re-lated, directly or even potentially, to the "spirit of capitalism" as defined by Weber and his school.

First, we have reached the general conclusion that the Protes-tant consecration of the world of men transformed the moral frame of reference affecting economic life. Sanctity, the supreme blessing of eternal life, was in the Protestant view a revelation more of the workshop than of cloister or castle. The world itself —and economic life was of course the central activity of the world—was both good and bad, but it was the critical area of concern. The Protestant saint must demonstrate his quality while living in the world and busying himself with its tasks; he is a social and total being and the high road to salvation which he travels advertises those positive aspects of the world which the Catholic tradition denies.

The most obvious and troubling problem tempting comment in the realm of economic affairs was that of rewards, especially the discrepancies of extremes: wealth and poverty. With pros-perity as with poverty, the Protestant urges the moral neutrality of rewards: both are absolutely God's will ("He giveth you riches, you get them not, it is not your own wisdom or travail that getteth them . . .";[64] "A rich man may be a good man, and a poore man may be wicked. Christ sanctified Riches, as well as Povertie . . .").[65] The saint need not *necessarily* be suspicious of prosperity ("prosperity" is defined as superfluity or abundance beyond "need" and "need" includes maintenance of depend-

---

[63] See Bernard Bailyn's excellent *The New England Merchants in the 17th Century* (Cambridge, Mass., 1955).

[64] *Works*, VIII, 28.

[65] Adams, *Works*, p. 860.

ents, servants, and inherited estate with all proper social appurtenances); similarly, poverty is neither positively to be sought, as in the Catholic tradition, nor, as in the later Capitalist tradition, is it a mark of damnation.

Yet throughout the works of the English divines runs a persistent theme of "let us labour to make our wayes more perfect, and we shall bee more perfect in our outward estate, we shall be better in our wealth."[66] Couched in pious injunctions about God's will and spiritual soundness as guides for all economic ambitions, there is a remarkably friendly attitude toward the possession, acquisition, and enjoyment of property. Combined with the generous interpretation of spiritually appropriate wealth, the principle *sunt dei dona ergo in se bona* seemed, indeed, often to let down all barriers to the great god Mammon. But not so. On the contrary, all possibility of ultimately viewing worldly prosperity as a reliable indicator of divine favor or the soundness of one's spiritual state is forestalled by the fundamental insistence (nagging common sense!) that the blessings of the world are distributed indiscriminately to the good and to the bad. If there is a tendency to see worldly prosperity as a likely accompaniment of Christian zeal, the much more usual and emphatic judgment is that by far the gifts of best quality and most quantity that the world can offer fall to the share of the wicked rather than the virtuous.[67]

The explanation for this melancholy state of distributed prosperity was of course in Matthew ("Ye cannot serve God and mammon"), but the English preachers worried constantly about the problem. Bolton argued that the wicked's proneness to wealth was owing to their lack of moral restraint in employing means to their ends.[68] Remarked Adams: "It is easie for that man to be rich that will make his Conscience poore."[69] In the final analysis, however, the source of this, as of every judgment, is God. Why does God permit the wicked to enjoy the worldly prosperity which the godly typically lack? He does so for two reasons: first, to reward the reprobate for whatever "civil" virtues

[66] John Preston, *The Saints Daily Exercise* (1613), p. 354.
[67] E.g., Bolton, *Works*, IV, 56; Downame, *op.cit.*, pp. 557-58.
[68] *Op.cit.*, p. 120.
[69] *Works*, pp. 862-63.

they possess, and, secondly, to compound their damnation, for they certainly are and will be damned, through their inevitable misuse of the good gifts of God.[70] Sibbes sums up briefly: "There is a pit a digging for the wicked; he flourisheth and bears out all impudently under hope of success, but his grave is a making, and his present prosperity will but aggravate his future misery."[71]

Under the onslaught of such opinion, wealth and success appear altogether to lose their attractiveness. So often linked with the wicked, they almost become wicked in themselves. Wealth is a web of temptation spun by Satan in which all but the spiritually heroic are bound to be ensnared. It is, of course, not the possession of wealth but the love of wealth which is the sin in man; but the argument repeatedly presented in this literature is that men, through the corruption of their nature, are so prone to the love of money, that the mere possession of money usually becomes a source of sin and spiritual decline.[72]

What is left? Where does the godly man, the Protestant saint, stand in the uncertain, challenging, and necessary world of economic man? With Aristotle, on the middle ground. The usual assumption is that the saint may properly seek and will probably possess a suitable competence in this life. Neither wealth nor poverty will characterize him. Downame had it "that the meane estate is much to bee preferred before the greatest prosperity . . . because it is most safe . . . The meane estate . . . preserveth us from forgetfulnesse of God, irreligion and prophanesse, which accompanieth prosperity, from the use of unlawfull meanes to maintaine our state, and from unpatiency, murmuring and repining against God to which we are tempted in poverty and adversitie."[73]

God's will in such economic matters may be inscrutable, and no rule of experience is quite reliable, but safety would seem to avoid extremes. The final, overwhelmingly magnificent reward, the gift of eternal salvation, was absolutely unrelated, or possibly

---

[70] Andrewes, *Works*, II, 33; Sanderson, *Sermons*, p. 163; Sibbes, *The Saints Cordials* (1637), p. 168; Downame, *op.cit.*, p. 378.

[71] *Op.cit.*, p. 168.

[72] See Adams, *Works*, p. 1147; Downame, *op.cit.*, pp. 372-75; Paul Baynes, *Briefe Directions*, pp. 330-31.

[73] *Op.cit.*, pp. 375-76. Cf. Donne, *Works*, III, 278-79: "You leave your nets if you leave your over-earnest greediness of catching."

negatively related, to economic rewards in this temporal world, and therefore such worldly rewards were in this ultimate context more a burden than a blessing. All of which theory is of course neither consistent nor quite honest; but to the real moral concern over the extremes of wealth and poverty and the attendant spiritual burdens of either economic injustice, the only possible solution was socialism, and socialism was a subliminal attribute of the Protestant mind, a fringe radicalism to be suppressed forcibly when it occasionally manifested itself in conscious social theory.

But if English Protestant divines were not consistent enough to be socialists, they were assuredly consistent enough to be generally anticapitalist. Of course, "capitalism" is a later socialist word and the free-enterprise exploitation of nature and labor which it denotes was in our period just emerging as a rational "system," and was not yet labelled. Consequently, the *substance* of capitalist practice and morality could be attacked before the Revolution produced a new orthodoxy that acquired a new sanctity with a conforming, defeated clergy. The social hiatus of the era of Reformation in England, the transitional and disintegrated character of Reformation economic theory, permitted a remarkable latitude of opinion and criticism. Neither manorialism nor capitalism was a working, dominant mode of economic life. The result was a consistent negativism from the pulpit. All forms of economic behaviour were condemned as either exploitative or, in the case of socialism, as dangerously visionary. Nearly every writer on the inequities of the existing economic arrangements began by insisting upon the iniquity of "those heretikes . . . which taught the unlawfulnesse of all earthly properties, seconded . . . in our times by some of the illuminate Elders of Munster. . . ."[74] Communism was strictly a doctrine for "the Consistorie of God, not . . . the Common pleas of men; in the Courts, not of Law, but of Conscience, in which onely it may fall out that the Civill owner may bee a spirituall usurper. . . ."[75]

Indeed, the one and the only attempt at a positive defense of "capitalism" was the pulpit defense of common law property

[74] Hall, *op.cit.*, I, 715.      [75] *Ibid.*

arrangements *against* the theoretical (and ancient) Christian ideal of community ownership. On the whole, private property was accorded a very weak justification in comparison with the later magnificent exculpation it was to receive from Locke; but the English Protestants before the Revolution were agreed that private property was a proven part of the *jus gentium* and had the authority of English tradition against the "fond imaginations" of radicalism. Perkins, discussing almsgiving, trotted out a common (rather backhanded and uneasy) vindication of property law based upon the word of God: ". . . from the words, *give to him that asketh* we may learne that it is the will of God that among his people there should be a proprietie of goods, and that all things should not be common in that behalfe: for the Lord would have some to have to give, and some to want that they might receive. . . . If any man think it was so in the primitive church because it is said, *they had all things common,* he is to know that that communitie was in such things onely as men had then freely given for the common good. And yet even then none was compelled or bound in conscience to give all his substance in that sort. . . ."[76]

There were occasional vague arguments about private property as a natural right[77] and citations of godly communities where private property existed;[78] but there was no real moral defense of the institution, except as more practiced than socialism. English Protestantism accepted without relish or imagination the legal basis of capitalist economy. Andrewes argued that *meum et teum* was a principle of economic life founded by Cain.[79] And he insisted not only that private property was a condition of sin, but that positive property law was not absolute —was a law of stewardship in the moral sense, under God's law.[80]

Sibbes agreed;[81] and Perkins pointed out that even "infidels before men are right lords of all their lands and possessions . . . and in the courts of men they are not to be deprived of them: but before God they are but usurpers: because they hold then

76 *Works,* III, 93.      77 Ussher, *A Body of Divinitie,* p. 329.
78 Whitgift, *Works,* I, 351-54.      79 *Works,* II, 248-49.
80 *XCVI Sermons,* p. 7.
81 *The Christians Portion* (1638), pp. 60-62; 91-99.

not *in capite*, that is, in Christ: neither have they any holy and right use of them. . . ."[82] Hall denied the propriety of killing to protect property.[83]

The ultimately vacuous moral character of the Protestant justification of private property is well seen in Gouge (perhaps the most "bourgeois" of the clergy in his social views) who defends the *basis* of ownership as possession—the right is a court right—and specifically denies the moral claims of godliness, industry, and creative labor: "Yea a faithfull and wise steward or other servant . . . may doe much more by his paines and care in getting and preserving the goods of the Family then his Masters. . . ."[84] In short, though private property is the only major distinctive aspect of capitalism defended by Protestantism, that defense is pragmatic, hesitating, ambivalent, and morally apologetic, or even dishonest. And it is essentially a defense not of innovation, but of the attitudes and the jurisprudence already established in the middle ages. There is absolutely no tendency in this literature which points to the liberalism of the modern world. The Scripturalism and basic religiosity of the English Protestants before the Revolution made such fictions as those created by Locke and his followers quite impossible. Yet, since the Protestants would not think seriously about this basic economic issue, they forfeited the game—a desperately important game—to secular intellects, and soon ended, as on so many social issues, by accepting the moral and intellectual initiative of the capitalist elite.

The Protestant mentality was firmer and more independent in dealing with the newer and more specific mechanisms of city capitalism. Everything from "unmercifull monopolies" to "unreasonable prices of merchants" comes under constant attack.[85] Mercantile and industrial operations are all brought under unfriendly scrutiny: they were the chief source of sabbath-breaking,[86] inferior workmanship, "private and secret conspiracies to

---

[82] *Works*, I, 300.    [83] *Works*, IV, 800.    [84] Gouge, *Works*, I, 177.

[85] E.g., Adams, *Works*, p. 6. Monopolies are defended when there is "Manifest equity, that where there hath been some great merit, or charge, or danger in the compassing of some notable work for a common good, the undertaker should be rewarded with a patent for a recured profit to himself" (Hall, *Works*, IV, 790).

[86] Greenham, *Works*, pp. 163-65.

rig markets and control prices,[87] and the nefarious practices of speculation in commercial instruments and products.[88] Even contract law was not looked upon with favor. William Ames pointed out that though "in all contracts, we should proceed according to right and good, not the letter or extreame rigour of the law, in which often times the most extreame injury is found," the rule in business life is craftiness and sharp practice, and therefore "Divine Law" should supervene to remedy the indigenous injustice of the market place.[89] The "common maxims current in the shops of trade, that things are so much worth as they can be sold for" is decried as the morality of Satan, "hony in your mouth . . . and poyson in your soule."[90] Indeed, profit itself is given no economically-feasible moral status: no margin for investment and expansion of the business is allowed, and personal wealth resulting from the process is a bad omen.[91] Business is properly a social service and is dangerous to the soul because of its temptations to uncharitable practice.

Finally and most important of all to the contemporary moralists concerned with specific capitalist practices in the towns (we have already discussed in the above section the wholesale indictments of capitalism in the counties, the "rack-renting," enclosures, depopulation, and so on) there was the issue of usury.[92] Of no other aspect of the rapidly-growing capitalism which was reshaping English society were the Protestant divines so aggressively and uniformly disapproving as of the taking of interest on loans. Compared with the Catholic legal casuistry developed from Aquinas through Cajetan's *Secunda Secundae Summae Theologica . . . cum Commentariis*, which succeeded in morally

---

[87] Hall, *op.cit.*, p. 791. Hall would like price to be set by "publique authority" at all times (*ibid.*, 787), and there is a general preference among the divines for a controlled market; no argument at all for a free market.

[88] Baynes, *op.cit.*, pp. 172-73.

[89] *Op.cit.*, pp. 232-38; cf. Hall, *op.cit.*, I, 794.

[90] Hall, *Works*, IV, 787; I, 717; cf. Sandys, *Sermons*, p. 70; Andrewes, *Works*, II, 252.

[91] See Hall, *op.cit.*, p. 787.

[92] See C. H. George, "English Calvinist Opinion on Usury, 1600-1640," *Journal of the History of Ideas* (October, 1957) for a general treatment of the subject (with bibliography).

condoning most loan mechanisms common to the European economy, the English Protestants were severe reactionaries.[93]

In their most latitudinarian mood, English divines would agree with Peter Baro that since "the use of money [is] manifold, and necessary for the traffiks of men, and that almost in every contract and bargains . . . it is plaine and evident that all gaine which is gotten by money is not to be condemned: yet a godly man must take diligent heed . . . least he abuse his moneye to the hurt of his neighbour: as it is an usuall practice amongst rich men. . . ."[94]

But suspicion of the money economy, and particularly of its credit arrangements, is merely the passive aspect of Protestant opinion. With bad grace, they grant, as Calvin had done, that the economic world makes practical demands upon Christian ethics which are very difficult to reconcile with Scriptural texts or good conscience. Clearly, they would prefer a simple farmer and artisan economy where no credit merchants are needed. They object not only to the money-lender who exploits the needs of the small man, but generally also to purely speculative and profit-tending loans among "the rich."[95] Usury is not, as it is today, a legal term to denote exorbitant interest charges: usury is the moral term used to condemn as uncharitable and parasitic any interest charges for the use of money. All efforts by the capitalist world to condone the practice as morally respectable because economically useful are treated by the leading clergy with contempt: "a sinne that hath many advocates and patrons" is still a sin.[96]

Henry Smith complained that taking interest on money was a sin receiving alarmingly-wide acceptance: "How many of this

[93] See Auguste Dumas, "Intérêt et usure," *Dictionnaire de Droit Canonique* (Paris, 1953), v, 1475-1518, for a discussion of the techniques of evasion of the canon law prohibition of usury; on the revolutionary casuistry of Cajetan, see Edgar Salin, "Kapitalbegriff und Kapitallehre von der Antike zu den Physiokraten," *Vierteljahrschrift für Sozial-und-Wirtschaftsgeschichte*, XXIII (Stuttgart, 1930), pp. 401-40.

[94] Peter Baro, *A Speciall Treatise of God's Providence* (1588), pp. 419-20.

[95] Greenham, *Works*, p. 41; John Udall, *The State of the Church of England*, pp. 11-14; Smith, *The Sermons*, pp. 78-79; Bolton, *Works*, I, 11-13.

[96] Greenham, *op.cit.*, p. 41.

City for all they are Usurers, yet would be counted honest men, and would fain have Usury esteemed as a Trade? . . . This is the nature of pleasure and profit, to make sins seem no sins, if one gain anything by them: but the more gainful a sin is, the more dangerous it is. . . ."[97]

The lender is "a legal thief," a "caterpiller, thief, and murtherer," the ultimate subverter of the Christian conscience. The divines insist that the implicit permissiveness of statute law regulating legal rates of interest is no moral approval of interest charges ("If God's law forbid thee, can any Law of man excuse thee?"[98]). Indeed, usury of *any* kind is "unnaturall" (in the Aristotelian sense); contrary to civil, canon, and common law traditions; denounced by the great ancient and modern theologians; a drain on the productive wealth of the commonwealth; condemned even by Mohammed![99] Above all, the preachers thundered, "the custome of sinning . . . hath made an apologie for [usury]"[100] which now the Protestant conscience in its terrible majesty must strip bare of what Calvin had called "new words in excuse of evil,"[101] and of what Thomas Adams cursed as the wit of "fine threads of distinction that . . . workes like a mole to digge . . . through the earth into hell."[102]

In this vehement denunciation of interest taking, the Protestant divines revealed most clearly their basic moral objection to "the spirit of capitalism." They could not tolerate any economic operation whose goal was primarily profit to the individual. Their economic ethic was entirely social and religious. For the economic man to be deliberately and self-consciously out for his own selfish good—any social benefit being derivative and an accident of economic organization—was anathema to the true Protestant saint. The money lender was the clearest moral case in point, the ultimate horrible social example. His usefulness to the community seemed far less than that of any other performer in the monied world of economic affairs. He was not

[97] *Sermons,* p. 78.
[98] *Sermons,* p. 87; cf. Henry Airay, *Lectures Upon the Whole Epistle of St. Paul to the Philippians* (1618), p. 846.
[99] Roger Fenton, *A Treatise of Usurie* (1611); Bolton, *op.cit., passim.*
[100] Fenton, *op.cit.,* p. ii.
[101] Calvin, *Commentarii in Quinque Libros Mosis* (1595), p. 356.
[102] *Works,* p. 454.

only a parasite in practical terms; more significant, his moral goal was antisocial and could in no way be said to have its justification in *vocatio*, being one of the few occupations specifically abjured by revelation and good authority. The point here is not to quarrel with the correctness of their economic view of the lender as a social *persona non grata*, but rather to see that the basic crime of which the usurer was convicted was his moral commitment to self, to profit as an end in itself, to a vocation not provably godly and socially constructive.

Finally, we return to assess the relation of the Calvinist calling to capitalism. The English Protestant view of vocation is arguably the most important concept in their ideology. Far more than Luther or Calvin, as befitted their relation to a more aggressive economic polity, they turned the generalized ideal of the calling into a particularized ideal of work in the world. The curious and significant fact about the enormous literature on the calling is that the particular or work-in-the-world calling occupies the center of English Protestant attention—so much so that the particular calling comes very close to becoming the spiritual, salvation-working calling as well as the moral, socially utilitarian vocation. In this process an ethic of work emerges unlike anything known to the West before.

The first emphasis of the English view is upon the social morality of the particular calling. Thus in its basic morality the Protestant vocational ethic is totally opposed to the individualistic social philosophy of emerging, and soon to be triumphant, bourgeois society. The moral incentives propounded by later liberalism, the Ben Franklins and Samuel Smileses of secularized middle class culture, the "Protestant" liberalism brilliantly set out for us in the novels of Richardson, Fielding, Dickens, and Thomas Mann—all of this flood of social morality based upon the priority of the individual's ego over the need of the group, was absolutely the antithesis of Reformation Protestantism. William Whyte, in his interesting book on *The Organization Man*, seriously mistakes the essence of the original "Protestant Ethic" by contrasting it with a "Social Ethic."[103] Indeed the "rugged individualist," whose loss in

[103] William H. Whyte, Jr., *The Organization Man* (New York, 1956), 6-7, and *passim*.

American life he laments, would have been considered by our Protestants as shockingly immoral as the feckless, hollow (and still essentially self-centered) "organization man."

Not only did the Protestant divines define vocation in terms of social utility, they also developed the precept of social good in specific criticism of those without a "lawful" calling. In general, this criticism was a great moral boon to the bourgeoisie and no help to the feudality. The frequency and virulence of attacks upon "idlenesse and luxurie," the "decline" of the (fictitious) hard-working nobility, the multiplication of "vagabonds that like beasts, know no other ende of their creation but recreation, but to eate and drinke and sleepe"—such indictments of those who "want the medicine of faithfull travaill" certainly tended to upgrade the middle as against the lower and upper classes.[104] Compared to the Roman Catholic hierarchy of vocations, which ranged all of the economically useful people in lower orders of spiritual and moral being, the English Protestant view was importantly revolutionary.

All such argument was essentially most welcome to the enterprising capitalist groups in England. They were given a moral status, by virtue of occupation, denied to them by the Catholic society of the past. They were even made to appear spiritually superior to the idle, luxury-encrusted nobility, and certainly to the idle, dispossessed hordes of the poor. Moreover, they were occasionally openly celebrated for their economic successes and social triumphs: "Cast up your bookes, O yee Citizens, and summe up your receits . . . and . . . acknowledge your selves deeper in the Books of God then the rest of the world . . . the wondefull plenty all of provisions both spirituall and bodily: You are the Sea, all the Rivers of the land runne into you: Of the land? Yea of the whole world. . . . Your Charters as they are large and strong . . . your forme of administration is excellent, and the execution of Justice exemplary, and such as might become the mother city of the whole earth. . . ."[105]

104 See John Prideaux, *Twenty Sermons*, p. 7; Dod, *A Plaine and Familiar Exposition of the 13th and 14th Chapters of the Proverbs of Solomon* (1609), p. 11; Adams, *Works*, p. 966.

105 Hall, *Works*, I, 721. See John Stow, *The Survey of London* (1598) for the significant new spirit of *moral* pride among the merchant oligarchy; one reason

Andrewes noted that "no where are the merchants Noble-men's fellowes and able to lend the Princes of the earth, so much as heer."[106]

Still, it must be insisted, capitalist enterprisers as such receive more abuse than praise. We have already discussed the pulpit's negative view of their methods of operation. As a class they are preferred to leisured aristocrats or idle vagabonds, but not to yeoman farmers or industrious laborers.[107] It is only as productive *workers*, as socially vital and community-oriented citizens, that they are praised. Further, the burden of proof of godliness and social utility is entirely on them, especially the successful among them. The pulpit is very suspicious of the success they sometimes praise in the merchants. Andrewes often complained of the arrogance of the rich and powerful who used their wealth to destroy "cobwebb-lawes" and "cobbwebb-divin-ity," to mock the admonitions to morality of "such meane men as we be."[108] The divines of Reformation England, as we have seen, attacked from many angles any orientation of life toward the increase of wealth, the satisfaction of "ambition" (always a pejorative word), or the display of self. They consistently favor a nonadventurous, nonindividualistic, and stable rather than mobile society. They do not urge young men to seek fortunes beyond the seas, or even to convert savages, but to cultivate their gardens. Man is to match his talents to his work and then remain at that work. Constancy in the calling is the righteous course of life and change of calling is permitted only if gross error in matching talent to vocation has occurred and greater service to society will result from a change.[109] Competition, that *summum bonum* of later bourgeois economic morality, is vigorously abjured.[110]

---

for the decline of pulpit prestige in London after 1660 was the fierce assertiveness of the merchant community which resented clerical lamentations over social failures.

106 *XCVI Sermons*, [ii].

107 Dod and Cleaver, *A Plaine and Familiar Exposition of the 11th and 12th Chapters of the Proverbes of Solomon* (1608), pp. 145-46; Fuller, *The Holy and Prophane States*, pp. 118-22.

108 *XCVI Sermons*, p. 1.

109 Bolton, *Works*, IV, 48.

110 Thomas Gataker, *Certaine Sermons* (1637), 141-42; Sanderson, *op.cit.*, p. 216.

Where, then, is the "spirit of capitalism" in its Protestant guise? It simply does not exist in England before 1640. There is a spirit of work, of frugality, of rationality in opposing waste and the misuse of economic resources,[111] but any push toward a society of individual profit-seeking, competition for economic rewards, and social mobility scaled to the economic pursuit of wealth, comes not from the ideology of Protestantism, but from the lay and secular world of capitalism *sui generis*. Above all, it is impossible to argue that Protestantism in any way encouraged a profit system when the massive, uniform bulk of sermon and tractate literature equated any desire for profit (as opposed to service) with covetousness: ". . . let us consider what moved Judas to betray his master: namely, the desire of wealth. . . ."[112] Any earnings above a fair maintenance of estate are to go directly to "the good of others . . . the releefe of the poore . . . the maintenance of the Church. . . ."[113] Downame demanded that any surplus of "talents" must go to "the glory of God in furthering the meanes of his worship. . . ."[114] The use of ~~~ ot increase in profits; it is nonsense to speak of ~eticism" as a Protestant idea. The use of profits , it is repeated over and over again, must be ie church. Money is to be spent, consumed; 't is of course enjoined to avoid the excesses :, and to preclude social pride or extrava- of riches is to be communicated: else God ..uc all rich."[115] The reward that accrues from a ...y calling faithfully pursued has immediate social and religious uses and is otherwise a danger; for "take heed of too much businesse, or intending it too much, or inordinately."[116] In fine, Protestantism opposed the profit system, encouraged gild and

---

111 L. B. Wright, *Middle-Class Culture* i ~ ~~ 228-96, is perceptive on this issue.
112 Perkins, *Works*, I, 193; cf. Donne, W
113 Perkins, *Works*, II, 127-28.
114 *Op.cit.*, pp. 688-89.
115 Greenham, *op.cit.*, p. 644.
116 Preston, *The Saints Qualification* :s-
tantism and Capitalism in Pre-Revolut is-
cussion. Cf. V. A. Demont, *Religion a* rk,
1952), pp. 13-34.

church interference in economic life, and, above all, placed the good of the group above the advantage of the individual.

The association of Protestantism with capitalism is nevertheless a unique and doubtless important historical fact. The creation of the financial, legal, and social techniques and goals of English capitalism has since Marx been recognized as the most precocious and possibly crucial economic process in the making of the modern world: and what happened in the sixteenth and seventeenth centuries in England triggered those vast social and economic explosions which have created and are creating revolutions of a magnitude comparable only to those which brought into being civilization itself. This economic revolution was linked to the religious revolution which is our concern, a linkage of both time and circumstance. Protestantism and capitalism had common enemies: the Roman Catholic hierarchy and feudalism. They shared the frustrations, dangers, and uncertainties of striving for self-confidence and social control in an age of disintegrating and disaffected elites and ideals. But though the ambitions of capitalist entrepreneurs and the ideals of Protestant religiosity often made common cause against the institutional and ideological bias of the past, reinforcing one another in their independent struggles, they could not share the future. For the new world taking shape was to be a world of business and science, perhaps the first civilization to dispense with religion as a primary concern for thinking humanity. There was no significant positive correlation between the philosophy of the bourgeoisie *qua* bourgeoisie and the religious idealism of Protestantism. There is certainly no evidence of dynamic, psychological, causal connection between Calvinism and either Weberian capitalism or the far more significant capitalism of "this worldly" predation.

# CHAPTER 5

## THE POLITICAL THOUGHT

## OF THE CHURCH:

## THE CRISIS OF REFORMATION

—✝✝✝—

"The history of political theory is not the history of a few isolated political classics, it is the study of a stream of influence which has flowed down from age to age, now deflected by some great event, now determining the course of events themselves; a stream whose own path may often be determined more by a boulder in its way than by a mountain on the horizon. After all, the history of political thought is history, and the tests ought to be historical rather than metaphysical."

—C. H. McIlwain, *The Political Works of James I*, xx

—✝✝✝—

### I. The Clergy as Political Theorists

POLITICAL THEORY is perhaps the most generally unstable of all Christian social ideas. From St. Paul to Suárez, Bellarmine, and the seventeenth-century English divines, Christian political thought has fluctuated between incommensurate ideals, following paths of least resistance. There is no Christian political ideal, but Christian theorists have always assumed there was, and political writing bulks large in the literature of all churches. On the whole, all Christian political theory in the West before the Reformation tended to be complaisant and tractable with reference to the established social order. Compromise with the powers that were, justification of the political status quo—these are the key ideas in the long history of Christian political thought before Calvin.

Of course there are exceptions. There were the few extremists in the medieval dispute over the powers of the Papacy relative to the Empire and to the feudal monarchies, there were Christian political radicals in fourteenth-century England and fifteenth-century Bohemia. But these occasional clerical flurries of opposition political theory soon subsided and the central theory, embedded in tradition, remained undiverted until the time of Reformation nationalist politics. In England, the reign of Catholic Mary Tudor and the resulting Protestant migrations to Strasbourg and Geneva produced a few new ideas in the publications of Christopher Goodman and John Ponet.[1] But still the mainstream of political thought, so brilliantly charted by McIlwain,[2] flowed on up to the developing political revolution in England. This revolution finally changed the whole course of Christian political thought by blocking off the main channel and forcing those new channels in which such thought still surges.

But to the student of political theory, the break with tradition that comes with the English Revolution of 1640 is so imposing, so much the chasm that divides medieval from modern political thought, that it is easy to look on the slower, conservative developments of the preceding century as unimportant.[3] For John Knox shares important ideas with Suárez, and Richard Hooker is in some ways closer to Engelbert of Admont than to John Locke. Yet a political revolution a hundred years before the Great Rebellion had destroyed the polity of medieval civilization and created a basis for the subsequent developments that have importantly shaped the modern world. Of the reaction of political theory to this Reformation and to all the accompanying social, economic, and institutional changes, the most extraordinary aspect is that sharper issues with the political ideals of the past were not joined. Papal authority had been rooted out of England, the Roman ecclesiastical hierarchy which had ruled the souls and helped rule the estates of the English for some scores of generations had been declared the embodiment of the antichrist; even the most holy of medieval institutions, the

1 John Ponet, *A Shorte Treatise of Politike Power* (1639); Christopher Goodman, *How Superior Powers Ought to be Obeyed* (Geneva, 1558).

2 See the classic *The Growth of Political Thought in the West* (N. Y., 1932).

3 See Perez Zagorin, *A History of Political Thought in the English Revolution* (1954).

monasteries, had been dissolved in crushing infamy. How could such an institutional upheaval leave basic political concepts relatively unchanged?

The answer, probably, is that the upheaval left the ruling classes relatively unchanged. The "mainstream" of political theory always mirrors the interests of the ruling classes. That is why the first real break in basic political theory came only when the political posture of the ruling classes was altered by revolution in England. Thus although there are isolated exceptions, such as the Strasbourg bred theory of Bishop Ponet's *A Shorte Treatise of Politicke Power,* which has its moments of originality, the overwhelming bulk of the literature confirms the tradition adhered to for a millennium in the West. Curiously, as we shall see later on, even the medieval theories of church-state relations were altered amazingly little, considering that the entire institutional basis of such theories had been destroyed in England. Indeed, the only new political concept to emerge before the English Revolution, the idea of "sovereignty," did so altogether outside the precincts of English religious theory, and amid the (justified) suspicions of the ruling classes.

From an historical viewpoint it is therefore not surprising that Protestants and Catholics differ least in general political theory. There are absolutely fundamental differences between them on other issues of social theory, but the Roman Catholic axis Aquinas-Bellarmine-Suárez is broad enough to include a large share of the political ideas common to English Protestants before 1640.

On the other hand, it is worth noting that the Anglican clergy were a far more homogeneous body in their political and legal precepts than were the English lay intellectuals. They produced no analogues to the radical speeches in the Stuart House of Commons. Nor can we discover any evidence for the often-alleged division of the Anglican pulpit into politically aligned factions of puritans and Anglicans.[4] While out of the

[4] Cf. Godfrey Davies, "Arminian versus Puritan in England, ca. 1620-1640," *The Huntington Library Bulletin,* v (1934), 157-79; "English Political Sermons, 1603-1640," *The Huntington Library Quarterly,* III (1939), 1-23. Margaret Judson, *The*

rich and complicated medieval legacy of law books and legal traditions (civil law, common law, mercantile law, ship law, natural law) a few secular minds like those of Cowell, White-locke, Bacon, Coke, and King James himself were busily fashioning concepts inimical to that essentially medieval constitution which the previous generation of Elizabethans (viz. Sir Thomas Smith) had restated without challenge, the English clergy were stubbornly refusing to abandon the policy of their ancestors. Why? After all, it had been a religious revolt which had ushered in the new age; Knoxian precepts from Geneva had altered the entire course of Scottish history; and in the reign of Mary Tudor the English clergy in exile had led the attack upon Roman Catholic polity.

But beginning in the reign of Elizabeth, the clergy changed decisively in the direction of caution, retrenchment, the *via media,* until by the reign of James it becomes startling to read their sermons and tracts on political issues alongside the far more probing and radical speeches, pamphlets, and treatises by their lay brethren. They are eternally searching for ambiguities, for meaningless locution, for ideas that will include all positions and mediate in the contemporary war of ideas.[5] They live in a dying world, in a vacuum of political thought created by the winds of contention blowing dangerously about them.

The explanation of this strange-seeming behavior of the

---

*Crisis of the Constitution* (New Brunswick, 1949) has done the ablest job of those who see the English clergy divided between "puritan" and "Royalist" (pp. 171-218; 311-49). She admits that "in any general history of political thought, no Puritan writing or preaching in England prior to 1640 deserves a place" (p. 321), but proceeds to assign the "puritan" clergy a vital role in the developing political opposition.

[5] Cf. George Mosse, "Puritan Political Thought and the 'Cases of Conscience,' " *Church History* (June, 1954) for a view of "puritan" political thought as "well attuned to effective political action. . . . Flexibility and practicality, as opposed to 'Utopianism' were to be the hallmarks of this Puritan approach towards building the godly society" (p. 110). See also Mosse, *The Holy Pretence: A Study in Christianity and Reason of State from William Perkins to John Winthrop* (Oxford, 1957). The fullest account of "Presbyterian Puritans" in Parliament and of the associated "Classical Movement" among the clergy in the reign of Elizabeth is set out in J. E. Neale, *Elizabeth I and Her Parliaments*; see also Neale's essay "The Via Media in Politics" in *Essays in Elizabethan History* (New York, 1958) and the still classic chapter by F. W. Maitland on the Anglican Settlement in *The Cambridge Modern History* (vol. 2; New York, 1934).

clerical Protestant who was so conservative in political thought, is probably somewhat as follows. First, from the time of St. Paul, Christianity has been very shy about making any original contributions to political theory: indeed, "render unto Caesar" would appear to be the principal contribution of Christ himself, and very seldom have Christian thinkers gone much beyond this minimum. Even St. Augustine is unoriginal as a political philosopher. Only when the papal monarchy had waxed mighty and saw practical challenges to its power had clerical theorists attempted original political concepts. But the medieval clerics' most important ideological achievement of a political nature was probably that of creating the ritual and sacrosanct Christian aura in which the struggling new monarchies were swaddled.[6] The general pattern is uniform: clerics placate the strongest elements in a given polity with suitably vague and usually derivative political concepts. Their main business has not been this world, and in this world political radicalism has been the last luxury they could afford.

Further, the authority of the Scriptures weighed more heavily upon the clergy than upon the laity. Until the English Revolution, all political theory, lay as well as clerical, was based upon the Scriptures, and of course the emphasis upon theocratic, divinely-appointed monarchy is significant in the Old Testament. The literal-minded Scripturalism of the English clergy certainly strengthened the cause of divine right monarchy. And the Pauline prescripts of the New Testament simply reinforced the monarchist tradition of the Old by urging complete obedience to the existing civil powers.

Now in the specific historical situation of the early seventeenth century, this general conservatism was amplified by the discouraging this-worldly tensions of a preparing revolution. All of the old fears were aggravated by the new intensity of change. The clerics had always been weak in a showdown fight with the lay state: the terrible experience of even so great and powerful a cleric as Pope Boniface VIII with Edward I and Philip IV

6 See the work of Percy E. Schramm, especially *Herrschaftszeichen und Staats symbolik; Beiträge zu ihrer Geschichte vom dritten bis zum sechzehnten Jahrhundert* (3 vols.; Stuttgart, 1954-1956).

THE CLERGY AS POLITICAL THEORISTS

was the perfect object lesson. The example of Henry VIII was more immediately unforgettable. One political fact was well known to all the clerics and was an intimate part of their institutional psychology: power was in the sword and the sword was wielded by the lay estates. Therefore, it was their primary political objective to keep the sword sheathed, or turned against their external enemies. But what to do when the state itself, secular institution against secular institution, begins to argue dangerously? It is one thing to have to draw the sword against heretics or lower class rebels, but when the ruling classes fall out—what then?

The fear of the clerics was ever-present and deep rooted: they dreaded the violence of political change. This fear and their long tradition of accommodation and political subservience gave their political thought a bias toward unreality. They wished not to offend any of the great powers around the throne, on the bench, or in Parliament. There is almost no evidence that the lack of clerical political opposition to the king and the extremely small clerical opposition to Parliament were the result of censorship.[7] Gardiner has shown that the High Commission at the height of the political excitement of the years 1634-1636 deprived only one minister for his political views.[8]

[7] Davies (*op.cit.*, pp. 17-19) and Judson (*op.cit.*, pp. 175, 311) argue that censorship made "Royalist" views triumphant and stifled the opposition. William Haller, *The Rise of Puritanism*, pp. 232-33, disagrees. There is very little contemporary evidence of effective censorship and very much evidence that "puritan" ideas were printed and reprinted in London. The difficulties encountered by Roger Manwaring in getting his "Royalist" political views published were as great as the obstacles to the publications of even radical political pamphleteers like Thomas Scott and Henry Burton. Indeed, it is a striking fact that the preachers labeled "puritan" by modern scholars published far more than those with other labels. Further, Professor Judson's own thesis is that the "puritan" clergy had no program of political opposition to Royalism, but merely argued ideas "supplementing and strengthening" in the religious sphere those of Parliament in the political (*op.cit.*, p. 327). Thus by her own thesis, the "puritan" clergy were not even trying to publish the sort of ideas which would stimulate such occasional outbursts as those of Scott or Burton. For the censorship issue in the "Arminian" controversy see John Rushworth, *Historical Collections* (7 vols.; 1682) I, 634-35; Clarendon, *History of the Rebellion*, I, 147-60.

[8] S. R. Gardiner, *History of England . . . 1603-1642* (10 vols.; London, 1883-1884), X, 224-25. For the deprivations of 1604-1605, Gardiner's figure of 300 is probably too high: see Usher, *Reconstruction*, II, 3; A. T. Hart, *The Country Clergy in Elizabethan and Stuart Times, 1558-1660* (London, 1958), p. 62, for estimates of 49 to 60.

Any conflict, the clerics felt, would weaken them and lead them into unknown and therefore treacherous paths. A war among the ruling classes would ruin the church: the hierarchy were utterly dependent upon the political favor of the monarchy, while at the same time the parish livings were owned by the gentry who dominated the Commons and whose ownership of the church was enshrined in common law.[9] The absolutely basic interests of the church—its very economic and political existence—were predicated upon the cooperation and common interests of gentry, king, and nobility. There could therefore be no political choice in such a conflict; the church had no independence, the only hope was in compromise, in the prevention of conflict.[10]

Such an historical situation could obviously not produce in the church any very enduring political thought. Looking back upon the Elizabethan and early Stuart church, one can see quite clearly that as an institution it had outlived its historically creative period: its greatness lay in its efforts to bring order and peace and some small charity into the predatory lay society of the middle ages. The political triumph of the church—really its most enduring monument—was its indispensable help in creating the English monarchy. But confronted by the new historical challenges of the sixteenth and seventeenth centuries, those revolutionary economic, legal, and political movements which shaped the bourgeois, secular state, the church could not possibly have survived whole, because its institutional form and spirit had been created in response to utterly different historical forces. The institutional helplessness of the church, so brilliantly described by Christopher Hill's monograph, is reflected in the massive, flabby body of clerical political thought.

Nevertheless, that political thought demands as much attention from the historian as do the "isolated political classics" of the period. For the political ideas of the pulpit are a prime source of the commonplace and generally believed—of the ideas

9 See Christopher Hill, *Economic Problems of the Church, passim.*

10 See James F. Maclear, "Puritan Relations with Buckingham," *The Huntington Library Quarterly* (February, 1958) for a good description of the Preston-Buckingham romance.

that ruled still in England, and against which any revolution had to struggle.

## II. Church and State

It is impossible satisfactorily to delimit the sphere of "political" theory, to separate it from other aspects of social thought. This is especially true in medieval and early modern history. For instance, we are about to discuss the ideas of church-state relations; but the Protestant concepts of "church" are so complicated that they will require many other discussions dealing with related issues.

In terms of the historical problems raised by the Reformation, one would expect to find the greatest concentration of clerical political theorizing on the anciently-disputed relations of the church to the lay estates. For a thousand years the clerical organization of Western Christendom had proved itself probably the most independent and ambitious church in its relations with the state that any society had ever produced. True enough, the hierarchies of church and state had been coordinated in the achievement and defense of their rulership of Western society; but any comparison with the church-state relations of other civilizations will reveal the relatively striking degree of conflict and opposition which characterized the relations of the great institutions of church and state as they developed in medieval Europe. Thus the weakness of the church vis-à-vis the state, which we emphasized in the preceding section, should also be considered in relation to its unique strength in the broader context of comparative church histories.

The general effect of Protestantism on the politics of Europe was greatly to weaken the institutional independence of the national church hierarchies. There are many reasons for this development, some of which we have discussed elsewhere: the rejection of the powerful political support of the papal monarchy, the attack on the spiritual superiority of clerical orders, the growing nationalism of the clergy themselves, and of course the necessity for the Protestant clergy to rely upon the state for the achievement and maintenance of their freedom from papal control. The obvious result of the greatly reduced institutional and economic power of the national churches was a weakening of their theoretical claims to independence. Calvin was unique among the Reformers of the sixteenth century in pressing the right of the church to a truly independent court system; the Protestants were generally far more friendly to statism. Elsewhere we have fully discussed the very important Protestant concept of society as essentially one, indivisible Kingdom of God.[11]

Therefore, we shall not be surprised to find in the following discussion that the Protestant pulpit in England was unanimous in rejecting Roman Catholic theories of independent (direct or indirect) political powers in the clerical hierarchy. Political power is unqualifiedly in the lay state. There are not two swords. The clergy are fully as much citizens as are laymen and are fully as much subject to the jurisdiction of the lay state; conversely, laymen are fully as much of the church as are clergymen. Predestinarian theology reinforced this concept: the Elect are one, eternal society permitting no qualifications of order or status or institution. What is left of the independent institution of the medieval church—the traditional vision of a church society essentially removed from the City of Man, leading to the very gates of the City of God—what is left and defended are the palpable traditions of clerical survival: the livings and courts and clerical assemblies which make up the (moribund) body of the Roman Catholic ideal. Thus Protestants defended the medieval church organization only in the way that laymen defended their property rights in common law, or various medieval privileges. The clergy did not defend their estates as in any sense apart from or beyond the juridical reach of the overarching state. In fact, the common law privileges of the laity were much more vigorously defended than the canonical privileges of the clergy against the new "sovereignty" principle of statism. That, of course, was to be a principal theme of the coming revolution.

This remarkable reorientation of English clerical opinion of the state did not mean that the English clergy were more "secular"-minded than their medieval counterparts or Roman

---

[11] See Chapter 2.

contemporaries. On the contrary, they made far greater moral demands of the state than had been true of Roman Catholic clerics. In joining forces with the state, they infused the new merger with the full measure of their Christian idealism and passion. Protestants did not retreat from society into the artificial purity of the monastic community; rather they smashed the old partitions and claimed for God the whole society of man. In their own minds (and quite desperately in their hearts) the essential nature of English society after the Reformation was a kind of theocracy. From Calvin through Laud, all the intense Protestants tried to view their states as God-centered and governed—though not priest-centered or governed. The Protestant clergy who surrendered political sovereignty to lay institutions in the fight against the Roman Antichrist, tried to convince themselves that the new polity was an harmonious Christian whole, undivided by political jealousy, led by modern Davids, and taking its spiritual direction from the pulpit.

One of the somewhat original theoretical developments from Protestant views of church-state relations was a new version of the ancient concept of the "social contract." The basic proposition of a "social contract" is to be found in Plato, Cicero, St. Augustine, and in the medieval theorists who derived from them; but the sixteenth century makes contract theories pivotal to the polemics of every party: Suárez and Buchanan argue the contract idea against the respective tyrannies of Protestant or Catholic monarchs.[12] The social contract serves these sixteenth-century political theorists as a weapon, as a dissolvent of allegiances, as an incentive to revolt for Huguenots against Catholic kings or for Catholics against Protestant kings. For the contract is almost invariably defined as having been violated.

But then Richard Hooker and the later English divines taught "liberals" the use of a theory of social contract which enshrined moral and historical precepts in the interest of a conservatively changing social order. Locke's theory of social contract owes very much to Hooker in this emphasis upon the rightness of the existing (yet new) social and political order.

12 See the excellent essay by Christopher Morris, *Political Thought in England: Tyndale to Hooker* (Oxford, 1953).

The literature and language upon which Hooker and his followers drew were in a sense more medieval than modern; they certainly owed more to such theorists as Manegold of Lautenbach and Marsiglio of Padua than to Calvin. For Calvin had no real theory of social contract—as Chenevière says of Calvin's theory: "Ces devoirs mutuels ne sont point conçus sous une forme contractuelle. Ce sont des devoirs créés par Dieu à la charge des gouvernés, indépendants les uns des autres; ce sont des ordres de Dieu: la non observation de ces devoirs par l'une des parties n'entraîne donc pas automatiquement la liberation de l'autre, puisque c'est envers Dieu que chacune des parties est obligée et non envers l'autre."[13]

The need for a revised social contract theory in the era of the English Reformation was to provide a somewhat more empirical and moral justification for historical change than could the more brittle divine fiat explanations of social relationships which prevailed throughout the middle ages; for even those medieval theories which preached "organic" or contractual concepts were mirrors of changeless hierarchy. The disadvantage of the radical sixteenth-century theories was that they tended to perpetual instability: "republican" attacks upon monarchy on behalf of the religious "out" group could end only in permanent civil war, the counterpart of permanent religious division.

The first step toward Locke's definition of social contract, as at once the will of the people and decisively defined by a property morality, was taken when Hooker insisted that the social group is sovereign in its political choices while at the same time necessarily obedient to its own traditions. Thus social change is morally respectable while revolution is morally irresponsible. The English Revolution was not fired by a *Vindiciae contra*

---

[13] Marc-Edouard Chenevière, *La Pensée Politique de Calvin* (Paris, 1937), p. 322. In the sectaries Barrowe, Greenwood, and Penry, one finds the continuation of the radical 'contract of the godly against tyranny' notions of Bishop Ponet's *A Shorte Treatise of Politike Power*. See *The Examination of Henry Barrowe, John Greenwood, and John Penrie* in *Harleian Miscellany* (1809), II, 37. Cf. Hans Baron, "Calvinist Republicanism and Its Historical Roots," *Church History*, VIII (1939), for a dissenting view of Calvin's political thought. See also Felix Gilbert, "Political Thought of the Renaissance and Reformation," *The Huntington Library Quarterly*, IV (1941), and John T. McNeill, *John Calvin on God and Political Duty* (N. Y., 1950), Introduction.

*tyrannos.* ". . . unto me it seemeth almost out of doubt . . . that every independent multitude, hath, under God's supreme authority, full dominion over itself, even as a man not tried with the bond of subjection as yet unto any other, hath over himself the like power. God creating mankind did endue it not wholly with full power to guide itself in what kind of societies soever it should choose to live."[14]

That was Richard Hooker; but so also is this: ". . . yea, albeit God do neither appoint the thing nor assign the person; nevertheless when men have established both, who doth doubt but that sundry duties and offices depending thereupon are prescribed in the word of God. . . . And therefore . . . as we by the law of God stand bound meekly to acknowledge them for God's lieutenants, and to confess their power his, so they by the same law are both authorized and required to use that power as far as it may be in any sort available to his honour. . . ."[15]

Thomas Bilson had earlier hinted at a similar idea of contract in emphasizing the king's coronation oath,[16] and declaring, "The Prince hath the same charge in the commonwealth that everie private man hath in his familie."[17] Thomas Beard, master at the Huntingdon grammar school where Oliver Cromwell was educated, interpreted the coronation oath to be as ". . . in every covenant and bargaine both parties are bound to each other by a mutuall bond to performe the conditions which they are agreed upon: the like is used at the coronation of Christian Kings, where as the people is bound and sworne to do their allegiance to their Kings: so the kings are also solemnly sworne

---

[14] *Ecclesiastical Polity*, VIII, ii, 5.

[15] *Ibid.* Cf. Walter Travers, the Presbyterian polemicist: "For as in commonwealthes . . . all the power is in the peoples handes who of ther free will choose magistrates unto them under whos authoritie they may often be governed: and afterwardes not all the people but only the magistrates chosen by them administer and governe the affaires of the commonwealthe. So it cometh to passe in the establishinge of the churche: So that when as yet ther were none set over them all, the authoritie was in all men's handes: but after that they had once given the helme into the hands off certain chosen men this power no longer belonged unto all but only to those who wer chosen by them to steare and governe the churche off God." *A Full and Plaine Declaration of Ecclesiasticall Discipline* ([trans. Cartwright, Zurich] 1574), pp. 54-55.

[16] Thomas Bilson, *The True Difference Betweene Christian Subjection and Un-Christian Rebellion* (Oxford, 1585), p. 251.

[17] *Ibid.*, p. 249.

to maintaine and defend true religion, the estate of justice, the peace and tranquilitie of their subjects, and the right and priviledges (which are nothing but the lawes) of the Realme."[18]

Archbishop Ussher developed exactly the same view of the contract between magistrates and people and accused the unfaithful magistrates of having committed a sin against God in failing to protect the "common good."[19] Ussher also likened the contract between the magistrates and the people to that in the church between ministers and people.[20] Sebastian Benefield stressed the political convenant as the basis of English government, but rather than emphasizing the mutual rights of governors and governed, he stressed the duty of allegiance under the covenant.[21]

None of the Protestant clergy used the contract theories to do (or to suggest) the revolutionary things for which Hobbes and Locke were later to be justly famous. They were far from Locke because they were faithful to the Christian tradition of suspicion regarding the moral basis of private property, and completely unwilling to conceive the origins of private property as presocial or that the social contract existed to protect property. Even less could they be related to the essentially atheistical social theory so brilliantly represented by Hobbes. For Hobbes made eloquent and logical a theory of covenant which the English clergy were opposing long before he began to publish his thoughts in the course of the Revolution. Bishop Andrewes perhaps best represents the typical feelings of the clergy about the Hobbes-like theorists whom he firmly labeled "Atheist" for propounding the fiction that ". . . there was a time when men wandered like beasts; after wandering they came into society; they ordained laws unto themselves to preserve their estate; these laws were not able to bridle them; by that mean they invented that there was . . . 'a just eye,' to see them even in secret, so that by this invention they might be afraid to do evil."[22]

[18] Thomas Beard, *The Theatre of God's Judgment* (1597), p. 13.
[19] James Ussher, *A Body of Divinitie* (1645), p. 301. This important work was written c. 1625.
[20] *Ibid.*
[21] Sebastian Benefield, *A Commentarie . . . of the Prophecy of Amos* (Oxford, 1613), pp. 175-76.
[22] Lancelot Andrewes, *A Pattern of Catechistical Doctrine*, in *Works*, II, 23.

Andrewes rejects such a theory of the origins of society, and such a theory of human nature, for reasons which lead us directly to consider formal church-state relations. To Andrewes, the original society was religious and social laws "came into the world a thousand years after religion,"[23] to check the "brutisnesse," the "folly and giddinesse," of all those people not changed by the divine miracle into *"populum tuum"*; the chosen of the religious covenant are the elect of the social covenant as well: "For there is, in Tuus, not onely that they be men, and not beasts; Freemen and not villains; Athenians or Englishmen (that is, a civill) not a barbarous people . . . but, that they be God's owne people and flock, and that is all in all. *His people*, because he made them . . . this is that, that sets the price on them. For over such a flock, so highly priced, so deerly beloved, and so deerly bought, it may well beseem any to be a guide . . . no leading, no leader too good for them."[24]

These rare words of passion drawn from Andrewes' quiet soul epitomize probably the most creative aspect of Protestant political theory: the rejection of the moral duality of church and state which led Roman Catholic prelates into a struggle for secular power in order to protect and expand the separated church society; and an equally emphatic rejection of the newer and popular ideas of Machiavelli which argued for the state as an amoral society. This was the general view of church-state relations held by the English clergy. From Bilson through Perkins to Gouge and Laud, there is a quite uniform pattern of ideas. The great enemies to this orthodox Protestant view are an unholy trinity that is clearly identified and endlessly pilloried: the Catholics, the "Machiavells," and the Separatists. Significantly, it is primarily on the issue of church-state relations (with its specific correlation to the issue of church government) that the Protestant radicals put themselves outside the pale of English orthodoxy. Robert Browne, because he argued for a gathered church of elect independent of the Commonwealth and reduced

---

[23] *Ibid.* Cf. Thomas Cartwright's opinion that "the church (was) before there was any commonwealth," *The Works of John Whitgift* (3 vols.; Cambridge, 1851-1853), III, 189.

[24] Andrewes, *XCVI Sermons* (1629), pp. 278-79.

the moral identity of the civil magistrate, seemed "Papist" to the ordinary English clergyman.[25] Thomas Cartwright and Walter Travers also tried to upset the balance between magistrate and minister as understood by the English; but after them this sort of radicalism virtually disappeared until the Revolution.[26] Even Henry Burton, though he attacked the bishops, was a vocal supporter of the English solution to church-state relations.[27]

Historians have too often used the word "Erastian" to denote the nature of English ideas about the position of the church in the state after the Reformation. The difficulty with that word is that it is used not only to describe the views of Erastus in his *Seventy-five Theses on Excommunication* (not Englished until 1659), but is also applied to the utterly different lay concepts of Hobbes and Selden.[28] Further, English divines almost never refer to the work of Erastus, and when they do it is to reject his only original idea: that the power of excommunication should reside with the civil authorities in a Christian polity.[29] We shall avoid the word altogether because it has too distinct a connotation of "secular"—it suggests a theory which makes church religion a subservient adjunct of the state and of "policy." In this sense—in the Hobbesian sense—"Erastianism" is the *bête noire* of the whole English clergy.

The point to be made here, and repeated, is that the English divines are fundamentally consistent in their views of the nature of the Christian Commonwealth, not because they subscribe to one of the continental schools of controversy—Erastian, Lu-

---

[25] See Robert Browne, *A Treatise of Reformation Without Tarying for Anie* (Middleburg, 1582), pp. 3, 13, 15. John Donne argued that separatists, papists, and "the temporisers, the statist" are all violators of *integritatem Jesu*, the "entireness" of "the dignity of Christ," *Works*, IV, 101.

[26] For Cartwright's opinions, see *op.cit.*, I, 22-25; III, 405-56; and for Travers, *op.cit.*, *passim*.

[27] Henry Burton, *The Baiting of the Popes Bull* (1627).

[28] See John Donne, *Works*, IV, 101, for evils of the "politician" cum "statis." Cf. W. K. Jordan, *The Development of Religious Toleration in England* (4 vols.; Cambridge, 1932-1940), II, 453-91, for a good brief discussion of Erastianism in England.

[29] Theodore Beza defended Calvin's strong views of an independent ecclesiastical discipline (*Institutes*, IV, xi-xii) and we doubt that for more than an insignificant fraction of the English clergy before 1640 Erastianism was not popular: Thomas Fuller tells us (*The Church History of Britain*, VI, 286-87) that Erastianism was a view liked by some laymen but by very few clergy.

theran, Calvinist, or what not[30]—but primarily because of the common and peculiar history of the English church. All the continental Reformers were known and quoted, and certainly Calvin was best known and most often quoted as the greatest of the "modern" divines;[31] yet the eclecticism of the English divines is amazing. When Thomas Bilson and William Perkins, or William Laud and William Gouge—who differ on many less significant issues in their interpretations of correct Protestant forms of worship or church politics—agree very clearly in their views of the nature of the Christian Commonwealth, and disagree with Genevan, Strasbourgian, Scotch, Dutch, and German Protestant theorists of church-state relations, they do so because their ideas are shaped by the particular problems and traditions of English history.

Two decades before Henry VIII broke the power of the Roman Catholic hierarchy in England, Edmund Dudley wrote on the religious character and functions of the monarch; what other Catholic polity in sixteenth-century Europe would have produced these words from a leading minister of state: "Then the roote of the love of god, which is to know hym with good workes, within this realme must chiefly growe by our sovereigne lord the king. And for the sewer and parfitt fastening of this roote in the king one thinge is very necessarie, And that is that all his subjects, spirituall and temporall, may see in ther prince that he hym self settith his principall delight and affection in the love of god, keeping his lawes and commandments. How motche shall that enforce and encorage the Bisshopps and other of the spiritualtie to be the verie Launternes of Lighte and to shew good examples to the temporaltie, and thei to folloo the same. . . ."[32]

The position of the king in relation to the church was of course strengthened with the coming of the Reformation: the

[30] Cf. H. F. Woodhouse, *The Doctrine of the Church in Anglican Theology, 1547-1603* (N. Y., 1954), pp. 154-68, for a discussion of the general relations of Anglican divines to the continental Reformer.

[31] The key passages quoted by English divines from Calvin's commentaries are from the *Institutes*, IV, xi and xx.

[32] Edmund Dudley, *The Tree of Commonwealth* (ed. D. M. Brodie, Cambridge, 1948), p. 33.

overthrow of the papal monarchy and the dissolution of the monasteries decisively weakened the institutional church politically and economically. In some ways the English Protestant redefinition of the church as coterminous with the commonwealth strengthened the king even more importantly. It is interesting to observe that so Catholic a prelate as Stephen Gardiner, in his *De Vera Obedientia*, written in 1535, could define the church as simply the "multitude of people, which being united in the profession of Christe, is growen into one bodie."[33] And the king was the head of that body. He was, as the *King's Book* of 1543 made clear, the supreme head of the Christian Commonwealth in a sense that neither pope nor emperor had ever been able to maintain in any of the Christian polities of the past. The English clergy could only compare the ecclesiastical posture of their monarch with that of the great Hebrew priest-kings in the tradition of Melchizedek.

The only interruption in the historical development of this revival of Hebraic kingship was the reign of the Catholic Tudor, Mary. It is the reign of Mary that explains the quasi-republican and presbyterian sentiments which infiltrated the England of Elizabeth. Ponet and Cartwright, though still taking a more positive view of magistracy than either the papalists or Luther, began to worry about the possible effects of an overweening authority over religion in the hands of an ungodly prince. Essentially, even Cartwright did not challenge the propriety of the peculiar Hebraic monarchy in England; but like Archbishop Sandys,[34] he was concerned that England have a Samuel, not a Saul.

Despite the fact that the monarch was a woman and not very religious or Protestant, the history of Elizabeth's reign greatly consolidated the general clerical view that the Christian Commonwealth in England was one society coterminous with one church and led by divinely-appointed princes to the glory of the nation and the salvation of the elect. Fear of Roman Catholics and Separatists as political, economic, and religious enemies produced a solid rallying to the national church.[35] All Protestant

[33] See Jordan, *op.cit.*, I, 49.
[34] Edwin Sandys, *Sermons* (1585), p. 27.
[35] Cf. Donne, *LXXX Sermons* (1640), p. 338; see Thomas Fuller, *op.cit.*, v,

ideas of the Christian Commonwealth in England were fundamentally conditioned by patriotism; by fear of Roman Catholic
national enemies; and by a full and unswerving identification of
the English prince with the English nation and therefore with the
leadership of the English church in the broad nonclerical sense
as well as in the narrower ecclesiastical sense. The perfect foil
for the theorists of English Protestantism was the view of church-
state relations developed by the greatest of the contemporary
Roman Catholic apologists, Cardinal Robert Bellarmine: " . . .
we have shown that kings hold first place among Christians, inasmuch as Christians are men, that is as citizens of an earthly
state, not as citizens of the heavenly kingdom and servants of
God, and as members of the Church. For in this respect Bishops
hold first place, and especially the supreme Pontiff; second
priests; third, deacons, and other ministers of the Church; last
laics, among whom kings and princes are numbered. . . . The
Church was governed most successfully by bishops and priests
alone."[36]

Thomas Bilson's *The True Difference Between Christian
Subjection and UnChristian Rebellion*, published in 1585, is an
amazingly comprehensive survey of what can be called the typical
English view of the Christian Commonwealth. Bilson is especially good at phrases that neatly make the distinctions between
church and state that Protestant Englishmen believed proper.
Thus preachers "direct unto truth" while princes "command for
truth."[37] Bilson strongly insists that the English are in no way

---

252-55, for interesting evidence of the clerical nationalism that made even Thomas
Cartwright an "English Champion" against "the Romish enemy in matters of doctrine," and "sensible with sorrow how all sects and schisms, being opposite to
bishops (Brounists, Barrowists, etc.) did shroud and shelter themselves under his
protection, whom he could neither reject with credit nor receive with comfort,
seeing his conscience could not close with their enormous opinions, and . . . ex-
travagent violences." Fuller explains Cartwright's Presbyterian ideas as the result
of an "active spirit" which "fell foul, in point of discipline, with those which
otherwise were of his own religion" when "the Romish enemy . . . was not in
the field."

[36] Robert Bellarmine, *De Laicis* (N.Y., 1928), pp. 77-78. Cf. C. H. McIlwain,
*The Political Works of James I* (Cambridge, 1918), pp. xxii-xxiii, for "the whole
sum of the Jesuit theory of Church and State" contained in a passage from Bellarmine's *Tractatus de Potestate Summi Pontificis*.

[37] Bilson, *The True Difference*, p. 124.

guilty of the Catholic imputation that they accept "the Princes will to be the rule of faith," cites the martyred courage of Protestants trapped in the lands of Catholic princes, and concludes, "For you holde opinion of Popes, that they cannot erre; we do not of Princes."[38] To bishops he denies all right "to beare the sword" and places them under the authority of the prince as are all other subjects.[39] Conversely, and most important, the power of the ruler to administer "correction and compulsion" is primarily a religious charge: the sword is given the prince by God to maintain true religion.[40]

Bilson, however, also shares something of Calvin's view that "the spiritual kingdom of Christ and civil government are things very different and remote from each other."[41] Because he is an Englishman, Bilson has sympathy with what Calvin regarded as the "Jewish folly . . . to seek and include the kingdom of Christ under the elements of this world. . . .";[42] but he has no sympathy whatever with the "Erastian" version of the Christian Commonwealth. There are many strong statements of the moral dependence of the civil power upon the leadership of the clergy: ". . . as in spiritual perfection and consolation the Preacher excelleth the Prince by many degrees, God having appointed Preachers and not Princes to bee the sowers of his seede, messengers of his Grace, stewards of his mysteries; so far externall power and authoritie . . . God hath preferred the Prince before the Priest, so long as the Prince commandeth that which God alloweth. . . . The Prince is bound to obey the Preachers worde, if he speak the truth and so is the Preacher bound to obey the Princes Lawes, if they be good."[43]

Again, consistent with Calvin's views, Bilson urges that "in effect kings must become religious and faithful members of the

[38] *Ibid.*, p. 125. Cf. Donne, "In other places we have seen the church settled so as that no man hath done or spoken anything against the government thereof . . . a settling by strong hand, by severe discipline and heavy laws; we see where princes have changed the religion; the church may be settled upon the prince or settled upon the prelates, that is, be serviceable to them and be ready to promote and further any purpose of theirs, and all this while, not be settled upon Christ" (*Works*, IV, 76).

[39] *Ibid.*, p. 127. Thomas à Becket is the prototype usurping cleric, *ibid.*, p. 483.

[40] *Ibid.*, pp. 129-34.     [41] Calvin, *Institutes*, IV, xx, 1.     [42] *Ibid.*

[43] Bilson, *op.cit.*, pp. 219-20. Cf. *ibid.*, pp. 257-60.

church to serve God in holines and righteousnes al the daies of their life. To believe the word that is preached, to frequent the sacraments that be ministered, to fear the Lord that is honored in al and above al . . . Kinges in respect of their calling must serve the church."[44]

To command the conscience, the Prince's "supremacy" by the law of the land must be morally justified: "Princes must be indured whatsoever they command, but not obeyed agaynst the faith or canons of the Church."[45] For although "the Prince is supreme . . . the Church bee superiour," and the supremacy has no power over the Scriptures, sacraments, faith, devotion, holiness, repentence . . . and such like Christian duties and vertues."[46] Finally, the spiritual health of the Commonwealth is insured by the essential Protestant reservation against all abuses —ecclesiastical and civil—in Christian society: "The right directors unto truth must be discussed by their doctrine not by their dignitie. . . . Absolute judge of truth neither Prince nor Priest may chalenge to bee. . . . Onely God must limit what is truth, and what error. . . . To discerne truth belongeth to all. God willeth all men to trie spirites. . . . The people must discerne teachers by their doctrine. . . . The church is not judge of the Scripture. . . ."[47]

Thus Bilson's political aphorisms, drawn from the meager stock of Christian tradition, strikingly sum up all that it was possible to contribute short of republicanism in the direction of checking "ungodly magistracy" with the individualism of the Protestant conscience. All of the divines tempered their theories of authority in the Christian Commonwealth with such self-assuring sentiments as these from Bilson: "The magistrate is no Governour of the conscience . . . Christ will not be subject to the voices of men . . . One man preaching trueth hath warrant enough against the whole worlde."[48] While the equally typical Calvinist caution against an excess of such radical precepts finds

44 *Ibid.*, p. 163.   45 *Ibid.*, p. 242.
46 *Ibid.*, pp. 166-71. And even when the ecclesiastical power of the supremacy is invoked, "The kingdom is not above the Church though the Prince punish wicked priests" (*Ibid.*, p. 219).
47 *Ibid.*, pp. 257-59.
48 *Ibid.*, pp. 533-36.

Bilson reminding his readers that ". . . if you advise the people to imitate the multitude of their fathers, you teach them the right way to hell . . . [for] all shall erre saving the elect."[49]

The famous dispute on the relations of church and state in the reign of Elizabeth was that between Thomas Cartwright and John Whitgift[50]—a curious debate about which generalizations are difficult to make because the positions are often inconsistently argued. Cartwright favored a Geneva-like polity of greater separation of church from state and greater authority in the clergy as opposed to the laity. Whitgift often represented the more radical Protestant view of the church as a "priesthood of all believers," even allowing laymen the right to preach and baptize on occasion.[51] He argued that he could ". . . perceive no such distinction of the commonwealth and the church that they should be counted, as it were, two several bodies, governed with divers laws and divers magistrates, except the church be linked with an heathenish and idolatrous commonwealth. The civil magistrate may not take upon him such ecclesiastical functions as are only proper to the minister of the church, as preaching of the word, administering of the sacraments, excommunicating, and such like; but that he hath no authority in the church to make and execute laws for the church, and in things pertaining to the church, as discipline, ceremonies, etc. (so that he do nothing against the word of God), though the papists affirm it never so stoutly, yet is the contrary most true, and sufficiently proved by men of notable learning. . . ."[52]

Cartwright, on the other hand, pressed for a much sharper separation of the spiritual from the secular society, which led Whitgift repeatedly to brand his views "papist": "The commonwealth," wrote Cartwright, "must be made to agree with the church, and the government thereof with her government. For as the house is before the hangings . . . so the church, being before there was any commonwealth, and the commonwealth coming after must be fashioned and made suitable unto the

49 *Ibid.*
50 See Whitgift, *Works*, for the texts of the debate.
51 *Ibid.*, II, 531.
52 *Ibid.*, I, 22.

church."[53] Cartwright was, of course, not only arguing for a presbyterian government in the church; he expressed a generally more democratic political outlook than can be found in orthodox Protestantism.[54] But courageous and sometimes bold though he was, Cartwright was too much an Englishman to be able to carry his political principles from the church into the state. He wanted it "granted that the government of one be the best in the commonwealth, yet, it cannot be in the church."[55]

Nevertheless, Whitgift frequently accused him of teaching political subversion of the monarchy in arguing the cause of presbyterian government for the church: for Whitgift insisted that the church was simply an aspect of the Christian society; the state was another aspect, and therefore innovation in one was inevitably innovation in the other. Cartwright attempted, rather lamely, to reply by urging a fictitious historical separation of the societies; and his arguments here were decidedly less typically Protestant than those which accepted episcopacy in the church as an historical expedient, much as they accepted the monarch in the state. For the most important and universal Protestant idea was that of the "priesthood of all believers," the reduction of the two Catholic societies into one. The genius of Protestantism was not democratic–tending in the political sense; the theology of election, which was basic to Protestantism as long as Protestantism conserved its creative fire, smothered whatever democratic ideology lurked in the religious individualism

[53] Ibid., III, 189. Whitgift charged that Presbyterians like Cartwright were intending a direct theocracy in which "you of necessity shut out the civil magistrate from all kind of government in the church," and which "may intermeddle in the offices of mayors, bailiffs, justices of peace, and indeed have an oar in every man's boat, and yet nothing hinder your pastoral office . . ." (ibid., III, 416, 427). See also ibid., I, 122. In Walter Travers, op.cit., 77-105, 185-88, the curious Presbyterian contradiction between the plea for separation of church and state and the demand that the ministry "prescribe all orders and degrees of men what they ought to doe, what is fitt for every one and what every man's dutie is: to declare the duty off kings and magistrates, to shewe the obedience off subjects . . ." (p. 97) is strikingly apparent. See Bishop Thomas Cooper, An Admonition to the People of England (1589), pp. 86-94, for a somewhat reasonable indictment of the Presbyterians ("Martin Marprelate" being the butt of his attack) as subverters of English common law and civil institutions. The hysterical 90's produced Richard Bancroft's Dangerous Positions and Proceedings (1593), which was, happily, representative of the views of very few.

[54] Ibid., I, 314-84; III, 274-75, 567-81.

[55] Ibid., III, 198.

of the new faith. Protestant religious "individualism" was socially theocratic and oligarchic both in ideal and practice; the rule of saints could never be the rule of masses. The dynamic of Protestantism was to be found essentially in its anticlericalism, a kind of moral equalitarianism whose social and political implications depended upon the future historical direction of specific national societies. Thus Cartwright's views were those of a small and vanishing minority in the church, destined to flourish only briefly in Massachusetts and more briefly still in revolutionary England.

To return to the mainstream of English political thought, let us consider the painstaking theories of church-state relations developed by the eminent Elizabethan, Archbishop Edwin Sandys. In the epistle to his *Sermons*, Sandys proclaimed his pulpit task to be one of teaching "the superiour how to governe, the inferiour how to obey: the Minister what to teach, the people what to learne: the Parliament what to establish, the Realme what to embrace: her Majestie and counsaile what to heare, Courte, Citie, and Countrie what to amend. . . ."[56] This modesty seldom deserted the Archbishop of York and he set out in sermons to Parliament and Court to clarify the nature of the Protestant polity. A principal emphasis is upon the Prince as "Our Samuel, our good and gratious governour," with frequent warnings that "God in his wrath for godly Samuel gave them wicked Saul," and the injunction to submit with "obedient hearts to the good governement of woorthie Samuel their natural Prince, their good and faithful magistrate."[57]

Sandys is one of the founders of the pulpit tradition which ascribed the essential nature of the English monarchy not to the unfortunate hereditary royal lines of Old Testament rulers, but to the great theocratic rulers such as Samuel, Melchizedek, Moses, David; for, while aware of the disasters resulting when princes are false to God and the state, Sandys argued that the rule of a successful Samuel ". . . doth teache what agreement, love, and liking should be betweene these two offices (of magistrate and minister) . . . The wisedome of God matched Moses

[56] Sandys, *op.cit.*, (3)
[57] *Ibid.*, pp. 27-28.

and Aaron, two brethren; the one the minister, the other the magistrate. . . . When the word and the sword doe joine, then is the people wel ruled, and then is God well served."[58]

Sandys was also eloquent on the new Protestant theme of the whole state as coequal with the visible church. He preached an organic theory of the Christian polity,[59] but though each group within the polity was assigned special functions, the religious quality of all functions—the calling of every man in the commonwealth—was given striking prominence. In a visitation sermon at York, Sandys reminded those clergymen who "suffer the sheepe for which Christ died to die for want of instruction" that "ye are fed by the sweate of other mens browes, ye receive things temporall without any corporall labour of your owne. But with what conscience doe ye this, if they which minister unto your necessities reape not that at your hands for which they minister? You can perhaps alleage many colourable excuses for your selves. But wil you alleage the same in the day when a strict account of stewardship shalbe required by him, that cometh to judge both quicke and dead?"[60]

In another connection, Sandys expanded the text "I regard not that which man doth regard" into an anthem of spiritual equalitarianism.[61] In addition to general sentiments concerning the religious equality of nonclerical Christians, the Archbishop preached the practical consequences of Protestant doctrine as it redefined the duties of magistracy. To judges on assize he declared, "If an Eclipse fall amongst you, the rest of England will be darkened with it. Ye are seene and wached of men and Angels. The world hath many eies, eares, and tongues. London, Westminster, the Innes of Court and Chancerie, from whence the best and most of you doe flow, are as a fountaine from whence should spring all true religion, all pietie, vertue and godlie conversation. If this spring bee corrupted, the rivers that flowe from it must needes bee polluted."[62]

In the sermons of Sandys, as in the writings of most of the English clergy, not only the king but all Christian magistrates are zealously urged to look to the state of religion in the com-

[58] *Ibid.*    [59] *Ibid.*, p. 85.    [60] *Ibid.*, pp. 215-16.
[61] *Ibid.*, p. 246.    [62] *Ibid.*, p. 203.

monwealth. The later Stuart disputes over Parliament's right to petition about religious affairs were a violation of the entire view held by English ministers of the duties of Christian magistracy. As with other matters in dispute between various elements in the state, Protestant theorists were at a complete loss when the constituted powers disagreed and argued and tried to force issues to a clear-cut political definition. For English Protestantism in ideal̶izing a polity of unity which laid *spiritual* ob- ̶ ̶ad no theory to explain the independent exist- ̶ ̶ic and social conflicts which would distort ̶ ̶s and set good Christians fighting amongst ̶ ̶ll of the clergy, in Sandys' words, "It apper- ̶ ̶s, to Magistrates, to them which are nowe ̶ ̶honourable Court of Parliament, by all good ̶ ̶ to see Gods house made cleane. . . ."[63]

̶ ̶ Hooker shared the views of Bilson, Sandys, and Whitgift; his *Ecclesiastical Polity* became for the generations before the Revolution the constitutional textbook of England's Christian commonwealth. The key problem was to define both the legal and the ideal position of the prince. The ideal definition consisted of analogies with biblical Samuel or David, a "nursing father" to the church. The legal situation of the prince in the church-commonwealth Hooker described as follows: "When . . . Christian kings are said to have spiritual dominion or supreme power in ecclesiastical affairs . . . the meaning is, that within their own precincts . . . they have authority . . . to command even in matters of Christian religion, and that there is no higher or greater that can in those causes over-command them. . . . But withal we must likewise note that their power is termed supremacy, as being the highest, not simply without exception of anything . . . where the law doth give him dominion, who doubteth but that the king who receiveth it must hold it of and under the law . . . we grant supreme authority unto kings, because supremacy is no otherwise intended . . . than to exclude partly foreign powers, and partly the power which belongeth in several

[63] *Ibid.*, p. 33.

unto others, contained as parts within that politic body over which those kings have supremacy."[64]

We could quote Hooker at very great length on all the aspects of church-state relations discussed in this chapter, but Hooker is easily available in print, has frequently been written about, and we are in danger of becoming repetitious. Probably the thing to be emphasized about Hooker is that, more than most theorists, he tried to combine the radical Protestant breakdown of the distinctions between clergy and laity with a somewhat medieval conservatism about the rule of law in the Christian polity. The more usual tendency of the pulpit theoreticians was to put all praise or blame for success or failure in the Christian commonwealth upon the moral character of magistrate or minister. Hooker completely accepts—indeed extols— the political structure of the Elizabethan church-state, yet never as an absolute; he points out that kings can be unworthy of trust, can ignore the essential and "natural . . . union of Religion with Justice," and that therefore only law—God's law and public law—is the absolute guarantor of the commonwealth.[65]

The most original, and along with Hooker the most respected and influential, of the Elizabeth theologians was William Perkins. His masterful dogma has frequently occupied our attention in this study. Some confusion is created in labelling Perkins a "puritan" when Presbyterians like Cartwright, Udall, and Travers are included in the group. For Perkins is more opposed to the idea of an independent clergy than almost any divine in Elizabethan England. If any of the prominent clergy could be termed "Erastian," Perkins would have to be one. In comparing the proper authority of the magistracy with that of the ministry, he declares the ministry to be inferior in many crucial respects: ". . . the Magistracie hath a power in it selfe, whereby the Civill Magistrate may command in his owne name . . . the Civill Government hath an absolute power to compell and inforce the out-

---

[64] *Ecclesiastical Polity*, VIII, ii, 3. For Hooker's view that the jurisdictional powers in England formerly belonging to the pope ("who by sinister practices had drawn it into his hands") have been "for just considerations by public consent annexed into the king's royal seal and crown . . . ," see *ibid.*, VIII, vii, 4.

[65] *Ibid.*, ii, 5; vi, 8; v, i, 2.

ward man; but the ministerie hath a power only to cownsell, persuade, exhort. . . . This power of the Sword is added to distinguish it from all private power . . . for the common good of mankind. . . . The Magistrate is the minister of God for . . . procuring the welfare of soule and bodie: which standeth in two things: first, true Religion: secondly, civill justice, both which are by Magistracie maintained. . . ."[66]

He continues in this vein of enthusiastic moral endorsement of the *de facto* nature of the English Reformation throughout his vast tomes: ". . . the Magistrate, which is the viceregent of the Lord, is the keeper or both tables; and therefore is to maintaine religion with the sword: and so may put to death Atheists, which hold there is no God, of which sort there are many in these daies: and heretikes, which malitiously maintaine . . . anything that overthrowes the foundation of religion in the Churches. . . ."[67]

Or again, in writing of the way Moses called on helpers to govern his people during the trek from Egypt, ". . . the Minister may teach and speake as much as hee will, or can; yet unlesse with the sword of the spirit there bee joyned the temporall sword of the Magistrate; to reforme mens lives, and to keepe them from open sinne against the law of God, and to urge them to the duties which the minister teacheth: surely, their teaching and preaching will be to small effect."[68]

Christian princes are "nursing fathers and nursing mothers to the Church" and all subjects are urged to pray for them, "that God would blesse them, and increase the number of them. . . ."[69] The ecclesiastical supervision of the Magistracy involves the duty to see that "the word is rightly taught, and sacraments dulie administrd; for else they have power either to reforme,

[66] William Perkins, *Works*, III, 536. Cf. William Gouge, *Works* (1627), I, 3-4, for exactly the same statement.

[67] Perkins, *Works*, I, 194.

[68] Perkins, *Works*, III, 149.

[69] *Ibid.*, I, 337. Perkins occasionally was troubled by the problem of a woman as prince, "for publike teaching is flatly forbidden to a woman," but he concluded, "Yet the person that in regard of sexe is inferiour, may have more excellent gifts, and so likewise may exercise authority and rule and . . . no records of time can shew a more happie regiment for blessings temporall and spirituall under any man, then we have long enjoyed under our noble Queene" (*Works*, III, 314).

or dispose such ministers as shall faile in their administration."[70] Finally, Perkins rejects any concept of the true English church as a "gathered" church in which only saints are members, for the Anglican ideal of the church as coequal with the commonwealth. Like the commonwealth, ". . . the Church containes as wel bad as good; hypocrites as well as sincere Christians; and therefore the best Churches neede Magistracie for the punishment of the evill doers, and the praise of them that doe well."[71] The distinguished John Reynolds, leader of the "puritan" faction at the Hampton Court Conference and one of the translators of the Bible, agreed with Perkins, Bilson, and Hooker in their definition of Supremacy, leaving the Elizabethan position remarkably clear and homogeneous.[72]

The Elizabethan theory which dealt with church-state relations was not basically altered by the generations of churchmen living under Stuart rule before the Revolution. Presbyterian theory virtually ceased to exist in England and the radical theories of separatist groups diminished in measurable influences. Of all the non-Anglican minorities, the Catholics in England were least effective. Few national churches have commanded a more general theoretical allegiance than the English church in the reign of James I. Although some scholars profess to have discovered a large brotherhood of opposition-minded clergy whom they label "puritan,"[73] there is little evidence that this opposition was directed against the norms of Anglican theory. In fact, the so-called "puritan brotherhood" were often the most enthusiastic champions of the Anglican orthodoxies: there is certainly some truth in the frequent contemporary charge that Montague, Cosin, and Laud represented "innovation" in the theories and practices of English churchmen.

---

[70] *Ibid.*, III, 538. Of course "the wickednesse and horrible rebellion of sundry persons in this age" (papists and Anabaptists) denies the just powers of the magistrate. Cf. Edward Dering: "The case is cleare, the Prince is a spirituall Magistrate. It belongeth unto him to reforme religion; he is the highest Judge in the Church of God, to establish that by law which the law of God hath appoynted" (*Works*, 167).

[71] Perkins, *Works*, III, 537.

[72] John Rainolds, *The Summe of the Conference . . . Touching the Head and Faith of the Church* (1584), pp. 669-74. For King James's own views of the ideal relation of the king to the church, see his very important and widely-read *Basilicon Doron* (ed. James Craigie; Edinburgh, 1944), pp. 49-51; 75o83; 145-47.

[73] E.g., Haller, *op.cit.*

Though there are really no new ideas contributed by the divines from Perkins to the Revolution, those theories which had been accepted were hammered home with an unprecedented volume of literature and with perhaps a shade more "statism" in their emphasis. If weight of words and richness of metaphor could have saved the English Protestant church polity from disruption, the Jacobean preachers would have had glorious success.

The principal themes are easy enough to represent. William Gouge set out the typical view: "Chiefe Governours are to take chiefe care for publique acts of piety. . . . I would the latter Popes of Rome had beene, and still were of that opinion. If they were, they would not usurpe such authority as they have done, and still do over Christian Princes, to the disturbance of their States. But to come to our owne time and country. King Henry VIII put downe the Popes authority, and began a reformation of Religion. Edward VI perfected that reformation. Queene Elizabeth restored it. King James and King Charles continued it. Thus by the divine providence this title *Defender of the Faith*, is most justly put into our Kings stile.

"To this end, namely to defend the faith, maintaine religion, and advance piety, hath God given them that supreme authority which they have, to be in all causes temporall and ecclesiasticall, over all persons in their dominions under Christ supreme Governours. He hath set them on his throne, and given them his owne title. . . . And to show that their authority is not onely for State policy, but also for Church piety, they are stiled Nursing Fathers of the Church; and they are made keepers of both tables."[74]

[74] William Gouge, *God's Three Arrowes* (1631), pp. 323-25.
Almost the same words and exactly the same ideas are in the sermons of John Preston (*Sermons*, 1630), p. 21; *The Breast Plate of Faith and Love* (1634), pp. 76-77). They are throughout the works of Richard Sibbes. Sibbes was fond of declaring: "The cure of the Common-wealth, and of the Church, is a duty belonging to the King . . . the Reformation both of Church and Common-wealth belongs unto the Prince. There is a generation which thinke that the King must onely take care for the Common-wealth; but they have also power to looke to Religion. Wee see Josiah doth it, hee is the keeper of both. Josiah . . . is a father, not onely to looke to the temporall state but to the church. . . . So that wee see, as a chiefe right, the ordering of the matters of religion, belongs to the care of the Prince" (*The Saints*

Even Henry Burton, whose two sermons attacking Laud and Montague in 1636 mark a kind of turning point in the relations of the clergy to the ecclesiastical hierarchy, was a staunch proponent of the basic Anglicanism we have been examining. In *The Baiting of the Popes Bull* he wrote: "Onely all lawfull Magistrates, as Kings and Princes, are as so many Viceregents of God Almightie, to governe and moderate their peculiar Dominions, in, for, and according to God, and his word; these be Gods Lieutenants here on earth, and therefore called Gods. Now give me leave to tell you, that the Jurisdiction of God Almightie here on earth is distinct from that of Christ. Gods Jurisdiction as Mediatour is in things Spirituall. These two Jurisdictions are not compatible, not coincident, or concurrent in their total extent in any one man. Onely the outward politie of the Church, both as touching persons, and causes Ecclesiastical are subordinated to God Almighties Lieutenants here on earth, as all supreame Magistrates: so that in this regard, those that are Christs Viceregents in common, as all faithfull Ministers of the Gospell . . . are for their persons, and outward estate subject to God Almighties Lieutenants set over them."[75]

Among the "royalist" clergy who opposed "parliamentary" radicals like Burton (the vast majority of the prominent clergy were unwilling to be a part of the struggle between king and Parliament), Robert Sibthorpe was one of the most troublesome. Yet in a famous sermon which Archbishop Abbot refused to license for its royalism, Sibthorpe remained faithful to basic precepts of English church-state theory: "The Church and State being so nearely united, that though they may seeme two bodies, yet indeed in some respects they may be accounted but as one, in as much as they are made up of the same men, which are differed only in relation to spirituall or civill ends. . . ."[76]

One of the most discussed books of the early seventeenth

---

*Cordials* (1637), pp. 73-74. See also his *Bowels Opened* (1639), pp. 300-01; *The Christian Portion* (1638), pp. 57-58. Cf. Richard Bernard, *Plaine Evidences* (1610), pp. 33-36).

[75] Henry Burton, *The Baiting of the Popes Bull* (1627), p. 50. See also his *For God and the King* (1636), pp, 35-36, for a comparison of the "feare of the Lord" with "feare of the King."

[76] Robert Sibthorpe, *Apostolike Obedience* (1627), p. 24.

century was Bishop Overall's treatise expounding his views on the proposed canons of 1606—canons which were never to receive royal assent. King James (and various others) found objectionable features in the *Convocation Book*,[77] but in the main it is a representative product of English clerical opinion. Though a good share of the *Book* was devoted to the familiar English attack on the "indirect" jurisdiction of the pope and an historical survey of the errors of the medieval papacy,[78] one of the principal intentions of the tract was to supply an account of the origins of civil and ecclesiastical authority to confute the Catholic theories of Robert Parsons and Nicholas Sanders. As might be expected, and as had been argued before by English divines, Overall found the origins of both church and state in the regimen of Adam: ". . . first, Adam for his time, and afterwards the heads of every family of the faithful, were not only civil governors over their kindred, but likewise had the power and execution of the priest's office; and . . . they were themselves instructed and taught from God. . . ."[79]

Overall agrees that the offices and functions of magistrate and minister are distinct,[80] and he emphasizes the fundamental position of Whitgift that "Christ left neither to St. Peter, nor to the bishop of Rome, nor to any other archbishop or bishops, any temporal possessions; all, that since any of them have gotten, being bestowed upon them by emperors, kings, and princes. . . ."[81] Yet by God's law, the law of Nature, and by all civil law, "as it was the duty of parents, so . . . was it of good kings and civil magistrates, to bring up their children and subjects in the true service and worship of God. . . ."[82]

Bishop Lancelot Andrewes, whose prestige in the church of

[77] See *Bishop Overall's Convocation Book, 1606* (Oxford, 1844), Preface (8), for a letter from James to Abbot complaining of the canon which seemed to make "God the author of sin . . . in saying upon the matter that even tyranny is God's authority, and should be reverenced as such."

[78] *Ibid.*, pp. 175-272.

[79] *Ibid.*, p. 5.

[80] *Ibid.*, pp. 34-35. Cf. James Ussher, *A Speech Delivered . . . at the Censuring of Certaine Officers* (1631), 5; and Robert Sanderson, *XXXVI Sermons* (1689), pp. 640-41.

[81] Overall, *op.cit.*, p. 158.

[82] *Ibid.*, p. 29. Cf. John Buckeridge, *A Sermon Preached at Hampton Court* (1606), Preface.

Elizabeth and James was unsurpassed, filled his sermons with such truisms of Anglican polity as have been described in detail above. Religion is the *first* concern of the magistrate, the prince, the civil polity; England was in need of David, not Saul, for Saul's great failing was that he did not put religion first.[83] However, in his great Latin polemic against Bellarmine, Andrewes argued that although the king's supremacy was in accord with God's law, the English church had not made a pope of the king, as Calvin had feared Henry VIII would do.[84]

Bishop Joseph Hall, whose militant social theorizing occupies a large place in this study, contributed nothing different to the literature on church-state relations, except perhaps for his frequent caution, best set out in the sermon "Christ and Caesar" delivered at Hampton Court in 1634, against a Machiavellian or too-Erastian view of religion as an instrument of civil policy: "Cursed be they that say, Religion is only to keep men in awe; and cursed be hee that sayes, There is any so sure way to keep men in awe, as Religion; Go ye crafty Politicks, and rake hell for Reasons of State; ye shall once find, that there is no wisdome, nor understanding, nor cownsell against the Lord. . . .

"Let the great Caesars of the world then know, that the more subject they are to Christ, the more sure they are of the loyalty of their subjects to them. . . . And if distressed Religion shall come with her face blubbred, and her garments rent, wringing her hands, and tearing her haire . . . wo be to the power that failes it. . . . Oh may it please your Gracious Majesty to shine unto these darksome corners, by improving your soveraigne authority, to the commanding of a learned and powerfull Ministry amongst them."[85]

In the period of political tension which built up under Charles I between the court and the Commons, and which led into Revolution, it is hardly surprising to discover that the theories of the clergy responded scarcely at all to the changed circumstances of their ideal polity. Presbyterianism and sectarianism began to reassert influence which the easier decades of

[83] Andrewes, *op.cit.*, pp. 268-69.
[84] *Responsio ad Apologiam Cardinalis Bellarmini* (Oxford, 1851), p. 38.
[85] Hall, *op.cit.*, III, 417. Cf. Andrewes, *Works*, II, 24.

the *via media* had minimized, and in the general political tur-
moil of pre-Revolutionary England a party of bishops, led by
the redoubtable Laud, provided a somewhat new emphasis upon
old ideas in defending the nature of their Christian commonwealth. But essentially, as argued earlier, the clergy were deeply
committed—intellectually, emotionally, and socially—to the
theories we have described and illustrated in this chapter.

Bishop John Cosin provides a good example of the intellectual effects of the political tension upon the group of prelates who felt that the disaffected were a menace to England's
Christian commonwealth. In general, Cosin was an orthodox
English Protestant. But in the notes he made for the *Book of
Common Prayer*, probably before 1640, he set down an almost
Erastian view of the relations of state to church: "But because
our Lord endued not the ministers of His kingdom with any
external power to constrain obedience, therefore the laws of
kingdoms and commonwealths have enforced the execution and
outward effect of that power which is instituted in the Scriptures. And in this respect, not the power of excommunication
alone, but of preaching and ministering the Sacraments, and
whatsoever else belongeth to the office of a minister in the
Church, is derived from the power of the Commonwealth; that
is, in our particular, from the imperial crown of this kingdom;
because it is exercised with effect outwardly, or doing the work
(though not of producing the inward end and purpose of con-
verting the soul) by laws enforcing thereunto."[86]

Just as Laud does, Cosin stresses "the better Christian the
better subject; and the more religious towards God and His
house, the more obedient towards the king and his laws";[87] both
do so because their worries are practical and political, bishops'
worries.

William Laud had not much time for theory, nor any conspicuous talent for writing his ideas. He was a politician, the
last of the great ecclesiastical statesmen in England. Most of his
theoretical work was done in prison and under the most trying
circumstances of debate. The anomaly of Laud's position is that

86 John Cosin, *Works* (Oxford, 1855), v, 412-13.
87 *Ibid.*, I, 111, 342.

his view of the church-state relations was closer to that of Calvin than was that of most of his colleagues in the church hierarchy, although he was singled out by the "Calvinist" opposition as the leading deserter from Calvinist orthodoxy. Laud believed in a clergy with a "liberal and free maintenance" and defended the restoration of tithes as the only feasible economic independence for the parish;[88] his orientation was heavily theocratic. In short, like Calvin, and unlike most English clerics, Laud believed in a considerable degree of separation of church and state, and in as much independence for the church as the legal and historical nature of Supremacy and the Settlement would permit.[89]

On the other hand, like Cosin and Montague, Laud was aware that "unity" was the watchword of his time of "Troubles and Tryal." And he was politically suspicious of the religious opposition. The whole religious theory of the English Christian commonwealth demanded agreement in the civil society. Therefore, Laud was quite justified in his belief that bad subjects were bad Christians. To those who charged him with "innovations," he replied: "I shall easily grant, that 'novations in religion are a main cause of distempers in commonwealths.' And I hope it will be as easily granted to me . . . that when great distempers fall into kingdoms and commonwealths, the only way to engage at home and get credit abroad is to pretend religion which in all ages hath been a cloak large enough to cover (at least from the eyes of the many) even treasons themselves. And 'for the present troubles' in Scotland, novations in religion are so far from being 'known to be the true cause,' as that it is manifest to any man that will look upon it with a single eye,

---

[88] Laud, *Works* (Oxford, 1847-1860), VI, Part I, 159-60; V, Part II, 601-03. See Trevor-Roper, *Archbishop Laud*, pp. 435-36.

[89] Laud, *Works*, I, 197; V, Part II, 613-15. Cf. Robert Sibthorpe, *op.cit.*, pp. 7-8: "Whosoever can put difference between the body and the soule, beweene this present transitory life, and that eternall which is to come, he shall easily understand, that the spirituall Kingdome of Christ, and the Civil government of Princes, are things of a different nature (*John* 18.36). And that the liberty of the soule from Jewish or over-numerous Ceremonies, and of the body from subjection, have no relation, nor cary any correspondency the one to the other, but that it is a Jewish error to inclose the kingdome of Christ under the elements of this world . . . sittence spiritual liberty may very well agree with civill bondage (1 *Cor.* 7.21) and it is not materiall whether thou be bond or free. . . ."

that temporal discontents, and several ambitions of the great men, which had been long a-working, were the true cause of these troubles; and that religion was called in upon the bye, to gain the clergy, and by them the multitude."[90]

When Lord Saye and Sele in 1641 reopened in Parliament the old charges of Cartwright against the bishops, the charges that they meddled too much in civil affairs, Laud answered at length in the tradition of Whitgift, declaring: "I know no bishop since the Reformation that hath been troubled with any (civil office) but only Dr. Juxon, when Bishop of London, was Lord High Treasurer of England for about five years. . . . As for the Star-Chamber, there were ordinarily but two bishops present, and it was fit some should be there: for that court was a mixed court of law, equity, honour, and conscience, and was composed of persons accordingly, from the very original of that court."[91]

Continuing, "As for the Council-table, that was never accounted a court, yet as matters civil were heard and often ended there so were some ecclesiastical too. But the Bishops were little honoured with this trouble since the Reformation: for many times no bishop was of the Council-table, and usually not above two. Once in King James's time I knew three. . . . Bishops, without neglect of their calling, may spend those few hours required of them, in giving them assistance in and to the fore-named civil affairs."[92]

Finally, Laud completed his defense of the church-state theory and practice from the days of Whitgift by adducing the singular elements of English history and the solid bias of Protestantism, as follows: "First, then, most true it is, that Bishops are 'called to preach the Gospel,' set apart to that work, but certainly they may . . . at all times (if they be called to it) give their best counsel and advice for the public safety of the State as well as their own."[93]

He cites the usual Protestant examples of godly men pursuing

[90] *Ibid.*, III, 298.
[91] *Ibid.*, VI, Part I, 176. Cf. *op.cit.*, I, 82, for the necessity of ecclesiastical courts.
[92] Laud, *op.cit.*, VI, Part I, 176-77.
[93] *Ibid.*, p. 179.

a "double" calling of mixed civil and religious obligation: St. Luke, physician and evangelist; St. Paul, tent-maker and apostle; then adds: ". . . do you think that Calvin would have taken on him that umpirage and composing of so many civil causes as he did order between neighbours, if so great sin had accompanied it? For he dealt in civil causes, and had power to inflict civil punishments in his consistory . . . or can you think that Beza would have taken upon him so much secular employment, had he thought it unlawful so to do?"[94]

Perhaps we might briefly summarize the main themes of the contrapuntal political theory we have tried to explain in this chapter. The principal theme is a development springing from the nature of the English Reformation: the clergy of England no longer represent an independent and European-wide church society. By Elizabethan days the facts of this new order of things have so deeply penetrated the consciousness of the English clergy that this group perhaps more than any other in England are the Queen's men—loyal and patriotic in parish, pulpit, diocesan conference, and national convocation. The political integration of the church into the organic whole of English society was neither in theory nor practice very difficult: Catholic barons and Presbyterian gentry were more of a problem than the hierarchy of the church which had earlier in the century owed allegiance to Rome and represented a supranational nexus of power and theory.

The transformation of the universal Catholic church into an English national church was the culmination of a process begun in the thirteenth century. But though the Reformation was a triumph for nationalism and for monarchy, it was not an apotheosis of statism or "Erastianism." For the national religious society was consistently viewed from pulpit and bishop's stool as a communion with Christ under the inspiration and leadership of a national clergy and a sacrosanct monarch—in other words, essentially as a theocratic society. The lost realities of ecclesiastical power were replaced by an ancient dream which

[94] *Ibid.*, pp. 181, 213-14. Cf., *op.cit.*, I, 5-7, for a discussion of the general relationship of ecclesiastics to the commonwealth.

conjured up an England ruled by a David or a Solomon, royal symbol of nationhood and of the whole Protestant vision of return to the biblical sources of Christian theory and historical practice.

Thus the mainstream of Protestant theory concerned itself with the evocation of the nature of the reformed Christian commonwealth as a national polity under God, a church as English as it was Christian. Ecclesiasticism was in the dominant view a relatively insignificant matter; the key elements in the ideal were the cooperation of King and clergy to the common end of creating an English Christianity. Church-state relations were in this process transmuted from their medieval form: there is no basis in Protestant theory for ideological warfare between the primate of the English church and the King of England. Therefore, this most vexing theoretical political problem of the previous centuries is largely by-passed in the minds of the majority of the clergy: their institutional role is primarily to preach the Gospel to the multitudes and to pray for the King. Evaded, as they have been since St. Paul, are the ultimate questions of justice and redress for the individual Christian suffering from bad preaching, evil neighbors, or a wicked King; this is done by invoking the mystery of the invisible communion of saints which will always distinguish out of the coterminal church-state society the children of God for final compassion and reward.

# CHAPTER 6

## THE POLITICAL THOUGHT

## OF THE CHURCH:

## THE DILEMMA OF MODERNITY

———————————✝ ✝ ✝———————————

"What power the king hath he hath it by law, the bounds and limits of it are known; the entire community giveth general order by law how all things publicly are to be done, and the king as head thereof, the highest in authority over all, causeth according to the same law every particular to be framed and ordered thereby. The whole body politic maketh laws, which laws give power unto the king, and the king having bound himself to use according unto law that power, it so falleth out, that the execution of the one is accomplished by the other in most religious and peaceable sort."

—RICHARD HOOKER, *Ecclesiastical Polity*, VIII, viii

"Sovereignty is sacred in it selfe; Authority even abstracted, is orient and illustrious. A ray, and representation of that great Majesty above."

—ROBERT BOLTON, *The Workes*, I, 4

———————————✝ ✝ ✝———————————

## I. Divine Right and Sovereignty

THE MASTERFUL ESSAYS of Figgis and McIlwain have long since made us familiar with the importance of the reign of James I in developing certain concepts of the constitutional position of the king in England.[1] These concepts, stimulated by the study of civil law and by the politics of the era of Reformation, involved principally legal redefinitions of the relation of the king

---

[1] J. N. Figgis, *The Divine Right of Kings* (Cambridge, 1914); C. H. McIlwain, Introduction to *The Political Works of James I*. See also E. A. Whitney, "Erastianism and Divine Right," *The Huntington Library Quarterly*, II (1939), 373-98, and M. Judson, *op.cit.*

to the courts and to the common law;[2] but of course the changed relation to the church (discussed in the last chapter) and certain general political definitions were subjects of clerical theorizing. To designate and sum up the theories propounded on the king's behalf, Figgis chose the somewhat unfortunate term "divine right." For all but wary students of political theory this term seems to imply that James began seventeenth-century absolutism by originating the idea of his divine appointment and responsibility, independent of law; actually, the idea that kings were selected by God and were ultimately responsible to God alone was a very old and familiar idea before James was born. In some ways, one of the greatest political achievements of Western medieval society had been the clerical propagation of the idea of divine right monarchy in this sense.

James's own interpretation of "divine right" theory varied with the pressures of political circumstances, and has been summarized by McIlwain.[3] In many ways, James was an ideal spokesman for the theocratic polity of Reformation England, a true David against the Roman Goliath, than whom, Professor McIlwain argues, there was "no more important opponent of the principles upon which the counter-Reformation rested and the wars of religion were to be fought."[4] Certainly James took very much to heart the role of priest-king assigned him in English Protestant theory.[5]

But what of the typical clerical view of "divine right" in the king? Did the clergy press to make the king *legibus solutus*, to

---

2 See William Holdsworth, *A History of English Law*, IV, 190-217.

3 *Op.cit.* McIlwain emphasizes, we feel unduly, the principal change as one of deserting "the reciprocal duties of *dominus* and *homo* so prominent in the medieval conception of English kingship," and its replacement "entirely by the Roman conception of a king *legibus solutus* . . ." (p. xlii).

4 *Ibid.*, p. lxxx.

5 The clergy were impressed by the religious views of the king published in the *Basilikon Doron* the year of his accession to the English throne. Curiously, Professor McIlwain fails to appreciate the integrity of James's Protestantism, which was unquestioned by the clergy; he writes: "James's real attitude toward Catholicism springs from the same root as his views on Puritanism. In both cases his hostility is more political than religious. . . . With the doctrines of the Pope, as well as those of the less extreme Puritans, he had little quarrel" (p. liii). James was, of course, nervous about *presbyterianism*; but he was sincerely, and altogether doctrinally, anti-Catholic. Cf. Constantin Hopf, *Martin Bucer and the English Reformation* (Oxford, 1946) for the influence of Bucer's *De Regno Christi*.

put prerogative above common law, to deliver his subjects into an "absolute, unquestioning, passive obedience no matter how tyrannous or oppressive the acts of that sovereign may actually become"?[6] Overwhelmingly, no; they did not. There were a few exceptions, of course. John Overall at one point argued for the legal omnicompetence of the king, even to a general "command" over property "when the necessity of the king and state did require it, according to the laws of the kingdom."[7] But even Overall insisted that kings were "notwithstanding that they had their kingdoms by succession . . . strictly bound to the observation of God's laws in their government, as Moses, Joshua, or any other judges or princes, elected, named, and appointed by God Himself."[8]

Trying to advance himself with the Court party, Robert Sibthorpe delivered a sermon at the Lent Assizes in Northampton supporting the king's loan of 1626 which was another exception —but the loan was licensed only after the archbishop had flatly refused to do so, bearing instead the imprimatur of George Montaigne, Bishop of London, the "least respectable of the prelates then living."[9] Sibthorpe argued for the most part in traditional terms of the organic commonwealth and the necessity for mutual duties ("Christians are bound in duty one to another, especially all Subjects, to all their Princes, according to the Lawes and Customes of that Kingdome wherein they live. . . ."[10]); but he also used some strong language about the power of the prince "to direct and make lawes, Eccles. 8. 3. 4. Hee doth whatsoever pleaseth him, where the word of the King is, there is power. And who may say unto him, what dost thou?"[11] Or again, "If Princes command any thing which Subjects may not

---

[6] *Ibid.*, pp. xlii-xliii. James disagreed with the proposition that "even tyranny is God's authority, and should be reverenced as such" in a letter to Abbot concerning the discussions of political theory in the Convocation of 1606. (See the Preface to Overall's *Convocation Book*, p. 8.) McIlwain makes rather too much of James's absolutist theories by ignoring the exceptions and frequent contradictions in the king's pronouncements on the subject.

[7] *Convocation Book*, pp. 23-30.

[8] *Ibid.*, pp. 20-21.

[9] S. R. Gardiner, *History of England*, vi, 206-07. For Abbot's detailed account of this whole incident, see C. H. Firth, *Stuart Tracts, 1603-1693* (N.Y., n.d.), pp. 309-50.

[10] Sibthorpe, *op.cit.*, p. 7.     [11] *Ibid.*, pp. 10-11.

performe; because it is against the lawes of 1. God, or 2. Nature, or 3. impossible; yet Subjects are . . . to yield a passive obedience. . . ."[12]

Obviously the few clergymen who tried to make something politically original and significant of "divine right" theory would approach some sort of theory of "sovereignty." The political concept of "sovereignty" was receiving increasing attention from European intellectuals.[13] But the English clergy did not like the idea because it was new and because its tendency was anti-theocratic and secular. Furthermore, they were quite as unconcerned about logic as were their lay counterparts. Almost every political theorist from Coke to Laud maintained logically-irreconcilable views of the relative authorities of various laws, parliament, the king.[14] Laud, for instance, argued that subjects could only be bound by law made in parliament;[15] at the same time, he agreed with the prevalent view that the king in his prerogative had a general power to act lawfully for the common good.[16] Obviously, either concept logically conferred a general legislative power, but there is hardly a theorist in England before 1640 who did not accept, as generations had accepted since the thirteenth century, the validity of both ideas. The traditional and persistent problem was to define which elements of law should be declared in council and with consent, and which by prerogative decree. God and "the people" were in either case the ultimate authority.

Professor Judson believes that two of the "royalist" clergy— Roger Maynwaring and William Dickinson—"proclaimed a theory of sovereignty."[17] We cannot quite agree (their ideas

12 *Ibid.*, p. 13. This theme of passive obedience to tyranny was generally agreed upon, but the context and occasion of it in this sermon caused the stir.

13 See G. L. Mosse, *The Struggle for Sovereignty in England* (East Lansing, Mich., 1950) for an interesting discussion of the growth of the concept among English lawyers and parliament men. See also Francis Wormuth, *The Royal Prerogative, 1603-1649* (Ithaca, N.Y., 1939); J. H. M. Salmon, *The French Religious Wars in English Political Thought* (Oxford, 1959), pp. 15-79.

14 See the interesting article by R. W. K. Hinton, "The Decline of Parliamentary Government under Elizabeth I and the early Stuarts," *The Cambridge Historical Journal*, XIII, No. 2 (1957).

15 Laud, *Works*, II, 234-35.

16 *Ibid.*, I, 99-101.

17 Judson, *op.cit.*, pp. 212-17. A good discussion. Cf. Eusden, *op.cit.*, pp. 172-80.

are both legally and politically contradictory, and the essence of "sovereignty" is the search for political and legal logic), but they did develop extreme opinions of the king's power. In a sermon which Laud thought contained things "which would be very distasteful to the people."[18] Maynwaring declared that "no Power, in the world, or in the Hierarchy of the Church, can lay restraint upon these supreames, therefore theirs the strongest. And the largest it is, for that no parts within their Dominions, no persons under their Jurisdictions (be they never so great) can be privileged from their Power; nor bee exempted from their care, bee they never so meane. To this Power, the highest and greatest Peere must stoope, and cast downe his Coronet, at the footstoole of his Soveraigne. The poorest creature which lyeth by the wall . . . is not without sundry and sensible tokens of that sweet and Royall care, and providence. . . . The Lawes, which make provision for their relief, take their binding force from the Supreame will of their Liege-Lord."[19]

William Dickinson, in a sermon preached before the judges at Reading, who urged him to have the sermon printed, had something of a legal concept of one aspect of sovereignty: ". . . to be *The Judge* is to be that Majesty and Architectonicall power, which out of its owne absolutenes setteth downe a law, and appointeth a publike measure . . . whereby all mens actions are to be squared and adjudged whether they be good. . . . The Latines have divers Phrases to express this power by, as *Jus Maiestatis, Jus summi imperii, Principatus, Arbitrium* . . . and (as the Hebrewes will have it) *Judex super nos*, a Judge over us . . . which words were spoken of Moses, who had a full power and command over the Israelites to order them by his Laws and Prescriptions. . . ."[20] Furthermore, Saul (whose reputation was high neither with Samuel nor with the English divines) was given not only Jurisdiction, "but *Dominium* over their persons and estates."[21]

---

[18] Gardiner, *op.cit.*, VI, 208.
[19] Roger Maynwaring, *Religion and Allegiance* (1627), p. 10.
[20] William Dickinson, *The Kings Right* (1619), (5). It is slightly surprising to find no mention of Dickinson or his sermon in the Commons Debates of 1621—or anywhere else that we have discovered.
[21] *Ibid* (6).

For all the excessive royalism of Dickinson's sermon, he certainly had no logical or legal concept of sovereignty. In this same sermon, in fact, he violates the key precept of the idea by dividing sovereignty—which is only united in God as the "source and fountaine of power and judgement"—among "a Father in his own Family, to a Land-lord amongst his Tenants and servants, to a King amongst his Subjects," or among "they who are Kings, and Law-givers, and Judges."[22] He views the Christian Commonwealth as an organic whole in which the king is a very great and fundamental power, but not a sovereign power in the sense of Hobbes or the lawyers.

Among the so-called "puritan" divines active before the Revolution, William Perkins, John Downame, and Robert Bolton all approached a concept of sovereignty ("puritans" generally vied with "Anglicans" in exalting the power and divine majesty of the king), though always with somewhat inconsistent theory. Perkins advanced a very high view of the royal prerogative, insisting, "God therefore hath given to Kings, and to their lawfull deputies, power and authority not only to command and execute his owne lawes, commanded in his word: but also to ordaine and enact other good and profitable lawes of their owne, for the more particular governments of their people. . . . And further, God hath given these gods upon earth, a power as to make these lawes and annexe these punishments. . . ."[23]

And he continued to discuss the "mitigation" of laws which was a power always and naturally in the hands of the magistrate to suspend and alter the execution of law ". . . with such discretion, as neither too much mitigation, doe abolish the law, nor too much extremity leave no place for mitigation"; this power was to be used in circumstances where the law of nature, the moral law, the written word, or ". . . when an inferiour law is overruled . . . by a higher law" should dictate the exercise of "this publike equity."[24]

A generation later, in a sermon preached at the Northampton Assizes of 1621, Bolton declared: "Soveraignety is sacred in it

22 *Ibid.* (9, 11).
23 Perkins, *Works*, II, 437. Cf. *ibid.*, III, 223.
24 *Ibid.*, pp. 437-38.

selfe; Authority even abstracted, is orient and illustrious. A ray, and representation of that great Majesty above.

"It also ennables the subject that receives it, with a remarkable splendour, and a kind of divine character. I have said you are Gods. . . . There are also by derivation, or deputation, some markes and impressions of that princely endowment stampt, and shining in the face and presence of every subordinate Magistrate. . . . Take Soveraignety from the face of the earth, and you turne it into a Cockpit. Men would become cut-throats and canibals one unto another. Murder, adulteries, incests, rapes, roberies, perjaries, witchcrafts, blasphemies, all kinds of villanies, outrages, and savage cruelty, would overflow all Countries. We should have a very hell upon earth, and the face of it covered with blood, as it was once with water."[25]

So extreme was Bolton's royalism that he wanted to bind even the conscience to political conformity, condemning for the sin of hypocrisy, "those, who though lawes and feare of danger against our State, yet harbour secret reprinings, murmurings, unthankefulnesse, and discontentments. Even a contemptuous thought of a King, or lawfull authority, is a sinne of high nature; and methinkes . . . is paralleled in *Ecclesiastes*, to the bloodinesse of actuall murther."[26]

But above all, the political theories of John Downame, one of the most widely-read and influential clergymen in England, expounded a concept of divine right monarchy that was fully as extreme as that of Dickinson or Manwaring. Downame pictured the king as absolute, as truly *legibus solutus*: he specifically put the king above all law, answerable only to God.[27] The People and their representatives in parliament had no legal check on this absolutism at all, "For what doth hee else who is advanced to this height of greatnesse, but Atlas-like beare upon his shoulders the waight of the whole common-wealth. . . . They are advanced indeed with the glorious titles of monarches . . . but what are they in truth but the great servants of the common-

---

[25] Bolton, *Workes*, I, 4-10. Cf. Donne, *Works*, v, 420.

[26] Bolton, *op.cit.*, IV, 72-73. This is a common enough theme among the clergy, but in a less intense form: cf. John Preston, *Sermons* (1630), pp. 24-25; Thomas Adams, *Works*, pp. 1008-09.

[27] John Downame, *The Christian Warfare* (1634), pp. 498-504.

wealth, who labour and take paines for the generall good? . . ."[28]

Or, in another suggestive image, ". . . a King in the common-wealth is like the soule in the body . . . and therefore he doth not lay upon his subjects its heavie burthens because he also is pinched with that waight which oppresseth them, he envieth not, but greatly rejoyceth in their prosperitie, because hee communicates with them in their contentment; and if for the good of the whole body of the commonwealth, he finde it necessary to receive, rather than take of their goods, that they may enjoy the rest with peace and comfort, he only croppeth them, or rather pruneth them, that they may grow the better. . . ."[29]

For all his sacrifices and parental devotion to his great family, this father-monarch, God's vice-regent, is rewarded only ". . . with ungratitude . . . the common people being naturally apt to condemne that in superiours, which being above their reach, they are not able to understand, and to mislike the present government, be it never so unblameable. Neither is it possible for any man to please all that ruleth many, or to doe that which is appectable unto God, and to gaine the applause of the vulgar people; seeing they are divided into as many phantasies as they have heads. . . ."[30]

The "puritan" Downame is thus the most articulate spokesman for the extremist Stuart view of divine right monarchy. Archbishop Laud probably never indulged his royalist proclivities to this theoretical extreme.

Indeed, such royalism as we have been discussing in the theories of Maynwaring, Overall, Perkins, and Downame was not at all the normal view of the clergy—nor of themselves for that matter!—who generally avoided explicit theorizing on the legal nature of "absolutism." The juridical maxims of Roman or common law books were eschewed in favor of biblical analogies; legal logic concerned them far less than the moral evocation of the responsibilities and glories of a Davidian throne in the Christian Commonwealth of England. The usual approach to the monarchy is, by modern taste, one of fulsome and fawn-

28 *Ibid.*, p. 500.
29 *Ibid.*, p. 499.
30 *Ibid.*, pp. 501-02.

ing adulation and praise: the person of the monarch is "sacred," his reign is "blessed," he is a "glorious Saint."[31]

For almost all of the clergy, such praise of the king was an expression of patriotism, of devotion to the Reformation, of antipathy to feudalism and to papalism. Sandys calls upon the English to, "Looke upon other princes at this day" who are evil in serving the Anti-Christ, in warring, in breaking covenants; and then to compare the godly majesty of the English throne.[32] In a passionate sermon, "The Citie of Peace," Thomas Adams paid this remarkable tribute to Stuart kingship: "While the State of Italy wants a King, all runnes into civil broyles. It is the happinesse of this Citie that there is no distraction. Not a King at Judah, and another at Dan . . . not the redde Rose heere, and the white there. We are not shuffled into a popular government; nor cut into Cantons, by a headlesse, headstrong Aristocracie: But *Henricus Rosas, Regna Jacobus*: in Henry was the union of the Roses, in James of the Kingdomes. Every King is not a Peace-maker; ours, like a second Augustus, hath shut the rustie doore of James Temple; so making Peace, as if hee were made of peace. . . . When hee was first proclaimed, what heard wee but peace? What heard the Nobles? A King that would honour them. What the Senators? a King that would counsell them. What the Schools? a King that would grace them. What the Divines? a King that would encourage them. What the rich? a King that would defend them. What the poore? a King that would relieve them . . . wee call our peace, the *Kings Peace* . . . Peace, Plentie, Trafficke, Learning, Administration of Justice, flourishing of Arts, preaching of the Gospell. . . . Like David, hee leads the Dance to heaven: and like Augustus makes a sweet spring wheresoever hee goes. . . . The Peace-maker doth both blesse, and is blessed; therefore let us blesse him, and blesse God for him, and hold our selves blessed in him.

Away then with those discontented spirits, that grudge these

[31] Or, in Bolton's apotheosis of Elizabeth and James, England is that blessed land ". . . where the Gospell shines with such glory, truth and peace, and under the kindly warmth and influence of two of the most glorious Starres that ever moved, or gave light in Englands Hemisphere" (*op.cit.*, I, 33); cf. Adams, *Works*, p. 641; Gouge, *Three Arrowes*, p. 367.
[32] Sandys, *Sermons*, p. 67.

outward rights, whether tributes of money, or attributes of Supremacie. . . . It is the mediate due to God, as prayers and praises are his immediate rents . . . perish his enemies, and upon his owne Head let his Crowne flourish. May not the Sceptor depart from Jacob . . . till Shiloh come againe. May his posteritie have a crowne on earth, when himself hath a crowne in heaven. Amen."[33]

The limits that clerical reasoning placed upon the theoretical power of the king were both timid and legally vague. Thomas Gataker, for instance, acknowledged that God "hath conferred an eminent power and authority upon them, a divine power representing and resembling his owne soveraignty,"[34] while arguing that the only limits on this sovereignty were the mortality of rulers and the supremacy not of positive law but of God's law.[35] The most constructive efforts to define divine right narrowly, within the framework of human law and human fallibility, were made by Richard Hooker, Thomas Beard, Lancelot Andrewes, and William Laud.

Hooker maintained that although "power is then of divine institution," there is no necessity for "a kingly regiment" *per se.* The power of monarchy had to be "either granted or consented into by them over whom they exercise (lawful power), or else given extraordinarily from God unto whom all the world is subject."[36] Once granted, of course, this power was hereditary unless there was a failure of heirs, when the power would revert to the people.[37] Finally, and most important of all, Hooker insisted England possessed a mixed or limited monarchy: ". . . I cannot choose but commend highly their wisdom by whom the foundations of this commonwealth have been laid; wherein though no manner, person, or cause be not subject to the king's power, yet so is the power of the king over all and in all limited, that unto all his proceedings the law itself is a rule. The axioms of our regal government are these: *Lex facit regem*: the king's

---

[33] Thomas Adams, *Works*, pp. 1008-09.
[34] Thomas Gataker, *Certaine Sermons* (1637), p. 75.
[35] *Ibid.*, pp. 87-93; 97-100.
[36] Hooker, *Ecclesiastical Polity*, I, x, 4; VIII, ii, 6; cf. the fragment of a sermon on Civil Obedience in *The Works* (2 vols.; Oxford, 1890), II, 583-84. Also cf. Bellarmine, *op.cit.*, 26-27.
[37] *Ibid.*, VIII, ii, 9, 10.

grant of any favor made contrary to the law is void. *Rex Nihil potest nisi quod jure potest.*"[38]

*Lex facit regem* is solid, majority opinion even in the reigns of Elizabeth and James! Such is the impressive inertia of medieval legal theory; indeed, great revolutions, first in the sixteenth-century church, then in the seventeenth-century state, were needed to overcome the ancient feeling for traditional law.[39]

Thomas Beard, in a popular treatise published in 1597 (the year the fifth book of Hooker's *Polity* appeared), quoted Plato, Cicero, Tacitus, and Pliny to the effect that "a Prince is not set over the law, but the law placed in authority above the Prince"; "the greatest Monarchs in the world," he declared, "ought to be subject to the law of God and consequently the lawes of man and of nature."[40] However, in terms of the medieval defense by common law as a basic individual right, as the redress which created "property" right, he seriously weakened his argument by treating all positive law as an abstract legal principle to guide princes away from the paths of tyranny; and by admitting the justice of the concept *Princeps legibus solutus est* "if there by any man that excelleth so in vertue above all others, that . . . no law is necessary . . . but where is it possible to find such a Prince so excellent and so vertuous, that standeth not in need of some law to be ruled by?"[41] This doctrine, in accepting the principle of the Philosopher Prince, led to Cromwell rather than to the proto-Liberalism which Hooker, Andrewes, and Laud championed in defending positive law as a private right.

We have already observed how thoroughly Andrewes objected to the Hobbes-like view of the origins of society;[42] it now remains to note his conservative view of royal authority, which drew for arguments upon the eighth book of Hooker's *Ecclesias-*

---

[38] Hooker, *op.cit.*, VIII, ii, 13. Though, of course, "The king is not subject unto laws; that is to say, the punishment which breach of laws doth bring upon inferiors taketh not hold on the king's person." (*Ibid.*, VIII, ix, 3.) Cf. Holdsworth, *op.cit.*, IV, 212-13.

[39] Cf. Bacon's opinion in *Calvin's Case* that "law is the great organ by which the sovereign power doth move," serving to make "the ordinary power of the king more definite and regular." (Holdsworth, *op.cit.*, IV, 201.)

[40] Beard, *The Theatre of Gods Judgement*, pp. 12-13, 17.

[41] *Ibid.*, p. 15.  [42] Chapter 4.

*tical Polity.*[43] Although Andrewes was discouraged with the effectiveness of these checks placed by "the laws of man" on tyranny, because their operation depended upon changes in "time, place, and person," he believed "the precepts of our religion we general to all alike; so that to the king as well as the subject we (can) say . . . 'it is not lawful for thee' . . . And so the prophets did not seek the favour of princes, but reproved them to their faces; and therefore this is that truth which is not ashamed, and is that truth which cannot proceed of man."[44]

To the question of whether wicked rulers should be absolutely obeyed, Andrewes answered no. Only to God was absolute obedience due, and to kings only "so far as their commandments are not repugnant to God's commandments."[45] Further, if a ruling prince does not possess certain moral qualities requisite to kingship—"a religious heart, high wisdome, heroicall courage, clemencie, like that of God, without measure or end"—then he only resembles a prince, a shadow lacking substance, a form without essence.[46] In sum, Andrewes' "constitutionalism" consists mostly of warnings against the menace of earthly gods who are idols in the state, of power uncommitted to God: "There be certaine Gods, heere below, aspire to glorie . . . and King Herod would be content to be made more than a man, and to heare *Nec vox hominum sonat.* And we beneath are too ready to sing it, otherwhile; to deifie those, that are on high, and give that (which) belongs to God on high, to Gods below. Now that earth is thus willing to entitle her selfe to heavens part, this brings all out of time."[47]

Archbishop James Ussher denied any specific divine appointment in the institution of monarchy. Obviously without civil magistrates ". . . neither Church nor Commonwealth can stand; yet are not their kindes, and number, and order so appointed of God but that men may make more or fewer, of greater au-

---

[43] Hooker's important eighth book was not printed until 1648, but from the manuscript copy in his possession Andrewes was familiar with Hooker's ideas. See R. A. Houk, *Hooker's Ecclesiastical Polity: Book VIII* (N. Y., 1931), pp. 109-10.

[44] Andrewes, *Works*, II, 50-51.

[45] *Ibid.*, II, 183.

[46] Andrewes, *XCVI Sermons*, p. 233.

[47] *Ibid.*, p. 125.

thority or lesse, according as the occasion of places, times, or the disposition of peoples, doe require."[48]

William Laud, although a statesman-prelate high in the counsels of Charles I, was no proponent of "sovereignty" nor of any of the extreme theories of divine right. His general view was theocratic in the English tradition,[49] and he was greatly impressed with the practical difficulties of absolutism and the kings' constant need for divine guidance and good counsel: ". . . for if any King think himself sufficient by his own virtue against the difficulties of a kingdom, by his own justice, and wisdom, and integrity, he will find by his loss . . . that he and all his vertue cannot long keep up, no, not a settled kingdom."[50]

More significant in limiting the concept of divine right sovereignty were Laud's views of law, parliament, and property, to be discussed later. Of these limitations, none is as important as his defense of property rights: ". . . although tribute and custom, and indeed subsidy, and all manner of necessary support and supply be respectively due to kings from their subjects by the law of God, nature, and nations, for the public defence, care, and protection of them; yet nevertheless subjects have not only possession of, but a true and just right, title, and property to and in all their goods and estates and ought so to have; and these two are so far from crossing one another, that they mutually go together for the honourable and comfortable support of both. For as it is the duty of the subjects to supply their king, so is it part of the kingly office to support his subjects in the property and freedom of their estates. . . ."[51]

This was to be the doctrinal heart of classic liberalism, as it had been the lawyers' reading of the medieval constitution since the thirteenth century. In no small part, the English Revolution was fought by the gentry who needed assurance that the kingly office really understood its obligations toward "the property and freedom of their estates."

[48] Ussher, *A Body of Divinitie* (1645), pp. 265-66.
[49] Cf. Laud, *Works*, I, 39-41, 188-205.
[50] *Ibid.*, I, 197. Cf. Laud, *op.cit.*, p. 44, with Sandys, *op.cit.*, p. 29 on the "secret lets and difficulties in public proceedings" which result from "evil counsel" and the "inevitable" nature of government.
[51] *Works*, v, Part II, 614-15.

## II. Law

*1. General Sentiments*

There is less legal theorizing in the work of the English clergy than one might expect from the facts of their education and the status of legal issues in their society. Maitland and Holdsworth have taught us to look upon the sixteenth and early seventeenth centuries as a crucial epoch in English legal development.[52] For this was the period when the conveniences of civil law precepts and procedures made a strong appeal to the bureaucrats confronted by the challenges of vast new social, political, and religious problems. Huge new areas of law making were opening up, and new courts—Star Chamber, Augmentations, High Commission—sprang up to administer this legislation. The supremacy of common law, of the medieval property law, was threatened.

The clergy, at least those with university degrees, were not only well read in Roman law, but in the High Commission they were reviving civil procedures and becoming practically embroiled in the broad constitutional struggle between common law on the one side, and prerogative and ecclesiastical courts on the other.[53] Further, they addressed hundreds of sermons to the men of the Inns of Court during these years which encompassed the legal battle between Coke's aggressive "prohibitions" and the relatively modest, defensive jurisdictional claims of Archbishop Abbot on behalf of the High Commission.[54] As Holdsworth says, though, "There are no great English writers upon the ecclesiastical law."[55] More significant, there is not really even a body of coherent, argued opinion on the great legal issues which agitated the lay intellectuals of the period. Abbot, when absolutely pressed to the wall by Coke, was capable

---

[52] See F. W. Maitland, *English Law and the Renaissance* (Cambridge, 1901); Holdsworth, *op.cit.*, IV, 217-93; and Holdsworth, *Sources and Literature of English Law* (Oxford, 1952), pp. 162-75, 228-38. See Eusden, *op.cit.*, pp. 41-54, 114-48.

[53] See R. G. Usher, *The Rise and Fall of the High Commission* (Oxford, 1913), an excellent monograph.

[54] *Ibid.*, pp. 208-21.

[55] Holdsworth, *Sources*, p. 229. The tracts of Whitgift's protégé, Richard Cosin, dean of the Arches, and Sir Thomas Ridley's *A View of the Civile and Ecclesiasticall Law* (1607), though competent products of the Doctors' Commons, are no exceptions to the rule.

of fighting back with the plea that Statute and Letters Patent and common use "tyme out of mynde" granted ecclesiastical jurisdiction over cases of heresy and schism; and from writers like Hooker and Laud came a series of confused legal bromides copied from outdated textbooks. Generally, the clergy were at their theoretical worst in dealing with law. Like all educated Englishmen, they respected the great common law, and as clerics they defended the existence of some sort of ecclesiastical law,[56] but their political timidity prevented ventures into either originality or cogent conservatism. They rejected the implications in the reality of sharp, constitutionally-significant clashes such as those of Bacon against Coke, or of Coke against Abbot. In attempting to ignore the facts of the great legal conflicts all about them, the clergy left the church with no theoretical posture on many vital issues—the spineless victim of tough-minded secular politicians who were very rapidly developing legal arguments of radical intention.

Perhaps the most usual sentiment about law expressed by the clergy was a deep, generalized, reverent regard. All law, considered in the abstract, seemed to the clerical mind a triumph of civilization. As Bullinger wrote in his *Decades*: "Now whosoever doth confer the laws and constitutions of princes, kings, emperors, or Christian magistrates, which are to be found either in the Code, or in the book of Digests or Pandects, in the volume of New Constitutions, or else in any other books of good laws of sundry nations, with these judicial laws of God; he must needs confess, that they draw very near in likeness, and do very well agree one with another."[57] Declared Archbishop Sandys, "Law is the life of the common wealth: and execution the life of Lawe."[58]

Such commonplace reverence for law, complemented by a reverence for monarchy, produced in clerical theory something

[56] The minor Presbyterian polemicist, William Stoughton, in a tract called *An Assertion for True and Christian Church Policie* (1604), argued for the abolition of all ecclesiastical courts as part of his general attack on episcopacy. He would grant the clergy no jurisdiction over even "spiritual" offenses. Strange print of the Genevan discipline!
[57] Bullinger, *Decades*, pp. 280-81.
[58] Sandys, *op.cit.*, p. 41.

analogous to the medieval feeling for law; this feeling had persisted into Tudor times among lay intellectuals like Sir Thomas Smith, but was disappearing in the theories of such great Jacobean lay intellectuals as Raleigh, Bacon, and Coke. As the years were soon painfully to demonstrate, this "constitutionalism" of the clergy was old-fashioned and ineffectual. But it was real enough to them, and sincerely professed. In a certain sense, one might say that clerical theory is a celebration of the constructive genius of the medieval achievement: they admired a whole galaxy of cultural heroes, all of the law books, judges, magistrates, kings, statutes, charters, and courts which had after a terrible struggle prevailed against the forces of feudalism, disorder, and paganism. In this context, where memories of feudal wars and the religious dangers of disunity were still fresh, we can better appreciate the conservatism of the clergy with respect to the old law—a law which had powerfully aided both the medieval and the reformed church in its struggle against barons, papacy, and sectarians.

Thomas Bilson and Thomas Beard expressed the almost universally-conservative view of the law in relation to monarchy by stressing the significance of the coronation oath, which promised the clergy and the people that their laws, customs, and liberties would be maintained and defended.[59] Richard Hooker, of course, in arguing that the monarchy in England was "limited," declared for ". . . the soundest, perfectest, and most indifferent rule; which rule is law; I mean not only the law of nature and of God, but every national or municipal law consonant thereunto . . . happier that people whose law is their king in the greatest things, than that whose king is himself their king."[60]

In his emphasis on defining law as multiple and discrete, the possession, the right, the custom of individuals and groups, rather than as abstract jurisprudence in the Roman sense, Hooker also held a thoroughly medieval view: ". . . there are in men operations, some natural, some rational, some supernatural, some politic, some finally ecclesiastical: which if we measure

[59] Bilson, op.cit., p. 251; Beard, op.cit., p. 13.
[60] Hooker, Polity, VIII, ii, 11-12.

not each by his own proper law whereas the kings themselves are so different, there will be in our understanding and judgment of them confusion."[61]

The vexed question of the king's prerogative powers received almost no attention from the clergy. Even the politically-oriented royalists, like Sibthorpe, spoke conservatively about the legal position of the monarchy, praying that "they which shall sway the Scepter of this Kingdome, will consider that Rulers also owe mutuall duties to their Subjects . . . to maintaine the fundamentall Lawes and Liberties of the Kingdome"; and while not stressing the *lex facit regem* theme of Hooker, they did view law as ". . . a medium betwixt the Prince and People: But whereas the Law is a mute Judge, and the Judge a speaking Law; so that those two are sometimes *termini convertibiles*; and the State can as ill stand without the one as the other; the Law restraining the Judges affection, and the Judge supplying the Lawes defect. . . ."[62]

On the other hand, William Perkins, though always concerned with the king's responsibilities to God, granted him a vast prerogative sanction: "God therefore hath given to Kings, and to their lawfull deputies, power and authority not only to command and execute his owne lawes, commanded in his world: but also to ordaine and enact other good and profitable lawes of their owne, for the more particular government of their people. . . ."[63] Even Sir Edward Coke and Sir John Eliot granted the king a vast prerogative as *pater patriae* to act with his prerogative, *pro bono publico.*[64] That was quite enough theory to sustain a *de facto* policy of absolutism.

Finally, it may be noted that William Laud vehemently, persistently, and probably truthfully, insisted he was no subverter

---

[61] *Ibid.*, I, xvi, 5. Perkins similarly defined "particular" justice as that "whereby we give every man his right or due" (*Works*, II, 148). To be sure, all positive law for both Hooker and Perkins was basically to uphold the commandments of the Two Tables (*ibid.*, pp. 531-32).

[62] Sibthorpe, *Apostolike Obedience*, pp. 22-25.

[63] Perkins, *Works*, II, 437.

[64] *Commons Debates: 1621* (eds. Notestein, Relf, and Simpson; New Haven, 1935), II, 228; the theories of Sir John Eliot are treated in R. W. K. Hinton, "Government and Liberty under James I," *The Cambridge Historical Journal*, XI, 1 (1953).

of law, or proponent of ". . . arbitrary or tyrannical government, contrary to law. I could not endeavour this; by knowledge and judgment going ever against an arbitrary government in comparison of that which is settled by law. I learned so much long ago out of Aristotle. . . . And ever since I had the honour to sit at the Council-table, I kept myself as much to the law as I could, and followed the judgment of those great lawyers which then sat at the board. . . . I did never 'advise his Majesty, that he might at his own will and pleasure levy money of his subjects without their consent in Parliament' . . . where a particular national law doth intervene in any kingdom, and is settled by mutual consent between the king and his people, there moneys ought to be levied by and according to that law. And by God's law, and the same law of the land, I humbly conceive, the subjects, so met in Parliament, ought to supply their prince where there is just and necessary cause. And if an absolute necessity do happen by invasion, or otherwise, which gives no time for counsel or law, such as necessity (but no pretended one) is above all law. And I have heard the greatest lawyers in this kingdom confess, that in times of such a necessity, the King's legal prerogative is as great as this."[65]

## 2. Positive Law

The declared laws, the written customs and privileges of "the people" and of the church, were in the epoch 1570-1640 undergoing searching analysis, discovery, and commentary;[66] but not by the clergy. There is not even any competent, detailed brief for ecclesiastical courts against the radical encroachments of common law writs. There is a great deal of complaint about the rapacity of lay impropriations of church livings,[67] yet no challenge of the important development by which this lay accumulation of church benefices and advowsons was protected in the laymen's property courts—the courts of the common law.

In theory, of course, all enacted and positive law was

---

[65] Laud, *Works*, III, 398-99. Cf. Sibthorpe, *op.cit.*, pp. 15-16; and Abbot on *meum et tuum* in *Stuart Tracts*, pp. 327-29.

[66] See Holdsworth, *op.cit.*, IV, 217-540; F. W. Maitland, *Roman Canon Law in the Church of England* (n.p., 1898).

[67] See Hill, *op.cit.*, pp. 14-168, 245-89.

"founded upon equitie and right (for otherwise they were no laws)" and "agreeable to, and as it were dependent on the law of God. . . ."[68] But as Bishop Cooper put it (in defending ecclesiastical law), "It hath beene alwayes dangerous to picke quarrels against lawes setled."[69] And law became "settled" when the lay estates and the monarchy wished it so. Consequently, when they commented on positive law, the clergy praised the legal status quo, however changing it may be and heedless of the seriousness of the social and political issues involved in the legal disputes; they confined their criticism to the safe and hoary traditions of accusations against the corruption of the lawyers, or complaints of inequities in the administrations of the laws. Thus Perkins agreed there was "good reason then that lawyers take the Divines advice, touching Equitie, which is the intent of the law";[70] and he found two kinds of men reprehensible: ". . . such . . . (as by a certain foolish kinde of pitty, are so carried away), that would have nothing but mercie, mercie . . . but fewe . . . offend in this kinde, mans nature beeing generally inclined, rather to cruelty than to mercy. . . . But in the second phase . . . another sort of men . . . have nothing in their mouthes, but the law, the law: and justice, justice. . . ."[71]

Bishop Hall many times spoke out eloquently on the principle of equality before the law: "Not only Fortune and Love, but even Justice also is wont to bee painted blindfold; to import that it may not regard faces. God says to every Judge as hee did to Samuel, concerning Eliah, Looke not on his countenance nor the height of his stature. Is an outrageous rape committed? Is blood shed? Looke not whether it be Courtiers or Peasants, whether by a Courtier or a Peasant; either of them cries equally loud to heaven. . . ."[72]

Yet when Perkins and the other divines were faced with clean violations, in the common law, of God's Scriptural law or of Christian equity as they understood it, they invariably engaged in rather shocking casuistry to defend the common law. Perkins justified the common law death penalty for theft, for example,

---

[68] Beard, *op.cit.*, p. 12. Cf. Donne, *Works*, II, 105.
[69] Thomas Cooper, *An Admonition to the People of England* (1589), p. 86.
[70] Perkins, *Works*, II, 441.     [71] *Ibid.*, p. 438.     [72] Hall, *Works*, I, 491.

although it violated both the more sensible Jewish penalty for violation of the eighth commandment and all precepts of Christian charity. Since Englishmen were much poorer than the Jews had been, he argued, theft was a "farre more grievous" sin in England than it had been among the Jews: "to steale a thing, but of some small value frome one in this country doth more endammage him, then a thing of great value would have done the Jews.

"Againe, the people of this country are of a more stirring and fierce disposition. . . ."[73]

In other words, as Andrewes rather uninvitingly put it, "As God's law supporteth the law of nations, so doth Christ plead for Caesar."[74]

The clerical writers, except for the presbyterians,[75] confirmed Holdsworth's judgment that the English king inherited all the broad jurisdictional powers of the pope in England ("less fettered than any other sovereign by the law of God or Nature") after the Reformation statutes became law. Bishop Cooper defended ecclesiastical courts and the English canon law on the grounds that should anything be done against church law, "the whole state of the lawes of this Realme will be altered."[76] Against the attacks of presbyterians he and the other divines used the same arguments in defending ecclesiastical law that they used in defending episcopacy: such attacks were essentially against the king and the commonwealth because the Reformation settlement provided no separation of church from state. All law was English law. Laud stated the usual argument well in his answer to Lord Say and Sele, maintaining that before the Reformation, ". . . Clergymen were governed by the Church canons and constitutions, and the common laws of England had but little power over them. Then in the year 1532 the clergy submitted, and an Act of Parliament was made upon it; so that even since the clergy of England, from the highest to the lowest, are as much subject to the temporal laws as any other men. . . ."[77]

[73] Perkins, Works, I, 64. Cf. also op.cit., II, 251-52.

[74] Andrewes, Works, VIII, 131.

[75] Holdsworth, History of English Law, VI, 220; Cf. Cartwright, op.cit., III, 278-79.

[76] Cooper, op.cit., p. 8.      [77] Laud, Works, VI, Part 1, 194.

## 3. God's Law and Natural Law

We have already indicated that the theory of the Protestant clergy insisted upon the ancient fiction of an hierarchy of laws reaching from the common law to the law of God, with the supreme moral law governing the precepts of all the lesser and derivative laws. Calvin supplied an inexhaustible source of inspiration to this concept, making the fiction respectable Protestant dogma: "Equity, being natural, is the same to all mankind; and consequently all laws, on every subject, ought to have the same equity for their end. . . . As it is certain that the law of God, which we call the moral law, is no other than a declaration of natural law, and of that conscience which has been engraven by God on the minds of men, the whole rule of this equity, of which we now speak, is prescribed in it. This equity, therefore, must alone be the scope, and rule, and end, of all laws."[78]

One of the most curious and distressing features of clerical legal theory is the attention which was lavished upon the precise definition and contemporary implications of the firmest of God's laws, the judicial code of Moses. The protracted debates upon the legal status and relevance of such an historically-anachronistic moral code were not, of course, intentional escapism—though they had the effect of escapism, which is seldom deliberate. Rather, they resulted inevitably from the clerics' peculiarly intense Scripturalism, their bookish isolation from real issues of social fact. The usual view was consonant with Calvin's opinion that although God "was pleased to become, in a peculiar manner" the "wise legislator" to the Jewish nation, nevertheless "in all the laws which he gave them, he had a special regard to their peculiar circumstances."[79] Bullinger went somewhat further, declaring that ". . . no Christian Commonwealth, no city or kingdom, is compelled to be bound to receive those very same laws, which were by Moses in that nation, according to the time, place, and state published and set out of old. Therefore every country hath free liberty to use such laws as are best and most requisite for the estate and necessity of every place, and of every time and persons: so yet

---

[78] Calvin, *Institutes*, IV, xx, 16.     [79] *Ibid.*

that the substance of God's laws be not rejected, trodden down, and utterly neglected. For the things which are agreeable to the law of nature and the ten commandments, and whatsoever else God hath commanded to be punished, must not in any case be either clean forgotten, or lightly regarded."[80]

John Whitgift agreed completely with Bullinger, and essentially with Calvin, but Cartwright's peculiar theocratic orientation (and admiration for Calvin's polity at Geneva) led him to interminable quarreling over the precise legal status of the Jewish law, and to unpleasant dicta: "But to say that any magistrate can save the life of blasphemers, murderers, adulterers, incestuous persons, and such like, which God by his judicial law had commanded to be put to death I do utterly deny. . . ."[81]

The whole protracted argument was absolutely fruitless; first, because no clerical interpretation of Mosaic law could possibly have influenced the English courts; and second, because once the principle of relativity of interpretation of the Decalogue was admitted, there could be no formula for deciding specific issues of law and penalty other than custom and use. A science of jurisprudence based on the Two Tables was one of Cartwright's wildest anachronisms.

Perkins also worried at some length about the problem of the binding force of Old Testament law, allowing almost complete freedom in the use of ceremonial law,[82] emphasizing the great distinctions between the moral law ("God's justice, in rigour, without mercie") and the law of the Gospel (which "offereth salvation to him that worketh not, but beleeveth in him that justifieth the ungodly").[83] He concluded that the laws of Moses were given by God and "directed" to the Jewish people. For other nations, particularly contemporary Christian Commonwealths, these judicial laws should be neither abolished nor totally binding: ". . . the safest course is to keepe the meane betweene both. Therefore the judiciall lawes of Moses . . . are of two sorts. Some . . . are lawes of particular equitie . . . [which] prescribe justice according to the particular estate and

80 Bullinger, *Decades*, II, 280.    81 Whitgift, *Works*, I, 270.
82 Perkins, *Works*, II, 538-39.
83 *Works*, III, 334.

condition of the Jewes Common-wealth and to the circumstances thereof. . . . A judiciall law may be knowne to be a lawe of common equitie, if either of these two things be found in it. First, if wise men . . . have by naturall reason . . . judged the same to be . . . necessary. . . . And the Roman Emperors among the rest, have done this most excellently, as will appeare by conferring their lawes with the lawes of God. Secondly . . . if it serve directly to . . . confirme any of the ten precepts of the Decalogue: if it serve to maintaine . . . the family, the commonwealth, the church."[84]

Richard Hooker, a prolific writer on the subject of Natural Law, the law of universal principle and reason, also supplied a revealing definition of the relation of positive law to the higher (non-Mosaic) law: "As for laws which are merely human, the matter of them is any thing which reason doth but probably teach to be fit and convenient; so that till such time as law hath passed amongst men about it, of itself it bindeth no man. One example whereof may be this. Lands are by human law in some places after the owner's decease divided unto all his children, in some all descendeth to the eldest son. If the Law of Reason did necessarily require but the one of these two to be done, they which by law have received the other should be subject to that heavy sentence, which denounceth against all that decree wished, unjust, and unreasonable things, woe. Whereas now whichsoever be received there is no Law of Reason transgressed; because there is probable reason why either of them may be expedient, and for either of them more than probable reason there is not to be found."[85]

In speaking of the various forms of God's higher law, there was a considerable confusion of terminology and definition among the divines, but no important disagreement. To Bishop Buckeridge, Natural law was God's law dimmed in lustre by the sins of Fallen Man.[86] To John Donne it was preeminently a "law in the heart; and of a breach of this, no man can be always ignorant."[87] To Cosin it was simply the universal law, the

84 *Works*, II, 520-21. Cf. James Ussher, *op.cit.*, p. 204.
85 Hooker, *Polity*, I, x, 10.
86 John Buckeridge, *A Sermon Preached at Hampton Court* (1606), *passim*.
87 Donne, *Works*, II, 106.

law that was no respecter of persons.[88] To Overall it was equivalent both to the moral law of the Old Testament and the doctrine of grace in the New.[89] And to Richard Sibbes, ". . . no man can dispence with Gods Law: this written word is alike in all: truth is truth, and errour errour, whether men think it to be so or no. Reason is reason, in Turkes, as well as amongst us. The light of nature, is the light of nature in any countrey as well as here. Principles of nature vary not as Languages doe: they are inbred things. And if Principles in nature be inviolable, and indispensable, much more is Divinity. . . . Therefore what is against nature, none can dispence withall. What is naught in one age, is naught in another, and for ever naught. There is no monarch in the world can dispence with the Law of Nature, or with the Divine Law of God. For the opinion of any man in the world, is not the rule which hee may comfortably live by, but the undoubted light of Christs written word."[90]

Generally, Lancelot Andrewes defined the law of Nature as "the Common Law of the World" which was "written in the hearts of all men"; he stressed that such law was, in conjunction with "God's Statute Law," the Scriptures, the only foundation of equity and justice in the world.[91]

All of these sentiments relate the commonplaces of clerical thought to the more esoteric Platonism, which was to flourish at Cambridge later in the century, as well as to the mainstream of eighteenth-century deism. But on one occasion, for which we can be grateful, the mask of other-worldly platitudes about God's law began to gall the saintly bishop, and for a moment the inevitable cynicism of the clergy shone forth splendidly: "What care men for sinne, if there by no action at the Common Law for it? None but Westminster-hall sinnes do men care for.

88 John Cosin, *Sermons*, I, 133.
89 Overall, *Convocation Book*, pp. 79-93.
90 Sibbes, *Yea and Amen* (1638), pp. 13-15.
91 Andrewes, *XCVI Sermons*, p. 159 et seq.; Andrewes often complained of the sloughing off of "law" in religion: "The name of the Law we looke strangely at: we shun it in our common talke. To this it is come, while men seeke to live as they list. . . . And we have gospelled it so long, that the Christian Law is cleane gone with us. . . . But . . . as Christ preacheth, so must we; and Law it is that Christ preacheth." (*XCVI Sermons*, p. 162.)

God saw it would come to this; Men learne no more duty, then *penall Statutes* did teach them. . . ."⁹²

## 4. Conscience

The Protestant conscience had a very important function in the clerical hierarchy of law: it was the mechanism by which God's law was known to the human being so that he could make proper moral adjustments to the positive law of his society. Obviously the great problem arose—never to be resolved—of the individuality of the conscience. If the individual's interpretation of divine law commanded him to act against evil positive law, how was such an eventuality to be squared with the doctrines of civil obedience and the divine right of magistrates? The radical Protestants, always the most logical in these matters, simply and firmly made the conscience the highest agent of law, trusting the individual's judgment of the right course of positive moral action above the Pauline platitudes enjoining obedience.⁹³ But it was Calvin, as usual, who supplied the basic Protestant precept of the political conscience to the English divines: "For if princes are to be obeyed, 'not only for wrath, but also for conscience' sake,' it seems to follow, that the laws of princes have dominion over the conscience. If this be true, the same must be affirmed of the laws of the Church. I reply, In the first place, it is necessary to distinguish between the *genus* and the *species*. For the conscience is not affected by every particular law; yet we are bound by the general command of God, which establishes the authority of magistrates."⁹⁴

Perkins wrote a great deal on the theme of human law and conscience, and his refrain is uniform: "Magistracie indeede is an ordinance of God to which we are subjectious but how far subjection is due, there is the question. For body and goods and outward conversation, I graunt all: but a subjection of conscience to mens lawes, I deny."⁹⁵

⁹² *Ibid.*, p. 847.
⁹³ See, for example, Robert Browne, *Reformation Without Tarying For Anie*, pp. 7-8.
⁹⁴ Calvin, *Institutes*, IV, x, 5. See Bellarmine's rather curious refutation of Calvin's "error" on this point (*De Laicis*, pp. 41-52).
⁹⁵ Perkins, *Works*, II, 527.

This identical idea echoes endlessly from all the pulpits in England. Archbishop Sandys warns all magistrates that if they "should command that which is impious and which God forbiddeth, in such cases we have our answere well warrented . . . It is better to obey God than men."[96] Decreed Archbishop Whitgift, "The liberty that God giveth to man, which no man ought to take from him, nor can if he would, is liberty of conscience. . . ."[97] The conscience as agent of God's law commands "passive obedience" to any bad laws of the magistracy, declared Richard Field, "passive obedience" to such as are "improfitable to the Commonwealth," but a "willing and ready obedience" only to those laws "such as are profitable and beneficiall to the societie of men to whom they are prescribed."[98] Bishop John Buckeridge went further, insisting that the sole law binding the conscience was that which was not only just and not forbidden by God, but also in "forma debita," "a due order of proceeding in Law-making," and for "a due end, Publicke good, and not private; for as a Tyrant herein differeth from a King. . . ."[99] And so on and on; the view appears in Robert Sanderson,[100] in James Ussher ("Doe their lawes binde the Conscience? As far as they are agreeable with the Lawes of God, they doe; but otherwise they doe not. . . ."[101]), and in Richard Sibbes.[102]

Perhaps the most striking defense of the power of civil law over the conscience was made by (the "puritan") William Gouge, who set out the following grounds for obedience for the sake of conscience: "Not that one man hath power over another conscience, this power is Gods Prerogative, but that God to whom all mens consciences are and ought to be subject, hath ordained the Powers, and requireth subjection to them. So as that which is done for *conscience sake*, is done *for the Lords sake*."[103]

96 Sandys, *Sermons*, p. 173.
97 Whitgift, *Works*, II, 570.
98 Richard Field, *Of the Church* (Oxford, 1628), p. 398.
99 Buckeridge, *op.cit.*
100 Sanderson, *Sermons*, pp. 74-75, 96-102.
101 Ussher, *op.cit.*, p. 266.
102 Sibbes, *Beames of Divine Light* (1639), pp. 69-75.
103 Gouge, *A Guide to Goe to God* (1636), pp. 287-88.

In another work, Gouge was more specific in applying this doctrine to compromise the moral position of the "conscientious objector": "Therefore a righteous man, if . . . he serve . . . under a King that is ever a sacrilegious man, he may rightly warre at his command . . . so that, perhaps, the iniquity of commanding may make the King guilty, but the order or serving may prove the souldier to be innocent."[104]

On the other hand, Bishop Joseph Hall probably stated the case for the conscience most eloquently: "Princes and Churches may make Lawes for the outward man; but they can no more bind the heart, than they can make it . . . the spirit of man therefore is subject only to the father of spirits . . . what coertion can any humane power claim of the heart, which it can never attain to know? . . . The Laws of men therefore do not, ought not, cannot bind your conscience, as of themselves; but if they be just, they bind you in conscience to obedience. . . ."[105]

Related to the discussion of conscience and law was some speculation, particularly by Perkins, about the problem of ends and means. Perkins' conclusion was that the conscience could be dictated to by the means proper to the desired end: "If we cannot doe the good thing that we desire, in the exquisite manner that we would, we must content ourselves with the meane; and in things which are good, and to be done, it is the safest course to satisfie our selves in doing the lesse, lest in venting to doe the more, which cannot be, we grow to the extremitie, and so faile or offend in our action. . . ."[106]

Or, as he expressed his casuistry in another connection, "The worker being acceptable unto God, the worke must needs be good also."[107] In other words, the godly can do no wrong. William Gouge agreed, though reluctantly. In seeking to justify the innumerable biblical incidents of low treachery practiced by heroes of the Hebraic-Christian tradition, Gouge argued that such deplorable acts were under "special direction from God." He recalled Christ's charge, "Be wise as serpents"; yet he also cited from classical sources, and with obvious admiration, those

---

104 Gouge, *Gods Three Arrowes* (1631), pp. 247-48.
105 Hall, *op.cit.*, IV, 828-29.     106 Perkins, *Works*, II, 116.
107 Perkins, *Works*, III, 170.

"generous Generals" who demonstrated "that undertaking a triall of vertue and valour, they would not get the victory by fraud. For they did not place honour and honesty simply in victory, but accounted victory base, unlesse it were obtained by honesty."[108]

On the whole, there is certainly more argument from the pulpit against "Policie," "Machiavellists," "Craftie politicians," and pride in asserting that "the godly have ever beene wiser than the politicke of the world,"[109] than there is argument for the wisdom of serpents. Protestant casuistry was far less flexible than that of the Jesuits, but it also was probably more convincing. There is no casuistry as effective as self-righteousness.

## III. Parliament and the Political Classes

### *1. Parliament*

Since even the intelligent and aggressive members of the House of Commons had no theory to explain the changing position of Parliament in the political structure of English society under Elizabeth and James, one would not expect the clergy to adapt their theories to the new facts.[110] The medieval "constitution" functioned in all English theory until the Revolution. Eliot and Phelips and a few others groped uncertainly toward a slightly altered view of emphasizing Parliament as a sort of mirror of "national will"; but essentially there are no ideas unknown to the medieval theorists. There is no republicanism, democratic thought, or approbation of the new concept of sovereignty. When these ideas came, in the course of the Revolution, they came out of the Revolution, not out of the religious thought of the pre-Revolutionary era.

In the controversy between Thomas Cartwright and John Whitgift, there is a very important discussion of the relation of the presbyterian church polity to English civil government. Cartwright argued that the ideal church polity he advocated

---

108 Gouge, *op.cit.*, 197-99.

109 Greenham, *The Works* (1612), pp. 838-39.

110 Curiously, there is no major treatment of the lay political theory which emerged in the period to the meeting of the Long Parliament. G. L. Mosse, *The Struggle for Sovereignty in England*, is a stimulating beginning.

must necessarily serve as a model for the state.[111] Then he reversed himself, and emphatically declared monarchy the best form of government in the commonwealth, though not in the church.[112] In yet another place, he tried to organize his confusion into a hybrid, theoretical monstrosity: "For the church is governed with that kind of government which the philosophers that write of the best commonwealths affirm to be best. For, in respect of Christ the head, it is a monarchy; and, in respect of ancients and pastors that govern in common and with like authority amongst themselves, it is an aristocracy, or the rule of the best men; and, in respect that the people are not secluded, but have their interest in church-matters, it is a democraty, or a popular estate. An image whereof appeareth also in the policy of this realm; for as in respect of the most honourable council, it is an aristocracy, and, having regard to the parliament, which is assembled of all estates, it is a democracy."[113]

From a strictly theoretical point of view it may seem surprising that Cartwright did not suggest the parallel (which seems obvious to us) of presbyterianism in the church and Parliament in the state. But such a theoretical alignment (indeed Cartwright *opposes* the "aristocracy" of the presbyter to the "democraty" of Parliament) was not made in England until the Revolution.[114] So Cartwright did almost nothing to exalt Parliament in relation to the king: less, in fact, than many staunch bishops of the church.

Archbishop Sandys expressed specific views of the powers and privileges of Parliament. He regarded Parliament as a maker of chains, that is, of "good statutes and lawes to holde all men within compasse,"[115] and he especially charged Parliament to use all good means and laws to "see Gods house made cleane,"[116] and to look into "the state of religion; the state of the Prince; and the state of the commonwealth."[117]

---

111 Whitgift, *Works*, III, 189.
112 *Ibid.*, p. 198.   113 *Ibid.*, I, 389-90.
114 In the Marprelate tract entitled *Oh Read over D. John Bridges* (1588), a very extreme view of the powers of Parliament vis à vis the king is assumed; but the satire of these tracts is so heavy it is hard to judge the seriousness of anything in them.
115 Sandys, *Sermons*, pp. 38-39.
116 *Ibid.*, p. 33.   117 *Ibid.*, p. 25.

Richard Hooker, as we have often observed, quite consistently emphasized the "representative" elements in medieval theory, and though he seldom discussed the nature of Parliament, no one was more flattering to the pretensions of the Parliament men: "The most natural and religious course in making of laws is that the matter of them be taken from the judgment of the wisest in those things which they are to concern."[118] The force of laws, he argued, comes not from the prince's power over the parliament, but from the parliament itself: ". . . from power which the whole body of this realm being naturally possessed with, hath by free . . . assent derived unto him that ruleth over them. . . ."[119]

From many pulpits Lancelot Andrewes urged the probity of Hooker's view. The summoning of popular assemblies for politico-legal action he declared to be consonant with the laws of God and Nature.[120] And for Richard Sibbes, parliaments existed to reform abuses: "Reformation makes all outward things fall into good rule, but they are to be called onely by the Authority of the Prince, and when a fit time and occasion requires . . . in that Josiah gathered a Councill in a time of publike disorder and . . . danger, here we learne that it is not onely lawfull, but many times necessary to gather assemblies and councils, for Reformation of abuses both in Church and commonwealth. . . ."[121]

William Laud's view of Parliament was neither original nor subversive. Of course he was accused, along with crimes against religion, of attempting to "subvert the rights of Parliaments." There is no evidence he was guilty of any such intent. On one occasion he spoke of Parliament as deriving "influence and

[118] Hooker, *Polity*, VIII, vi, 10-11; I, x, 7-8.
[119] *Ibid.*, VIII, vi, 11.
[120] Andrewes, *Works*, v, 153; to the king in 1606 he proclaimed: "There is no people under heaven may better speak for the use of assemblies than we; there was nothing that did our ancestors the Britons more hurt, saith Tacitus of them, nothing that turned them to greater prejudice than this one, that they met not, they consulted not in common, but every man ran a course by himself of his own head; and this was the greatest advantage the Roman had of them, they were not so wise as to know what good there was in public conventions." (*Ibid.*, pp. 145-46, 207.)
[121] Sibbes, *The Saints Cordials* (1637), pp. 74-75.

power from the King"[122] (a correct view of one vital aspect of the expanded council of the medieval constitution); but in his famous debate with the Jesuit, "Fisher," he avowed that ". . . there are divers businesses of greatest consequence, which cannot be finally and bindingly ordered, but in and by parliament; and particularly the statute laws, which must bind all subjects, cannot be made and ratified but there . . . And again . . . the supreme majestrate in the state civil may not abrogate the laws made in parliament. . . ."[123]

Further, Laud took the neo-medievalist position that there was no possible opposition in the interests of Parliament and king. Indeed, the rights of Parliament are best preserved by "the greatness and power of their king; that so he may be the better able, against all foreign practices, to keep up the honour as well as the safety of the nation . . ."; conversely, and not inconsistent with conservative (medieval) theory, "Parliaments are the best preservers of the ancient laws and rights of this kingdom."[124] As Trevor-Roper has shown, Laud got into trouble precisely because he was an able and doctrinaire conservative living in a revolutionary epoch.[125]

In the era of the Reformation, one of the main theoretical problems of Parliament's position in the constitution concerned the relation of that body to religion and the church. The Reformation had been largely enacted by statute, so the difficulties were inherent in the whole constitutional nexus of the components king-in-parliament. No one doubted that the king as head of the church and divine right father of the commonwealth had extremely broad prerogative powers to defend and regulate the religious establishment. Sir Edwin Sandys in 1621 even granted that the king had statutory authority (35 Elizabeth) to "alter religion when he pleaseth."[126] But Pym and Eliot used the Reformation statutes to claim precedent for Parliament's right to advise the king and the bishops on matters of religion affecting the welfare of the generality, or the safety of the state. Pym based the contended right of Parliament to restrain papists and other heretics

---

[122] Laud, *Works,* I, 101.
[123] *Ibid.,* II, 234-35. Fisher was a pseudonym for Percy.
[124] *Ibid.,* III, 433.
[125] Archbishop Laud.
[126] *Commons Debates, 1621,* II, 285.

by penal laws on "the instinct of nature" which justified "politic states, amongst which monarchy is the chief" in acting to "preserve itself" from rival, subversive allegiances.[127] In 1629 Pym was claiming more, arguing for parliamentary interference on the theory that Parliament spoke for the general will: "And howsoever it is alleged that the Parliament are not just judges in matters of faith, yet ought they to know the established and fundamental truths, and the contraries unto them; for Parliaments have confirmed acts of General Councils, which have not been received until they have been so authorized; and Parliament have enacted laws for trial of heretics by jury. The Parliament punished the Earl of Essex for countenancing heretics; and there is no Court can meet with this mischief but the Court of Parliament. The Convocation cannot because it is but a provincial Synod, only of the jurisdiction of Canterbury, and the power thereof is not adequate to the whole kingdom; and the Convocation of York may perhaps not agree with that of Canterbury. The High Commission cannot, for it hath its authority derived from Parliaments, and the derivative cannot prejudice the original, the judgment of Parliament being the judgment of the King and of the three estates of the whole Kingdom."[128]

Sir John Eliot, in the same crucial year, declared Parliament had no intention "to deal with matters of faith" but merely wished to serve to "confirm" the established truths of "fourscore years" of religious profession, and to warn of the dangers of "Popery and Arminianism."[129]

This extremely complicated and potentially dangerous speculation about the relations of Parliament to religion was—true to form—avoided almost entirely by the English divines.[130] Hooker stated very well what was certainly the almost universal

[127] *Ibid.*, pp. 461-63.

[128] *Commons Debates for 1629* (ed. Notestein and Relf; Minneapolis, 1921), p. 21.

[129] *Ibid.*, pp. 24-28.

[130] A very few exceptions can be found. Pym stated that one Dr. William Beale, a notable "Royalist," had asserted in a sermon that the king had the power to make laws without parliament and moved that he be made to account for his error (Gardiner, *op.cit.*, IX, 111-12; see also Mosse, *op.cit.*, p. 49, for the views of Maynwaring, Matthew Wren, and Isaac Bargrove).

clerical view: "In matters of God . . . it were unnatural not to think the pastors and bishops of our souls a great deal more fit than men of secular trades and callings; howbeit, when all which the wisdom of all sorts can do is done for devising of laws in the Church, it is the general consent of all that giveth them the form and vigour of laws . . . laws could they never be without consent of the whole Church, to be guided by them. Whereunto both nature and the practice of the Church of God set down in Scripture, is found every way so fully consonant; that God himself would not impose, no not in his own laws upon his people by the hand of Moses, without their free and open consent. Wherefore to . . . determine even of the church's affairs by way of assent . . . the parliament of England hath competant authority."[131]

In his debate with Lord Say and Sele—one of the last hearings the polity of Henry VIII and Elizabeth would receive—Laud restated Hooker's position defensively.[132] Even episcopacy Laud justified *jure ecclesiastico*, by the laws of the realm confirmed in Parliament.[133]

## 2. The Political Classes

The Protestant saint is never directly encouraged to become a citizen of the ancient Athenian or modern English ideal: a politically and socially thoughtful and active person. The saint has a calling to work in, England to glorify by service and piety, heaven as an immediate and ultimate destination. But a truly political being, a critic and thinker in legal, constitutional, and social terms he is not. The saint is given absolutely no en-

[131] Hooker, *Polity*, VIII, vi, 11.
[132] "I will not dispute it here, what power a lay assembly (and such a Parliament is) hath to determine matters of religion . . . before the Church hath first agreed upon them. Then, indeed, they may confirm or refuse. And this course was held in the Reformation. But originally to take this power over religion into lay hands is that which hath not been thus assumed, since Christ to these unhappy days . . . I meddle not here with the King's power. For he may be present in Convocation when he pleases, and take or leave any canons as he pleases, which are for the peace and well ordering of the church; as well as in Parliament, take or leave any laws made ready for him, for the good and quiet of his people. But if it come to be matter of faith, though in his absolute power he may do what he will, and answer God for it after; yet he cannot commit the ordering of that to any lay assembly, Parliament, or other. . . ." (*Works*, VI, Part 1, 142-43.)
[133] *Ibid.*, pp. 42-44.

couragement to aspire to Parliament or to the Bench or to a commission of the peace; nor is he urged to agitate, however patriotically, in the restricted political arenas of county or town. Nevertheless, the continuity between the Protestant political activism and intellectual fertility of political thought in the epoch 1640-1660 and the political passivism and intellectual sterility of the clergy before 1640 is by way of the newly-defined saint. For it was by insisting upon the spiritual autonomy and individuality of the saint, independent of existing hierarchies in church and state, that the Protestants succeeded by indirection and inversion in creating a new kind of citizen class. This Protestant idea eventually and inevitably transformed socially ordinary people, politicians, judges, county J.P.'s, even a few nobles, into a self-confident citizenry who in the excitement of the revolutionary dislocation of the old order began to think for themselves. This creation of a new citizen class is the political essence of the revolution of 1640-1660; it is the permanent achievement upon which the future was built. And of course such an expansion of the citizenry, of the politically involved, came out of no equalitarian ideal, no confidence in "the people" —which is one reason the radicalism of the Revolution is so startling. The political alchemy of Protestant sainthood is elusive because it is essentially a "psychology," a state of mind, rather more than a theory. It is the intense level of individual spirituality which creates the healthy egotism that can challenge sacrosanct status and orthodoxy in the very name of God. The "opiate" effects of religious sanctions are finally dissolved in the new acid of Protestant psychology. But the old order was safe enough from direct criticism in terms of the implicit equalitarianism of Protestant thought.

"In the question of the people," Whitgift pronounced, "there are three things especially to be noted: their inconstancy, their flattery, and their curiosity."[134] They are also ignorant, deceitful, and drunken.[135] Cartwright charged Whitgift with "the papists' manner of speaking, in saying that the people be 'ignorant and unlearned' ";[136] but Whitgift spoke for the overwhelm-

134 Whitgift, *Works*, III, 567.
135 *Ibid.*, I, 372-82.     136 *Ibid.*, III, 273.

ing majority of the Protestant clergy. Calvin, the inexhaustible fountain of so many Protestant theories, was no democrat. To him the world was inundated by "the private vices of multitudes," and consequently, "human affairs have scarcely ever been in so good a state as for the majority to be pleased with things of real excellence."[137] John Downame warned against courting "the applause of the vulgar people; seeing they are divided into as many phantasies as they have heads, the which are not only divers, but expressly contrary to one another"; and this mass instability, he observed, could result in rebellion and confusion.[138]

Andrewes cautioned Parliament to insist upon orderly assemblies, for "if Demetrius getteth together his fellow-craftsmen, they may of their own heads rush into the common hall, and there keep a shouting and crying two hours together, not knowing most of them why they came thither—and yet thither they came."[139] Gouge similarly warned against "the folly of such Governours as wholly apply themselves to the fancie of their people, yea though it be against the Lord and his word. This was . . . (the) folly . . . of Pilate, who to please the people, against his conscience, delivered Christ to be crucified."[140] Such antidemocratic sentiments are continual, commonplace, and shared by all factions among the clergy. There are exceptional incidents of dissent in Cartwright and Donne, but only among the Separatists is there a real predisposition to democratic-tending theory.[141]

Once the great majority of people had been dismissed with scorn and fear, the clergy proceeded to consider the political classes proper: the gentry, the town elite, the nobility. There is a vast quantity of comment on the manners, morals, and fitness to rule of the ruling classes. A great deal of this comment is critical, even abusive. There is a large ingredient of clerical smugness, of pulpit pomposity based partly upon the long-established immunity of the laity to the fulminations of such

---

137 Calvin, *Institutes,* Dedicatory Epistle, p. 32.
138 Downame, *The Christian Warfare,* pp. 501-02.
139 Andrewes, *Works,* v, 147.
140 Gouge, *The Works,* i, 9.
141 E.g., Robinson, *The Works,* iii, 62-63.

professional pessimism. To the modern reader it is surprising to encounter what superficially appears wholesale social attack by the pulpit on the worthies of old England. Few contemporary preachers would think of attacking their ruling elites with such dogmatic self-confidence. But the Reformation pulpit was concerned with saving souls, and this process was verbally rude; furthermore, for all the abuse of the ruling classes, there was no challenge to their absolute, God-directed mandate to rule.[142] Therefore the criticism was entirely for the edification of the ruling classes and was part of both Protestant moral monism and of the ancient Christian value scheme which insisted on the moral advantages of periodic breast-beating and contemplation of one's sins at the behest of the clergy. Professor Owst writes thus of the medieval English pulpit: "Finally, that habit of ruthless satire and penetrating criticism in sermons, which did so much to undermine the authority of the Church, worked in similar fashion against the strongholds of feudal privilege. A continuous stream of scorn and reproof for all the current sources of pride and prestige in medieval society poured forth from the pulpits. The ears of the people must have grown quite familiar with homiletic phrases that often sounded to them like so many threats of destruction for the powerful and the rich. Hence, for better or for worse, we must acknowledge the sermons, however little so intended, as a primary literature of secular revolt, and their authors as the heralds of political strife and future social liberties."[143]

But the obvious fact is the converse. The traditions of this literature, generations upon generations, made it quite innocuous: it heralded no real change or challenge, but served mostly to ventilate the collective conscience of those Christians embarrassed by the permanent anomaly of an ethic of love and brotherhood forced to accommodate a predatory, hierarchic society.

[142] William Perkins even defended the lack of virtues in the "children of Nobles" because "dignities doe run in discent, and the posterity is honoured in the name of the auncestours, but principally for the vertues of the auncestours" (*Works*, II, 150).

[143] G. R. Owst, *Literature and Pulpit in Medieval England* (Cambridge, 1933), p. 236.

In castigating the nobility, King James himself was fond of the pulpit style: the ". . . fecklesse arrogant conceit of their greatnesse and power: drinking in with their very nouris-milke, that their honor stood in committing three points of iniquity: to thrall, by oppression, the meaner sort . . . to maintaine their servants and depenters in any wrong . . . and for any displeasure, that they apprehend to be done unto them by their neighbour, to take up a plaine fude against him. . . ."[144]

James did not regard "the naturall sicknesse" of the nobility as a serious handicap to successful rule; and his magistracy would correct all and balance out the evils indigenous to the various classes. But Richard Hooker looked upon the deficiencies of the nobility as a more serious problem, for ". . . the whole body politic wherein we live should be for strength's sake a threefold cable, consisting of the king as a supreme head over all, of peers and nobles under him, and of the people under them; so likewise, that in this conjunction of states, the second wreath of that cable should, for important respects, consist as well of lords spiritual as temporal: nobility and prelacy being by this mean turned together, how can it possibly be avoided, but that the tearing away of the one must needs exceedingly weaken the other, and by consequent impair greatly the good of all?"[145]

Many of the clerics condemned the excesses of privilege. Thomas Beard found "corruption and perversitie" everywhere; with the governing classes providing leadership in iniquity.[146] John Dod cried shame upon those who "devising gay toyes . . . are but unprofitable burdens of the earth,"[147] and Paul Baynes deplored the "gallancy which they (though falsely) thinke much making for their Lords glory."[148] Downame was especially severe

---

[144] *Basilikon Doron*, pp. 83-85.

[145] Hooker, *Polity*, VII, xviii, 10. Richard Bernard makes his "Wilfull-Will" confess, "I stood too much upon my birth, and Gentry, as too many this day doe . . . I tooke it for granted, that my Gentrie stood in idlenesse, pleasurable delights, hawking, hunting, and haunting tavernes, drinking of healths, whiffing the tobacco-pipe, putting on a new and variety of fashions in Hat and in haire . . . in boasting and bragging, in cracking of oaths, in big looks, great words. . . ." (*The Isle of Man* [1627], pp. 180-81.) And George Herbert condemned the same list of privileged excesses ("The Country Parson," Chapter 32, *Works* [Oxford, 1941]).

[146] Beard, *op.cit.*, pp. 3-5.

[147] Dod and Cleaver, *A Godlie Forme of Householde Government* (1612), p. 63.

[148] Paul Baynes, *Christian Letters* (1620), No. 3.

on the vanity of the leisured class, "seeing therefore this worldly Nobility is of no excellence"; but he was ambivalent, as were all the divines, for he simultaneously praised the concept of a blood nobility which conferred its graces and talents from generation to generation.[149] Indeed, the clergy even stressed a kind of ancestor worship and chided the current generation with defaulting on the legacy of their blood and broad acres. "Thinke with a reverend courage of your noble Ancestors . . . shew your selves the legitimate and true borne children of such fathers," cried Thomas Adams.[150] Robert Sanderson declared to the aristocracy, "You usurp their Arms, if you inherit not their Vertues. . . ."[151]

There is, in fact, a curious vein of social atavism in the clerical commentary on the mores of the aristocracy: the old chivalric virtues of prowess at arms and *gloire* come in for a surprising amount of nostalgic praise from the pious men of the pulpit. This is probably simply because the past was frequently created golden out of whole cloth, to emphasize the evils of the present— "the age of iron, and rusty too," as Donne wrote it. Robert Bolton employed his powerful language in its full glory to excoriate patrons of church livings, courtiers, the idle gallant, all of them poor substitutes for the great warrior nobility of the past.[152] Thomas Scott protested the rigging of elections to Parliament by the great lords through their control of tenants.[153] Fuller, in his entertaining *The Holy and Profane States*, contributed a veritable lexicon of desirable and undesirable traits of aristocracy, emphasizing the magic of "ancient parentage" and the failings of sons to live up to the demands of their high calling.[154]

The court nobility were sometimes criticized as such, apart from their class as a whole. The most impressive critic was Bishop Hall; his language was extremely vitriolic. "Of all men under heaven," he cried in a sermon before James, "none had so much need to pray as Courtiers . . . They are set upon the

[149] Downame, *op.cit.*, pp. 490-97; 653-54. Cf. Perkins, *Works*, II, 150.
[150] Adams, *Works*, p. 1084.
[151] Sanderson, *XXXVI Sermons*, pp. 212-13.
[152] Bolton, *Workes*, I, 157-214.
[153] Scott, *Vox Populi* (xii-xiii).
[154] Fuller, *The Holy and Profane States*, pp. 141-317.

hill, and see the glory of the kingdomes of the earth, but I
feare it is seene of them . . . the more need, the lesse devotion."[155]
Further, "Yee great men wring the poore sponges of the Com-
monaltie into your private purses, for the maintenance of pride
and excesse,"[156] while "alas, I see some care to be gallant, others
to be great, few care to be holy."[157] Hall also admitted to a
general distaste for the ruling classes: "I confesse, I cannot
honour blood without good qualities. . . . I speake boldly, our
Land hath no blemish comparable to the mis-education of our
Gentry. . . . Learning is for Priests, and Pedants; for Gentlemen,
pleasure. . . . I shame and hate to think, that our Gallants hold
there can be no disparagement, but in honest callings."[158] (It
is possibly true that in these wholesale condemnations of gentry,
nobility, merchants, and lawyers, the clergy were venting their
corporate spleen, the general frustration of clerical impotence.)

In addition to the mass of vituperative comment on the ruling classes as such, there was a large literature dealing with
the ruling classes in office, the magistracy. We have already indicated that there is virtually unanimous assent to Calvin's dictum
that "The first duty of subjects towards their magistrates is to
entertain the most honourable sentiments of their functions,
which they know to be a jurisdiction delegated to them from
God, and on that account to esteem and reverance them as God's
ministers and viceregents."[159] Andrewes considered, not without reason, that the orderliness of good government was a
"miracle."[160]

Nevertheless, there came from the pulpit a certain amount
of rather caustic comment on the failings of the office holders.
Archbishop Sandys declared the state to be full of bribe-takers,
spoilers, and ungodly magistrates.[161] Downame condemned the
money nexus ("What is there which is not corrupted with silver
and gold?") that permits "friends bought with gifts" to allow the
ambitions to "mount up into the seate of eminencie."[162] "Heretofore," complained Downame, "men were preferred unto offices

---

[155] Hall, *Works*, III, 173.    [156] *Ibid.*, p. 417.    [157] *Ibid.*, p. 446.
[158] *Works*, I, 393-95.    [159] Calvin, *Institutes*, IV, xx, 22.
[160] Andrewes, *XCVI Sermons*, p. 276.
[161] Sandys, *Sermons*, pp. 103-04.    [162] Downame, *op.cit.*, p. 210.

THE DILEMMA OF MODERNITY

for their service, sufficiencie; and desert; but now the usual entrance unto them is by large gifts . . . Now what wonder is it if these men who entred into their places by bribing, doe in the execution of them live by extorsion?"[163] Lawyers are the chief culprits.[164] In his endless tirades against the "lewdnesse of the time," the irascible Thomas Adams attacked the timidity of magistrates who went in fear of "great men," the "beasts of the Heard," and in "cowardly darknesse" refused to "oppose your strengths to his oppressions."[165] Fuller singled out as a paragon among ministers Sir Thomas More, who, "though some years Lord Chancellor of England, scarce left his son five-and-twenty pounds a year more than his father left him. . . ."[166]

Finally, it need hardly be added, "it is impossible to resist the magistrate without, at the same time, resisting God himself";[167] for all must "learn not to scrutinize the persons themselves, but may be satisfied with knowing that they are invested by the will of the Lord with that function, upon which he has impressed an inviolable majesty."[168] The judgement of Calvin stood without exceptions in England.[169] Rebellion was an ungodly act with a history of the darkest misdeeds and inevitable, terrible retribution.[170] Tyrants were to be dealt with only by God, at His own sovereign pleasure; "having lived in other men's blood," went the general theory, "he dies commonly in his own."[171] To be sure, other people's revolutions, in Bohemia, Holland, Scotland, and France, were defended cautiously for here those in revolt were only trying to prevent tyrants from carrying out their nefarious designs to "alter their State, and evert their ancient Lawes."[172] This is perfectly illogical of course: in defending the Protestant revolts of which they approved, the English were using the same arguments Roman Catholics were employing

[163] *Ibid.*, pp. 210-11.    [164] *Ibid.*, p. 211.

[165] Adams, *Works*, pp. 346-47.    [166] Fuller, *op.cit.*, 169-70.

[167] Calvin, *Institutes*, IV, XX, 23. Cf. Sheldon S. Wolin, "Calvin and the Reformation," *American Political Science Review* (June, 1957).

[168] Calvin, *Institutes*, IV, XX, 29.

[169] Even John Robinson, the separatist, in condemning the views of the Baptist, Thomas Helwys, supported the orthodox opinion of the powers of magistracy, *Works*, II, *passim.*

[170] See Beard, *op.cit.*, pp. 193-213, 230-35.

[171] Fuller, *op.cit.*, p. 325.    [172] Bilson, *op.cit.*, pp. 516-21.

against Protestant states. But it is seldom indeed that the English divines felt impelled to speak with favor about any rebellion anywhere. For their almost exclusive concern was with "the manifold complots and treasons both at home and abroad that have beene conspired and attempted against our Prince and State, by profane men stirred up by the Devill. . . ."[173]

## IV. Nationalism and War

The patriotism of the English clergy was as deep and colorfully verbal as that of the laity. Perhaps the most striking superficial distinction between Roman Catholic and Protestant clergy is in the latter's militant nationalism. The explanation of Protestant nationalist zeal is not far to seek: Protestantism came into being the lusty creation of English statism and the international political and spiritual claims of Catholic imperialism were from the outset the major threat to Protestant ideals. The fierce chauvinism of the English clergy, like that of the Dutch clergy, was maintained at a high pitch by the will to survive the alliance of Spain and the Jesuits.

Still, one ought to ask why a genuine sentiment for international Protestantism did not arise to combat international Catholicism. The fate of French, Flemish, and Bohemian Calvinism is ample evidence of the failure of any such sentiment to develop depth or intensity. Protestantism failed to develop an international outlook—even vis-à-vis Roman Catholicism—because of its parasitic political morality and the explicitly national structure of its ecclesiastical polity. If the Roman Catholic Church was the child of the Roman imperium, the Protestant churches were the children of European nationalism.

Nationalism in seventeenth-century England deserves far more scholarly attention than it has received: it may, indeed, constitute the most important element in the social consciousness that ended in revolution. On the one hand, as Professor Mac-Caffrey has insisted in his recent monograph on Exeter, for most individual Englishmen "the greater universe of England and Englishmen loomed hazily" beyond the realities of their tradi-

[173] Perkins, *Works*, III, 399.

tional communities, and England was in many respects a land of confederated medieval communities.[174] On the other hand, the tight oligarchies of town and county were exclusively and consciously hierarchical, and a dynamic popular culture and religion were breaking down the entrenched particularism of both London and the provinces, giving to the masses in England a new sense of dignity and brotherhood.

This process may well mean that the essential ideology around which all of the forces of opposition and revolution clustered in the seventeenth century was neither Protestantism nor secularism, but nationalism. Surely it is no coincidence that England in this century is the land at once of intensest nationalism and of major revolution. When Protestantism was fragmented in the crucible of civil war, with Scotch Presbyterianism more of a threat to Cromwell than Irish Catholicism, with class and particularist interests threatening to dissolve the Protestant enthusiasm which had supported revolution, the revolutionary parties in Parliament and Army could summon mass support for the New Model regiments and Pym's mobs by propaganda like that of *The Souldiers Catechism* published by Parliament in 1644; by such propaganda, "the love I beare to my Countrey" became the transcending appeal for sacrifice and revolutionary zeal.

But though nationalism may be the rallying sentiment of the Revolution, the core ideological resource which made possible the execution of the King and war with Holland, a major precursor of that nationalism is discoverable in the Protestant hatred of Catholicism, a hatred based more upon political propaganda than theology. "Eighty-eight" and the Gunpowder Plot are the twin symbols—endlessly evoked—of English jingoism *cum* Protestantism. "Jesuit" and "Spanish" are interchangeable epithets for a common evil in two aspects: the Anti-Christ and the Armada. (Indeed, so basic was the nationalist ingredient in English religious fervor that an attempt had been earlier made by Bancroft and others to discredit presbyterianism by identifying it with "foreign" influence from Geneva and Scotland.)[175] The strength and depth of anti-Catholic feeling (anti-presbyter-

174 Wallace T. MacCaffrey, *Exeter, 1540-1640* (Cambridge, Mass., 1958), pp. 1-2.
175 Bancroft, *Dangerous Positions*, p. 3.

ian sentiment was neither strong nor widespread by comparison) surpassed even such modern evidences of paranoia as the Communist bogey-man in America. The true measure of this feeling is not to be gauged by scholarly polemics like Andrewes' *Tortura Torti,* or his *Responsio ad Apologiam,* or Thomas Morton's *A Catholike Appeale,* but rather by the thousands upon thousands of words and phrases of hate and fear in the sermons and tracts of the period. The major impact of this propaganda was usually directed against the general theories which underlay the bull *Regnans in excelsis* and Bellarmine's "indirect power"— theories which to the English seemed responsible for the many plots against their monarchs and in effect the foulest treason and incitement to political assassination: "This geer . . . but newly raked up from hell," as Andrewes expressed it.[176] There is not space to quote the endless samples of clerical vituperation characteristic of this very important form of nationalism: they are common coin, never out of circulation and adding up to a high national fund of revolutionary potential.

In addition to such religiously-oriented zeal for English nationhood, the clergy encouraged a remarkable degree of secular, vulgar, intense patriotism. They did homage to the pantheon of English kings, and compared glorious reigns like those of Henry II, Edward I, Henry V, and Henry VIII with the far lesser or positively unsavory accomplishments of foreign princes.[177] There are expressions of simple parochial and ignorant distrust of foreigners.[178] And there was at least one English clergyman maddened by the new fever, a veritable Cato, crying for the destruction of Spain. This was Thomas Scott: "Thinke what a happinesse, what a glory it is for England to have wars with Spaine, sith Spaine in the Lethargy of our peace, hath very neer undermined our safety, and subverted our glory; and let us dispell those charmes of security, wherein England hath bin too long lull'd and enchanted asleepe . . . and our swords cut those tongues and pens in pieces, which henceforth dare either

---

[176] Andrewes, *XCVI Sermons,* p. 863. Cf. Donne, *Works,* v, 420: "King James is lawful king in all his dominions and therefore exempt from all foreign jurisdiction over him."

[177] Sandys, *Sermons,* pp. 67-68.

[178] Perkins, *Works,* III, p. 73.

to speake of peace, or write of truce with Spaine. . . . Warres, warres, then yee (with cheerfull hearts and joyfull soules) let us prepare our selves for warres: That our Brittaine, the beauty of Europe, as Europe is the glory of the world, lie no longer exposed to the apparant danger and mercilesse mercy of this Castillian Rat, of this Crocodile of Italy, of this Vulture of Germany. . . ."[179]

England is to Scott a "sleeping lion," "one people of the same Language, Religion, Lawes, governed by the same Gracious and good King . . . *Unum cor, Unam viam* . . . our Brittaine so famous of old for her triumphs and many victories over other Nations. . . ."[180] And with the curious logic of most violent nationalists, Scott urged every sort of imperialist endeavour, from the conquest of the Spanish empire to peaceful union with Scotland (which, says Scott, only King James had the vision to appreciate!).[181]

Though Scott stands almost alone in his hysterical enthusiasm for war, most of the clergy spent time urging the lawfulness of war under certain circumstances. Calvin had permitted nations to take up arms for "public vengeance," "against any hostile aggression," and, in general, in the pursuit of any "just" war.[182] The definition of a just war is left entirely to the king, and no one, of course, may properly refuse to serve him in whatever he declares to be a just cause for military action. In their view of the morality of war, Protestants differed scarcely at all from the Roman Catholics: only in ignoring the issue or condemning the justice of crusades against the Moslems were they original.[183] The Anabaptists—rejected by all of the national Protestant confessions—were the only pacifists and were roundly abused for it.[184] To be sure, Lancelot Andrewes and William Perkins occasionally spoke out against "peace-breakers," and even the belligerent Gouge joined Beard, Adams, and Hall in rejecting war except as "a desperate medicine"; and the clergy were almost unani-

179 Thomas Scott, *Vox Coeli* (1624), pp. xii-xiii.
180 *Ibid.*, p. 60.
181 *Ibid.*, pp. xvi-xvii.
182 Calvin, *Institutes*, IV, xx, 11.
183 Cf. Bellarmine, *op.cit.*, pp. 57-73; Chapter 26.
184 E.g., Cosin, *Works*, I, 114-15.

mous in praising the good peace of the Stuarts.[185] But such sentiments were surely a minimum concession to the Christian ethic of love.

Of course the Old Testament was a mine of inspiration for the bellicose instincts of clerical nationalists. "Gods people may make warre," cried Perkins, "not onely by way of defence; but also, in assault upon their enemies. . . ."[186] Gouge, who argued that the good end justifies evil means, concluded that "Lawfull warre well waged proves prosperous."[187] However, it was necessary to caution that the Lord "seeth it meet sometimes to suffer enemies to have the better over his people," and that "concerning the difference of religion betwixt Protestants and Papists, we are not to judge of it by event and successe in warre."[188]

A good deal of comment on the proper conduct of war, on the ethics of warfare itself, issued from pulpit and clerical press. There is almost nothing said of chivalric ethics; and indeed, there is a large volume of condemnation of any form of private revenge, ordeal by combat, or duelling;[189] but the problems of soldier relations and treatment of the enemy in victory are discussed. The "common soldier" is told to obey the orders of his superiors, and, since the "courses of war are so complicated . . . and private soldiers have neither the calling nor ability to dive into such mysteries," he is not to worry about larger issues.[190] Paul Baynes declared, "The strength of the common soldiers is as much, yea farre more in the wisdome and power of their Leader, then in their owne valour and furniture."[191] Gouge agreed, and accounted "a good Generall . . . worth ten thousand others. . . ."[192] There is little evidence in all this pointing to the

[185] See Andrewes, *XCVI Sermons*, pp. 185-89; Gouge, *Gods Three Arrowes*, pp. 350-67; Perkins, *Works*, III, 19; Beard, *op.cit.*, p. 294; Hall, *Works*, III, 424; IV, 110.

[186] Perkins, *Works*, III, 176.

[187] Gouge, *op.cit.*, pp. 289; 212-96.

[188] *Ibid.*, 269-77.

[189] E.g., William Ames, *Conscience with the Power and Cases Thereof* (1639), pp. 182-84; Gouge, *Gods Three Arrowes*, p. 219; Perkins, *Works*, II, 120; Fuller, *op.cit.*, pp. 131-35.

[190] Fuller, *op.cit.*, p. 129.

[191] Paul Baynes, *The Spirituall Armour* (1620), pp. 2-3.

[192] Gouge, *op.cit.*, p. 288.

extraordinary political and social agitation of rank and file soldiers in Cromwell's regiments!

Gouge preached much on the dignity of the warrior and
complained of public apathy in forming and training numerous
city artillery companies.[193] Bishop Cooper defended the church's
fish-eating prejudice on the grounds that "there is no state of
men, that doth so much furnish this realme with sufficient
numbers of mariners for our navie, as fishers do"![194] The soldiery
about whose dignity and calling the clergy talked at some length,
were understood to be citizen-soldiers, the largely fictional ancient militia of freemen led by the knights and barons of the
realm in public defense against invasion. The hard truth of the
wars of their age—wars fought by mercenaries for pay and without honor—most of the clergy ignored.[195] Thus the morality
they preached for the conduct of war was unreal and unavail-
ing. When Thomas Adams demanded that "soldiers should be
generous and gentle in victory" and fight only for justice and
peace, and urged that "Piety and Policy are not opposites," he
was speaking platitudes that bore little relation to existing and
very real problems.[196]

It is a sad commentary on the endless social congruity of Christian ethics that the brilliant and moving words written by
Erasmus against war should have moved so few hearts. Only the
outcast radicals, the victims of history, as it were, could see the
cheap casuistry in the thousands of clerical platitudes about
"just" wars and "honourable" soldiers. But of course this failure
of the Christian ethic has been a permanent feature of all of the
major confessions, and is so still.

193 Gouge, *The Dignitie of Chivalrie* (1626), pp. 38-47.
194 Cooper, *An Admonition*, p. 107.
195 Cf. Fuller, *op.cit.*, p. 130.
196 Adams, *Works*, pp. 1071-82.

## CHAPTER 7

## THE ENGLISH PROTESTANT

## AND THE FAMILY

—————————✝✝✝—————————

Whatever Hypocrites austerely talk
Of puritie and place and innocence,
Defaming as impure what God declares
Pure, and commands to some, leaves free to all.
Our Maker bids increase, who bids abstain
But our Destroyer, foe to God and Man?
Haile wedded Love, mysterious Law, true sourse
Of human ofspring, sole proprietie,
In Paradise of all things common else.
By thee adulterous lust was driv'n from men
Among the bestial herds to raunge, by thee
Founded in Reason, Loyal, Just, and Pure,
Relations dear, and all the Charities
Of Father, Son, and Brother first were known.
　　　　　—JOHN MILTON, *Paradise Lost*, IV

—————————✝✝✝—————————

### I. Sex and Christianity

IN A WAY THAT WAS UNIQUE among the major religions, Christianity took the monogamous family under its particular protection and sponsorship. By thus sanctioning monogamy as the basis of family life and the sole outlet for sexual need, Christianity achieved a compromise between the two tendencies evident in all the sophisticated religions: the tendency positively to support sexual activity in terms of its product, the survival of the species, and the tendency negatively to limit it or even altogether to deny it in deference to the values of ascetic thought and practice.

In the religions of nonliterate peoples—the so-called nature religions—the positive or fertility principle bulks by far the larger of the two tendencies; at the same time, these religions

concern themselves with the regulations, often extremely numerous and burdensome, governing sexual conduct within the
group, occasionally even evidencing an ascetic way of thinking.
Yet the whole ascetic tradition in regard to sex—the tradition
which encourages the denial of all normal or overt sexual satisfaction so that other more important and principally spiritual
satisfactions will be gained—certainly achieves fullest expression
in the religions of history, especially in those which have survived
longest and gained the largest followings. Among these religions,
and within the religions' various groups and sects, there are differences of emphasis on this subject. So much, however, can be
said of Christianity as a whole: relative to its fellow inheritors of
the same religious tradition, Judaism and Mohammedanism, it
tends to asceticism on the sexual as on other issues. Its consistent
and implacable adherence to monogamy as the only approvable
marriage relationship is probably more closely connected to this
ascetic bias than to any other single aspect of its philosophy.

Though the pressure of the ascetic tendency is evident even in
Christianity's concept of marital chastity, Christian sexual asceticism comes to its full flowering only in the religious hallowing
of the life of strict celibacy. The absolute Christian preference
for celibacy over any type of marriage is already apparent in the
Gospels and, for a long period at least, time only adds more
prominence and clarity to this preference. Virginity in the female
becomes in itself a virtue and its preservation against odds a
basis for sanctification. Celibacy in the male becomes the first
and primary mark of that peculiar dedication to the duties of
religion and the demands of the spirit which the life of monasticism embodies. Finally, in the Christian church which dominates unchallenged through more than a thousand years of the
history of Western Europe, celibacy becomes a requirement for
ecclesiastical position and preferment.

The ideological tension between asceticism and relative non-
asceticism is undoubtedly the most important single aspect of a
Christian philosophy of the family: the particular resolution of
this tension achieved in any Christian creed determines the
status which family life as such will occupy in the total system
of values. But a number of other significant issues are also in-

volved, for even where celibacy has been most sharply exalted above marriage in spiritual value, Christian creeds have nonetheless dealt extensively with the proprieties of relationship between society and the family and among the family's individual members.

By all odds, in regard to the breadth of application and the amount of attention paid to it by the spokesmen of Christianity, the most significant of these secondary topics of discussion concerns the status and role of the wife in the family. Since in the vast bulk of the social thinking of history the words "wife" and "woman" have been virtually interchangeable (the role of wife subsuming, for the most part, the total role of woman), all definition of one tends also to define the other. Much has been said of the influence of Christianity in exalting and dignifying, relative to previous and surrounding situations, the status of woman; and when Christianity is compared on this score with the other great historical religions, much deserves to be said. Even if the basis of Christianity's support of monogamy is primarily in the ascetic tradition, at least an incidental consequence has been an atmosphere more congenial to the dignity of woman than that afforded by those faiths which permit or encourage polygyny. And, again relative to the other major historical faiths, the body of tradition surrounding the origins of Christianity grants to a great number of women unusually prominent and praiseworthy functions. In Gospel Christianity, moreover, the spiritual equality between men and women—the equal accessibility of the boon of salvation through confirmation in the faith—is more than not denied: it is emphatically affirmed.

Yet it must be acknowledged that even from the relevant commentary in Gospel Christianity, woman still emerges as the second sex and as socially, ecclesiastically, and, in a less specific sense, mentally and morally inferior to man. To be sure, most of the positive assertions of this viewpoint are to be found in the Pauline Epistles and have been interpreted by some as a flooding in of a more formally Judaistic position on the subject (though in other respects Paul is seen as peculiarly the antagonist of Judaistic influence). But even the three Synoptic Gospels, by implication if not direct statement, are at least not incompatible with

Paul on the position of women in the Christian community. However important women may have been as aides and subsidiaries in this earliest Christian drama, the roles of real authority and prestige were all occupied by men, and the whole structure of belief found its apex in a masculine Messiah and a deity whose total masculinity was not relieved (as it tended to be even in many historical faiths) by the presence of a consort. Moreover, the tribal tradition from which Christianity emerged, and whose presence was especially prominent in the early days of the faith and in the recurrent outbursts of sectarianism, provided a solid social basis for concepts of equalitarianism regarding the relationships between man and man; but the uncompromising patriarchal character of the tradition could only reinforce the inequalities between man and woman. It is altogether logical, therefore, that the social radicalism of initial Christianity (its penchant for questioning and attacking existent patterns of social hierarchy) should be less evident in this than in any other area of human relationship.

This concept of the inferiority of women, already present in the first beginnings of Christianity, tended only to be strengthened and expanded by the ideological and institutional development of the faith during the centuries immediately following its emergence and establishment. There was not, of course, a total absence of countercurrents. For what benefit it was to women in their usual role as wives, Christianity never departed from the maintenance of monogamy as the only suitable form of marriage. Through martyrdom or other dramatic acts of piety, considerable numbers of women—though never nearly as many women as men—came to be recognized as saints within the church. Finally, nunneries offered, at least to women of relatively exalted birth, an alternative to marriage; for those few who came to rule over them as abbesses, they provided positions of great prestige and a degree of authority superior to that of many men.

So much the Christian church afforded to women during the first thousand years of its history in the West. How then can the major influence of this history on the status of women be described as negative? The factor principally responsible for this evaluation is the increasing emphasis, during these early centuries of the growth of Christian thought, upon the ascetic theme, and particularly upon sexual asceticism. It was asceticism, to be sure, which was responsible for the nunnery and which therefore gave to a minority of women the opportunity of some choice in life, but for the majority of women the very existence of the nunnery further underlined the relative degradation of their role, peculiarly dedicated as it was to the rites of sex. One needs no very intimate acquaintance with monastic literature to be aware that when the men of religion attacked sex, they intermediately or by consequence attacked women as well.

As the Christian church became an established institution in Western Europe, moreover, there was a total exclusion of women from all ecclesiastical positions or ritual functions within it. Even compared to the way other major historical religions treated women, Christianity may be said to have cut off women wholesale from institutional roles. With the entirely incidental exception of the life of the nunnery, no office in the Western Christian church could be held by a woman, and no essential ritual required and very few even permitted performance or supervision by a woman. In the origin and maintenance of this ecclesiastical boycott of the female, the pressure of the ascetic tradition was no doubt largely instrumental, together with the related desire of Christian leaders to distinguish sharply their faith from preceding and contemporary pagan cults—cults which were more extensively involved with the fertility principle and thus far more dependent upon the services of women both as priestesses and devotees.

Everything we have been developing here attains a climax of organization and logic, if not intensity, in the writings of St. Thomas Aquinas. Thus it forms a part of that focal Roman Catholic doctrine around which so much of our comparison between Catholicism and early Protestantism has been revolving. The view of marriage of Thomistic Catholicism is readily defined in terms of the double standard of morality which we have found to occupy so important a place in medieval Roman Catholic philosophy. This double standard, as we have noted, grants to the religious life, and especially the monastic life, a higher spiritual value *per se* than to the life of the world; and the religious life, whether monastic or ecclesiastical, is properly celibate. In consequence, marriage automatically becomes, even at best, a concomitant of a lower, less demanding, and spiritually less rewarding type of Christian life.

There is no question that marriage is accepted, defended, and even hallowed in Thomistic Catholicism, but the whole structure of argument indicates that marriage is tolerated as a means to other ends than a liking or an admiration for the practice in itself. Defended from the social standpoint, marriage is a means to produce children: thus marriage is an absolutely indispensable ingredient of the life of the human community and even compatible with the life of individual perfection. (St. Thomas assumed, for instance, that reproduction occurred in Paradise and provided there a basis for sinless marriage.) Yet what is really sponsored here—and what is really hallowed in the Roman Catholic matrimonial sacrament—is not marriage but reproduction for which marriage supplies the means.

Marriage is also defended from the standpoint of the life of the individual in the world of fallen men; but it is defended much more grudgingly and with no sense of hallowing, as a means to ease the human burden of concupiscence, or as a remedy for sin. "It is better to marry than to burn"—through emphasis on this Pauline statement, marriage is very nearly damned with faint praise.

Turning now to the second topic with which we are primarily concerned, that is, the nature, status, and function of woman, one finds in the philosophy of St. Thomas virtually the strongest and most unqualified Christian assertion of her inferiority. From the writings of the Angelic Doctor, woman, as a group and generality, emerges inferior to man in every aspect of her being. Physiologically she is inferior, since St. Thomas perpetuates the Aristotelian concept of woman as a misshapen or half-formed man.[1] The relative weakness of her reason is emphasized,[2] and from this weakness follows the greater susceptibility

---

[1] St. Thomas Aquinas, *Summa Theologica*, I, q. 99, a. 2, ad. 1.
[2] Aquinas, *Summa Contra Gentiles*, III, 123.

of her soul to the disorder of sin.[3] God is asserted to have created her as a helpmate for man in only one essential function, the process of reproduction. Another man, St. Thomas contends, would have been more suitable as a companion or helpmate in all other regards.[4] (St. Thomas, it should be noted, thus cuts short at its root any emphasis on the companionable aspect of marriage.) And even in the process of generation woman's role is that of an inferior: man is the active principle of generation, woman the passive; man provides the form of the newly created being, woman only the matter.[5]

Woman's status in the Thomistic system is in accord with her asserted incapacities. As a child, she is subject to her father. As an adult, she is subject to her husband, whose power over her is limited only by the absence of the power of life and death. The husband is specifically granted in the *Summa Theologica* the right to correct his wife with corporal punishment in case of need.[6] He is assigned control over the financial affairs of the household and the wife is cautioned, along with children and serfs, not to give alms without her husband's permission.[7] The woman's authority over her children, which is at the start a secondary authority in the line of family command, is further weakened by St. Thomas's contention that, absolutely speaking, the father is to be loved by his children more than is the mother. "For father and mother," he writes, "are loved as principles of our natural origin. Now the father is principle in a more excellent way than the mother, because he is the active principle, while the mother is a passive and material principle."[8]

Although assured that she is not a slave in the home of her husband (Aristotle, indeed, had said no less), woman, in a different instance, is compared with slave to her own limitation and the slave's advantage. Whereas the slave is not necessarily a slave by nature, the woman, in whatever circumstance she may find herself, is always by her nature a subject to some man.[9] For

---

[3] Aquinas, *Sum. Theol.*, III (Supplement), q. 4, ad. 5.
[4] *Sum. Theol.*, I, q. 92, a. 1, c.
[5] *Summa Contra Gentiles*, IV, 11; *Sum. Theol.*, II-II, q. 26, a. 10, ad. 1.
[6] *Sum. Theol.*, III (Supplement), q. 62, a. 2, ad. 1.
[7] *Sum. Theol.*, II-II, q. 32, a. 8, c.
[8] *Sum. Theol.*, II-II, q. 26, a. 10, c.
[9] *Sum. Theol.*, III (Supplement), q. 39, a. 3, ad. 4.

the slave there is the possibility of escape from dependence and tutelage to freedom; for the woman there is none.

Before completing this brief analysis of the development of Roman Catholic concepts concerning the place and status of women in the church and in society, some mention should be made of the cult of the Virgin. Certainly this cult is the product of a long historical pressure to relieve or balance the stark masculinity of Christianity and to introduce into it some of the feminine qualities familiar to the cults of paganism. Perhaps in a vague and general way the existence of the cult enhanced the position of women in the Christian church, for the Virgin could at least provide an intimate focus for their devotions and a peculiar evidence of triumph for their spirituality. But any other lines of influence or consequence are extremely hard to trace or to make firm. By its very nature, the cult of the Virgin offered support only to those two feminine roles which were already best established and most highly valued in the hierarchy of ecclesiastical and social respectability: those of the ascetic—the nun—and the mother. From the honor tendered to a Virgin Mother, the conjugal role, the role of the wife as such, could borrow no reflected glory.

The signal break which Protestantism makes with this entire Roman Catholic tradition is in its insistence on the virtual universality of the human need for and the human right to marriage. Here is another aspect of the Protestant flight from the Roman Catholic double standard of morality and the related rejection of the Roman Catholic program of asceticism. Concerning the Protestant sponsorship of marriage, and especially the sponsorship of the marriage of the clergy, the question has been raised whether the logical mechanism involved is the Protestant's more emphatically positive view of marriage or more emphatically and generally negative view of human nature. The negative view can no doubt be traced in Protestant literature; and marriage is not infrequently excused in the Pauline manner as a remedy for sin. Yet in relation to the background of attitude we have been discussing, the Protestant emphasis appears primarily positive. Marriage is accepted as part of the ordinary life of ordinary people in the world, and, as we have noted many times already, a central tenet of Protestantism is that the fullest reaches of religious experience must be totally available to just such ordinary people living ordinary lives. Thus, just as Protestantism sees no dichotomy between sanctity and the following of a legitimate worldly calling, so there is no dichotomy between sanctity and marriage. Not only *may* the Protestant saint be married, but in all probability he *will* be married, and he will express and realize his sanctification in his marriage relationship as fully as in any other activity of his life. The pull of such an attitude as this, particularly when compared with the prejudice inherent in Christian asceticism, is clearly and markedly toward a more positive estimate of the value and dignity of marriage. This fact will become established beyond reasonable doubt, we feel, as we proceed to analyze in some detail the nature of the English Protestant response to marriage and the family.

## II. Marriage

The English Protestant attitude toward marriage and the whole area of human sexuality is not a matter of simple and unqualified statement. Here as elsewhere in this literature one finds that well-nigh universal characteristic of Christian thought: the simultaneous existence of contradictions, where a viewpoint is always a more or less unstable balance between opposites. Among individual English Protestant divines there were considerable differences of emphasis on this subject. Yet all agreed in one respect at least: they upheld the common Protestant position that all men, including those called to the ministry, were allowed to marry; associated with this view was their repudiation of the moral value of vows of chastity. We have previously noted the vehemence of the general English Protestant opposition to monastic life, and all such opposition includes an attack upon the primary monastic vow of celibacy. Gouge can serve as a representative of this universal opinion: ". . . it is accounted a Doctrine of devils to forbid to marry. For it is a Doctrine contrary to God's word, and a Doctrine that causeth much inward burning and outward pollution, and so maketh their bodies, which should be temples of the holy ghost, to be sties of the devill . . . Contrary . . . is the impure and tyrannicall restraint of the Church of Rome, whereby all that enter into any of their holy orders, are kept from mariage . . . Six thousand heads of infants were found in the ponds of a religious house . . . Devillish must that doctrine needs bee, which hath such devillish effects. Well did he wish, that wished that all they who cannot containe, would take heed how they doe rashly professe perfection, and vow virginity."[10]

Despite the universal resistance of English Protestants to vows of virginity and the forced celibacy of the clergy, some still clung to a fairly clear preference for virginity as a more suitable condition for the individual with a special religious gift, tending to see in the capacity to remain celibate a token of superior moral endowment. Hooker, for example, speaks of single life as "a thing more angelicall and divine" than married life and follows Roman Catholic doctrine in "excusing" marriage, as it were, solely on the basis of its generative function.[11] Herbert's acceptance of the marriage of the clergy is highly qualified by considerations of policy and of human frailty. He declares: "The Country Parson considering that virginity is a higher state than matrimony, and that the Ministry requires the best and highest things, is rather unmarryed than marryed. But yet as the temper of his body may be, or as the temper of his Parish may be, where he may have occasion to converse with women, and that among suspicious men, and other like circumstances considered, he is rather married then unmarried."[12]

Echoing Hooker, Cosin, too, refers to single life as "a thing more angelicall and divine" than marriage. He writes that "he [Christ] was a virgin Himself, and His Mother, she was a virgin . . . and married life itself seems to be but an imperfect state. The state of perfection is virginity, so much commended by our Saviour, so highly esteemed by St. Paul."[13] Yet Cosin goes on to say that "marriage is an honourable estate in all men ["all men" here marks the degree of distinction between Cosin's

10 Gouge, *Works*, I, 107.
11 Hooker, *Polity*, v, 74, i.
12 Herbert, *Works*, pp. 236-37.
13 Cosin, *Works*, I, 56.

position and that of Roman Catholicism, since from so inclusive
a category even the clergy are presumably not excepted], a
state ordained by God Himself in paradise, a state without
which there can be no society in this world durable. . . ."[14]

These three commentaries represent the extreme limit in
English Protestantism of the ascetic tendency as it relates to
marriage, for, in comparison with the bulk of thinking on the
subject, they are plainly exceptional concepts. Even Fuller, who
devotes a chapter in his treatise, *The Holy and Profane States*,
to "The Constant Virgin," switches the basis for any preference
of the celibate over the married state from a simply moral or
spiritual to a more nearly practical one. He writes: "She [the
'constant virgin'] chooseth not a single life solely for itself, but
in reference to the better serving of God. A single life is none
of those things to be desired in and for itself, but because it
leads a more convenient way to the worshipping of God, especially in time of persecution. For then, if Christians be forced
to run races for their lives, the unmarried have the advantage,
lighter by many ounces. . . . Yet in all her discourse she maketh
an honourable mention of marriage. And good reason that virginity should pay a chief rent of honor unto it, as acknowledging
herself to be a *colonia deducta* from it. . . ."[15]

It is the privilege and comfort rather than the self-sacrifice
and arduousness of virginity which Fuller emphasizes. He concludes his analysis by noting that "the way to heaven is alike
narrow to all estates, but far smoother to the virgin than to the
married."[16]

That marriage and celibacy are at least moral equivalents
and equally part of that general universe of indifferent things
which God decreed as the domain of Christian liberty is the
central and dominant theme of English Protestant thinking on
the subject. Of the monastic vows of both poverty and chastity,
Perkins complains that "they abolish Christian liberty in the
use of the creatures and ordinances of God, as riches, and marriage, meate, drinke, apparrell; making that necessarie which

[14] *Ibid.*, p. 48.
[15] Fuller, *Holy and Profane States*, pp. 56-57.
[16] *Ibid.*, p. 61.

God left to our libertie."[17] Proclaims Adams: "God honoured marriage, in making the first woman from Adam; and he honoured it againe, in marrying the best woman to Joseph. There is no such fountaine of comfort on earth, as marriage; whether for Societie, or for Posteritie. The marriage was contracted before his [Christ's] conception and solemnized before his Nativitie. Thus hee that would take flesh of a virgin, did yet grace marriage. . . . If the same God had not beene the authour and blesser of marriage as well as of virginitie, he would not have countenanced virginitie by marriage."[18]

Occasionally one finds a comment in this literature which more than accepts the moral equivalence of virginity and marriage—which suggests or asserts the superiority in godliness of the latter over the former state. Thus Perkins argues: "Marriage of its selfe is a thing indifferent, and the kingdom of God stands no more in it, then in meates and drinkes: and yet it is a state in itselfe, farre more excellent, then the condition of single life. For first, it was ordained by God in Paradise. . . . Again it was instituted upon a most . . . solemne consultation among the three persons in the holy Trinity. . . . Marriage was made . . . by God himselfe, to be the fountaine . . . of all other sorts and kindes of life, in the Commonwealth and in the Church."[19]

Rogers remarks that "God hath . . . given grace to them [who marry] either Minister or private person, more than to them, who in pride and hypocrisie, or in blinde intention have vowed against it."[20] Robinson is even more explicit in his preference for marriage as a pattern of Christian life. "God hath ordained marriage, amongst other good means," he writes, "for the benefit of man's natural and spiritual life." He rejects all implication of the peculiar value of virginity: ". . . this is, indeed, the very dregs of Popery, to place special piety in things either evil, or indifferent, at the best; as is abstinence from marriage, and the marriage bed; which is no more a virtue, than abstinence from wine, or other pleasing natural things. Both marriage and wine are of God, and good in themselves; either of them may in their

---

[17] Perkins, *Works*, I, 535.    [18] Adams, *Works*, p. 1234.
[19] *Works*, III, 671.
[20] Richard Rogers, *Seven Treatises* (1630), p. 233.

abuse, prejudice the natural or spiritual life: neither of them is unlawful, no not for them which simply need them not: which also not to need, argues bodily strength in the one, but a kind of weakness in the other."[21]

Marriage, then, as it is presented in English Protestant writings, has clearly advanced in moral status relative to its position in Thomistic Catholicism. Of this contrast in viewpoints English Protestants were well and perhaps excessively aware. Gataker declares: "Marriage is Honourable. . . . Yea so Honourable (saith Chrisostome) that a man may with it ascend to the Episcopall Chaire. . . . The Marriage Bed (saith the Apostle) is of itselfe free from filth. . . . What need they be ashamed (saith Chrisostome) of that that is honourable? . . . But saith the Spirit of Satan speaking by these Men or Beasts rather; Marriage is dishonourable: disabling men to holy offices. . . . And the Marriage Bed is filth, luxurie, uncleanesse, pollution, obsceneness, etc. And it is better for some men to commit Whoredome, than to contract Marriage. . . . A point . . . well-pleasing Whore-master Priests, who, instead of one wife, might have dealing with six hundred Harlots. . . . Thus they strive to dishonour that that God hath honoured, to disgrace that that he hath graced; preferring that before it . . . that God most of all detesteth and abhorreth."[22]

In English Protestantism vis-à-vis Roman Catholicism, more than this change in the evaluation of marriage has occurred, however: the character and function of marriage are also differently interpreted. Thomistic Catholicism, as we have seen, finds the primary, indeed, the sole essential purpose of marriage in its reproductive aspect; the companionable needs of man would be better served, declares St. Thomas himself, by association with another man. English Protestant divines, on the other hand, though of course they do not ignore the basic biological service of marriage, almost always couple with this service at least an equal and often a superior emphasis upon the importance of companionship between a man and wife. Thus Sandys declares that marriage was ordained by God first and most im-

[21] Robinson, *Works*, I, 239.
[22] Gataker, *A Good Wife* (1637), pp. 167-68.

portantly as an honourable estate for all mankind, in terms of the "mutual societie, helpe and comfort" which it affords.[23] Ussher maintains that the creation of Eve proves that "man is naturally desirous of the society of woman and therefore that Munkeries, Nunneries, and Hermitages are unnaturall, and consequently ungodly." He continues the argument in question and answer fashion: *"What is the end why she [woman] was made?* To be a help unto man. *Wherein?* First, in the things of this life by continuall society. . . . Secondly, in this life, for generation. . . . Thirdly, in the things of the life to come, even as they which are heirs together of the grace of life. And now a fourth use is added, to be a remedy against sin, which was not from the beginning."[24]

Gataker, in listing the functions performed by the "good wife" for her husband, similarly emphasizes her companionable over her biological role:
"A good wife being . . .
The best Companion in Wealth;
The fittest and readiest Assistant in worke;
The greatest comfort in crosses and griefes;
The onely warrantable and comfortable meanes of Issue and Posterity;
A singular and soveraigne Remedy Ordained by God against Incontinency;
And the greatest Grace and Honour that can be, to him that hath her."[25]

Gouge declares the ends of marriage to be three: first, propagation; secondly, the avoidance of fornication; and thirdly, "that man and wife might be a mutuall helpe one to another." The importance of this last condition is indicated by the variety of services which Gouge finds it involves: "An helpe as for bringing forth, so for bringing up children; and as for erecting, so for well governing the family. An helpe also for well ordering prosperity, and well bearing adversitie, an helpe in health and sicknesse. An helpe while both live together, and when one is

23 Sandys, *Sermons*, p. 279.
24 Ussher, *Divinitie*, pp. 106-07.
25 *Op.cit.*, p. 166.

by death taken from the other. . . . No such helpe can man have from any other creature as from a wife; or a woman, as from an husband."[26]

Though the sacramental character of marriage was denied by English Protestantism,[27] the bond of marriage was nonetheless assumed to be virtually unresolvable and the partnership between husband and wife properly to be life-long. Divorce was countenanced, but only on the single Scriptural basis of one partner having committed adultery. It is generally insisted that the right of divorce is equal in both partners, "for in regard of the bond of marriage," Perkins notes, "they are equally bound one to another."[28] There is a difference of opinion in this literature, however, as to whether the remarriage of the innocent partner in a divorce action should be sanctioned. Perkins himself is liberal in his interpretation of Scriptural provisions on the subject: "The phrases of Scripture used by the Holy Ghost concerning mariage after divorce, restraining it to some cases, and allowing it in others, seeme to take it for granted, that after lawfull divorce, it is no sinne to marrie againe. . . . The innocent partie is not to be punished for the wilfulnesse of the offender and therefore the partie that is faultlesse may with good conscience marrie again, after lawfull divorce."[29] John Reynolds writes an entire treatise defending this same proposition.[30] Andrewes, however, refuses to admit the legitimacy of a second marriage even for the innocent party, "for then it would follow, that the party offending would not, upon reconciliation, be received again by the innocent to former society of life, without a new solemnising of marriage insomuch as the former marriage is quite dissolved, which is never heard of and contrary to the practice of all Churches."[31]

In view of the concept currently abroad of the peculiar concern of all varieties of puritanism with sexual sins or with the general sinfulness of sex, it is interesting to observe how rela-

26 *Works*, I, 122-23.  27 E.g., *ibid.*, p. 72.
28 *Works*, III, 70.  29 *Ibid.*
30 John Rainolds, *A Defence of the Judgment of the Reformed Churches That a Man May Lawfullie Not Onelie Put Awaie His Wife for Her Adulterie, but Also Marrie Another* (1609). This was written in opposition to Bellarmine.
31 Andrewes, *Works*, XI, 106-07.

tively little these sermons emphasize such matters. It is accepted doctrine, naturally, that legitimate sexual activity must be confined entirely within the institutional boundaries of marriage. Yet the attitude toward sex in marriage is essentially positive. Perkins, for example, in insisting upon the equal spiritual value of all human acts which are performed in godliness and specifically by the godly, declares that "deedes of matrimonie are pure and spirituall . . . and whatsoever is done within the lawes of God though it bee wrought by the body, as the wipings of shoes and such like, howsoever grosse they appeare outwardly, yet are they sanctified."[32] In another treatise he does complain that "they abuse their libertie" who use "the marriage bedde intemperately."[33] In a stronger tone, Bolton cautions that the marriage bed "ought by no meanes to be stained . . . with sensuall excesses, wanton speeches, foolish dalliance." "Even in wedlock," he continues, "intemperate . . . lust; immoderation and excesse is deemed both by ancient and moderne Divines, no better than plaine adultery before God."[34] A sentence with similar import is contributed by Robinson. "As a man may . . . be drunken with his own wine," he writes, "so may he play the adulterer with his own wife . . . by inordinate affection and action."[35]

As is abundantly evident in these sermons, however, the only real concern with sex as sin is reserved for extra-marital sexuality, for fornication and especially for adultery; in both these instances it is as much the disturbance of social order involved as the simple sexuality which constitutes the heinousness of the sin. Nonetheless, there are certainly no stronger condemnations of the sin of adultery anywhere in Christian literature than in the writings of the English Protestantism of this period. Andrewes lists at length the many separate sins which, all combining in the breach of the marriage contract, constitute the peculiar viciousness of the act: "1. It [adultery] is of all sins most brutish, and maketh us come nearest the condition of beasts . . .

---

[32] *Works*, I, 391.     [33] *Ibid.*, p. 59.
[34] Bolton, *Works*, IV, 243.     [35] *Works*, I, 242.

"2. It taketh away the heart . . . it quite extinguisheth the light of reason . . .

"3. It is of all sins most inexcusable; other sins may have some vizard or colour, but God having ordained a remedy for this, which is marriage . . . he that will not use the remedy is without excuse.

"4. It is against the church; for whereas God made marriage an holy institution, and a resemblance of Christ and His Church, it is a contempt of the ordinance of God, by making it unholy and unclean . . .

"5. It is against the commonwealth . . .

"6. It is against the whole state of mankind; for whereas marriage is for increase of mankind, they that commit adultery shall not increase. . . ."[36]

The listing continues further, and at the end of the discussion Andrewes remarks that adultery is "forbidden Lev. XVIII. 20, and punished with death of both parties. . . . And though the politic laws of men have not made it so yet by the judgment of all divines, it is capital."[37]

Perkins also comments on the desirability of a capital penalty for so capital a crime: "Now if adulterie bee so grievous a sinne, worser then theft, etc. then, we must wish that in all places, it were so severely punished as theft is [that is, with the death penalty]; so would families be reformer, and become good Seminaries, both for Church and commonwealth."[38] The Old Testament's matching of the crime of adultery with the penalty of death is not, contends Downame, "a meere judiciall law . . . but a law of common equity."[39]

Yet, a gentler note is occasionally struck. Hall, for example, at some length and with great fervour, urges the husband of an adulterous wife to forgive his spouse her sin, if she has sincerely repented of it, and to restore the marital bond.[40] The same possibility of forgiveness and reconciliation lies at the root

---

[36] *Works*, II, 233-34.

[37] *Ibid.*, p. 245. For the sensational Essex divorce case which did little credit to the principles of Andrewes, Bilson, Neile, and Buckeridge, see Gardiner, *History of England*, II, 166-75.

[38] *Works*, III, 53-54.

[39] Downame, *A Treatise of Swearing* (1609), p. 187.

[40] Hall, *Works*, I, 328-29.

of Andrewes' objection to the remarriage of the innocent party in a divorce action.

Acts and behavior which cluster around and are assumed to contribute to illicit sexuality are subject to some scrutiny in this literature. Having pointed out that Christ saw fit in the Sermon on the Mount to condemn equally not only the overt act of adultery itself but the hidden desire to act, the mere looking at a woman to lust after her, Perkins moves then to include in this same category of condemnation a whole area of lascivious stimuli: Now, as looking to lust is here forbidden; so by proportion are all other like occasions unto adulterie: as first, reading of unchast and wanton books . . . using light and wanton talke. . . . Secondly, the acting of all such Plaies and Comedies, the matter whereof is the representation of the light behaviour of men and women. . . . Thirdly, the wearing of vaine and light attire, whereby others are provoked to cast their eyes upon them unto lust. . . . Fourthly, mixt dauncing of men and women . . . for therein is more occasion . . . unto lust. . . . Fifthly, evill companie. . . . Sixthly, the pampering of the bodie with daintie meates, or strong drinkes; this was the sinne of Sodome. . . . Seaventhly, Idlenesse and lazinesse, in not employing the body in some honest calling, for thereby also is lust incited."[41]

Ussher makes almost the same listing of enticements to lust (and hence to adultery) in dress and entertainment and warns the Christian against indulgence in them. His indictment of stage plays is particularly severe: ". . . Interludes, and Stage-Playes . . . offend against many branches of this Commandement [the seventh] . . . in the abuse of apparell, tongue, legs, countenance, gestures, and all parts almost of the body. For besides the wantonnesse herein used . . . the man putteth on the apparell of the woman, which is forbidden as a thing abominible . . . much filthinesse is presented to the beholders, and foolish talking, and jesting, which are not convenient. Lastly, Fornication, and all uncleannesse (which ought not to be once named among Christians) is made a spectacle of joy and laughter. . . ."[42]

41 *Works*, III, 54.
42 Ussher, *Divinitie*, p. 280.

Since Ussher, incidentally, cannot in any feasible definition of the group be included among the number of English Protestant "puritans," it is evident that in this concern with the sins of sexuality we are not dealing with any peculiarly "puritan" preoccupation. More important, however, is that in the literature as a whole, particularly when the absolutely immediate area of adultery is excepted, attention to such matters is of strictly minor significance in comparison with the space and condemnatory zeal devoted to almost any other type of sinful behavior which might be named—usury, for example.

### III. The Status of the Wife in the Family

In the absence of an ecclesiastical hierarchy divorced from family involvements, the family becomes for English Protestantism the basic social unit both for church and state. It is not only, as it had traditionally been in Christian thought, a "little commonwealth": it is also a "little church." Gouge remarks that "a family is a little Church, and a little commonwealth, whereby tryall may be made of such as are fit for any place of authority, or of subjection in Church or commonwealth. Or rather it is as a schoole wherein the first principles and grounds of government and subjection are learned. . . ."[43] In urging families to a regular performance of devotional duties in the home, Perkins declares that, "These families wherein this service of God is performed, are, as it were, little Churches, yea even a kinde of Paradise upon earth."[44]

The family is a little commonwealth, then, a little church, the first and primary school for training in all the aspects of a Christian life. In relation to its status in Thomistic Catholicism, moreover, the dignity of the family as a social institution is additionally enhanced by the English Protestant insistence that proper performance of the duties appertaining to one's place in the family is at least a worthy and virtually indispensable part of the total calling of every individual. Such duties can, and indeed for most members of the family customarily do, constitute the worldly calling in its entirety. As Gouge explains,

[43] *Works*, I, 610.  [44] *Works*, III, 670.

since the family as a school for church and commonwealth is an absolutely essential foundation of the total social welfare, "the private vocations of a family and functions appertaining thereto, are such as Christians are called unto by God, and in the exercising whereof, they may and must employ some part of their time." He further contends: "This is to be noted for satisfaction of certaine weake consciences, who thinke that if they have no publike calling, they have no calling at all . . . a conscionable performance of household duties in regard to the end and fruit thereof, may be accounted a publike worke. Yea, if domesticall duties be well and thoroughly performed, they will bee even enough to take up a man's whole time. . . . So a wife likewise, if she also be a mother and a mistris, and faithfully endeavour to doe what by virtue of those callings shee is bound to do, shall find enough to doe. As for children under the government of their parents and servants in a family, their whole calling is to be obedient to their parents and masters, and to doe what they command them in the Lord. Wherefore if they who have no publike calling, bee so much the more diligent in the functions of their private callings, they shall be as well accepted by the Lord, as if they had publike offices."[45]

English Protestantism assumes that the family, in being a "little commonwealth," will have a government, a structure of authority and subordination, within itself. Further, this government will properly correspond to the patriarchal pattern traditional in Western philosophy from the time of Aristotle. "A Family," says Perkins, "is a naturall and simple Societie of certaine persons, having mutuall relation one to another, under the private government of one."[46] The "one" in this case signifies the husband and father, and the subordination of wife to husband in household government is an absolutely universal postulate in this literature; this we shall shortly observe in greater detail.

But though the general outlines of this patriarchal theme may have been, at least until recently, an almost constant element in Western thought, time has subjected the view to various

45 *Works*, I, 10-11.
46 *Works*, III, 669.

manners of presentation and degrees of emphasis. Relative to
its statement in Aristotelianism and even in Thomistic Catholicism, for example, the theme in English Protestantism appears
to be definitely muted; and by regarding mutually-sustaining
companionship as a principal, if not the principal, end of marriage, it tends toward improvement of the wife's status. Indica-
tive of how far this modification of patriarchal dominance could
proceed is the reference in one English Protestant treatise on
family government to the single essential division in the family
between "the Governours" (husband and wife collectively) and
"those that must be ruled" (the children and the servants).[47]

Nonetheless, as the wife is considered in relation to the husband in these writings, her proper subordination to him is consistently maintained. Again and again, in treatises on the family
and incidentally in connection with other arguments, the Christian wife is reminded of her duty to be subject to her husband.
"The husband is he which hath authority over the wife," writes
Perkins, "they twaine beeing but one flesh, hee is also the head
over the wife."[48] Gataker comments that in the family "the
Husband is the superiour, and the wife the inferiour . . . the
Husband is as the head, the wife as the body."[49] "Many common
graces and good things are requisite both for husband and wife,"
Robinson declares, "but more especially the Lord requires in
the man love and wisdom; and in the woman subjection."[50]

The traditional Christian view is followed, too, in the conception that the wife's subjection to the husband is not merely
a punitive subjection—the product of Eve's greater transgression
in the engendering of the Fall—but is a natural subjection as
well—the product of a basic and God-decreed inferiority in the
structure and status of the female which is signified by the
woman's secondary or derivative creation. Field explains: "Yet
because the man was not of the woman, but the woman of the
man; the man was not created for the woman, but the woman
for the man, who is the glory of God, the woman's head and
every way fittest to be chiefe commaunder in the whole Family

---

[47] Dod and Cleaver, *A Godlie Forme of Householde Government*, p. 30.
[48] *Works*, III, 691.
[49] *Marriage Duties* (1637), p. 188.     [50] *Works*, I, 240.

and household. Hereupon Adam the father of all the living, was appointed by the God that made him, to instruct, guide, and direct those that should come of him, even in the state of nature's integritie. . . . And when he had broken the Law of his Creator . . . and recomforted with the promise, that the seede of the woman should breake the Serpents head: he was to teach his children the same thing and [was] sanctified to be both a King to rule in the little world of his owne Family: and a Priest, as well to manifest the will of God to them of the same."[51]

Robinson likewise notes that the second source of woman's subjection to man—Eve's transgression—did not create or establish the yoke she wears but merely made it painful: "The woman in innocency was to be subject to the man: but this should have been without all wrong on his part, or grief on hers. But she being first in transgression . . . hath brought herself under another subjection, and the same to her more grievous; and in regard of her husband, often unjust; but in regard of God, always most just; who hath ordained that her desire should be subject to her husband . . . who by her seduction became subject to sin."[52]

Thus the assumption in English Protestantism is, first, that the husband's dominance in the family is founded on a differentiation in nature between men and women, so that one sex is suited for rule and another for subjection. The inferiority of female nature, however, is more a matter of fragmentary statements and occasional phrases in these sermons than of careful analysis. Women are commonly called the weaker sex, but the exact quality of this weakness is never precisely defined. Hooker, in speaking of women, refers to "the imbecility of their nature and sex," but examines the issue no further.[53] Perkins points to the greater "outward excellence and dignitie in the person of a man then of a woman."[54] Robinson touches on the difference in capacity between the sexes when he writes: ". . . the husband must walk with his wife as a man of understanding . . . which God hath therefore afforded him, and means of obtaining it, above the woman, that he might guide and go before

51 Field, *Of the Church*, p. 410.   52 *Works*, I, 241.
53 *Polity*, v, 73, v.   54 *Works*, I, 151.

her, as a fellow heir of eternal life with him. It is monstrous, if the head stand where the feet should be. . . . Yea, experience teacheth how inconvenient it is, if the woman have but a little more understanding (though he be not wholly without) than her husband hath."[55]

Bolton similarly observes that "the husband by the benefit of a more manly body; tempered with naturall fitnesse for the soule to worke more nobly in; doth, or ought ordinarily outgoe the wife in largenesse of understanding, height of courage . . . moderation of his passions, dexterity to manage businesses, and other naturall inclinations and abilities to doe more excellently. . . ."[56]

Though it is commonly assumed that the inferior status of women is associated with some type of inferiority in femininity as such, the status is also seen as an institutional entity in itself, without reference to the qualities of the persons involved. In counselling wives to honor their husbands, for example, Gouge reminds them that this honor is due regardless of the adequacy or inadequacy of the particular husband to whom it is rendered. The office must be honored, even when the person cannot be. He further states: "For the evil quality and disposition of his heart and life, doth not deprive a man of that civill honour which God hath given unto him. Though an husband in regard of evill qualities may carry the Image of the divell, yet in regard of his place and office, he beareth the Image of God: so doe Magistrates in the Commonwealth, Ministers in the Church, Parents and Masters in the Family."[57]

Gataker likewise admonishes the wife "in holy wisedome and godly discretion to learne to know her place and her part . . . yea though she be herselfe of a greater spirit, and in some respect of better parts, though she bring much with her . . . yet to acknowledge her husband as God hath appointed him, to bee her superiour as he is her husband and her head."[58]

Where it is noted in the literature, the confinement of women to a status of virtually perpetual minority, established in the law of the time and particularly exemplified in the limitations upon

[55] *Op.cit.*, 240.   [56] *Works*, IV, 245.
[57] *Works*, I, 160.   [58] *Marriage Duties*, pp. 189-90.

a woman's right to hold or control property, meets with nothing but approval. Thus Gouge remarks at length: ". . . neither the law of Nations, nor of the land where we live give the wife a property. By the common law mariage is a gift of all the goods and chattels personall of the wife to her husband, so that no kinde of property in the same remaineth in her. And all personal goods and chattels during mariage given to the wife, are presently *ipso facto* transferred . . . to the husband. . . . Yea, her necessary apparell is not hers in property. While shee remaineth a wife, she is (to use the law phrase) *under covert baron*. She can neither let, sell, alien, give, nor otherwise of right make anything away . . . while her husband liveth without his consent. . . . This restraint of wives . . . is not against the law of God. . . . Nay, it is agreeable to the Law of God, and grounded thereupon."[59]

So thoroughgoing in this literature is the statement of the woman's inferiority to the man and of the wife's subjection to her husband that it hardly seems possible that a more extreme formulation of the viewpoint could be made. Yet, as one carefully compares this doctrine on the nature of woman and the status of the wife with that enunciated by the spokesman of medieval Roman Catholicism, St. Thomas Aquinas, one finds that English Protestant opinion contains definite and significant elements of liberalization. It must be assumed that St. Thomas accepts the universal Christian concept that a kind of basic spiritual equality exists between man and woman since salvation is available to both sexes. Yet he makes such extensive use of the sharp and invidious Aristotelian distinction between the masculine and feminine natures as, logically speaking, to bring into question his support of even so primary a Christian tenet. Moreover, save for one comment to the effect that some women are more virtuous than many men,[60] we know of no passage in his works where he labors to correct the impression that the social, intellectual, and physiological inferiority of women, which he so strongly stresses and so richly illustrates, leads to or entails a spiritual inferiority as well.

[59] *Works*, I, 175.
[60] *Sum. Theol.*, III (Supplement) q. 39, a. 1, ad. 1.

English Protestant writers do not state the natural inferiority of women so extremely. In the effort to marshal evidence of women's inferiority, they make absolutely no reference, for example, to the thoroughgoing debasement of the sex which the Aristotelian viewpoint involves; instead, they employ exclusively the concepts of the Old and New Testaments, which are philosophically much more moderate. To be sure, English Protestantism conceives that some degree or type of natural inferiority distinguishes the woman from the man and that this inferiority is properly reflected in the wife's subordination to her husband. But many of the comments on woman's natural as well as institutional inferiorities tend more to minimize than to maximize these differences, and the natural inferiority in particular is often so vaguely defined or so understated as virtually to disappear. Thus Gouge, staunch upholder of patriarchal supremacy though he is, speaks of "that small inequality which is betwixt the husband and wife." He continues: ". . . for of all degrees wherein there is any difference betwixt person and person, there is the least disparity betwixt man and wife. Though the man be as the head, yet is the woman as the heart, which is the most excellent part of the body next the head, farre more excellent than any other member under the head, and almost equall to the head in many respects, and as necessary as the head. As an evidence, that a wife is to man as the heart to the head, shee was at her first creation taken out of the side of man where his heart lieth; and though the woman was at first of the man created out of his side, yet is the man also by the woman. Ever since the first creation man hath been borne and brought forth out of the woman's wombe. . . . Besides, wives are mothers of the same children, whereof they are fathers . . . and mistresses of the same servants whereof they are master . . . and in many other respects there is common equity betwixt husbands and wives. . . ."[61]

Lest such ascription of women's natural inferiority be thought to imply any degree of spiritual inferiority as well, English Protestants carefully assert the opposite. Perkins briefly notes

[61] *Op.cit.*, p. 160.

that "holinesse and righteousness" are not peculiar to men alone but are common to men and women alike, and that both sexes are equally the image of God in this regard.[62] Adams develops the same theme more fully: "The woman hath many adversaries, that disdaine her competition with man. Some will not allow her a soule; but they bee soulelesse men. God *in his Image created them*, not *Him* onely, but him and *Her*. . . . Some will not allow her to be saved; yet the Scripture is plaine; *Shee shall be saved by child-bearing*. . . . Though Christ honoured our sex, in that he was a man, not a woman: yet hee was borne of a woman, and was not begot of a man. And howsoever wicked women prove the most wicked sinners: yet the worst and greatest crime that ever was done, was committed by man, not by woman; the crucifying of our Lord Jesus; not a woman had a hand in it. . . . In a word, God in his Image created them both on earth, and God in his mercy hath provided them both a place in heaven."[63]

Bolton, after having spoken of the male's superiority in mentality and physique, immediately reminds the masculine reader that "his wife hath as noble a soul as himself." He continues: "*Soules have no Sexes*, as Ambrose saith. In the better part they are both men. And if thy wives soule were freed from the frailty of her sexe, it were as manly, as noble, as understanding, and every way as excellent as thine own. . . . Let the husband then be so farre from . . . contemning his wives worth, for the weaknesse of her sexe; that out of consideration that her soule is naturally every as good as his owne; onely the excellencie of its native operations, something damped, as it were, and disabled by the frailty of that weaker body, with which God's wise providence hath clothed it upon purpose, for a more convenient and comfortable . . . serviceableness to his good; that I say, hee labour the more to entertaine and intreat her with all tendernesse and honour, to recompence, as it were, her suffering in this kinde for his sake."[64]

Sibbes even ventures to suggest that women tend in general to be more responsive than men to the appeal and stimulation

[62] *Works*, I, 151.   [63] *Works*, pp. 1133-1134.
[64] *Works*, IV, 245-46.

of religion, thus indicating a kind of spiritual superiority as a sex; he writes: "For the most part women have sweet affections to religion, and therein they oft goe beyond men. The reason is, Religion is especially seated in the affections: And they have sweet and strong affections. Likewise they are subject to weaknesse, and God delights to shew his strength in weaknesse. And thirdly, especially child-bearing women bring others into this life with danger of their own, therefore they are forced to a nearer communion with God, because so many children as they bring forth, they are in peril of their lives."[65]

In the Thomistic argument, on the other hand, the spiritual status of women is further weakened, for his entire system of thought tends to imply the existence of a close and mutually-sustaining relationship between virtue and authority. As the representative of a firmly-established, hierarchical church in a stable and hierarchical society, he tends not only to prescribe that there should be, but also to find that actually there is, a positive correlation between the virtues of an individual and his position or authority. As we have already frequently observed, complacency of this sort in regard to the parallelism of social and spiritual hierarchies is by no means a characteristic of the English Protestant literature we are studying. In his analysis of the husband and wife relationship, Gouge, for one, specifically denies the appropriateness of any such linkage between dignity and virtue: "A wives subjection to her husband, answerable to the Churches subjection unto Christ, is an evidence that shee is of the Church guided by the same Spirit that the Church is. For it cannot bee performed by the power of nature, it is a supernaturall worke, and so an evidence of the Spirit.

"Wherefore, O Christian wives, as your husbands by their place resemble Christ, so doe you by your practise resemble the Church. Of the two this is the more commendable: for that is a dignity, this a vertue. But true vertue is much more glorious than any dignity can be."[66]

In establishing a terminus to the inferiority of the wife, St. Thomas does no more than refer to the Aristotelian dictum

[65] Sibbes, *Riches of Mercie*, pp. 9-10.
[66] *Op.cit.*, p. 201.

that a wife is not a slave. Though one may assume that as a
Christian he always intends that any human authority he establishes or confirms shall be viewed as subordinate to and hence
limited by the supreme authority of God, nowhere does St.
Thomas specifically apply this cautionary principle to a husband's authority or a wife's subjection. English Protestant ministers, on the other hand, who concern themselves with analysis
of the domestic proprieties, usually note carefully that a wife's
duty to her husband must be defined within the context of her
superior duty to God. There is a "restraint" on wifely obedience,
says Gouge, consisting in the fact that wives "may not be subject
in any way to their husbands that cannot stand with their subjection to the Lord."[67] A wife's submission, Gataker observes,
must be understood in terms of the necessary limitation "that
it extend not itselfe to anything against the Will and Word of
God."[68] And Downame comments that "the husbands government and the wives subjection must be in the Lord . . . if he
commandeth what God forbiddeth, or forbiddeth what God
commandeth, he is not to be obeyed."[69]

A more important instance of how the English Protestant
sermons differ from Aquinas' writings on the status of women
is to be found in the discussion of wife-beating. We have seen
in that last section of the *Summa Theologica*—which was completed by a disciple after the death of St. Thomas, but presumably on the basis of notes which he had left—that the husband is granted the right to chastise his wife corporally; indeed,
his authority over her is limited only by the absence of the
power of life and death. Wherever the issue is raised in English
Protestant literature, however, this right is emphatically denied
to the husband. Perkins, for example, having queried "whether
the husband may correct the wife," replies to his own question
in this manner: "Though the husband bee the wives head, yet
it semeth he hath no power nor libertie granted him in this
regard. For we read not in the Scriptures any precept or example
to warrant such practise of his authoritie. He may reproove and

[67] *Ibid.*, p. 16.
[68] Gataker, *Marriage Duties*, p. 197.
[69] Downame, *The Plea of the Poore* (1616), p. 109.

admonish her in word onely, if he seeth her in fault. . . . But he may not chastise her either with stripes or stroakes."[70]

Gouge makes an essentially identical statement[71] and Fuller comments, concerning the Christian husband's treatment of his wife, that "all hard using of her he detests, desiring therein to doe, not what may be lawful but fitting. And grant her to be of a servile nature, such as may be bettered by beating; yet he remembers he hath enfranchised her by marrying her. On her wedding day she was, like St. Paul, free born, and privileged from any servile punishment."[72]

It would at first glance appear impossible to increase or exceed the scope and rigidity of the English Protestant position on the wife's inability to own or control property. But even in this area St. Thomas had succeeded in extending patriarchal authority beyond the generous boundaries drawn by English Protestantism: he had specifically denied the wife's right to give alms out of community property without the explicit consent of her husband. Though the general tenor of English Protestant assertions on the husband's supremacy in the control of property might suggest that the wife is at least discouraged from doing otherwise, she is nowhere specifically forbidden. In the single instance where the issue is discussed, moreover, a strong opposition to this conservative view is registered. Thus Downame writes: ". . . God the first Instituter of mariage, gave the wife unto the husband, to bee, not his servant, but his helper, counsellor and comforter. The which duties she is bound to performe, not onely in respect of temporall affaires, but also of those things which appertaine to godlinesse and everlasting happiness; and therefore if hee neglect religious and charitable duties, shee is not onely bound to moove and persuade him unto them, but also, if hee still neglect them, to doe them herselfe for him, lest the sinne and punishment be not onely upon him, but also upon her and the whole familie."[73]

[70] Works, III, 692.
[71] Op.cit., pp. 224-25.
[72] Holy and Profane States, p. 35.
[73] Downame, op.cit., pp. 119-20. But for the decline of women's property rights in common law—a decided regression from female legal status in Canon law—see Holdsworth, op.cit., III, 185-98, 520-33; VII, 376-81.

We have previously seen Aquinas' argument, which follows the lead of Aristotle, on the duty of a child toward his parents: since in conception and generation the father is the active principle, giving the child its form, and the mother the passive, providing only its material substance, it is the duty of the child to love and honor the father more than the mother, the formal cause being in all senses superior to the material. The one English Protestant who touches on this subject, John Gouge, specifically denies the Thomistic thesis. He writes: "The first point then to be noted is, that children beare an equall respect to both their naturall parents, and performe duty to both alike. The law expressly mentioneth both, *Honour thy Father and thy Mother.* . . . Many reasons there be to inforce this point.

"1. Both Parents are under God, a like meanes of their children's being. Children come out of the substance of both alike.

"2. The care and paines of both for the good of the children is very great . . . one way or other the childe is equally bound to both and accordingly God's law maketh no difference betwixt them . . .

"Though there be a difference betwixt father and mother in relation to one another, yet in relation to their children they are both as one, and have a like authority over them."[74]

Though, as we have seen, English Protestants continue to maintain the patriarchal pattern long established in Christianity by affirming the chief magistracy of the husband in the household, a subordinate magistracy for the wife is also clearly defined and certainly more fully developed as a theme than in Thomistic literature. Gouge declares that "in generall the government of the family, and of the severall members thereof, belongeth to the husband and wife and both." To support his viewpoint that wives ought to participate in such government, he notes that St. Paul "layeth it expressly to their charge that they *governe the house.*"[75] And Perkins declares: "The Goodwife or Mistresse of the house is a person which yieldeth helpe . . . in government to the master of the familie. For he is . . . the prince and chiefe ruler; she is the associate, not onely in

74 *Op.cit.*, p. 274.
75 *Ibid.*, p. 151.

office and authoritie, but also in advise and counsell unto him."[76]

The whole emphasis upon companionship between husband and wife as a principal, if not the principal, function and goal of marriage—a prominent element in these English Protestant sermons, as we have observed—contributes to this view of the wife as a coadjutor of her husband and an effective deputy in the management of family affairs. The companionship of marriage, moreover, is seen as an active and not a passive entity; it is a mutually sustaining partnership in work and enterprise. For wifehood is a calling, the English Protestant maintains, with a multitude of tasks attached which are sufficient to keep a Christian woman fully and honorably occupied through all her days. Concerning the nature of the woman's calling, Gataker writes: "It is no shame . . . for a woman to be house-wifely, be she never as well-borne, bee she never so wealthy.

"For it is the woman's trade to be; it is the end of her creation; it is that that she was made for. She was made for man and given to man, not to be a play-fellow or a bed-fellow, or a table-mate, onely with him (and yet to be all these too) but to bee a yoake-fellow, a work-fellow, a fellow-labourer with him, to be an assistant and an helper unto him, in the managing of such domesticall and household affaires . . .

"Art thou to make any choise of a wife? Choose thee an house-wife. It is no shame for thee though thou beest welthy, to seeke her at the wash-house. . . . Seeke her at the needle, at the wheele, at the spindle. It is no disgrace for any to be found and taken at such imployments."[77]

Again, in a fashion which serves well to climax and to close this topic, Gataker proclaims the function of wife as helpmate: "It is not Good, saith God, for man to bee alone; I will make him an Helpe, or an Assistant; not a mate onely, but an helper; not a companion onely, but an assistant too. Man being a creature of the kinde, not of those that love onely to a flocke . . . and live together . . . but of those that desire to combine and

---

[76] *Works*, III, 70.

[77] *A Marriage Prayer* (1637), p. 128. In Berthold of Regensburg's catalogue of vocations for the Catholic world (*op.cit.*) it should be noted that the work of the woman in the home is completely ignored; it has not the status of a vocation.

worke and labour also together. . . . Now behold here a fit, and
a ready helpe. . . . For who fitter to help man, than shee whom
God himselfe hath fitted for man and made for this very end
to be a fit helpe for him? I will make him such an helpe saith
God, as shall be meet for him: one that shall bee as his match
. . . one that [is] in all parts and abilities in a manner as himselfe. . . . And certainely as there are offices not a few, that none
can in many cases so fitly performe about a man, as a wife may:
so there is no helpe that he hath, or ordinarily can have, so ready
at all times at this helpe. . . ."[78]

In eliminating the monastic pattern of life, English Protestantism, like Protestantism in general, did close off to women an
alternative to marriage and a road to prestige available to Roman Catholic women. Moreover, English Protestantism was no
less adamant than the earlier Christian creed in forbidding to
women the performance of routine ecclesiastical functions. In
fact, it may be that in insisting upon the impropriety of baptism by lay persons, English Protestantism more decisively excluded women from the ecclesiastical area than Roman Catholicism had done. Perkins observes that "it is not warrantable by
God's word for a woman to administer the sacrament of baptism," and he confirms the further prohibition that "women . . .
are not allowed to preach, no not in . . . case of necessitie, when
men are wanting."[79] "And for women," Robinson similarly declares, "they are debarred by their sex, as from ordinary proph-
esying, so from any other dealing [in the church] wherein they
take authority over the man."[80]

Yet even in this highly conservative area of English Protestant
thought, there is evidence of a significantly greater liberalism
than characterized the Roman Catholic viewpoint. Perhaps the
most important single change in this direction is the diminu-
tion in concern for women's ritual uncleanness. This concern
is incident upon Protestantism's rejection of the ascetic tradition
and its higher evaluation, relative to Roman Catholicism, of
human sexuality as a whole. A significant symbolic indication

[78] *A Good Wife*, pp. 161-62.
[79] *Works*, III, 313-14.
[80] *Works*, II, 215.

of this change can be found in the total redefinition in the Anglican liturgy of the meaning of the ceremony of churching: from a rite of purification in the Judaistic pattern it became an expression simply of thanksgiving.[81] The status of women in religious life is also enhanced by the general agreement among English Protestant divines that it is the responsibility and privilege of wives to share with their husbands in the supervision of domestic devotions. Perkins explains that, where the truths of religion are concerned, "although [a woman] may not teach publikely, yet [she] may teach at home, and in the absence of [her] husband, it is her duty to teach her children."[82] Even more generous in attributing religious functions to women is this statement by Robinson, with which he would appear to qualify considerably the Pauline dictum commanding women to silence in the church; also qualified is his own judgment about the issue, quoted above: ". . . they [women] may make profession of faith, or confession of sin, say amen to the church's prayers, sing psalms vocally, accuse a brother of sin, witness an accusation, or defend themselves being accused, yea, in a case extraordinary, namely where no man will, I see not but a woman may reprove the church, rather than suffer it to go on in apparent wickedness, and communicate with it therein. . . . Neither is there respect of person with God in the common duties of Christianity."[83]

But then Robinson ultimately became a separatist, and Protestant separatists and sectarians tended to be notably more responsive to the religious capacities of women as a sex than were the great established bodies of Protestantism.[84]

## IV. The Status of the Child in the Family

Characteristic of English Protestant as compared with Roman Catholic thought was a general increase in the prestige and significance of the family unit. Where the wife and mother gained in this change, the child can perhaps be said to have lost somewhat in social stature and independence.

[81] See Hooker, *Polity*, v, 74.    [82] *Works*, III, 314.
[83] *Works*, II, 215-16.
[84] See K. V. Thomas, "Women and the Civil War Sects," *Past and Present* (April, 1958).

In the Roman Catholic system, the church was so distinct and so supremely important an institution that the child was encouraged to find in it a focus of loyalty superior even to the family in its force to command allegiance. Hence in Catholicism the child was free, as it were, to choose between two areas of duty. St. Thomas Aquinas specifically grants to a minor the right to enter a religious order with or without parental consent,[85] and in the event of the church's solemnization of a marriage, that marriage is held valid even in the face of parental opposition.[86]

In English Protestantism, on the other hand, the child's primary and almost his only circle of society is the family; and within the family his subordination to parental dictate and guidance is strenuously affirmed. There is a total absence of institutional resource for the expression of rebellion against parental authority. Indeed, such rebellion is seen to constitute as profound a crime as any of which human nature is capable; yet, also, it is seen as a crime to which human nature is especially prone. Robinson observes: ". . . surely there is in all children, though not alike, a stubbornness, and stoutness of mind arising from natural pride, which must . . . be broken and beaten down; that so the foundation of their education being laid in humility and tractableness, other virtues may, in their time, be built thereon. This fruit of natural corruption and root of actual rebellion both against God and man must be destroyed."[87]

The child's propensity to rebelliousness, urge and command numerous English Protestant divines, must be checked by the frequent application of corporal punishment. "He that will not use the rod on his child," Fuller warns, "his child shall be used as a rod on him."[88] In considering the possibility of the child's "refusing or abusing correction," Gouge extends parental discipline to the ultimate severity and repeats the Calvinistic dictum that children who are obstinate in resistance to their elders incur the proper penalty of death: ". . . when they will be no whit bettered [by correction], but still run on in their lewd

[85] *Sum. Theol.*, II-II, q. 189, a. 6, c.
[86] *Sum. Theol.*, III (Supplement), q. 47, a. 6, c.
[87] *Works*, I, 247-48.     [88] *Op.cit.*, p. 40.

courses, and rather waxe the worse for being corrected. This may be counted the highest pitch of a child's rebellion: for this is the last meanes which a parent can use to reclaime his childe from desperate courses. If this prevaileth not, the law of God requireth, that a parent should give up his childe into the hand of the Magistrate, that he may be put to death."[89]

Perkins appeals to the Pauline injunction, "Now I say that the heir, as long as he is a child, differeth nothing from a servant" (Gal. 4:1), as a basis for this further comment: ". . . the father hath authoritie to dispose of his childe. This is the law of Nature, and the law of Nations . . . children in respect of their bodies, are the goods of their parents. In this respect the Jews are permitted to sell their children, Exod. 21:7. And so sacred a thing was the authoritie of the parent, that he which rebelliously despised the same, was put to death."[90]

In specific applications of such general decrees regarding parents' authority, however, qualifications and variations tend to emerge in these writings, and the apparent absolute becomes the actual relative. In two areas of discussion may this process be observed at work: in the analysis of how properly to choose a marriage partner and a calling. In the first choice, the usual assumption is that parental consent is not merely desirable but absolutely necessary to a valid marriage. The strongest statement to this effect is Perkins': "In the marriage of the child the parent is the principall agent, and the disposer thereof . . . the parent hath authoritie . . . to give and bestow his childe, and to take wives to his sonnes. . . . Whether the father may command his childe to marrie? *Ans.* Presuppose two things; one, that the commandement is without compulsion: the second, that the father knows what is for the good of the child: then I answer, that he may command his child to marry, and to marry a person thus or thus qualified. . . . Whether a marriage made without and against the consent of parents, be a marriage or no? *Ans.* It may be called a politicke or civill marriage, because it is ratified in the courts of men, according to humane lawes, and by this meanes the issue is freed from bastardy. Neverthelesse it is not

89 *Op.cit.*, p. 263.
90 *Works*, II, 269.

a divine or spirituall conjunction or mariage (as it ought to be) because it is flat against the commandement of God."[91]

In the course of his argument on this subject, Perkins takes pains to point out "the impietie of the Roman religion," for in the family "it puts downe the authority of the father: for it ratifieth clandestine contracts."[92] He sums up his viewpoint with the unqualified assertion that "the consent of parents, that is of father and mother, I hold it requisite of necessitie to mariage: for the authoritie of parents must not be resisted or violated."[93]

Though Perkins does hedge round and considerably limit his grant of power to parents to command a marriage, he appears to reserve to them an absolute right to forbid a marriage of which they disapprove. The rigor and detail of his statement on this subject are, however, exceptional in the literature. One does find occasional brief comments of a similar tone, such as Dod's remark that "every Christian childe must bee his father's servant . . . especially in mariage."[94] The official ecclesiastical position on this issue was considerably milder and terminated parental privilege at an "age of consent," as is indicated by the following item in a list of inquiries to be made of parish clergy by supervisory visitors: "Whether hath your Minister, either with License or without, married any . . . before their parents and governors (the parties being under the age of twenty-one years) have testified their consent?[95] Furthermore, though Hall strongly commends the desirability of parental consent in marriage, he maintains that a marriage without such consent must be considered valid, not only legally but in the eyes of God.[96]

Even while preaching children's obedience to parental wishes in the choice of marriage partners, English Protestant divines command parents to consider carefully "the natural inclination of their children" in such matters.[97] Dod points out that parents must know that "they have not this rule and authoritie over their children that they may chuse whether they will let them

[91] *Ibid.*    [92] *Ibid.*    [93] *Works*, III, 684.
[94] Dod, *Ten Commandements*, p. 193.
[95] Andrewes, *Works*, XI, 117.
[96] *Works*, IV, 845.    [97] Dod, *op.cit.*, p. 203.

marrie or no, or when they list, and whom they list: but . . . that they have rule over their children under the Lord. . . . Now God . . . commandeth them to permit . . . every one to marrie that is disposed to marrie."[98] Gataker makes a particularly eloquent plea to the same effect: "A Father may finde out a fit wife, and thinke such a one a meet match for his Sonne: and her Parents may bee also of the same minde with him . . . and yet it may be, when they have done all they can, they cannot fasten their affections. As Faith, so Love cannot be constrained. As there is no affection more forcible; so there is none freer from force and compulsion. The very offer of enforcement turneth it off into hatred. There are secret lincks of affection, that no reason can be rendred of: as there are inbred dislikes, that can neither be resolved, nor reconciled. When Parents have long beaten the bush, another oft, as we say, catcheth the bird: affections are set some other way, and cannot bee removed."[99]

A companion to the problem of the child's marriage is that of his placement in a calling. Here, too, one finds the double and to some extent contradictory emphasis: first, on the primary authority and responsibility of the parents, and second, on a proper concern for the inclinations and aptitudes of the child. "Touching the callings of children," Perkins remarks, "they are to be ordered . . . at the discretion of parents"; again he calls attention to the "impietie" of the Roman church in its giving "liberty to children past 12 or 14 yeares of age, to enter into any order of Religion [and hence into a self-chosen calling] against the consent of their parents."[100]

Yet even Perkins, that particular champion of parental privilege, having enunciated a rule concerning callings—"Every man must choose a fit calling to walke in; that is, every calling must be fitted to the man, and every man . . . to his calling"—then cautions parents to pay due heed to the abilities and interests of the child himself. "Parents cannot do greater wrong to their children, and the societie of men," he says, "then to apply them

[98] Dod and Cleaver, *A Godlie Forme*, pp. 316-17.

[99] *A Good Wife*, p. 138. It is interesting to contrast the Protestant emphasis on love in marriage with the "Courts of Love" and love-in-adultery traditions of chivalric ethics.

[100] *Works*, II, 269.

unto unfit callings . . . for this is as much, as . . . to set the members of the bodie out of their proper places."[101] When parents choose a profession for their children, declares Fuller in a similar vein, they must follow the children's own inclinations, for "when they set Abel to till the Ground, and send Cain to keep sheep . . . drive some to school and others from it, they do violence to nature, and it will thrive accordingly."[102]

Thus, though these sermons provide children no institutional resource to which to turn when there is conflict between them and their parents, English Protestant divines are certainly free enough with cautioning and moderating advice to parents so that, if such advice were respected and followed, parental guidance might continue but parental tyranny would be avoided. Aptly illustrating this policy of hedging parental authority with moral restraints is the following commentary by Gouge upon a text from Paul, "And ye fathers provoke not your children to wrath" (Eph. 6:4): *"Parents are as well bound to duty as children* . . . though parents bee over their children, and by them cannot bee commanded, yet they are under God: and he it is who hath enjoyned them their duty . . .

"The authority which parents have, is not so much for their owne advancement, as for the better governing of their children, which being so, their very government is a duty. . . . Wherefore let Ministers follow this patterne of the Apostle, and carry an even hand towards all of all sorts: let them not be partiall in laying all burden on children's necks, and none on parents . . . Parents are flesh and bloud as well as children, and as prone to transgresse in their place, as children in theirs. Yea, Ministers ought of the two to be more earnest in urging parents to performe their duty, because they are under no such power and authority as children are. Feare of parents authority keepeth children much in awe. There is no such thing to keepe parents in awe. They will be more ready therefore to take the greater liberty, if by feare of God, and by a good conscience, they bee not kept in compasse."[103]

[101] *Works*, III, 758-59.
[102] *Op.cit.*, p. 41.
[103] *Op.cit.*, p. 88. The good divines of England were as concerned about the duty of maternal breast feeding (no wet-nursing) of infants as was Rousseau later

## V. The Status of the Servant in the Family

Within this literature, almost the entire discussion on the status of the servant and of the general condition of servitude takes place in the context of the analysis of family relationships. It is assumed, on one hand, that the family, whose structure and proper functioning the English Protestant is concerned with, will include servants; on the other, it is assumed that the servants will be part—albeit the least and lowest part—of the family community. This domestic focus of the subject of servitude is more wholesale and precise than in either Aquinas or Aristotle. It clearly indicates that it is the hired family servant rather than the slave or serf whom the English Protestant has primarily in mind in his pronouncements on the nature of the role.

Too well-known to require elaboration is the Aristotelian concept of the division of mankind: into the small elite who are by nature free and the vast majority who are by nature slave (even though, regrettably, natural truth had not always been confirmed by historical circumstance). The slave, moreover, is strictly instrumental: he exists only as a means to the good of the master; he has and can have no end or purpose within himself. Though the Christian division between the saved and damned was as sharp, and in some senses as given or assigned, a division as Aristotle's, there was a complete shift in the ground and appurtenances of this division; and, initially at least, Christianity rejected any possibility of a linkage between the worldly condition of an individual and the eternal destiny of his soul. St. Paul and subsequently maturing Christianity recognized the validity of slavery as a social institution, but the reflection of any natural and, above all, spiritual inferiority in the status of slavery was specifically denied.

As we have repeatedly observed, it must be assumed that Aquinas embraced, at least implicitly, the basic concepts of Christian theology. One such concept is that even those who wear the worldly livery of a slave may wear the crown of spiritu-

and as are our Freudians now. See Ussher, *Divinitie*, p. 262; Perkins, *Works*, III, 693; Bolton, *Works*, IV, 198; Pricke, *The Doctrine of Superioritie* (1609); Dod, *Ten Commandements*, p. 200; Smith, *Sermons*, p. 28.

ality. Yet in his explicit commentary Aquinas moves toward a surprising contiguity with Aristotle. Due in part, no doubt, to his own emergence from and acceptance of an hierarchical and status-involved society, Aquinas may be said to embody a compromise between the tendency toward social equalitarianism, found in initial and basic Christianity, and the intensive inequalitarianism—whose rankings directly coincide with a particular ethnocentric bias—of Aristotelian philosophy. For example, Aquinas finds the source of servitude (whether of serf or slave) not in perfect but in fallen nature. It is a state which in one sense is not natural to man but is the product of sin. Yet for the present and observable world, he clearly accepts the Aristotelian distinction between those who are by nature free and those who are slave. He does admit, as Aristotle did, that some who are not slaves by nature are so by circumstance; but he appears to believe confidently that the great majority of those who in his time and place are institutionally slaves or serfs are so in accord with their natural deficiencies.

Since, as he must, he grants to the serf or slave the possession of an immortal soul which is potentially capable of salvation, Aquinas cannot retain Aristotle's completely instrumental view of slavery. Self-contained within the slave as well as the master is an end or purpose superior to any other that may be served. Hence it is logically necessary for St. Thomas to argue that the condition of the natural slave is good, not for the master alone but also for the slave: the latter in his weakness can be guided and helped by the wisdom of the former and thus both may more readily arrive at their salvation. Still, the capacity of the natural slave is asserted by St. Thomas, as by Aristotle, to be less than that of any other grouping of mankind (specifically less than that of the free-born woman, for example). In such a system, where capacity tends to be so closely linked to good deeds and good deeds to virtue and virtue at last to salvation, the share of the serf or slave in salvation (like the share of the woman) would appear to be directly diminished as basic capacity is diminished or denied. While on one occasion Aquinas makes a small effort to interrupt this sequence of logic where women are concerned,[104] he never pauses to do so for the great servile mass at the foundations of his society.[105]

How does the English Protestant concept of the servant compare with these Aristotelian and Thomistic concepts? As we have seen, the attention of the English Protestant is primarily centered on the hired house servant, the apprentice, and the agricultural hand, all of whom are visualized as members, by contract, of the family circle. He does deal to some extent with the slave as well, but the discussion of chattel slavery constitutes a separate topic which we shall consider later. Since the servant-master relationship is one of contract—a relationship between individuals, each of whom essentially is free—the English Protestant is not compelled with the same force as was Aristotle or St. Thomas to find a natural basis for servitude in some sharp differentiation of character or capacities. Not that it is argued that this difference in status is wholly an accidental or adventitious matter: the positions of master and servant are callings like any other and it is assumed that in each case there will be aptitudes appropriate to the role. But never in English Protestantism is there any talk of the presence of rationality or spiritual substance in one nature and its relative absence in another; even though endowed with different combinations of the same ingredients, master and servant are conceived to be equally gifted with all those traits of body, mind, and soul which are essential simply to humanity and to humanity's capacity for salvation.

The decisive equalitarianism of English Protestantism is, of course, that very equalitarianism of basic Christianity: the refusal to concede any connection (except possibly a negative one) between position on earth and God's boon of salvation in eternity. The tendency in Aquinas, which we have noted many times, to construct some type of positive correlation between heaven's and earth's rewards is completely and explicitly swept away. For, as English Protestants repeatedly remind the Christian, there is no respect of persons with God. Speaking specifi-

104 Aquinas, *Sum. Theol.*, III (Suppl.) q. 39, a. 1, ad. 1.
105 See *Commentarium in Libros IV Sentiarum.*, II, d. 44, q. 1, a. 3, c; III, 81; *Sum. Theol.*, II-II, q. 57, a. 3, c; III (Suppl.), q. 52, a. 1, ad. 2. *De Regimine Principum*, I, 1.

cally to those masters, who, accustomed to the favoritism of the world, tend to forget God's even-handed justice, Gouge cites again the often-quoted phrase: "Neither is there respect of persons with him," he cautions, and in these words he finds the proof and guarantee of "God's just and equall manner of proceeding with all men of ranke and degree soever." "Wherefore, O Masters . . . remember that albeit as Master and Servant ye differ, yet ye are both men, and before God, all one."[106] At another point in his argument he assures the Christian servant of the complete spiritual validity and value of the status he occupies and the work he performs: "Everyone of what estate and degree soever hee bee shall bee rewarded of God for every good thing hee doth, be it great or small. Therefore every servant shall be rewarded of God for every good service. . . . As God accepteth not men because they are free, so neither rejecteth he them because they are bond. It is not the person, but the worke that he regardeth."[107]

Contractual though the relationship between master and servant may be for English Protestantism, and firmly held in the context of Christian spiritual equalitarianism, it is in its worldly character a relationship of enormous authority on one side and profound abasement on the other. Within the family group there is no inferiority to match that of the servant, and though the master of a servant is not granted the magistrate's power of life and death over a subject, his control in other regards (as in its intimate and intrusive quality) exceeds the magisterial. Servants are consistently ranked lowest in the family hierarchy. Ames defines the status of the servant as being sharply different from and markedly lower than that of the child: "Servitude is much different from the state of a child. First, in respect, it is not from nature . . . but either undertaken by voluntary consent, or else imposed by way of punishment. Secondly . . . servitude doth aime directly at the good of the Master, and not of the Servant. Thirdly . . . servants are bound to doe all kind of worke. Fourthly . . . servants owe their perpetuall endeavours without all distinction of time. Fifthly, that in all things, chil-

[106] *Op.cit.*, p. 386.    [107] *Ibid.*, p. 98.

dren are more tenderly, and favourably to bee used than Servants."[108]

"No inferiours are more bound to obedience then servants." Gouge observes; "it is their main, and most peculiar function, to *obey their masters.*"[109] A number of English Protestants specifically command servants to accept corporal punishment from their masters without resistance or complaint, even where such punishment is admittedly unjust. In Gouge's discussion of the subject, a servant questions, "Shall I suffer myselfe wrongfully to be beaten, when I can helpe myselfe and hinder it?" The writer answers him: "Servants may not bee their owne Judges, whether their correction be just or unjust: for men are so prone to soothe themselves, and to extenuate the evill actions which they doe, as if they be not corrected till they thinke it just, they would never bee corrected."[110]

Describing the "good servant," Fuller argues, if not for the same reasons at least to the same effect: "Just correction he bears patiently, and unjust he takes cheerfully; knowing that stripes unjustly given more hurt the master than the man. . . ."[111]

Though the English Protestant may be said to have rejected not only the Aristotelian concept of natural slavishness as an individual's biological endowment, but also the Thomistic compromise with this concept, he altogether endorsed, at least for the voluntary servitude of the household servant, the naturalness of the institution of servitude. Also maintained was the traditional Christian association between the painfulness of this, as of any human situation, and the tragedy of the fall—hence the association between servitude and sin. "Mastership and service are lawful," Andrewes asserts, and the lawfulness of the relationship is based primarily on the fact that "servitude came first into the world for punishment."[112] Pricke remarks that the lot of the servant is a hard one in the world "by reason of the inward pride, whereby every man hath a desire to be advanced above others: as also for that by the light of nature, we all love libertie, and hate bondage and servitude as a punishment for sinne."[113]

[108] Ames, *Conscience,* pp. 159-60.
[109] *Op.cit.,* p. 337.    [110] *Ibid.,* p. 343.
[111] *Op.cit.,* p. 51.    [112] *Works,* ii, 188.    [113] *Op.cit.,* p. 68.

The whole hierarchical structure is further confirmed when it is proclaimed that the master, like the magistrate, must be viewed as the embodiment in his office, though not in his person, of the supremacy of God over the whole of humankind. Declares Pricke, "The master taketh his authoritie over the servant, from no creature in heaven or earth, but onely from God himselfe."[114] For Gouge, "[The] master's place and power . . . is God's appointment: God hath placed them in his stead, and in part given them his power: they are the Deputies and Ministers of God, and therefore in Scripture the title [Lord] is after a peculiar manner given to them."[115] During his analysis of the nature of the servant's role, Gouge takes pains to reject decisively "the opinion of Anabaptists, who teach that all are alike, and that there is no difference betwixt masters and servants." To the Anabaptist argument that "it is against nature for one to be a servant, especially a bond-servant of another," Gouge replies: "To grant that it is against that absolute and perfect nature wherein at first God created man, and that it came by sin, yet is it not against that order and course of nature wherein God hath now settled man. God hath turned many punishments of sin, to be bounden duties, as that man's eating bread in the sweat of his brow."

Having cited the Anabaptist object that "this subjection is against the liberty that Christ purchased for us," he concludes with the typical Pauline precept: "It is not. For the liberty is from the curse and rigor of the morall law . . . but not from those degrees which God hath established betwixt man and man, for the good of mankinde. Wherefore thou art not made a Christian, that thou shouldst be proud, and scorn to serve."[116]

On the subject of chattel slavery as such, there are few comments in this literature and they are mostly brief and incidental. Perkins, the only writer who devotes any particular space or thought to the matter, hazards an opinion that "the . . . question is, whether bondage, in which some are Lords, others bondmen, or slaves, may stand with Christian religion? *Answ.* It may, in

114 *Ibid.*, p. 70.
115 *Op.cit.*, p. 333.
116 *Ibid.*, pp. 321-22.

the Countries where it is established by positive lawes, if it be used with mercie and moderation."[117]

Turning principally to Old Testament history and judicial commentary to buttress his position, Perkins states in another treatise his definite support for the legality and Christian propriety of slavery. Upon examination of his argument, however, one finds that the slavery whose legality he accepts is also that of the Old Testament and not the far more wholesale and drastic servitude of Roman and later Western law. The conditions and limitations with which Perkins surrounds the institution completely remove it from the Aristotelian category and make possible only partial contact between his idea of a type of slavery compatible with the Christian conscience and the Thomistic concept. Where it is established by positive laws, he writes, men may with "good conscience" have bondmen; this "power and right" must be used with moderation, however, subject to these seven conditions: "I. That the master have not over his servant the power of life and death. . . . II. That there be not libertie granted him to use his servant at his owne will and pleasure in all things; for this was not granted by the law of God to his owne people: Exod. 21:26. . . . III. That the power be not enlarged to the commanding of things against piety or justice, for in these cases a man must rather obey God then men: Act. 4:19. IV. That masters doe not take libertie to make separation of those their servants that be maried . . . or of those that be parents from their children. . . . V. That the masters doe not take libertie to put over their servants to ungodly and unbelieving masters. . . . VI. That they doe not bind them to perpetuall slaverie, and never make them free: Exod. 21.5. . . . VII. That the servitude be not procured and retained by force; for it is a more grievous crime to spoile a man of his libertie, then of his riches."[118]

Fully aware of the deviance between his viewpoint and that of Aristotle, Perkins explains that servitude is a result of the fall and is not, as for Aristotle, a natural condition of man, "for

[117] *Works*, II, 267.
[118] *Works*, III, 697-98.

all men by nature are equally and indifferently free, none more or lesse than others."[119]

That Perkins does not approve but merely tolerates even the highly qualified form of slavery he has been defining is indicated by a summary statement, in which he advises that "where this kind of servitude is abolished, it is not to be again received or intertained amongst Christians, specially considering, it is a far more milde and moderate course to have hired servants."[120]

In balance, then, Perkins' comments on chattel slavery are considerably more negative than positive; he clearly prefers, on moral grounds, the contractual master-servant relationship characteristic of his own seventeenth-century English society. Ames makes a brief but more emphatic attack against "perfect servitude" as a violation of basic human liberties and rights.[121] It is Sanderson, however, whose rejection of slavery, or at least of the slave trade, is the most uncompromising and resolute: "Lands, Houses, Cattel, and other like possessions made for man's use, are the proper subject-matter of trade and commerce. . . . But that Man, a Creature of such excellency, stamped with the Image of God, endowed with a reasonable Soul, made capable of Grace and Glorie . . . should become merchantable ware. . . . I suppose had been a thing never heard of in the world to this hour; had not the overflowings of Pride, and Cruelty, and Covetousness, washed out the hearts of Men, the very impressions both of Religion and Humanity. It is well, and we are to bless God, and under God to thank our Christian Religion and pious Governours for it; that in these times and parts of the world, we scarce know what it meaneth. But that it was generally practised all the world over in some former ages, and is at this day in use among Turks and Pagans to sell men: ancient Histories and modern Relations will not suffer us to be ignorant."[122]

In assaying the English Protestant posture on voluntary or involuntary human servitude in relation to that of earlier bodies of thought, one final quality of it should be mentioned. Although, as we have seen, much space and moralizing logic are

[119] *Ibid.*, p. 698.    [120] *Ibid.*    [121] *Op.cit.*, p. 160.
[122] Sanderson, *XXXVI Sermons*, pp. 451-52.

spent upon the subject of the servant's duties to his master, very nearly equal attention is devoted to the reciprocal duties of the master toward his servant. This is a subject in which Aristotle had no interest whatsoever and in which Aquinas was not greatly involved (though the apologist can always cite for him the churchmen's necessary general concern for the spiritual welfare of all Christians). But no English Protestant who has anything to say on the servant's role and his proper subjection to his master neglects to pronounce a resounding barrage of caveats against the master's misuse or abuse of his authority. Modifying or even directly contradicting two points made by more disciplinarian commentators on the extent of the servant's subordination to his master (the servant's marked inferiority to the child in the family and the master's right to employ corporal punishment in dealing with him), Smith makes the following observations concerning the duties of masters: "And therefore the Housholder is called *Pater familias* . . . because he should have a fatherly care over his servants, as if they were his children; and not use them only for their labour, like beasts.

"Besides, the name of a servant doth not signifie suffering, but doing; therefore Masters must not exercise their hands upon them, but set their hands to work. . . ."[123]

Andrewes lists as one among the duties of the master that he not be "sharp and bitter"; he also directs the master to provide his servants with adequate "meat, drink, and clothes, or wages agreed upon." It is the master's further duty to shape commandments to his servants in such a fashion that they are "lawful," "possible," "profitable to some good purpose," and "proportionable to time, place, and person."[124] Perkins has much the same to say: "The master is a member in the family, which . . . beareth rule over the servant. And his duty stands principally in three things.

"First, to make a good choice of his servants . . .

"Secondly, to enjoyne them labour and not to require more of them, then their strength will beare. The master is to rule over the servant in *justice* . . .

[123] Smith, *Sermons*, p. 26.   [124] *Works*, II, 188-89.

"Thirdly, to recompense the diligence . . . of his servant, and that three waies

"First, by giving him his due of meate and drinke for the present . . .

"Secondly, by paying him his hire in the end of his service . . .

"Thirdly, if the servant . . . be sicke, the master's care must be by all meanes . . . to procure his recovery."[125]

Gouge, whose extensive treatment of the subject we have seen, also contributes to this final aspect of the matter. He writes that the relation between master and servant has been made by God, who "hath set each of them in their severall and distinct places for the mutuall good of one another."[126] Inspired by Paul's statement that, "Knowing that your Master also is in Heaven: neither is there respect of persons with him," Gouge concludes his chapter on the duties of masters, hammering home the point that since both master and servant are equally subject to God and to God's assignment of their respective duties, the master is ultimately as much a subject as the servant. This is so for two reasons: "The first reason which declareth the subjection of Masters, in that they have a Master over them, putteth them in minde of that account which they are to make . . . of the well using of their authority, and of their carriage toward such as are under them: For they are but as Stewards over fellow servants: every one of them therefore shall have this charge, *give an account of thy Stewardship* . . .

"The second reason . . . declareth an equality betwixt Masters and Servants in relation to God. As God is the Master of Servants, so is he the Master of Masters also. As Servants are the Lord's freemen, so Masters are the Lord's servants. In this respect, they who are made Rulers, and they who are under them, are called fellow-servants. For howsoever in outward dignity, there is a great difference between Master and servant, yet as the Servants of God they are of a like condition, and in many things may be accounted equall: especially if both be of the same faith, and so brethren in Christ."[127]

125 *Works*, III, 696-97.
126 *Op.cit.*, p. 99.
127 *Ibid.*, p. 385.

Built on Paul but moving in its fullness and passion considerably beyond the Pauline emphasis, a single passage succeeds not only in summarizing Gouge's viewpoint on the master-servant relationship, but also in summing up the kind and manner of thought which at once inspires and limits the whole English Protestant concept of authority.

## CHAPTER 8

## THE ENGLISH PROTESTANT

## AND THE CHURCH

━━━━━━━━━━━━━━━✝✝✝━━━━━━━━━━━━━━

"Gods Church is a well governed estate. Therein is a King: a just, wise, and potent King. . . . Therein are righteous lawes, excellent priviledges, and all things requisite for a well ordered politie, all tending to the good of the subjects. For it is the estate whereof God taketh most care.

"They therefore that seeke to take away order, and to bring confusion into the Church, doe much dishonour this kingdome and the King thereof, who is not the author of confusion but peace. So do they also who professe themselves to be members of the Church, and yet live as if they were without law, in no kingdome, under no government. . . .

"Gods Church is not yet perfect. This is true of both parts of the Church, militant and triumphant. . . . Shall now particular Churches which . . . may be proved to bee true Churches bee denied therein? They who will abide in no Church but in that which is perfect, may wander from Church to Church and finde none on earth to abide in. . . . All here on earth is in part, all is imperfect. . . . They that thinke themselves perfect are for the most part further from perfection."

—WILLIAM GOUGE, *A Guide To Goe to God*, 51-53

━━━━━━━━━━━━━━━✝✝✝━━━━━━━━━━━━━━

## I. The Historical Setting

WE HAVE LONG AGO and many times observed that Christianity is a system filled with ideological tensions. Part of its vitality and historical dynamic is due to this fact—that always simultaneously present within it are contradictory concepts and tendencies upon which varying circumstances and compulsions can work in a number of ways.

*306*

One of the most historically significant of these tensions is that between the force which presses toward the individual's intimate, immediate, and unique contact with deity, and that which presses toward externalizing, regularizing, and institutionalizing such contacts. As faith and as church, Christianity has been at odds with itself both logically and historically. Yet since, except for fleeting patches of times, one can scarcely be said to have existed without the other, both forces would seem essential to their common survival and success. The mutual interdependence of mutual hostilities—no absolutely stable situation can emerge from such a relationship, and so it is that one of the prominent lines of change in Christianity has been the periodical readjustment and recombination of these two ingredients.

The massive institutionalization of Roman Catholicism clearly represents an extreme of achievement in this direction. Of logical necessity, therefore, insofar as it differs here from Roman Catholicism, Protestantism as a whole can only represent some movement in the opposite direction. In the effort to break through the wall of institutionalism which a thousand years of dominance had raised around this Roman Catholic form of Christianity, Protestantism inevitably called upon those solvents of all worldly dignity and organization which always exist in the heart of the faith. There was the turning back by Protestant revivalism to the institutional simplicities, the well-nigh complete absence of institutionalism which characterized Gospel Christianity. There was the appeal by Protestant personalism to the living force of the individual conscience, the inner and particular sense of truth, against the dead weight of tradition and authority.

In no universal or categorical way, of course, was Protestantism anti-institutional. The absolute need for an institutional shell, to protect and confine the quicksilver of belief, was fully recognized by all forms of Protestantism. At the beginning of the movement, it would appear, the conscious desire was simply to revive and reform an old and decadent institution by means of a new truth and to replace an outworn unity with a living one. Thus it was in good part despite itself and its initial purpose that Protestantism was carried as far as it eventually was in the direction of disunity and institutional impotence. The real force of Protestant anti-institutionalism was meant to be used in one direction only—against the bulwarks and redoubts of Roman Catholicism—but the energy involved in the destructive effort carried over into the area of reconstruction, and Protestantism was prevented from rebuilding for itself—even though the wish to do so indubitably was present—anything like the solidity of institutional structure which encompassed the creed of imperial Rome.

On the problem of institutionalism, the history of English Protestantism has long been recognized as a peculiar case in the history of Protestantism as a whole. The first break with Rome was accomplished by a monarch for political and economic reasons alone. It resulted in a church which—while it adequately represented the growing desire and capacity of a nation to define its area of total sovereignty and to resist any foreign intrusion, notably that of Roman Catholic religious imperialism—answered none of the other complaints or criticisms motivating the Protestant upsurge. Henry VIII merely established a national Roman Catholic church not unlike that which by other and more gradual and indirect techniques French and Spanish kings succeeded in creating for their own realms. It is a tribute to the complexity of the Protestant movement in general, and to the particular depth and tenacity of its roots in England, that English religious change did not stop here but went on to create, despite the disfavor of a Henry and the active persecution of a Mary, an English church which was as decisively Protestant in doctrine as any other.

Yet the peculiar history of the English church certainly left its mark on the institutional framework of English Protestantism. The political rather than religious emphasis of the origins of the English church, its unique dependence for its first emergence upon the fiat of a monarch—these aspects of its background are no doubt largely responsible for its relative conservatism as an institution, which persisted despite the eventually complete and relatively radical Protestantization of its doctrine. With the exception of misguided and tragic Mary, the monarchs of England from Henry through Charles I were individuals of moderate religiosity at most, whose primary interests were the better securing and maintaining of the political unity and stability of their domains. Without implying any necessary quality of Machiavellian craft in their policies—since with the religious arguments at hand it was easy enough to identify a monarch's interests with the interests of the deity—one may still declare that their first view of the church was an instrumental one: as they saw it, a central purpose of the church was to strengthen and confirm the structure and policies of the state. In a religious age—in an age of religious disputatiousness, especially, as the sixteenth and seventeenth centuries surely were—strong discipline, definite hierarchy, set rituals within the church, in short, the church's fairly rigid institutionalization, were all likely to meet with the approval and sponsorship of the monarch and his coterie, so long as the subordination of religious to political authority (wherever the two might conflict, at least) was securely maintained. It is well for the servant of the strong to be himself a man of strength, possessed of a capacity for governance which, while being always subject to control from above, is not liable to dispute from below.

For the church to be as fully as possible an efficient servant of the state, it had not only to be strong: it had also to be unified. It had to be entirely integrated with the state so that all those who were citizens of the nation were at the same time members of the nation's church. With this primary and essentially political purpose in mind, the same English monarchs who encouraged the institutional rigidity of the church and the narrow following of traditional ways also encouraged doctrinal breadth and even slackness, so that the maximum number of believers, agitated and torn apart by the doctrinal disputes of their time, might find it feasible to join in common worship within a common church. The state was understandably far more interested in the formalities of adherence to the institution than in the intricacies of the inner belief. One nation, one church—this was the monarchical ideal. From Henry to Charles I (with Mary again put aside), a fairly consistent king's policy was directed toward this ideal and sought to achieve it by establishing, first, a church which was English; second, a church which served the state; third, a church which within itself was strong enough to maintain discipline and put down dissent; and, finally, a church which achieved universality by the subordination of doctrinal differences to ecclesiastical conformity.

Speaking absolutely, it is irrelevant to the political concerns we have been analyzing that the English church should be Protestant. Henry sought to continue the old belief, as we have noted, but as much because he thought this would better balance or neutralize the unsettling effects of other changes as from purely religious convictions. The politically-minded might claim some advantages in Roman Catholic doctrine, because of its long association with the kind of ecclesiastical organization and interior discipline which, properly subordinated to the state, might best serve the state. Yet despite Henry, whose opposition was, after all, not consistently strenuous, England became increasingly a Protestant nation.

The advance of the new creed was subsequently furthered not only by the pressure of purely religious enthusiasms, but also by political events and political leaders—beginning dramatically in the reign of Edward. The rivalry with Catholic France and Spain, the miserable reign of Mary, Elizabeth's long struggle to maintain her throne against foreign, and always Catholic, treachery and intrigue—this is the charged political atmosphere which contributed directly to the success in England of the faith of the Reformers. Once the surge toward Protestantism was underway, monarchs and their agents were quick to recognize that, simply as a faith, it was as fully capable as any other of guarding their position and pretensions and supporting their primary interest in political stability. It would be a mistake, therefore, to attempt to delineate any sharp or consistent difference between a court party on one side and a religious party on the other. Points and moments of friction there were, but the area of cooperation was far broader than the area of conflict.

Indeed, the overriding quality of the history of the English church during the seventy years of our survey is one of harmony. Its institutional framework had been firmly set in the relatively conservative pattern which its origins had determined; its doctrine was unequivocally Protestant. Further, both the political and religious leadership of England pursued equally, if from somewhat different standpoints, the same objective of ecclesiastical unity. We are dealing, in short, with the golden age of the *via media*, the period in the history of Protestant England which above all others was characterized by a sense of religious community.

This is not to say, however, that dissenting notes were altogether absent. No more in England than elsewhere had the Protestant conscience been set free to accept complacently and universally a single kind of religious belief and a single manner of religious practice. Within the church disputes arose, principally about institutional matters, and to a much lesser extent about doctrinal ones. Despite the earnest efforts of churchmen and statesmen both, separations from the church occurred. We have not ignored these matters nor shall we do so in this chapter. But we do feel that many scholars, too much involved with the cataclysm which was to close this period of relative religious calm, have read back into it an intensity of dissension which really was not there. Partly to balance this undue attention to division we choose to emphasize the peace.

## II. The Nature of the Church

We turn now to consider in detail certain issues, primarily institutional rather than doctrinal in focus, which were subjects of discussion and dispute in this literature. English Protestant writers were enormously interested and involved in such matters (the nature of the church, the place and function of its ministry, its proper government, the determination of a suitable ceremonial with which to clothe its doctrines); most spent a great deal of space and energy upon them, and some were entangled in them almost to the exclusion of all other concerns. So vast is the material directly or indirectly related to problems of this type that we can hope only to give a surface sense of it and to point out the principal lines of argumentation. In each instance we shall attempt to define a central or a dominant point of view—a *via media*—and to set it off against a traditional Roman Catholic concept on one side and radical Protestant and separatist thinking on the other. For each issue we shall also attempt to evaluate how stable a compromise the *via media* had actually achieved—how little or how much pull, from within the confines of the unified church, the *via media* had made possible toward either the right or the left extremes.

We shall consider first the nature of the church.[1] The Roman Catholic position on this subject had long been clear and solidified. The church was, without apology or qualification, simply the institutional structure of Roman Catholicism, huge, spreading, and complex as it had come to be through more than a thousand years of building. It was the priesthood, with its special privileges and powers, the elaborate hierarchy, the system of sacraments, the ceremonials, the cathedrals which celebrated and proclaimed the whole in spires of stone. It was all-embracing: it extended across baronies, duchies, and through and across the growing sense of nationhood in Western Europe. Ideally, had it had the power and resource, it would have extended—as an institution, primarily—through and around the world. It was all-embracing not only in this horizontal sense of a spreading outward over area, but also in the vertical sense of a spreading downward into the population of the area it dominated. The Roman Catholic Church sought thus to bring everyone into at least a formal membership and into contact with its sacramental system which it conceived to be an absolutely essential means to the salvation of any individual.

By virtue of its doctrinal acceptance of a double standard of religiosity, the policy of Roman Catholicism was made more lenient. In accordance with the maximum demands of the upper level of this double standard, a place was surely provided in the Roman Catholic Church for those whose religious impulses were intense beyond any possible compromise with the full interior fervor of belief or with any substitution of the appearance for the reality of devotion. There was surely a place for saints in the Church of Rome. And yet the lower level of this

[1] See Wilhelm Pauck, "The Idea of the Church in Christian History," *Church History* (September, 1952).

same double standard—by far the larger, more commodious and hospitable area of the two—provided accommodation for those whose Christianity was often merely a matter of automatic, unchosen admission to the specific organization, the mechanical performance of a few ceremonials, and the payment of stipulated fees.

The acceptance of this kind of Christianity was not the product of despairing resignation to the weakness of the flesh and the limitations of circumstance; that formalistic adherence was sufficient for the church and for the majority of Christians had come to be a positive concept, entirely integrated into the total system which saw in these masses a necessary and inevitable foundation for the ecclesiastical pyramid. The nature of Roman Catholic missionary policy during the middle ages and into the modern period shows that such was indeed the viewpoint. The essence of conversion consisted in one ceremony—baptism. Hence it was possible for thousands to be made Roman Catholics—and presumably to be brought thereby within the circuit of salvation—at the point of a sword or by the mere command of a monarch who had been won to the faith. It is well known and often documented that Roman Catholicism was able to blend in ceremony and even in doctrine into other, principally pagan, religions. Having thus become an amalgam of old and new, it could more easily attract and hold the unenlightened in another facet of the endorsement of a world of compromise. In this world the earth-bound might live out wholly dutiful lives, while those few who were able to endure the heights could breathe the headier atmosphere of undiluted truth.

The problem for Protestantism was much more complicated. We have again and again commented upon Protestantism's rejection of the Roman Catholic double standard and its insistence on the sole validity of a single standard of religiosity and morality to which all who could be considered truly Christian must adhere. Logically speaking, outside of this standard with its requirement of the thorough penetration of faith into every thought and action of the believer's life, there was for Protestantism no Christianity at all. There was no second-best Christianity; there was everything or nothing; there was a saint or a reprobate. The Protestant conceived, moreover, in perhaps a more thoroughgoing fashion than the Roman Catholic, that in the society of the world the saints were few and the reprobate many. The strict logic of his position pressed strongly toward the ancient Gospel pattern of the church—if it could indeed be called a church at all—as simply the foregathering or the company of the faithful. Protestant literature of all types assures us that where two or three of such faithful have come together to pray and worship there the church is fully, and in some senses *most* fully, present.

Yet for many reasons the great leaders of Protestantism could not follow this road of strict logic to its ultimate conclusion. They never even tried to do so and they energetically opposed any others who made the attempt. They were church builders as well as faith restorers, and each of their churches was to be, at least in its own area of provenience, as all-inclusive and solidly institutional—though not on as grandiose and commanding a scale—as the Roman Catholic Church had been and was. As an institution, then, the Protestant church was admittedly intended to enclose both saved and damned.

Protestant apologists generally presented two reasons for this continuance of the Catholic Church's institutional and all-inclusive nature. First, they argued, no man could take it upon himself to decide who among his fellow men were the reprobate and who the saved; even the saved might be unaware of their own condition and through much of their lives might exhibit to themselves and to others the surface characteristics of the reprobate. Therefore, all should be exposed to the influence of the faith—of the Word, most importantly—which emanated from the church. In this way, all the saved would eventually be brought, if not to full knowledge of their salvation, at least to full readiness for it.

The second reason was more directly institutional and practical: though the reprobate would remain reprobate however long they were subjected to the church's inspiriting agency, went the argument, they should nonetheless be so subjected. This is necessary for the greater glory of God through the absolutely universal publication of His will and judgment, and for the greater peace of society through such confinement and restraint of the wickedness of the reprobate as the discipline of the church could provide.

Hence just as Roman Catholicism maintained the all-inclusiveness of the church by conceiving its division into two horizontal strata—a saintly, typically clerical, elite at the top and the mass of the laity at the bottom—so Protestantism, in its major forms, accomplished the same purpose by conceiving this division more in terms of two vertical sections, as it were: an invisible church of the elect and a visible church which included both the elect and the damned.

Yet no structural metaphor—none of various images of mechanical partitions between the invisible and the visible church —accurately represents this Protestant idea. For, involved in the concept of the invisible church is not separateness but inwardness, and an inwardness which does not subsist as a distinct kernel within the heart, but is a living principle interpenetrating the whole body. The invisible church is the real vitality, the essential soul of the visible church. This is no new idea, of course. It is as old at least as Augustine and represents another product of Protestantism's conscious effort to revive and reestablish concepts and policies from what were presumed to be the purer origins of the faith.

In its concept of the nature of the church, English Protestantism fully represents the typical view of Protestantism as a whole. There is a virtually universal acceptance of the division between a visible and invisible church: one is organized and institutionalized and national and its membership ideally includes all those who by citizenship are Englishmen; the invisible church within the visible is composed only of the company of the elect, whoever they may be. Gouge notes this double significance to the Protestant of the church: "Church according to the notation of the Greeke word signifieth an assembly called together. It is in Scriptures by a propertie attributed to them who are called to God.

"This calling is two fold:

"1. *Outward*, which is common to all that make profession

of the Gospell: in this respect it is said, *many are called and few chosen.*

"2. *Inward,* which is proper to the elect. None but they, and all they in their time shall both outwardly be called by the word to a possession of Christ, and also inwardly and effectively by the spirit to beleeve in Christ and obey his Gospell. This is stiled *an heavenly calling,* which is proper to the Saints. These make that Church whereof Christ is properly the head. . . ."[2]

Despite his primary concern with the visible and institutional church, Hooker also acknowledges the existence within it of the invisible congregation of the elect: "That Church of Christ, which we properly term his body mystical . . . can [not] . . . be sensibly discerned by any man, inasmuch as the parts thereof are some in heaven already with Christ, and the rest that are on earth (albeit their natural persons be visible) we do not discern under this property, whereby they are truly and infallibly of that body. Only our minds by intellectual conceit are able to apprehend that such a real body there is. . . . And as those everlasting promises of love, mercy, and blessedness belong to the mystical Church; even so on the other side when we read of any duty which the Church of God is bound unto, the Church whom this doth concern is a sensibly known company . . . [a] visible Church. . . ."[3]

That in the outward or visible church both the elect and the reprobate shall be included is stated repeatedly by these writers. Having cited the fact that both Cain and Abel made offerings to the Lord, Perkins proceeds to argue: "Hence we learne, that the Church militant is a mixt . . . companie of men . . . true beleevers and hypocrites mingled together . . . the good shall never be quite separated from the bad, untill Christ himselfe doe it at the last judgement. . . . This beeing so, let no man therfore be afraid to joyne himselfe to the visible church; neither let any that are in it goe out of it, because the bad are mingled with the good. . . ."[4]

Adams similarly states that "this visible Church is a mixt company of men, professing the faith . . . in it are both beleevers

---

[2] Gouge, *Works,* I, 21.  [3] Hooker, *Polity,* III, 1, ii-iii.
[4] Perkins, *Works,* III, 16.

and hyprocrites, corne and tares: it is a band of men, where be some valiant souldiers and many cowards."[5] And Ussher observes that "the visible Church . . . consisteth of good and bad, as at the beginning we may see it did in Cain and Abel; whereupon our Saviour compareth the Church to a net, in which are fishes good and bad."[6]

The logic of this English Protestant point of view on the nature of the church presses directly and strongly toward a superior valuation of the invisible over the visible church. As compared with the Roman Catholic background, the whole of English Protestantism is characterized by this movement away from the institutional and toward a more spiritual concept of the church. Yet within the boundaries of English Protestantism itself there are clearly differences of emphasis on the subject of the church. Indeed, the overt and conscious drawing out of certain consequences of this central Protestant idea is primarily, though by no means absolutely, a preoccupation of the so-called "puritans." Thus it is Gouge who states (page 316) that the invisible church alone, the inward church, is the church of the elect "whereof Christ is properly the head."[7] For Perkins, the company of the faithful constitutes the essence and reality of the church. "To beleeve the Church," he writes, "is nothing els, but to beleeve that there is a company of the predestinate made one in Christ, and that withall we are in the number of them."[8] Adams maintains that the visible church is only called a church "from the better, not from the greater part,"[9] that is, from the existence within it of the company of the elect or the invisible church. Sibbes argues to the same effect that "the visible church hath tearmes of excellency put upon it sometimes, but it is in regard of the better part. As gold unrefined is called gold because gold is the better part."[10] Ussher, however, who is not numbered among the "puritans," proclaims as decisively as anyone that true membership in the church is limited to the elect alone. "Who are the true members of the Church militant on earth?" he asks, and then replies: "Those alone who as liv-

---

[5] Adams, *Works*, p. 557.    [6] Ussher, *Divinitie*, p. 397.
[7] Gouge, *loc.cit.*    [8] *Works*, I, 301.    [9] *Works*, p. 557.
[10] Sibbes, *Bowels Opened*, p. 340.

ing members of the mystical body . . . are by the Spirit and
Faith secretly and inseparably conjoyned unto Christ their
head. . . . Truly and properly none are of the Church, saving
only they which truly beleeve and yeeld obedience . . . all which
are also saved."[11]

An interesting aspect of English Protestantism's relative down-
grading of the institutional church is the general insistence that
the visible church, as it exists in the world, is fallible in its
judgments, has erred in the past, and may well continue to do
likewise in the future. There was in this regard a conscious
opposition of English Protestant to Roman Catholic opinion,
and though not all English Protestants contributed actively to
the progress of this argument, no one opposed its course. Laud,
indeed, in his conference with the Jesuit protagonist, Fisher,
presents some of the fullest and longest statements on the subject. He does, to be sure, tie his discussion somewhat narrowly
to a refutation of the Roman Catholic position, attacking most
vigorously the claimed infallibility of popes and Roman Catholic councils, and leaving rather more of a quality of infallibility
than certain other Protestants might grant to the institutional
church as a whole.[12] Chillingworth extends the argument further: beginning at the point where Laud leaves off—the insistence upon the actual commission of errors by Roman Catholic
officialdom—he goes on to state that errors may and do enter
into Protestant churches too. "No church," he says, "may hope
to be secure from all error simply, for this were indeed truly to
triumph over all."[13]

Again, however it is the so-called "puritans" who make the
most sweeping and emphatic declarations on this topic. Preston,
for example, having rejected Roman Catholic claims to infallibility for their church and their pope, concludes with the comment that "not to be capable of errors, is the inseparable attribute of God himselfe . . . which cannot bee said of any creature.
. . ."[14] Perkins writes with notable certainty that "all visible
churches upon earth . . . are subject to Apostasie." This can

[11] *Op.cit.*, p. 189.
[12] Laud, *Works*, II, 13, 21-22, 29, 285-86.
[13] Chillingworth, *The Religion of Protestants*, p. 281.
[14] Preston, *Sermons* (1630), p. 88.

be so, he explains confidently, despite the equal certainty that "true beleevers cannot fall away": "In the visible church on earth, there are foure kinds of beleevers. The first are they, which heare the word without zeale, and they are like the stone ground. The second are they, which heare, know, and approve the word. The third are they, which heare, know, and approve the word, and have a taste of the power thereof, and accordingly yeeld some outward obedience. The fourth are they, which heare, know, approve and keepe the word, in that they beleeve it, and are turned unto the obedience of it. The three first may fall quite away. The fourth cannot. And by this meanes it comes to passe, that visible churches upon earth may fall away: because of them that professe the faith, three to one may utterly fall away."[15]

Both Preston and Perkins contrast to its considerable disadvantage the church as an institution with the true source of faith and salvation in God alone and in the word of God. Preston counsels Christians "to take up nothing meerely upon trust, not to thinke things are so onely because the Church hath said it; this foundation is too sandy for us to build our faith upon, that should be built upon the rocke which is the word of God. . . ."[16] Perkins concludes an elaborate allegorical treatment of the story of Sarah (who, as the mother of God's chosen, is seen to represent the church, the mother of all Christians) with the declaration: "The use is, to teach us all to honour the Church as our mother; but to worship God alone, who is the father of our soule. The Church cannot make her selfe our mother, nor us her children, when she will: but it is God that must speake the word, then are wee made: hee must beget us by the power of his spirit, and ministerie of his word."[17]

Occasionally manifesting itself in this literature is an attitude potentially even more subversive of ecclesiastical institutionalism than any of the viewpoints we have considered. It takes the form of a doubt or question as to whether membership in the visible church of England, or for that matter in any visible

[15] *Works*, II, 287.
[16] *Sermons*, pp. 19-20.
[17] *Works*, III, 89.

church, is really essential to salvation. One meets with a more positive form of this problem in such relatively rare souls as Donne and Chillingworth who, in speaking of the breadth of God's love and understanding, overstep the boundaries of specific sects and creeds. But there is also Perkins' interesting comment that "an hypocrite may bee in the visible Church . . . and bee taken for a true member of Christ, when as a man indeede regenerate may be excommunicated, and ends his life before he be received againe. . . ."[18]

The separatist impulse is the final product of the tension of ideas we have been considering. For, the separatist goes only one more step along the line of Protestant logic to assert the need—this invisible church being admitted to be the true reality of the visible—for a greater actual conformity between the two churches. But we have scarcely touched on English separatists in this study; hence the numerous divines whose sermons we have read prove that it was at least feasible for Protestants to live both with the particular conceptual system we have been discussing and within the confines of English Protestant institutionalism. Indeed, English Protestants achieved on this as on so many other subjects a *via media* of viewpoint, consisting in this case of three generally acknowledged propositions: first, the church was two-fold in character, combining both a visible and an invisible element; second, while from the religious standpoint the invisible element was superior to the visible, from the ecclesiastical standpoint the relationship was in a sense reversed; hence, third, institutional separation must not and could not properly be the outcome of a division which was essentially interior and spiritual. What conscious departure there was from this *via media* consisted more in conservative agitation over possible unsettlement and rebelliousness contained within the viewpoint than in any pushing of the claims of the authority of the invisible over the visible world.

## III. The Ministry

The differences between Roman Catholicism and Protestantism in their concepts of the place and function of the ministry in

18 *Works*, I, 360.

the church are so well known and have been so often publicized
that they require only the most cursory comment here. For the
Roman Catholic, the priest was a specially dedicated, specially
endowed individual who, particularly in his sole capacity to
officiate in the miracle of the mass, served as an essential inter-
mediary between the laity and God. For the Protestant, on the
other hand, the priest, or more properly, the minister, was indeed specially called and specially trained, but only to serve as an
aid and guide to those who must in all important regards find
God and salvation for themselves. Luther enunciates this absolutely universal Protestant doctrine by his declaration of the
priesthood of all believers. It can also be stated in terms of the
sole priesthood of Christ the Redeemer and the derivation of the
minister's role from the merely publicizing and inspiriting function of certain disciples.

The basic Protestant attitudes we have indicated here and the
many consequences which flow from them are altogether evident
and clear in the writings of English Protestantism. Thus Luther's
assertion of the priesthood of all believers is strongly reaffirmed,
directly or indirectly, in this literature. Even Cosin, the extreme
conservative on all ecclesiastical issues, remarks that "in a spiritual sense, though not in regard of public offices in the Church,
we are all priests, the whole assembly of people, as well as the
chief minister himself."[19] Sibbes argues that, though Christ is
the only true and original priest, all who truly participate in
Christ participate also in the power of this priesthood. "He hath
washed us in his blood," he writes, "and made us . . . Priests."[20]

Thus English Protestantism, like Protestantism in general,
brought clergy and laity more closely together in the church by
exalting first the spiritual status of the laity. There is scarcely
an argument or a topic of discussion in all of English Protestantism which, relative to Roman Catholicism, does not in some
fashion serve to improve the position of the worshippers *vis à vis*
the directors of worship. One need only refer to the Protestant
concept of the saint, which completely disentangles possession of
the grace of God from institutional considerations of any sort, to

[19] Cosin, *Works*, III, 353.
[20] *Beames of Divine Light*, p. 51.

see from how many directions and in how many ways this tendency to dignify the laity was encouraged. The turning away from ecclesiastical authority to Scripture and the ordinary man's reading and understanding of Scripture as the ultimate grounding of religious truth—contentions which will be analyzed more fully hereafter—are another aspect of this same kernel of ideas. Chillingworth likewise opposes the dogma of papal infallibility with the common Protestant recognition that all right-thinking men are capable of coming to the fundamentals of the Christian faith themselves in the absence of ecclesiastical aid; in doing so, he makes a statement which is unrepresentative of English Protestantism as a whole only in the peculiar confidence and intensity of its rationalism: "You [the Roman Catholic antagonist] say again confidently, that *if this infallibility be once impeached, every man is given over to his own wit and discourse*: which . . . if you mean by discourse, right reason, grounded on Divine revellation and common notions, written by God in the hearts of all men, and deducing, according to the never failing rules of Logik, consequent deductions from them, if this be it, which you mean by *discourse*, it is very meet and reasonable and necessary that men, as in all their actions, so especially in that of greatest importance, the choice of their way to happinesse should be left unto it and he that followes this in all his opinions and actions . . . follows alwaies God; whereas he that followeth a Company of men, may oft-times follow a company of beasts."[21]

To be sure, the closer conjunction between laity and clergy can be accomplished by a second means as well: by diminishing, again relative to Roman Catholicism, the position of the clergy. And certainly these English Protestant writings contain numerous references to the sole priesthood of Christ and the consequent inappropriateness of applying any of the special attributes entailed in Christ's priesthood to a particular group of men, however gifted in human terms they may be. Thus Perkins writes: "In the old testament there were many priests one following another in continuall succession, but of the new testament there is one onely reall priest, Christ Jesus God and man,

---

21 *Op.cit.*, Preface.

and no more. . . . Indeed he hath his ministers to teach men his will: but a deputie to offer sacrifice in his stead he hath not. . . . Indeed all Christians are priests to offer up spirituall sacrifice, but it is the propertie of Christ alone to offer an outward and reall sacrifice unto God. . . ."[22]

"Let us know," says Dering, "these two things both to bee done by Christ for us, that is, both to make intercession, and to purge our sinnes, in neither of which works, let us attribute any thing to any other, except wee will robbe Christ of the glorie of his Priesthood. . . ."[23]

Departure from the Roman Catholic concept of the priest and the priesthood is further signalized in these sermons by the general use of the term "minister" rather than "priest" to designate the ecclesiastical personage in question. One is aware, admittedly, that there is some contention about the matter in English Protestantism, particularly at the beginning of the period we are studying. In the report of the dispute between Whitgift and Cartwright there is a reference to Cartwright's protesting of the continuing use in the Church of England of the priestly title. Replies Whitgift: "The name of priest need not be so odious unto you as you would seem to make it. I suppose it cometh of this word *presbyter*, not of *sacerdos*, and then the matter is not great."[24]

Hooker, however, has already conceded the point. A little grudgingly at first, he writes that he terms the ministers of the Gospel in the English church presbyters rather than priests, "because in a matter of so small moment I would not willingly offend their ears to whom the name of Priesthood is odious though without cause." A few lines later, nonetheless, he confesses that "in truth the word *Presbyter* doth seem more fit, and in propriety of speech more agreeable than *Priest* with the drift of the whole Gospel of Jesus Christ."[25]

Neither "presbyter" nor "priest" is the word principally encountered in these sermons; it is instead, as we have noted,

---

[22] *Works*, I, 219. Cf. Pauck, "The Nature of Protestantism," *Church History* (March, 1937) Pauck, *The Heritage of the Reformation* (Boston, 1950), pp. 27-33.
[23] Dering, *Works*, p. 591.
[24] Whitgift, *Works*, III, 350.
[25] *Polity*, v, 78, iii.

"minister" or "the ministry." "Preacher" and "pastor" are other common terms. Avoidance of the controversial word of priest is not absolute nor universal, to be sure. Even a "puritan" writer may occasionally employ it in other than a hostile sense,[26] and so aggressively Protestant a sermonizer as Ussher uses it fairly often and without embarrassment. The preference in this literature, however, is clearly for those terms which have no involvements with Roman Catholic ecclesiasticism. Except with such extreme conservatives as Cosin or Montagu, the older word, when used, is not allowed to retain any flavor of its former eminence and significance.

As always in this literature, once one point has been made about it, one seems compelled to turn around and make its opposite. For even though the English Protestant decisively rejects the quality of magic or superhuman power which adheres to the Roman Catholic concept of the priesthood, and even though, to symbolize this basic rejection, he tends to avoid even the term of priest, nevertheless to the position of the minister and the office of the ministry he attaches enormous virtue and dignity. Those very "puritans" who most adamantly repudiate the attributes of the Roman Catholic priesthood are also those who tend to devote most space and passion to asserting the value of the ministerial function. "The dignity of the Ministers function," Gouge declares, "is in a spirituall respect so great, as no calling in the world can be comparable unto it." He unfolds his viewpoint further: "I would not be understood to speake only of outward respect, for our master is heavenly, our calling . . . our message spirituall and heavenly: accordingly must the respect bee which is given unto us; which is diligently to attend unto our message. Willingly to follow our directions, to account our comming welcome, our feete bewtifull, in heart to esteem us as Gods Angels, yea as Christ himselfe."[27]

For Bolton, "The feet of Gods faithful Messengers [that is, His ministers] are so beautifull in the eyes of discerning Christians . . . that they intertaine them into their affections with speciall reverance as Angels of God, nay in an holy sense, even

26 Dering, *Works*, p. 457; Adams, *Works*, p. 934.
27 *Works*, II, 258.

as Christ Jesus himselfe."[28] Perkins speaks of ministers as "Angels" or as "Ambassadours . . . sent from the high God," and of "every true Minister" as "Gods Interpreter to the people, and the peoples to God" or as "the divine and spirituall interpreter."[29] Ministers, says Sibbes, are "Christs mouth." "Christ is either received or rejected in his Ministers."[30]

Adams even states what is otherwise and in regard to any other kind of calling never suggested in this literature: that the eternal reward coming to the good minister will be greater than that coming to the good Christian who performs a lesser function: "*We shall shine* and that with no ordinary glory; but *As the Starres*: and this not for a time; but, For ever and ever. . . . I would shew you the differences of Glory, which are heere implyed, *Good Men shall shine as the Firmament*: but, *Good Ministers, as the Starres*. If I be not deceived, the Starres have a brighter glory than the Firmament."[31]

This emphasis upon the importance of the minister and his work is by no means a monoply of the so-called "puritans." Bilson, for example, insists that "in spiritual perfection and consolation the Preacher excelleth the Prince by many degrees"; ministers he refers to as the messengers of God's grace and the "stewards of his mysteries."[32] Cooper speaks of the clergy of the Church of England as those who "have brought unto this realme, the same light of the gospell, the same trueth of doctrine, the same way of salvation, that the Apostles brought to the people of God in their time. They are the mouth of God, whereby hee speaketh to us and calleth us to his knowledge, as hee did his chosen by other in the Primitive church."[33] And Sanderson maintains that because the minister is "Gods Embassadour," therefore "a slander or other wrong or contempt done to a minister . . . is a sin of an higher strain than the same done to a Common Christian . . . as reaching unto God himself. . . ."[34]

Though the Roman Catholic concept of the uniquely sacerdotal capacities of the priesthood is rejected by English Protes-

28 Bolton, *Works*, IV, 205.    29 *Works*, III, 431.
30 *Bowels Opened*, pp. 142-43.    31 *Works*, p. 81.
32 Bilson, *The True Difference*, p. 219.
33 Cooper, *An Admonition*, p. 4.
34 Sanderson, *XXXVI Sermons*, p. 23.

tants, there is still a general acceptance in this literature of the minister's possession, in a very substantial sense, of the power of the keys—the power to absolve the repentant sinner from the burden of his guilt, or at least to signalize to him the reality of God's forgiveness. Some differences of interpretation are evident. While certain conservative writers are more concerned with the statement of this power in its maximum fullness, though still within the limitations which Protestantism places on it,[35] divines of "puritan" inclinations tend to emphasize these limitations instead and to remind believers that all effective absolution of sin must in the long run be accomplished by God alone. Yet Perkins' definition of the minister's power of the keys is surely universal English Protestant orthodoxy: ". . . authoritie is given to a Minister of God, *to redeeme* a man penitent from hell, and damnation: not that he is the meanes of working out this redemption, for that wholly and onely is Christ himselfe: but he is Gods instrument and Christs instrument. First, *to apply* those meanes unto him: Secondly, *to pronounce* his safetie and deliverance when these meanes are used. Here is the principall honour of all, belonging to that calling: and it is the greatest that ever was vouchsafed to any creature Man or Angel: for it is a plaine Commission, *to goe and deliver such a man from the power of hell*, and to redeeme him into the state of Gods children, and to make him heire of Heaven. . . ."[36]

English Protestant divines frequently lash out—and here too it is the "puritans" among them who do so most frequently and with greatest vigor—at the disrespect and even active scorn of the minister and the ministerial calling which they feel to be prevalent in their time. The old theme of the inevitable affliction of the godly through persecution by the ungodly is now applied to these leaders and prime exemplars of the godly. Bolton observes that "the conscionable Minister is an ordinary and eminent Object, whereon prophanenesse, and policy: hatred to be reformed and conformall Popery; hell and the world, doe execute the extremity of their rage and poyson."[37] "This Land,"

35 See especially Montagu, *Appello Caesarem*, p. 316.
36 *Works*, III, 437.
37 *Works*, IV, 167.

Gouge similarly complains, "and the greater sort of people therein, have in these dayes highly provoked the Lord by disgracing and abusing his Ambassadours. For we are made as the filth of the world, the off-scouring of all things."[38] So confident is Gouge of the world's antagonism against the godly minister that he advises ministers who receive other treatment to question the quality of their work. "All that are of the world," he writes, "will doe what they can against them [ministers] . . . let them not look for such respect at the worlds hands, as earthly Ambassadours find: if they find such, they have cause to suspect themselves. It is to bee feared, that they seeke too much to please the world."[39]

The function of the minister, as English Protestants conceived it, has become fairly clear from the preceding discussion. As was the Roman Catholic priest, the English Protestant minister is a mediator between God and the laity; but his mediation is inspirational, guiding, and assisting, rather than mystical, supernatural or authoritative. The minister is named for what he does: he ministers; he helps. Having in the course of an argument identified the ministry and the church, Adams makes a neat statement of the viewpoint: "They [the Papists] say, the holy Ghost useth the authoritie of the Church to beget Faith in our hearts: We say, he useth the Ministry onely, not the authoritie."[40]

Yet the ministry of the church, the ministry of the ministers, remains for the English Protestant an extremely important factor in the spiritual destiny of every individual; after God's will expressed through predestination and God's word spoken in His Scriptures, it is the most important factor. For the vast majority of individuals, indeed, the services of the minister are seen to constitute an absolutely essential aid and stimulation to the conquest of the flesh and the winning of salvation. In a sense, therefore, the Protestant concept of the minister thrusts upon him a greater burden of responsibility for the welfare of his flock than the Catholic priest has had to bear. The minister's is a strenuous, penetrating role; he cannot only passively offer but

[38] *Works*, II, 258-59.    [39] *Ibid.*, p. 265.    [40] *Works*, p. 67.

must also actively motivate to accept. Compared to the Roman Catholic priest, the quality and effectiveness of his work, and hence his own value as a co-worker with God, come to depend far more upon his personal ability and self-directed actions and far less upon the automatic functioning of his office. There is in consequence a renewal of the old pressure upon the minister —which had once proceeded so far as to produce the Donatist heresy—to be in every sense that perfect instrument of God and to exhibit in himself the marks of God's grace and power.

Thus ideas and ideals of ministerial character and behavior were set up, especially in those early days of English Protestantism, full of many enthusiasms as they were. Being certainly beyond the immediately practicable and perhaps even beyond the ultimately possible reach of actuality, such ideas and ideals became also sources of bitterness and dispute. It was not that the ideals themselves were challenged or found unacceptable by any group within the Church of England: they were praised and generally desired by all. But because of two issues there was established a scale of differences along which the divines can be variously located. First, there was an issue of how much and what kind of emphasis should be placed upon the ideal, and an occasional question about its exact definition. More important— since this measure tends more adequately to distinguish a group of conservatives whose interest was defense of the ecclesiastical status quo from a group of aggressive Protestants whose interest was further reform—was a matter of the degree and type of reaction aroused by any failure in the actuality to rise to the ideal.

Strenuous complaint against the incompetence of ministers in the Church of England is, as one might expect, a relative monopoly of the so-called "puritans" among English Protestant divines. For one comment of this type from a recognized conservative, we have a large number from representatives of the reforming school. Hooker does speak somewhat of "that threefold blot or blemish of notable ignorance, unconscionable absence from the cures whereof men have taken charge, and unsatiable hunting after spiritual preferments" which, he felt, too much characterized the ministry of his church.[41] But how much sharper is this attack by Travers on ministerial failings: ". . . yt is a mervell how that ther be everywhere so many withe us both corrupt in doctrine and defiled in life and conversacion. For how many Papistes be ther now a dayes that even fiften yeeres after the reformacion off religion occupy the place of ministers in the church . . . How many also be ther admytted to the government off the church off most wicked life and ungodly behavior. . . ."[42]

In passage after passage the later "puritan," Dering, achieves much the same level of combativeness on this issue. He speaks of the "idle, prophane, unlettered, and unskillfull Pastors" who afflict the Church of England, "Feeders, but of themselves, not of thy flocke: Teachers and Doctors, who have mouthes but speake not, eyes but see not."[43] He refers to some preachers who "are . . . so corrupt, that they will sell the trueth for a mourning gowne." Complaining further, he says: "Let a man bee never so blinde . . . yet you shall find some preacher will commend his sight; if a man were as blacke as the blacke horse spoken of in the Apocalypse . . . yet hee shall finde a blacke Prophet with a blackemouth, and a head-long tongue, to make him as white as white wool."[44]

With almost equal sharpness Bolton inveighs against those false prophets "who out of their owne . . . lying visions, cry peace unto the consciences of unholy men [and] for want of a Conscience or courage, applaud and secure the great Ones of the world, in the unblessed sunshine of their outward glory, and unsanctified greatnesse."[45] Even the moderate Perkins finds occasion to lament the number and variety of inadequate ministers in the English church, ministers who are "as unsavourie salt" since they "doe not, or cannot dispense Gods word, for the seasoning of mens soules." Among these are "the blind watch-men that have not knowledge: and dumbe dogges that cannot barke" as well as those who, knowing and preaching

[41] Polity, II, 31, V.
[42] Travers, A Full and Plaine Declaration of Ecclesiasticall Discipline, p. 64.
[43] Works, pp. 133-34.     [44] Ibid., pp. 553-54.
[45] Works, IV, 157.

good doctrine, yet spoil the salutary effect of it by their "ungodly and scandalous lives."[46]

Obviously, then, certain English Protestant divines expressed a sense of imperfection, even grievance, on the issue of the competence of ministers. This attitude, at least when vigorously stated, was bound to be met by defensive and counter-aggressive reactions, particularly by those divines who were most directly responsible for the institutional functioning of the English church. Typical of this conservative response to criticism is a passage from Andrewes, in which he flings the epithet of Donatist at those presumed perfectionists who complained about the absence of personal virtue in the ministry of the Church of England: "For, an error it is, an old worne error of the *Donatists*: and but new dressed over by some *fanaticall Spirits*, in our dayes, that teach in corners. One, that is not himselfe inwardly holy cannot be the meanes of holinesse to another. And where they dare too, that: One, that is not in a state of grace, can have no right to eny possession or place. For, they of right belong to none, but to the true children of God: that is, to none but to themselves.

"Fond ignorant men! . . . they that by the *Word*, the *Sacraments*, the *Keyes*, are unto others the conduits of grace, to make them fruitful in all good workes: may well so be, though themselves remaine unfruitful, as doe the pipes of wood or lead, that by transmitting the water, make the garden, to beare both herbes and flowers, though themselves never bare eny. . . . Sever the office, from the men. . . ."[47]

These currents of criticism and defense or counter-criticism are fairly easy to trace in this literature and following them, one is able to separate with relative accuracy the "puritan" from the conservative group. Yet the effort to distinguish between these parties becomes much more difficult, if not impossible, when the basis of differentiation is positive principles rather than such essentially negative reactions. All English Protestants really agree, for instance, that personal virtue and a very special competence are at the least extremely desirable ministerial at-

[46] *Works*, III, 24.
[47] Andrewes, *XCVI Sermons*, p. 696.

tributes; indeed, to the good minister they are absolutely essential. Andrewes himself lists as the first of the duties of the minister that he should be "an example in his life."[48] Ussher declares it to be part of the contract which a minister makes with his people that he must shine "before them by an holy example."[49] Surely, then, there is nothing exceptional in Perkins' statement on the same subject: "All ministers therefore, as they would see any fruits of their ministerie, let them first sanctifie themselves, and cleanse their hearts by repentance, before they presume to stand up, to rebuke sinne in others."[50]

Certain divines of "puritan" inclinations actually complain vociferously of the presumed lack of virtue in many ministers of the English church. Yet for all that, no one of them insists that the possession of this quality is completely necessary for the sufficient, if not most efficient, performance of the minister's duties. All, in short, ultimately abide by the directive of Andrewes that the person of the minister and his office must be distinguished. Thus Hildersam, a "puritan," maintains that "a man may be a Preacher of Gods sending, though he be an hypocrite, and have no truth of grace in his heart."[51] Downame similarly contends that "the Ministerie of the Word is Gods ordinance, which dependeth not upon the worthinesse of him who delivereth it, neither is it made voide and uneffectuall by his unworthines, but it hath its vertue . . . from the blessing of God, and from the inward operation of his spirit. . . ."[52] And Perkins too, though he is among those who most emphatically assert how desirable it is for the minister himself to be a man of grace and virtue, denies as unequivocally as Andrewes that this is necessary. "Whereas wholesome doctrine out of Scripture

---

[48] *Works*, II, 194.     [49] *Op.cit.*, p. 301.     [50] *Works*, III, 450.

[51] Hildersam, *CLII Lectures*, p. 805. Even this statement by Travers is notable only in the breadth of the competence demanded and in the intensity of expression: "And yet here [in ministers] is not any common or vulgar knowledge and zeale of religion to be required but speciall and singular above all men. For ther is none so small a function in the churche that doth not as it were exempt them out off the number of other men and joyning them as it were neerer to God doth lay a necessitye upon them beinge placed in higher degree to shine and give example unto others and stir them up by ther meanes, to all vertewes and godlynes" (*op.cit.*, p. 62).

[52] Downame, *Warfare*, p. 174.

is a note of a true Prophet," he writes, "it teacheth us that we may lawfully use the ministerie of those men, whose lives and conversations be evill and offensive, if so be their doctrine be sound and good. . . . the vertue and efficacy of the Word and Sacraments administered by men, is not from the Minister, but from God."[53]

How significant in the minister's life is the calling—the sense of special summoning and dedication to the responsibilities of his office? Here is another area of discussion where, within a broad context of general agreement, differences of detail in emphasis and analysis may to some extent be equated with a factional difference between conservative and "puritan." Involved here is something more than the mere belonging to and working in a calling which, in the Protestant view of things, appertains to every Christian who fills a role or performs a job in the world. As the duties of the minister are extraordinary, so his sense of calling must also be extraordinary. Even the conservatives admit so much, though—befitting a group so largely involved in the practical problems of administration and in establishing and maintaining, particularly, workable standards for admission to the ministry—they tend to understate the interior and hidden quality of the ministerial sense of calling and to translate it as much as possible into the external testimony provided by a man's talents and training. Thus, having observed that since the minister's position is an honour which "no man must take . . . unto him unless he be called," Andrewes then confidently counsels the potential minister that his calling may best be known to him merely through "his talents." There are, he advises, three orderly, obvious, and measurable procedures through which the individual enters into the ministry: "*a*. having this calling, and *b*. having in the university where this was taught, his bringing up, and *c*. having the laying on of hands of the company of eldership."[54] Sanderson makes a similar sober statement of the matter: "Divines teach it commonly, and that truly, that every man should have an inward Calling from God, for his particular course of life: and this in the Calling

[53] *Works*, III, 241.
[54] *Works*, II, 192-93.

of the Ministry is by so much more requisite, than in most other Callings, by how much the business of it is more weighty than theirs, as of things more immediately belonging unto God. . . . We are to know, therefore, that to this inward Calling there is not of necessity required any inward, secret, sensible testimony of Gods blessed sanctifying Spirit to a mans soul . . . [but only] these three things now specified, viz. the Inclination of their nature, their personal Abilities, and the care of Education. If it shall please God to afford any of us, any farther gracious assurance than these can give us . . . we are to embrace it with joy . . . as a special favour: but we are not to suspend our resolutions for the choice of a course, in expectation of that extraordinary assurance; since we may receive comfortable satisfaction to our souls without it, by these ordinary means, now mentioned.

"For, Who need be scrupulous, where all these concur?"[55]

One may observe, however, a subtle shift away from this conservative posture, toward what may be called a "puritan" one; this is evident even in Ussher's declaration that there is a sinful "theft" by the minister of the perquisites and honors of his occupation "when he presseth into his Calling uncalled . . . being neither qualified with gifts, nor willing to imploy those he hath for the good of the people."[56] The shift consists partly in the emphasis upon the moral urgency of the question of whether the sense of calling is present or absent and partly in the addition of something beyond the external gifts: the wholly inward element of "willing." A passage from Perkins reveals this insistence on the primary and essential inwardness of the phenomenon. He maintains that "the callings of the Ministers of the Gospel must bee manifest to their owne consciences" since "they are to speak in the name of God, and this they cannot doe, unless they know themselves to be called." The minister must have "the assurance of his calling" if he is to pray for "the assistance of Gods Spirit in the teacher," which alone can make his work effective.

Not that there is an entire turning away from the elements

55 *Op.cit.*, pp. 220-21.
56 *Op.cit.*, p. 301.

Andrewes spoke of; there is not a subtraction or a substitution, but rather an addition and a consequent reevaluation of the relationship among the several elements. How can men know that they are called by God to be ministers? They may know, answers Perkins, by their possession of three things: ". . . the testimonie of their consciences, that they entred not for praise, honour, lucre, but in the feare of God . . . a faculty to doe that for which they have a desire and will . . . the Ordination of the Church, which approves and gives testimonie of their will and ability. Hee that hath these things, is certainely called of God."[57]

"Wouldst thou know whether God would have thee to goe or no?" Perkins elsewhere summarizes. "Then thou must aske thy owne conscience, and aske the Church, for if thou be heartily willing, and be fully and worthfuly qualified, then God bids thee go."[58]

All English Protestant divines concur with Andrewes in their view that the prerequisites to the ministry consist essentially of three elements: the calling, the necessary education, and the approval of the church. But by emphasis upon the inward character of the calling, by talk of the absolute need of the individual conscience to speak out in the choice of this highest of all callings, and by insistence on the minister's assurance not so much of the church's as of God's choice of him, it is possible for certain English Protestant divines, and notably for certain "puritans," to move considerably from the conservative and cautious position of an Andrewes. It is obvious that Bolton, for example, is meeting Andrewes in conscious combat when he writes: "Give me a Minister, admirable for the profoundnesse and variety of as much knowledge as you will . . . yet, except he be further sanctified with an experimentall insight into the great mystery of Godlinesse, and into the particularities of that heavenly science of saving soules . . . well may he carry away the credit of a great scholler, and a famous Preacher with the greater part: but I doe not see, how he shall ever be able to purchase in the hearts . . . of discerning Christians the honour and reverence of a good Pastour."[59]

[57] *Works*, II, 159.　　[58] *Works*, III, 462.　　[59] *Works*, IV, 163-64.

The "good Pastour" must be called, then, and called inwardly, and sanctified to his work through his calling. Only those "whose calling may bee knowne to bee of God,"[60] ought to be summoned and educated and authorized to serve in His public ministry.

A final topic concerning the definition of the good minister and his proper role in the church remains to be considered. This is the question of how much and in what manner the good minister must be a preaching minister. We are confronted again with a situation we have encountered many times before: a large and basic area of common viewpoint within which exist differences of approach and precise statement which serve roughly to divide a conservative from a more aggressively Protestant group. All English Protestant divines agree that the good minister should be a preaching minister; they all agree that the distinction between Roman Catholic priest and Protestant minister consists at least partly in this: that the primary job of the Roman Catholic priest is to officiate in the sacrifice and the miracle of the mass and thereby to mediate between divinity and the laity, whereas the primary job of the Protestant minister is, through preaching to pour into his listeners the Word and the power of the Word, thus arousing and heartening each to make his own particular rendezvous with God. The capacity to preach well, then, is an ideal placed before the minister by all English Protestant sermon-writers. The difference between one group of Protestant divines and another appears only in two subsidiary aspects of this ideal: first, the reaction to the church's inability to assure that all its ministers have such a talent; second, the question of an exact definition of good preaching.

As in all the problems we have been dealing with, the "puritan" position is marked off by a relatively strong statement of the demands of the ideal, and by relatively aggressive and constant criticism of the church's failure to satisfy these demands. The conservative position is marked off by a defensive response to such criticism and by the insistence that where departure from the ideal is a matter of necessity and not of choice, it must be condoned and worked with rather than attacked. Thus

[60] Dering, *Works*, p. 605.

Whitgift becomes a typical representative of the conservative viewpoint in declaring: "One thing I must advertise you of . . . that, although I wish that all ministers were able to preach, yet that being impossible (as the state is now, and always for the most part hath been), I think the administration of the sacraments may be committed to those to whom the office of preaching is not committed. . . . And therefore reading ministers (if other things be correspondent) not to be rejected."[61]

Hooker's comment on the subject plainly shows his institutional interest: "We say . . . of the minister of God, 'publicly to teach and instruct the Church is necessary in every ecclesiastical minister, but ability to teach by sermons is a grace which God doth bestow on them whom he maketh sufficient for the commendable discharge of their duty.' That therefore wherein a minister differeth from other Christian men is not as some have childishly imagined the 'sound preaching of the word of God' but as they are lawfully and truly governors to whom authority . . . is given . . . according to the order which polity hath set, so canonical ordination in the Church of Christ is that which maketh a lawful minister as touching the validity of any act which appertaineth to that vocation."[62]

Andrewes, spokesman as he is for the *via media*, bewails the furor and states the essential insignificance of the dispute: "It were a folly to fall to comparisons . . . as the fond fashion now adaies is, whether is better. Prayer or Preaching; the *Word*, or the *Sacraments*. What needs this? Seeing we have both, both are ready for us. . . . It may be (who knowes) if the one will not worke, the other may. . . . In case it be not; yet have we offered to God our service in both, and committed the successe of both to Him."[63]

The far more common theme in this literature, however, is not this condoning of the absence of a talent in some ministers; rather, it is the assertion, without qualifying excuses for the unable, of the need for and the value of good preaching. Both Anglicans and "puritans" participate in this latter kind of commentary. Ussher, for example, speaks eloquently of a good ser-

61 Whitgift, *Works*, III, 52.     62 *Works*, II, 226-27.
63 *Op.cit.*, p. 542.

mon's power to stir and to disturb a man: "Which is the cause,"
he continues, "many men desire not to come where the Word
is taught, because it galls their consciences, and desire the masses
rather, because they say the *masse bites not*: They desire a dead
minister that would not rub up their consciences. . . ."[64] Hall
refers to the unique capacity of a sermon "to divide the Word
aright; to apply it to the conscience of the hearer; and in an
authoritative way to reprove sin, and denounce judgement
against sinners; to lay forth the sweet promises of the Gospel
to the faithful and penitent."[65]

What especially constitutes the distinction of the "puritan,"
therefore, is the active and aggressive criticism of those ministers
who preach not at all or else incorrectly, or of the church for
permitting such incompetent ministers to officiate within it.
One finds the peculiar quality of the "puritan" temper, for instance, in such a directly combative comment as this by Cartwright: "Another fault there is in the whole service or liturgy
of England, for that it maintaineth an unpreaching ministry;
and so consequently an unlawful ministry; I say it maintaineth,
not so much in that it appointeth a number of psalms and other
prayers and chapters to be read, which may occupy the time
which is to be spent in preaching . . . as for that it requireth
necessarily no thing to be done by the minister which a child
of ten years old cannot do as well and lawfully as that man
wherewith the book contenteth itself."[66]

Peculiarly "puritan," too, is the use of the harsh phrase or
epithet—"dumb dogges that cannot barke" is a common example—to refer to the ministerial derelicts who cannot or will
not preach. And Perkins surely exhibits his "puritan" proclivities in denouncing such inability not as a mere negative lack

---

[64] *Eighteen Sermons*, pp. 127-28.

[65] Hall, *Works*, IV, 839. Sibbes, the "puritan," adds very little to such emphasis
and praise when he declares that the sermon alone should be used as a tool of
compulsion by the church: "Other courses to punish men in their purse, or imprison them, or the like, may subdue them to outward conformity, but if we
would bring their soules to Heaven, let us indeavour to enlighten their understandings to see the danger they are in . . . there will be no need of any other
compulsion. . . . We are not to looke to gaine all by preaching: those that withstand it are sent by it with the more just damnation to Hell, but those that doe
belong to him are gained that way." (*Beames of Divine Light*, pp. 271-73.)

[66] Whitgift, *Works*, II, 454-55.

of talent, but as a positive "sinne against their neighbours."
"And not onely not to preach at all," he concludes, "but to
preach negligently is utterly condemned."[67]

Another fairly clear monopoly of "puritan" divines is the
formulation and publicizing, as an ideal for the good minister,
of that style of preaching which is somewhat vaguely designated
by its champions as "plain." Perkins is the principal spokesman
for the doctrine of the plain sermon. He writes: "Here first we
are to observe the properties of the Ministry of the Word. The
first, that it must bee plaine, perspicuous, and evident. . . .
Againe, that kinde of preaching is to be blamed in which there
is used a mixed kinde of variety of languages, before the unlearned . . . in this kinde of preaching wee doe not paint
Christ, but . . . our owne selves. It is a by-word among us: *It
was a very plaine Sermon*: And I say againe, *the plainer, the
better.*"[68]

Plain preaching, to Perkins and the few other "puritans" who
trouble themselves with this matter, must be primarily and overwhelmingly founded on the Scriptures. Dering invokes the
image of the "faithfull Minister, like unto Christ, one that
preacheth nothing but the word of God."[69] Says Bolton: ". . .
assuredly [the heart of the true Christian] feeles . . . itselfe more
soundly comforted, and truely Christianized . . . by one Sermon
woven . . . out of a feeling soule by the strength of meditation
. . . supported . . . by the true, naturall, and necessary sense of
the Word of life, managed with the powerfull incomparable
eloquence of Scripture . . . then with a world of generall, com-
mon-place, declamatorie discourses . . . though they should be
stuffed with the flower and quintessence of all the Arts, humani-
ties, Philosophies. . . ."[70]

The second positive quality of "plain" preaching, as its supporters define it, is that it must have power; it must be moving
to the emotions and rousing to the will. "The word preached,"
writes Perkins, "must pearce into the heart."[71]

The plain sermon, however, is perhaps more sharply, more
distinctively, and certainly more combatively defined by what

[67] *Works*, I, 55.  [68] *Works*, II, 222.  [69] *Works*, p. 456.
[70] *Works*, IV, 161.  [71] *Works*, II, 222.

it is not than by what it is. It is repeatedly opposed to the "scraping and patching together of the unprofitable Pompe of a selfe-Sermon,"[72] and "the vaunting of wit, memorie, and learning, by fine contrived sentences, multiplication of quotations, varietie of allegations of Fathers, Schoole-men and other learning."[73] This plain style of sermonizing likewise involves resistance to the use of foreign phrases, and especially of Greek and Latin, in pulpit oratory. "Neither the words of Arts, nor Greek and Latine phrases and quirkes must be intermingled in the sermon," Perkins admonishes, since such strange words "disturbe the mind of the auditours [and] hindereth the understanding of those things that are spoken."[74] At least potential in this doctrine, constructed so largely of negatives as it is, is the general capacity for belligerence. This is well exhibited in the following complaint by Bolton: ". . . one reason, why in this glorious Noone-tide of peace and profession, we have so many Preachers, and little planting of grace, is because we have so few truly skillful . . . in the . . . practice of that high and supernaturall Art of soul-saving. Because the Word is not handled with that conscience, feeling, and affection; but formally, and Frier-like: for selfe-praise, and private ends."[75]

Perkins, whose commentary on the subject of plain preaching is by far the most extensive, makes two points clear which should be noted before we close this topic. The first is that this doctrine, as he formulates it, is not antagonistic to learning as such or in any general sense. Perkins specifically defends the doctrine from any imputation of an encouragement to igno-

---

[72] *Works*, II, 210.    [73] *Works*, III, 13.    [74] *Works*, II, 670-71.

[75] *Works*, IV, 164. The confidence which the champions of plain preaching felt in the righteousness and thorough respectability of their cause is indicated by Bolton's citation of King James himself as one of the formulators of the principles involved. "Since the ancient Fathers preached dayly, how happeneth it," Bolton queries, "that many respected great Schollars in these times, preach so seldome?" He replies as follows to his own question: "First, one Reason may be an affected humour of man-pleasing, or selfe-preaching; which is ambitiously pursued, and mightily prevailes abroad in the world.

"This King James out of his deepe and Princely wisedome, conceived to be the cause of so many dayly defections from our Religion, both to Poperie and Anabaptism. He calls it a light, affected, and an unprofitable kind of teaching, which hath beene of late yeeres too much taken up in universitie, Citie, and Country: In which (saith he) there is a mustering up of much reading, and a displaying of their owne wits, etc. . . ." (*Works*, II, 209-10.)

rance: "If any man think that by this means barbarisme should be brought into pulpits, hee must understand that the Minister may, yea and must privately use at his libertie the arts, Philosophy, and variety of reading, whilest he is in framing his sermon: but he ought in publike to conceale all these from the people, and not to make the least ostentation. . . ."[76]

He remarks somewhat testily in another treatise that "it is no point of the greatest learning to use the sayings of Fathers and Poets in preaching; and they which use it not, refraine therefrom, not because they cannot doe it, but because they dare not mingle the sayings of men with the word of God."[77] The second point of moment he makes is that his doctrine of plain preaching does not involve the rejection of eloquence in sermons. "Rhetoricke is a warrantable, good, and lawfull art," he insists. "They . . . that holding the contrary, do say . . . it is unlawfull, goe against the common practice of the Scripture, and the rules of common reason."[78] The foundation of Christian eloquence, he maintains, is in the Scriptures. He has chosen no mean model, it must be confessed, for it is out of such respect for the Scriptures and for Scriptural eloquence that in his own time that noblest of monuments to the English language, the King James version of the Bible, was created.

For all the furor and aggressiveness that such a "puritan" at least as Bolton embodied in his pronouncements on plain preaching, it is difficult for the modern reader of these sermons to make any organized distinctions between plain preaching and its opposite—clear as its opposite might be to those who set up the rules. Indeed, Andrewes is the only English Protestant divine of whom one can say with relative security that here was the enemy, stylistically speaking, whom Perkins, Dering, and Bolton appear to have had in mind; but even Andrewes has come down to us not in the possibly more flowing line of his finished sermons, but in the inevitably somewhat crabbed scratchings of the author's and auditor's notes.[79] It is certainly

[76] *Works*, II, 670.     [77] *Works*, III, 208.     [78] *Works*, III, 93.

[79] Andrewes did feel his manner of preaching to be a target of the criticisms involved in the program of plain preaching; this is indicated by his reference to certain "imaginations" regarding the manner of delivery of sermons prevalent among some over-precise and rigid English Protestants. "They must hear no Latin,

impossible to make any consistent division on this basis between Anglicans and the so-called "puritans." Representative "puritan" writers employ sources of wisdom and anecdote in their sermons other than those which are strictly Scriptural; Anglican and all other English Protestant divines invariably set their sermons in a Scriptural context and cite Scriptural far more than non-Scriptural references.

If one seeks in simplicity and directness of approach the criteria of the style in question, then Sanderson was surely a plain preacher and Ussher as well. If one would emphasize the power of a sermon, its moving or emotional quality, then Hall and even Ussher on occasion were at least as plain preachers as any others. And if plain preaching is both these qualities plus eloquence, that is, simply great preaching, then who in this period is a greater preacher than John Donne? Obviously there was an issue here and even something of a quarrel but, as with so many of these matters, when one attempts to tie the problem down to actual realities and instances, it is hard, from this distance at least, to discover what the fuss was all about.[80]

## IV. The Scriptural Foundation

The view that Scripture is the primary and final source of authority and truth in Christianity, though it is one of the elements in the "puritan" doctrine of plain preaching, is by no means limited to a group of extremists in English Protestantism. Against the background of Roman Catholicism, Protestantism as a whole is indeed characterized by this emphasis, which constitutes an essential ingredient of its revolutionary *élan.* Opposing an entrenched institutionalism by appeal to an older and purer truth before and beyond it, Protestantism was forced by the very logic of its position into a peculiar reliance upon Scripture. Hence the thorough Protestantism of the Eng-

---

no Greek," he notes, "nor none of the Apocrypha . . . Nor any thing alleged out of the Jews Talmud. . . . But especially no heathen example or authority—for which allegations of the ancient Fathers I have often dealt—a matter which the Primitive Church never imagined unlawful." (*Works*, VIII, 56.)

[80] Cf. W. Fraser-Mitchell, *English Pulpit Oratory from Andrewes to Tillotson* (1932); A. F. Herr, *The Elizabethan Sermon* (Philadelphia, 1940).

lish church of this period is reaffirmed by the divines' absolutely universal acceptance of Scripture as the Word of God over any and all merely human authority or tradition.

To English Protestant divines, the errors of Roman Catholicism in this area of dispute consist particularly in two deviations from a proper estimate of the supreme validity of Scripture: in the tendency to value so-called traditions equally with Scripture; and in the endeavor to confirm Scripture through the church rather than the church through Scripture. All divines who touch upon such matters take pains to reject these two errors and to affirm their opposites. Hooker, for example, joining Scripture to man's "natural understanding," argues that "they both jointly . . . be so complete, that unto everlasting felicity we need not the knowledge of anything more than these two may easily furnish our minds with on all sides; and therefore they which add traditions, as a part of supernatural necessary truth, have not the truth, but are in error."[81] Whitaker similarly declares that "all things appertaining to faith and morals may be learned . . . from Scripture, so as that traditions are in no way requisite."[82] And Ussher asserts that "the bookes of holy Scripture are so sufficient for the knowledge of Christian Religion, that they doe most plentifully contain all Doctrine necessary to salvation . . . whence it followeth, that wee need no unwriten verities, no traditions or inventions of men, no Canon of Councels, no sentences of Fathers, much lesse Decrees of Popes, for to supply any supposed defect of the written word. . . ."[83]

The superiority of Scriptural over merely ecclesiastical authority is likewise universally maintained by English Protestant divines. Bilson states simply that "the Church is not judge of the Scriptures,"[84] and Ussher writes that "any authority that the Church hath, it must prove it by the Scriptures therefore the Scripture dependeth not upon the Church."[85]

---

[81] *Polity*, I, 14, v.

[82] Whitaker, *A Disputation of Holy Scripture Against the Papists* (Cambridge, 1849), p. 515.

[83] *Divinitie*, p. 18.   [84] Bilson, *op.cit.*, p. 258.

[85] *Op.cit.*, p. 12. Whitaker only makes the point more insistent and explicit when he explains: ". . . we do not acknowledge, receive, promulge, commend the

Though exceptional in the extent of his defensive concern for the institutional structure of the English church and correspondingly sensitive to what he considers any undue emphasis by Protestant extremists upon the authority of Scripture, even Laud in his positive statements does not depart notably from the above viewpoint. His analysis of the relationship between tradition, or the church, and Scripture is one which securely preserves the ultimate logical supremacy of the latter over the former. He writes: "And since it is apparent that tradition is first in order of time, it must necessarily follow that Scripture is first in order of nature; that is, the chief upon which faith rests and resolves itself. . . . A beginner in the faith, or a weakling, or a doubter . . . begins at tradition and proves Scripture by the Church; but a man strong . . . in the faith . . . proves the Church by Scripture."[86]

Tradition is necessary, he argues, not because Scripture is insufficient, but "because it is deep, and so can be mistaken, if any man will presume upon his own strength, and go single without the Church."[87] He affirms, as any "puritan" might have done, that the Church of England is founded decisively and narrowly in Scripture. He claims, moreover, that those Roman Catholic elements she has eliminated do not possess the requisite Scriptural sanction. Addressing the Jesuit, Fisher, he declares: "The Church of England grounded her positive articles upon Scripture, and her negative do refute these, where the thing affirmed by you is not affirmed by Scripture, nor directly to be concluded out of it. And here, not the Church of England only, but all Protestants agree most truly and most strongly in this, 'That the Scripture is sufficient to salvation and contains in it all things necessary to it.' . . . And have we not reason then to account it, as it is, the foundation of our faith."[88]

---

scriptures to all its members; and we say that this testimony is true, and should be received by all. . . . But we deny that we believe the scriptures solely on account of this commendation of them by the church. For we say that there is a more certain and illustrious testimony, whereby we are persuaded of the sacred character of these books, that is to say, the internal testimony of the Holy Spirit, without which the commendation of the church would have with us no weight or moment." (*Disputation*, pp. 279-80.)

[86] Laud, *Works*, II, 114-16.     [87] *Ibid.*, p. 117.     [88] *Ibid.*, pp. 61-62.

Why this English Protestant preference for Scripture over all other sources of religious authority? Because Scripture alone is seen to be the authentic word of God, whereas traditions and the church are both fallible in the human quality of their origins. "A man is not bound to receive any thing in Religion," says Hildersam, "upon the credit of any man whatsoever, till he have tried and examined it by the Scriptures."[89] Sanderson finds it "prejudicial to . . . that freedom we have in Christ, to give [servile] honour to any other man, but the man Christ Jesus only; or to any other writings than to those which are in truth the Oracles of God, the holy Scriptures of the Old and New Testament."[90] Mere men, moreover, are prone to the perpetration and the perpetuation of mistakes. "For the heart of man which drinketh in errour," observes Dering in rejecting the validity of traditions, "is very bound with olde customes . . . measuring truth which is pure and holy, onely by time, which is corrupt and evill . . . nature also hath enflamed our affections to love to much our Fathers waies."[91]

Men cannot be left to themselves nor to anything simply human, Whitaker contends, in the pursuit of religious truth. In civil affairs, which pertain to "this life," custom and natural reason are very important. But they are "of no avail in religion," for in this realm men are "blind by nature and cannot without the divine words and laws rightly worship God, or attain to life. Wherefore they are by no means to be left to themselves but must be bound to certain and written laws."[92]

English Protestants share with Protestantism as a whole the insistence that Scriptures be translated into the vernacular and be made universally available to all Christians. Special pleading for the encouragement of universal literacy is an interesting further consequence of this position among a number of English Protestant writers.[93] The problem of interpreting Scripture is variously but almost always confidently encountered. The most common argument is this, stated as follows by Whitaker: ". . . our fundamental principles are these: First, that the scrip-

[89] Hildersam, *op.cit.*, p. 59.    [90] *XXXVI Sermons*, p. 306.
[91] *Works*, pp. 216-17.    [92] *Op.cit.*, p. 612.
[93] Cf. Morton, *op.cit.*, pp. 150-51; Ussher, *Divinitie*, p. 27.

tures are sufficiently clear to admit of their being read by the people and the unlearned with some fruit and utility. Secondly, that all things necessary to salvation are profounded in plain words in the scriptures. Meanwhile, we concede that there are many obscure places, and that the scriptures need explication; and that, on this account, God's ministers are to be listened to when they expound the Word of God, and the men best skilled in scripture are to be consulted."[94]

Heresies arise, Ussher argues, not from the darkness of the Scriptures but from the "naughty hearts" of those who lack "an humble and godly affection for the Word."[95] They spring "not of Scripture," Perkins similarly maintains, "but are darke cloudes which spring out of the blinde hearts of hypocrites given to pride and singularitie."[96]

It is evident that on the basis of the positive tenets of Scripturalism as a viewpoint or an emphasis, no line of demarcation can be drawn between Anglicans and "puritans" in English Protestantism. Nevertheless, one exclusively non-"puritan" preoccupation can be defined in this area of discussion. This is the overt concern with what is conceived as the prevalence within and without the Church of England of an overly enthusiastic Scripturalism—a Scripturalism which permits or fosters criticism of the structure and practices of the Church of England. Thus Hooker quarrels with those believers who would "draw all things unto the determination of bare and naked Scripture" and in the process entirely abate "the estimation and credit of man." "For the scope of all their pleading against man's authority," he concludes, "is to overthrow such orders, laws and constitutions in the church, as . . . if they should . . . be taken away, would peradventure leave neither face nor memory of Church to continue long in the world. . . ."[97] "Those men are in a great error," says Sanderson, "who make the holy Scripture the sole rule of all humane actions whatsoever." He further declares that "the stirs that have been long since raised and are still upheld by the factious Opposers against our Ecclesiastical Constitutions, Government, and Ceremonies . . . had been long

[94] *Op.cit.*, p. 364.    [95] *Divinitie*, p. 23.
[96] *Works*, I, 392.    [97] *Polity*, II, 7, ii-iii.

ere this wholly buried in silence, or at leastwise pretty well quieted if the weakness and danger of the error whereof we now speak [that is, excessive Scripturalism] had been more timely discovered. . . ."98

Cosin, too, displays this same embattled conservatism in his attack upon "this bragging age . . . this vainglorious generation that . . . can quote Scripture[s] so fast . . . or use them for a colour to make the world think they are such goodly professors . . . or bring them forth to hold argument against Christ, or against His Church." To use Scripture in this manner is "the devil's way."99 Laud likewise finds reason to warn against those "many rigid professors" who exalt Scripture "to the neglect and contempt of the Church, which the Scripture itself teaches man both to honour and obey." "Atheism and irreligion" gather strength through the excesses of this kind of Scripturalism and the consequent weakening of ecclesiastical authority.100

Hooker, Sanderson, Cosin, Laud—all who have been quoted on this subject—are more than Anglicans; they are conservative Anglicans, representing a group which is beginning to emerge from this analysis as more sharply defined and readily identifiable than the "puritans" themselves. Thus the conservative Anglican defines himself here by the negative evoking of an image of narrow Scripturalism to which he is opposed. As has often happened in discussing previous disputes, however, the positive form of this image among those who presumably entertained and fostered it cannot really be found. Though in the course of particular arguments certain "puritan" divines may momentarily occupy a position allied to this which their conservative opponents attribute to them, their conscious and specifically advertised posture is one, not of exclusive, but only of primary reliance on Scripture. Preston, for example, cites Scripture as merely one, though the greatest, among no less than four sources of religious and moral truth available to man; and he joins with Hooker in numbering a "Law of Nature" ascertainable through human reason as yet another item on the

98 *XXXVI Sermons*, pp. 63-65.
99 Cosin, *Works*, I, 73-74.
100 *Works*, II, xv-xvi.

list.[101] Sibbes, in a gesture of the utmost generosity, throws open all the doors of learning and declares: "*All things are ours*, therefore truth; wheresoever we finde it, it is ours: we may read Heathen Authors. Truth comes from God, wheresoever we find it, and it is ours, it is the Churches; wee may take it from them as a just possession . . . we must not make an Idoll of these things, but Truth, wheresoever we finde it, is the Churches; therefore, with a good conscience wee may make use of any humane Author."[102]

Among "puritans" in the English church there is no specifically wholesale rejection of the value and authority of the Fathers. As, we have seen in our discussion of plain preaching, certain "puritans" do criticize what they feel to be excessive use in sermons of references to the Fathers. Reacting to such criticism, spokesmen of the more conservative Anglican position occasionally protest that this "puritan" passion for Scripturalism comprehends the total annihilation of "the testimonie and consent of the Primitive Church and the ancient learned Fathers."[103] Yet in actual fact, almost all the "puritan" ministers whose writings we have perused do not hesitate to quote extensively, when it suits their purposes, not only from the early Fathers but also from the later writers of the Schools. Making a principle of practice, Perkins himself, that prime champion and essential definer of plain preaching, freely grants in one sermon that "it is both lawfull and necessarie, for the defense of truth, that men of sound judgment and pietie study the writings of the Fathers" and even "Popish Commentaries and postils."[104] He pronounces in another treatise what amounts to the universal English Protestant viewpoint on the issue: "There be two kindes of writings in which the doctrine of the Church is handled, and they are either *Divine* or *Ecclesiasticall*. Divine are the bookes of the olde and new Testament, penned either by Prophets or Apostles. And these are not onely the pure *word* of *God*, but also the *scripture of God*: because not only the

---

101 *The Saints Qualification* (1634), pp. 180-83.
102 *The Christians Portion* (1638), pp. 68-69.
103 Cooper, *An Admonition*, pp. 70-71.
104 *Works*, III, 236.

matter of them; but the whole disposition thereof, with the style and the phrase was set downe by the immediate inspiration of the holy Ghost. And the authority of these bookes is divine, that is, absolute and soveraigne . . . and beeing the only foundation of faith, and the rule and canon of truth.

"*Ecclesiastical* writings are all other ordinary writings of the church consenting with Scriptures. These may be called the word or truth of God, so farre forth as their . . . substance is consenting with the written word of God . . . their authoritie in defining truth and falsehood in matters of religion is not soveraigne, but subordinate to the former: and it doth not stand in the authoritie and pleasures of men and Councels, but in the consent which they have with the Scriptures."[105]

## V. Sacraments and Ceremonies

In regard to the sacramental system, the most significant aspect of the Protestant break from Roman Catholicism is the reevaluation of the nature and efficacy of that key sacrament in all Christianity, the Eucharist. The doctrine of transubstantiation, with its emphasis on ministerial sufficiency, is replaced in the early forms of Protestantism by one type of ideology or another which emphasizes the spiritual state of the recipient. The reduction of the sacraments from seven to two is simply another, and a lesser, aspect of the same general Protestant tendency to interiorize religion.

The English Protestant position on the Eucharist is defined first and most importantly by its decisive and unqualified repudiation of the doctrine of transubstantiation. "The real presence of Christ's most blessed body and blood is not therefore to be sought for in the sacrament," says Hooker, "but in the worthy receiver of the sacrament."[106] The extension leftward of English Protestant sacramentalism is terminated at the Zwinglian reduction of the communion service simply to a memorial significance. "In this sort wee acknowledge Sacraments to be *signes*," Ussher declares, "but bare signes wee denie them to bee: *seales* they

105 *Works*, I, 122.
106 *Polity*, v, 67, vi.

are, as well as signes of the Covenant of grace."[107] "A Sacrament is that," Perkins similarly asserts, "whereby Christ and his saving graces, are by certaine externall rites, signified . . . and sealed to a Christian man."[108]

Though some differences of emphasis can be detected on this point, it is generally agreed in English Protestantism that not even the two sacraments which remain in the Protestant system —baptism and the Eucharist—are absolutely essential to salvation. Asserts Hooker: "Now the law of Christ which in these considerations maketh baptisme necessary, must be construed and understood according to rules of natural equity . . . And (because equity so teacheth) it is on all parts gladly confessed, that there may be in divers cases life by virtue of inward baptism, even where outward is not found."[109]

"Baptisme," Ussher likewise declares, "is a high Ordinance of God . . . and not to be neglected . . . yet where God denieth it . . . there comes no danger from the want of the Sacraments, but only from the contempt of them."[110]

Even Laud, who on this as on other issues exhibits a rare and extreme conservatism, takes care not to cut himself off entirely from the general stream of English Protestant opinion. Replying to Fisher on the matter of the Church of England's continuance of infant baptism, he writes that "it may be concluded directly out of Scripture, both that infants ought to be baptized, and that baptism is necessary to salvation . . . (in the ordinary way of the Church, without binding God to the use and means of that sacrament, to which He hath bound us). . . ."[111]

The less significant the issue, the more intense will be the disagreement: this often appears to be the most secure generali-

[107] *A Sermon Preached Before the Commons . . . 1620* (1631), p. 15.
[108] *Works*, I, 71.
[109] *Polity*, v, 60, v.
[110] *Divinitie*, p. 419. Perkins adds nothing except a further detail in argument when he writes: "The covenant of grace is absolutely necessarie to salvation . . . but a Sacrament is not absolutely necessarie, but only as it is a proppe and stay for faith to leane upon. For it cannot entitle us into the inheritance of the sonnes of God, as the covenant doth, but onely by reason of faith going before, it doth seale that which before was bestowed upon us . . . Therefore the want of a sacrament doth not condemne, but the contempt is that which will condemne a man." (*Works*, II, 73.)
[111] *Works*, II, 66-67.

zation regarding the differences and disputes which ruffle the calm of this English Protestant literature. Arguments between individual divine and individual divine or between faction and faction tend to be sharper and far more frequent in the ecclesiastical or institutional than in the doctrinal area; and where these ecclesiastical issues are themselves concerned, a common viewpoint tends to characterize the fundamentals of purpose and nature while tensions cluster around the incidental matters of precise interpretation and conduct. On the important subject of the function of the sacraments in the life of the church and of the Christian, for example, there is, as we have seen, very widespread and solid agreement in English Protestantism. But the details of conduct of these sacraments and other ceremonial and liturgical matters provoke more numerous and more considerable differences than may be found anywhere else in the church or in the church's literature. We are dealing here in good part with obvious and indisputable facts and the student who hopes to trace in English Protestantism a line of cleavage which will lead straight from the origins of the church to the decisive rift of revolution in 1640 is certainly well advised to turn first to these ceremonial and liturgical disputes. The institutional conservatism of English Protestantism has, after all, been best exhibited in the past as in the present in the relatively greater pomp and circumstance attaching to her services. There is a long and fully-documented history of opposition to this elaborate ceremonialism by more intense or radical Protestants within and without the English church. Laud's program, finally, interpreted so often as that last burden of official pressure which produced open rebellion in response, had as it principal content the effort to enforce on a more or less recalcitrant ministry the observance of every last jot and tittle of ceremonial and liturgical conformity.

Yet though ceremonialism is the area of the most severe and the most nearly steady factional antagonism in the Church of England during the period of our survey, we have nonetheless come to feel in the process of our research that here again too much rather than too little has been said; too many students have tended to draw lines of demarcation too sharply between opinion and opinion and group and group and have too generally made absolutes of what are actually only relatives. At least in the decades of English Protestant history with which we have been concerned (which are for these scholars the crucial decades), no single line of development for viewpoints on ceremonialism and liturgy can effectively or accurately be formulated. Within the English church, that is, there is no clearly defined official posture which meets in any process of growing distance and hostility a radical posture. There are arguments; there are incidents; there is even a culminating quarrel of serious proportions; but the active burden of antagonism is borne in each instance by a few individuals only—an extreme minority, it would appear from the evidence we have been considering, among the total body of the English Protestant ministry. These few individuals, furthermore, are primarily concentrated in two distinct and fairly widely separated periods, one close to the beginning of our time span and the other close to its end.[112]

A high level of argumentative tension in regard to ceremonies and liturgy, as in regard to many of the other ecclesiastical issues we have been discussing, is encountered in that grouping of polemics and polemicists symbolized by the *Book of Discipline* (attributed to Travers), the *Marprelate Tracts*, and the Whitgift-Cartwright exchange. A final, though much gentled, echo of this early agitation comes to us through accounts of the Hampton Court Conference. Evident in these various writings and reports is a real and bitter conflict between an intensive Protestantism which sought to eliminate all vestiges of external ceremonial with any link to the Roman Catholicism of the past, and an official position which, more than the preservation of these vestiges, sought merely their allowance where other circumstances appeared to dictate their expedience. The tone

[112] The list of "puritan" liturgical issues is a long one if all the protests are put together as a party manifesto; however, each "puritan" has his own pet notions: the usual excitement is over matters such as no surplice or cap, no cross or interrogatives in baptism, the communion table in the center aisle, no baptism by women, no confirmation, no ring in marriage, no kneeling at communion, no bowing to the name of Jesus, and the iconoclastic opposition to crosses, images, screens, and pictures in church. Cf. Hooker, *Polity*, Book v, *passim*. See also H. Davies, *The Worship of the English Puritans* (Westminster, 1948).

and manner of the intensive Protestant (the "puritan") approach is illustrated in a statement in the *Book of Discipline* on the vestiarian issue. The author begins mildly enough by remarking that "to binde the Mynesters to any certen fashion of forme of apparell hath no grownde off any precept off the gospell or commandement out off the word of god." But he quickly makes it plain that what he has in mind is no atmosphere of permissiveness wherein those who objected to the surplice might be free to dispense with it; he means, rather, an absolutism which would have forbidden its use to all. These garments "are . . . the invencions off men," he writes, "and of what men but even off such which have soughte to paint and adorne with these colors the shame of ther whorishe idolatrie and superstition . . . they take . . . allmost all ther massing apparell by a foolishe and ridiculous imitation: that having an alter and a priest they might not want apparell for the stage."[113] Cartwright couches his argument on the vestiarian question in much the same terms of embattled intolerance. Concerning the ministerial garments to which he takes exception he writes that "no authority by the word of God, with any pretence of order and obedience, [can] command them, nor make them in any wise tolerable, but by circumstances they are wicked and against the word of God."[114]

Cooper, one of those who entered into the fray at this time in defense of the Church of England's constitution and discipline, is essentially correct, then, when, in connection with this very dispute, he points out that the plea for permission of exception tends readily to become a demand for an opposite conformity. "At the beginning," he notes, "some learned and godly Preachers, for private respects in themselves, made strange to weare the Surplice, Cap, or Tippet, but yet so, that they declared themselves to thinke the thing indifferent, and not to judge evil of such as did use them. Shortly after rose up other defending that they were not thinges indifferent, but destayned with Antichristian idolatrie, and therefore not to bee suffered in the Church."[115]

[113] Travers, *Discipline*, p. 128.  [114] Whitgift, *Works*, II, 73.
[115] *Op.cit.*, pp. 160-61.

Quoted in his controversy with Whitgift, Cartwright again and again reveals himself to be as little a friend of compromise in his position as Laud was later to be in his. The form of the liturgy of the Church of England, as embodied in the Communion Book and in the Book of Common Prayer, is, he asserts, "taken from the church of antichrist"[116] and "is full of corruptions."[117] Replying to the frequently employed official argument that the appropriate authorities may authorize as ecclesiastical ceremonial or liturgy whatever is not repugnant to the Scriptures, Cartwright insultingly remarks: "But their craft is plain; wherein they deceive themselves standing so much upon this word 'repugnant'; as though nothing were repugnant or against the word of God, but that which is, expressly forbidden by plain commandment: they know well enough, and would confess, if either they were not blinded or else their hearts hardened that, in the circumstances each content, wherewith we justly find fault, and they too contentiously for the love of their livings maintain, smelling of their old popish priesthood, is against the Word of God."[118]

The official response to all this early controversy about ceremonies and liturgy is summarized entirely in two points made repeatedly by Whitgift. First, on Christian liberty regarding things indifferent: "No devil, no idol, no pope, can so defile the nature or form (not being contrary to the scriptures) of any of God's creatures, that the liberty of a christian man should be taken away in using and not using them."[119]

The second statement is on the right and business of the church as a public body—and specifically of the officers of the church—to choose arbitrarily from among these indifferent things certain ceremonies to symbolize in religious services the fact of the church's unity and order: "That which is appointed in the church by a lawful magistrate, and by lawful authority, for order and decency," Whitgift maintains, "doth edify, as other orders do ... what is comely and decent is not every man's part to judge, but the magistrate's, and such as have authority in the church."[120]

---

116 Whitgift, *loc.cit.*    117 *Ibid.*, III, 336.    118 *Ibid.*, p. 335.
119 *ibid.*, II, 55.    120 *Ibid.*, p. 58.

Hooker's lines of argumentation and his purpose follow those of Whitgift: "Let our first demand be . . . that in the external form of religion such things as are apparently . . . effectual and generally fit to set forward godliness . . . may be reverently thought of. . . . Neither may we in this case lightly esteem what hath been allowed as fit in the judgment of antiquity and by the long continued practice of the whole Church; from which unnecessarily to swerve, experience hath never as yet found it safe."[121] Meeting head-on the "puritan" charge of the Romishness of certain ceremonies, he declares that "what ceremonies we retain common unto the church of Rome, we therefore retain them, for that we judge them to be profitable and to be such that others instead of them would be worse."[122]

Careful analysis of the reports of the Hampton Court Conference reveals three principal observations relating to this matter. It is first of all made absolutely clear that the nature of the division between an Anglican and a "puritan" party within the Church of England was then, as it had always been, not doctrinal but almost entirely ecclesiastical or institutional. Also, in comparison with the era of Travers and Cartwright, the temper and mood of the controversy at this time had been greatly altered on both sides toward moderation and mutual forbearance. Finally, the preservation of the political structure and stability of the church was a central concern to the conservative party; as Whitgift and Hooker had long since readily acknowledged, defense of the church's ceremonials and liturgy was only a corollary of defense of the church's authority.

Recalcitrance of certain of the ministry on some of these ceremonial and liturgical issues does not cease with the Hampton Court Conference, of course, nor is there an end to official pressure in the direction of a more nearly perfect conformity. One finds Andrewes still defending the "customs" of the church from their attackers long after the conference is past. He remarks in some annoyance upon the contentiousness of these critics: "For with some all is not worth a rush, if they see not farther than their fellows, nay their betters, then; if they find not somewhat

121 *Polity*, v, 6, ii.    122 *Ibid.*, iv, 4, ii.

to find fault with, if it be but a ceremony. And to pick a quarrel with a ceremony is easy. A plausible theme, not to burden the Church with ceremonies; the Church to be free, which hath almost freed the Church of all decency."[123]

Yet how cautious he is, withal, in his defense, how intent upon soothing rather than irritating the sensitive. Customs, he points out, do not concern "*credenda*, points of doctrine," but only "*agenda*, matters of practice."[124] Only those customs which the Apostles and the Primitive Church approved does the Church of England maintain; there is, he argues, no better example for the church.[125] Finally, no custom can be considered valid which does not coincide with Scripture. "Nor do we even them [customs] with, much less oppose them to that which is written," he assures his readers, "Never any custom against that; no custom that comes from the will or wit of man, against Scripture which comes from the wisdom and will of God."[126]

Sanderson, too, spends a great deal of space and thought defending the Church of England's ceremonies from criticism by those whom he identifies as the "anti-ceremonian Brethren." His arguments follow closely the already-classic line of English Protestant reasoning in this area. The customs of worship in a Christian church are indeed externals and matters of indifference, he declares, and it is one of the grosser errors of papists and of popes that they "stile their Decrees and Constitutions Oracles" and "require subjection both to their Laws and Persons, as of necessity unto salvation."[127] Nonetheless, church authorities, and specifically English church authorities, have a right to establish certain of these customs of worship as requisite to the proper conduct of religious services; conformity to such customs becomes then "so necessary, that neither may a man without sin refuse them, where Authority requireth; nor use them, where Authority restraineth the use." He further assures the Christian reader that no shadow of popish error or any "impeachment to Christian Liberty" is here involved. "Our

---

[123] *Works*, v, 408.    [124] *Ibid.*, p. 410.    [125] *Ibid.*, pp. 412-13.
[126] *Ibid.*, pp. 410-11.    [127] *Op.cit.*, p. 304.

Church," he writes, "hath sufficiently declared her self by solemn protestation . . . that by requiring obedience to these ceremonial Constitutions, she hath no other purpose than to reduce all her Children to an orderly uniformity in the outward worship of God; so far is she from seeking to draw any opinion either of divine necessity upon the Constitution, or of effectual holiness upon the Ceremony."[128]

Both papists and "puritans," therefore, abuse Christian liberty, the first by understating and the latter by overstating it. "The earnestness of my desire," Sanderson declares, "[is] to contain within some reasonable bounds of sobriety and duty, those of my brethren, who think they can never run far enough from superstition, unless they run themselves quite out of their allegiance."[129] Considered in their totality, Sanderson's statements on the ceremonial issue are notably rational and moderate and hence, to the modern reader at least, notably compelling.

The most important point which emerges from our investigation of ceremonies, however—important because so little recognized—is not so much the moderation of the conservative party, nor the primarily formal or expedient basis on which it chose to take its stand. It is the almost total absence, once the period of Travers and Cartwright is passed, of militancy on the question and, indeed, in most instances of any considerable involvement with it among representatives of the so-called "puritan" contingent. Of the great number of divines of the Church of England whose sermons have been left to history and whom history has chosen to designate as "puritans," only a minority concern themselves to any extent at all with this subject and the principal preoccupation of those who do is the urging of moderation upon both extremes in the dispute. Perkins, to be sure, does warn against beguilement by that particular Romish error: the pursuit of salvation through outward ceremonial instead of inward grace.[130] Having pointed out else-

---

[128] *Ibid.*, p. 12.    [129] *Ibid.*, p. 318.

[130] ". . . take a view of the profession that is used among the people of England, and it will appeare, that they place their whole religion for the most part in the observation of certaine ceremonies. The manner of most men is to come to the place of assemblies, where God is worshipped, and there mumble up the Lords prayer, the Commandements, and the Beleefe in stead of prayers, which

where that "the love of God and of our brethren are the two highest degrees of good workes" while "the outward worship of God . . . commeth in the last place," Perkins complains again that "the practice of men is otherwise; generally they are more forward in outward ceremonies then in the main duties of the love of God and of their brethren." They are "like to the Pharisees, who passed over judgement and the feare of God, and were very strict in tything mint and rice. . . ."[131]

Though critical of the majority of English Protestant Christians, such comments are only very glancingly and indirectly censorious of the English Protestant Church itself and of its constitution and customs. Sibbes does not even participate in such cautious criticism as this; in regard to ceremonies he speaks altogether positively of the Church's continuance in the path of rectitude so boldly plotted by Luther and the other pioneers of Protestantism. "Therefore we are to praise God," he concludes, "for the liberty of the Church at this time, that we have the Word of God to rule our consciences, and that other matters are not pressed on us but as matters of decencie and order."[132] Adams' comments on ceremonial matters exhibit that distaste for all extremes, whether "puritan" or conservative, which constitutes the essence of the *via media*. He advises: "There bee certaine royall Lawes, which Christ and his Apostles made for eternall use: to the observation whereof all Christian Nations and persons are unchangeably bound. And there bee some rituall things, which were at the first convenient but variable according to the difference of the times and places. Strictly to impose all these circumstances on us, were to make us, not the sonnes, but the slaves of the Apostles. That is a fond scrupulositie, which would presse us in all fashions with a conformitie to the primitive times: as if the Spouse of Christ might not weare a lace or

---

being done, God is well served thinke they: whereas in the meane season they neglect to learne and practice such things as are taught them for their salvation by the Ministers of Gods word. . . . But wee must know, that there is no soundnesse of religion, but grosse hypocrisie in all such men; they worship God with their lippes, but there is no power of godlinesse in their hearts." (*Works*, I, 198-99.)

[131] *Works*, III, 49.
[132] *Beames of Divine Light*, pp. 264-66.

border, for which she could not plead prescription. . . . Let us keepe the substance; for the shadow God hath left us at liberty. But yet when we looke backe upon those first patterns, and finde a rule of discipline fit for the present times; in vaine wee should studie a new, that are so well accomodated with the old."[133]

Directly attacking those troublesome spirits who "love truth well, but not peace," Adams elsewhere pleads again for the "middle way": "It is the nature of our controversies to fight peremptorily at both ends, whiles truth and pietie is left in the middle, and neglected . . . The divisions of a few, and that about the huske of Religion, Ceremony, cannot redound to the condemnation of a whole Church. In Gods judgement it shall not."[134]

Finally, the "puritan" firebrand Downame virtually equalizes in Pharisaical shallowness those who place the essence of religion in the performance of ceremonies with those who unduly agitate for the elimination from the Church of England of those few remaining ceremonies: ". . . as though it were enough to be free from superstition, though we be destitute also of all true religion . . . to be zealous against ceremonies, and to be key-cold in embracing the substance truth, faith, mercy . . . brotherly kindnesse and the rest."[135]

Concerning customs of worship or ceremonies, therefore, the evidence clearly shows that during these halcyon middle years between Cartwright and Laud there was a large measure of mutual adjustment and agreement among all contributors to the English Protestant literature. Undoubtedly there were ministers who persisted throughout this time in stiffly and noisily dissenting from all adjustment on ceremonial matters, for although the strident voice of such is not much heard in the sermons of the period, both conservative and "puritan" writers bear witness (and almost always regretful witness) to its exist-

[133] *Works*, p. 931.    [134] *Ibid.*, p. 742.

[135] Downame, *Warfare*, p. 1055. In terms of logic if not the total and exact content of his argument, Sanderson had said little else than this when he observed that "it is superstition to forbid that as sinful, which is in truth indifferent, and therefore lawful; as well as it is superstition to enjoyn that as necessary, which is in truth indifferent, and therefore arbitrary." (*Op.cit.*, p. 305.)

ence. On the response to dissent on liturgy and ceremony, moreover, there was undoubtedly so much difference between conservative and "puritan" divines: the former were interested
first of all in defense and preservation of the ceremonial pattern
as it had been established (their very nature as conservatives
is defined, after all, by their defense of all aspects of the status
quo). The "puritans" were primarily interested in maintaining
a sufficient breadth of tolerance in the church so that some
deviation in "indifferent" things might be permitted while
agreement on the fundamentals of the faith continued to hold
firm the circuit of the ecclesiastical community.

Yet the hope and expectation of compromise on existing
differences were always focal in the thought of the sermonizers
of these middle decades—which were the decades also of the
*via media*, the middle way—and both the conservative and the
"puritan" occupiers of the English pulpit were continually reminding their listeners that disputes about ceremonies were of
small moment beside the common bond of the faith which embraced all true Englishmen. At the Roman Catholic critic who
charges the English with being "some Puritans, some Protestants" and with being torn apart by wrangling over "ceremonies
and outward discipline," Airay flings the confident response:
"Now for our difference about ceremonies, and outward discipline, I wish we were all like minded in these things. . . . But
for the substance of doctrine, and grounds of religion, wherein
is it that we are not like minded?"[136]

The problem of set as against impromptu prayer had been
and was to become again a matter of open contention and even
rupture between conservative and more radical Protestants.
From the literature of this middle period, not just a preference
for compromise but a solidly common viewpoint appears to
have been achieved on this liturgical issue. Ussher, for example,
speaking of the Lord's Prayer, specifically commends the employment both of the set form of the prayer, and, on other
occasions, of other and impromptu words to express the same
sentiments in the same spirit. In arguing the general proposition
on set and informal prayer, he observes that though a set form

[136] Cf. Airay, *Lectures*, xxv, 2.

of prayer is necessary "to help the weaker and ruder sort of people especially," it must not be so employed as to make men "sluggish in stirring up the gift of prayer in themselves according to divers occurents, it being incident to the children of God, to have some gift of prayer in some measure."[137] And Perkins, whose approval of impromptu prayer may be assumed on the basis of his "puritanism," displays a similar breadth of concept when he writes: "Now considering set praier is Gods ordinance, and the imperfections of man require it . . . I doubt not to affirme the same to be both profitable and necessarie; whereby we may see how blinde and rash they are, who tearme set prayer an abominable Idol . . . here we see, that it is meete and necessarie we should have some set forme of prayer in our hearts."[138]

The well-nigh universal and total destruction of the religious art of English churches after the establishment of the Reformation—so much bewailed by modern esthetes and art historians—is sufficient to indicate the extensive and general nature of the iconoclastic viewpoint in English Protestantism.[139] The literature we have surveyed only confirms and makes even more emphatic this architectural impression. By far the largest share of the comment in these sermons on the plastic or pictorial representation in churches of religious subjects is wholly and violently antagonistic. All such products of an earlier religious enthusiasm tend to be consigned to the single category of idols and are even seen to represent the hated heritage of papistry. "As for the painted and carved images of the Papists," Perkins asserts, "we utterly detest them, as Idols."[140] To be sure, most of this condemnation of idolatrous practices occurs in the writings of "puritan" divines, but these same "puritans" are completely self-assured in the conviction that what they have to say is the bed-rock doctrine of the entire English church. "And therefore commendable is the practice of the Church of England," remarks Perkins again, "that suffers not in places that

---

[137] *Divinitie*, p. 381.

[138] *Works*, III, 119-20.

[139] For the effects of English Protestant iconoclasm see the Introduction to Lawrence Stone's *Sculpture in Britain: The Middle Ages* (1955).

[140] *Works*, II, 223.

serve for use of religion, images either painted or carved. . . ."[141]

Fully as wholesale a repudiator of all things reminiscent of or conducive to idolatry as any "puritan" is Ussher. The second commandment, for example, he maintains is a hazard to the Christian worshipper "to paint Christ for the remembrance of his death." An image "can only represent the man-hood of Christ, and not his God-head, which is the chiefest part in him, both which Natures being in him unseparable, it were dangerous by painting the one apart from the other, to give occasion of Arianisme . . . or other heresies."[142] Even the conservative Andrewes observes that "there hath been good riddance made of images" from English churches, since they were the devil's devices to distract the Christian from the true and proper worship of God.[143] Laud himself, though he attacks unauthorized image-breaking, does not venture to condone the presence of images in churches. Only Sanderson speaks a cautious word or two in defense of the propriety of such use of religious images. First interested, like Laud, in discouraging the destruction of images by overzealous individuals without official sanction, Sanderson goes on to admit that it is his personal opinion that statues and pictures may be permitted in churches "for the adornment of God's House and for civil and historical uses, not only lawfully and decently, but even profitably."[144]

To find in the writings of English Protestantism, after the brief era of Travers and Cartwright, so little heat or pressure on any side on these liturgical and ceremonial issues is to render all the more extraordinary and, as it were, *sui generis*, the episode of Laud. His arguments in this area are roughly the same in logic as those which the representatives of the official or conservative position had always employed, but the tone of their presentation has now greatly altered. What was in Andrewes or Sanderson moderate defensiveness and persuasive rationality has become in Laud aggressive absolutism—the expression of a firm and bureaucratic temperament bent upon stating a policy determinedly and determinedly assuring that the policy is also carried out. Where in Andrewes, Sanderson, or even Whitgift can

[141] *Works*, I, 685.  [142] *Op.cit.*, p. 231.  [143] *Works*, v, 56.
[144] *Op.cit.*, pp. 34-35.

one find such a pronouncement as this which Laud places in the mouth of Charles I? ". . . forasmuch as we are given to understand, that many of our subjects being misled against the rites and ceremonies now used in the Church of England, have lately taken offence at the same, upon an unjust supposal that they are not only contrary to our laws, but also introductive into popish superstitions; whereas it well appeareth unto us upon mature consideration, that the said rites and ceremonies . . . were not only approved of, and used by . . . learned and godly divines . . . at the time of the Reformation under King Edward the Sixth . . . but also again taken up by this whole church under Queen Elizabeth. . . .

"And albeit since those time for want of an express rule therein, and by subtle practices, the said rites and ceremonies began to fall into disuse, and other foreign and unfitting usages by little and little to creep in; yet forasmuch as in our own royal chapels, and in many other churches, most of them have been ever constantly used . . . we cannot now but be very sensible of this matter, and have cause to conceive that the authors . . . of these jealousies . . . aim at our royal person, and would fain have our good subjects imagine that we ourself are perverted, and do worship God in a superstitious way, and that we intend to bring in some alteration of the religion here established."[145]

Hitherto unexampled in English Protestant history is this sense of concern and urgency at the official level; from this new sense Laud's program of Thorough arose. The old provisions regarding uniformity in liturgy and ceremonial are restated and reinforced in his Canons, both as they applied to Scotland and to England, and new ones are added. What Whitgift and Bancroft never ventured to spell out as a requirement—the placement of the communion table at the east end of the church —Laud does not hesitate to demand. Having insisted "that one form of the worship of God in the blessed Trinity be used in all churches in the kingdom; and that in all meetings for divine worship before sermon, the whole prayers according to the Liturgy be deliberately and distinctly read," Laud goes further

[145] In the introduction to his *English Constitutions and Canons* (*Works*, v, 607).

yet: he forbids, in the face of the entire moderate temper of the church before this time, all employment of impromptu prayer. "Neither shall any presbyter or reader," this Canon provides, "be permitted to conceive prayers *ex tempore* or use any other form in the public Liturgy or service than is prescribed, under the pain of deprivation from his benefice or cure."[146]

More than reaffirming old or stating new requirements, of course, there was the matter of the rigor of enforcing existing provisions. Although the record of deprivations during Laud's administration does not indicate that he made or was forced to make extensive use of this extreme disciplinary measure, nonetheless an atmosphere of pressure and threat hung heavy over the Church of England. The *via media* which had shone brightly but a little while before was effectively concealed by the shadows of the coming storm.

## VI. Church Government

We have been considering many issues around which controversies clustered during the seven decades of our survey. In the differences of viewpoint, the extremes may be appropriately designated by two labels: *conservative* for those viewpoints primarily concerned with defense and maintenance of the established ecclesiastical pattern; and *puritan* for those primarily concerned with the statement and implementation of a more aggressively Protestant policy. The principal points of tension on all these issues we have found to be consistently concentrated at the two termini of our span of coverage: the beginning (the period of Travers and Cartwright) and the end (the period of Laud). In between lies the large area of the *via media*. By far the major bulk of the literature we have read positively contributes to the *via media*; and by far the major number of divines, both thorough Anglicans and "puritans" alike, actively participate in its spirit.

Of all the controversies of this period, the only truly church-shaking one (the controversy regarding the structure of church

[146] *Works*, v, 597.

government and the relationship of church to state) is almost entirely limited, so far as clerical pressure from within the Church of England is concerned, to the beginning of the period. This makes it all the more obvious how impossible it is to abstract from this history of the church and its literature any single line of consistently present and steadily incrementing difference between two groups. Of the English Protestant divines of any considerable influence, the only ones avowedly presbyterian in sentiment are Travers and Cartwright, with Udall as a less significant though more severely suffering fellow-combatant; it can be said that only from them does the concept of church-state relations—most clearly formulated by Hooker and overwhelmingly characteristic of English Protestant thought as a whole—receive any notable degree of challenge.

This presbyterian quarrel is linked, to be sure, with disputes about other and principally liturgical and ceremonial matters. The Travers and Cartwright position can be simplified into the argument that the purity of ecclesiastical policy and discipline is guaranteed only when churchmen and not statesmen are directly and exclusively in charge of church affairs. Hence, as contemporary conservatives like Bancroft and Whitgift could contend that the presbyterian agitation threatened to weaken or overthrow not only bishops and the episcopal system but the king and civil magistracy as well—threatened, in short, utter Anabaptism—so it was possible for later conservatives to contend, or at least to suggest, that agitation about ceremonial or liturgical practices in the Church of England threatened utter presbyterianism. The sole basis of real bitterness at the Hampton Court Conference, for example, was this continuing fear among conservatives that behind the anticeremonial head, which could be entertained and parlayed with, dragged an inert but still living presbyterian tail. And "no Bishop, no King," protested James, who had good reason to feel strongly on the subject.

As one follows this conservative argument in support of episcopacy, one finds that, like so many other arguments we have analyzed, it contains within it elements of both absolutism and moderation, even contradictory elements which give to it the restless, dialectical quality so typical of religious polemics in general. There is, to begin with, the customary confidence that the institutions and practices in question—specifically the position of bishops in the English church—may be traced to the very origins of the faith: to the original superiority in place, power, and privilege of the Apostles in relation to certain presbyters, for example, whose ministerial functions they supervised and guided;[147] or at least to a distinction in responsibility and function between two orders of presbyters as established by the Apostles.[148] Some apologists even seek so far as the Old Testament to discover further shoring for this governmental structure of the English church.[149] From these Judaistic and Apostolic origins the episcopalian polity is seen by its defenders to have been continually maintained within the church. "A thousand five hundred years and upward," Hooker writes, "the Church of Christ hath now continued under the sacred regiment of bishops. Neither for so long hath Christianity been ever planted in any kingdom throughout the world but with this kind of government alone; which to have been ordained by God, I am for mine own part even as resolutely persuaded as that any other kind of government in the world whatsoever is of God."[150]

In the stiff-necked and aggressive manner peculiar almost to himself alone, Laud sums up the matter by proclaiming that "the calling of bishops is *jure divine*." To this he adds the climactic observation that "from the Apostles' times, in all ages, in all places, the church of Christ was governed by bishops: and lay-elders never heard of, till Calvins new fangled device at Geneva."[151]

Though the pattern of reasoning we have been considering might seem logically and inevitably to lead to just such a statement as Laud's, which asserts not merely the justifiability of episcopacy but its unique and unmatched rectitude as well, most English Protestant conservatives do not choose to carry the

[147] See Andrewes, *Works*, II, 356; Overall, *Convocation Book*, pp. 145-57; Hooker, *Polity*, v, 78, iv-v; Field, *Of the Church*, p. 498.

[148] See Archbishop Hutton on episcopacy in Strype, *Whitgift*, III, 227-28.

[149] See Bernard, *Plaine Evidences*, pp. 215-16; Overall, *Convocation Book*, p. 124.

[150] *Polity*, VII, 1, iv.

[151] *Works*, VI, 44.

matter by any means as far. The argument from Apostolic example is not usually so boldly translated into an argument from divine right; and it is frequently diminished in its force by the additional citation of expediency. Thus Whitgift, a foremost champion of episcopacy, advises: "It is necessary that among the clergy some should be in authority over the rest; and therefore there may be both archbishops and bishops. But I know you will answer that there may be government without these degrees: then say I unto you again, Stand not so much in your own conceit: this order is most ancient in the church . . . it hath the pattern from the practice of the Apostles (all which hath been shewed before), it is most meet for this state and kingdom, and therefore be not wilful in a new device, the trial whereof was never as yet, the manner whereof is unknown to yourself, and the end no doubt mere confusion."[152]

Cooper chooses even more decisively to occupy an historical or relativist position on the question of church government and presses the charge of absolutism, so usually attached by modern students of the subject to the episcopalian party, against the presbyterian adversary instead. He writes: "All those Churches, in which the Gospell in these days, after great darkensse, was first renewed, and the learned men whome God sent to instruct them. I doubt not but have been directed by the spirite of God to retaine this liberty, that in external government, and other outward orders, they might choose such as they thought . . . to be most convenient for the state of their Country, and disposition of the people. Why then should this libertie, that other Countries have used, under anie colour bee wrested from us? I thinke it therefore great presumption and boldnesse, that some of our nation, and those whatsoever they thinke of themselves, not of the greatest wisdome and skill, shoulde take upon them to controlle the whole Realme, and to binde both Prince and people, in necessity of conscience, to alter the present state, and to tie themselves to a certaine platforme devised by some of our neighbors, which in the judgement of many wise and godly persons is most unfit for the state of a Kingdome, or

152 *Works*, ii, 263.

to be exercised under a Christian Prince that defendeth the Gospel. . . ."[153]

While firmly upholding the episcopal pattern of church government, conservative policy, in the time of this presbyterian agitation, also allowed itself a number of admissions and explanations calculated to be conciliatory to the opposition. Whitgift points out, for example, that the distinction between bishops and presbyters is only an administrative and not a ministerial one. "It is not to be denied," he writes, "that there is an equality *quoad ministerium*: touching the ministry; for they have all the power to preach the word, to minister the sacraments: that is to say, the word preached, or the sacraments ministered, is as effectual in one (in respect of the ministry) as it is in another. But *quoad ordinem et politicam*: touching order and government, there always hath been and must be degrees and superiority among them."[154] And though Whitgift has strong words to speak on the evils of "popular government" in the church, which he conceives to be an element in the presbyterian interpretation of the lay eldership, he nonetheless maintains for the congregation a certain right to participate in the election of its pastor: "The people are for the most part rude and ignorant, careless also in such matters, and more meet to be ruled than to rule . . . These and a great number more reasons may be alleged why the people are to be secluded from the election of their pastors: and yet do I not so utterly seclude them from such elections, but that, if they have anything to object against him that is to be ordained, they might be heard; which order is prescribed in the book of making ministers; and that is as much as can be required." He further concedes that in other circumstances and other churches more generous or "democratic" practice in this regard is equally admissible. Those churches by whom election of ministers is "safely committed" to the congregation he does not condemn, "for I only speak of the present estate of this church of England."[155]

The essential moderation of even this conservative defense of the government of the Church of England is evident again in a summarizing statement by Hooker: "We boldly . . . set down

[153] *Op.cit.*, pp. 84-85.    [154] *Op.cit.*, p. 265.    [155] *Works*, I, 468.

as a most infallible truth, 'That the Church is at this day law-fully, and so hath been sithence the first beginning, governed by Bishops, having permanent superiority, and ruling power over other ministers of the word and sacraments.' "[156] Though lawful, the polity of the Church of England is not *the* only law-ful polity. That there is nothing absolute or resistant in all circumstances to modification in government by bishops Hooker himself specifically allows: ". . . bishops, albeit they may avouch with conformity of truth that their authority has . . . descended even from the very Apostles themselves, yet the absolute and everlasting continuance of it they cannot say that any com-mandement of the Lord doth enjoin; and therefore must ac-knowledge that the Church hath power by universal consent upon urgent cause to take it away, if thereunto she be con-strained through the proud . . . and unreformable dealings of her bishops."[157]

The active defense of episcopacy is principally the preoccupa-tion of those divines who may be designated, partly because of this function, as conservatives. Yet once the period of Travers and Cartwright is passed, antipresbyterianism is not a significant aspect of the writings of those many English Protestant divines who, for other reasons, have come to be known as "puritans." Downame is cited by Bernard as a supporter of the Scriptural basis of episcopacy[158] and he confirms the judgment of his Angli-can colleague by demonstrating, in the manner and wording of the archiepiscopal dedication of one of his treatises,[159] his thorough respect for the privileges of ecclesiastical officialdom. Another "puritan" and one notable for the frequent aggressive-ness of his approach and argumentation, Adams, too, stands out as a staunch defender of episcopacy. The church, he says, was founded and has continued ever since on the basis of inequality. Equality in government breeds only disorder: "Take away dif-ference, and what will follow, but an Anabaptisticall ataxie or confusion? . . . Without order, Faith itselfe would be at a losse. . . . Therefore is our Ministry called Orders, to shew that

[156] *Op.cit.*, 3, i.   [157] *Op.cit.*, 5, viii.
[158] Bernard, *Evidences*, p. 216.
[159] Downame, *Warfare*, Dedicatory Address.

we are bound to order above other Professions. This orderly distinction of Ecclesiasticall persons is set downe by the Holy Ghost, 1. Cor. 12, placing some as the head, other as the eyes, other as the feet: all members of one Body, with mutual concord, equall amitie, but unequall dignitie. To be a Bishop then, is not a Numerall, but a Munerall function; a priority in order, a superiority in degree. All Ministers of Christ have their due order, some are worthy of double honour. Farre be it from us sinners, to grudge them that honour whereof God himselfe hath pronounced them worthy."[160]

Thus the "puritanism" with which we have principally dealt —the "puritanism" of the whole span of time between the Travers-Cartwright agitation of the 1570's and 1580's and the terminus of our study in 1640—has no overt affiliation whatsoever with the presbyterian position. During Laud's administration some presbyterian sentiment came to exist among certain of the English clergy, as is indicated by the 1641 publication of the famous presbyterian pamphlet. Of its authors, five English Protestant preachers who called themselves collectively "Smectymnuus," none of them is numbered among the contributors to the literature we have surveyed. This revival of presbyterian ideas can no doubt be traced in part to some continuing stimulation from the earlier English ferment, as well as to encouragement from the more immediate Scottish example. But the major factor in the resurgence of the old agitation appears to us to be the development of so much antagonism to current ecclesiastical policy among the more desperate of the dissident clergy that it finally seemed impossible to them that any lesser remedy than the wholesale reform of church government would suffice. Hooker himself had said, after all, that "the Church hath power . . . upon urgent cause" to do as much.

Only three of the "puritans" we have encountered—Travers, Cartwright, and Udall—have clear ties to the presbyterianism which its contemporaneous opponents and detractors and some modern analysts have so widely and loosely attributed to the whole "puritan" tendency. The ultimate ecclesiastical radical-

[160] *Works*, pp. 932-33.

ism of separatism, similarly interpreted as a frequent, if not a usual, ingredient of "puritan" mentality, has been found, in terms of the highly inductive procedure we have followed, to be even less characteristic of the movement. We have made no special study of English separatism, of course—a complex phenomenon associated with a variety of doctrines and ecclesiastical policies ranging from relatively extreme deviance in doctrinal as well as institutional regards to the simple stress on congregational independence without major doctrinal departures from the established viewpoint. Robinson is the only separatist we have quoted in detail, and among the English separatists of our period he has appeared to be the individual most germane or necessary to our study because he represents the only influential voice of separatism. Differing in no essential doctrinal regard from his former colleagues in the Church of England, Robinson merely carried one item in this general belief—the emphasis on the ultimate sole reality of the invisible church, the communion of the saints—to the point of advocating and finally practicing (in his church abroad) a greater congregational exclusiveness than was compatible with the all-embracing, nationalistic policy of the English church. He carried it, in short, to the point of "separating."

Now it can be argued that in doing this Robinson merely actualized what was strongly potential in English "puritanism" as a whole. We have long since observed that in English "puritans" as a group, relative to English non-"puritans" as a group, there is something of this same tendency to concentrate on the invisible church and on the inevitable God-given "separateness" of the saint, both of which Robinson invokes as a basis for his decision to seek an institutional separateness. Yet a number of additional facts militate against so straightforward a line of connection. First of all, whatever may be said of differences in emphasis between one Protestant group and another, the central viewpoint here—the reality of the invisible church, the reality of the communion of the elect—is English Protestant orthodoxy. Second, Robinson is only one English separatist; he happens to be a Calvinist in theology and a decided predestinarian. Most English separatists as individuals and most English separatist ideologies move strongly in an Arminian direction. It is as logical, therefore, to argue that Montagu or Cosin in the English church are peculiarly allied with separatism, because of their Arminian tendencies, as to argue that "puritans" are, because of their somewhat special interest in the communion of the saints.

The actual fact of the matter is that, with the exception of Robinson, all the English Protestants we have read are not only nonseparatist but antiseparatist as well; that is, insofar as they deal with the tendency at all, they actively combat it. If there is any difference between "puritans" and Anglicans in this regard, it is that the former are more violently and noisily antagonistic to separatism than the latter, in part perhaps because they are aware of the charge occasionally flung against them by more aggressive opponents that they are otherwise. This is no mere matter for "puritans" of protesting against calumny, however, for one cannot read their writings without acknowledging the deep and complete sense of devotion which they felt to the idea of the unified national church. Even those two principal presbyterian "puritans," Travers and Cartwright, repeatedly indicate that their desire is not to depart to form another church on the basis of their program but rather to enforce it as policy upon the church to which they already and inviolably belong.[161]

Though a mark of later "puritan" reformers continues to be the existence of some spirit of criticism regarding what are considered certain abuses and inadequacies in the Church of England, the sole validity for Englishmen of the Church of England is always specifically accepted and championed. Thus Perkins states what is a universal English Protestant opinion: "Now although these corruptions and deformities were in the Jewish

---

161 See Fuller, *Church History*, v, 252-55, for interesting evidence of the clerical nationalism that made of even Thomas Cartwright an "English champion" against "the Romish enemy in matters of doctrine," and "sensible with sorrow how all sects and schisms, being opposite to bishops (Brownists, Barrowists, etc.), did shroud and shelter themselves under his protection, whom he could neither reject with credit nor receive with comfort, seeing his conscience could not close with their enormous opinions, and . . . extravagant violences." Fuller explains Cartwright's presbyterian ideas as the result of an "active spirit" which "fell foul, in point of discipline, with those which otherwise were of his own religion" when "the Romish enemy . . . was not in the field."

Church, yet our Saviour Christ made no separation from it but came and preached both in their temple and synagogues. . . . And hence wee gather, that the practise of al those men in our Church, which separate themselves from all assemblies for the wants thereof, holding that our Church is no Church, that the grace which is wrought by the preaching of the word among us, is nothing els but a sathanicall illusion, that Sacraments are no Sacraments, I say, that their practice is condemned by our Savior Christ's conversing among the Jewes . . . and therefore we cannot in good conscience disjoyne ourselves from the Church of England."[162]

In sum, even though he may admit the existence of errors in the Church of England, the "puritan" writer still maintains that since these errors are not within or against the foundations of the faith, there can be no lawful departure from this particular visible church. "Untill the Church separates from Christ," Adams admonishes, "we must not separate from it."[163] Bolton credits separatism and the disaffection which leads to separatism to the machinations of none other than Satan: "Satan gaines very much by the division of Christian hearts. . . . He labours mightily . . . by vexing their judgements with Opinionativenesse . . . and thoughts of Separation, to drive them by degrees from divorce of judgements . . . to disaffection . . . to faction . . . to schisme. . . . The powers of darkenes, and all sorts of profane men cannot possibly be better pleased, or the blessed Spirit and good men more grieved: then to see . . . Gods children to be at variance. . . . It infinitely concerns all those which have given their names to sincerity, to labour every way to keepe the unity of the Spirit in the bond of peace."[164]

And so it is that even for that most "puritanical" of "puritans," the mettlesome Bolton, the way of separatism is the way of Satan, while the way of God is the way of the *via media*.

97.

*PART III*

PROTESTANTISM AND REVOLUTION

"God usually visits a people when some horrible crying sins raigne amongst them; as first Atheisme. . . . So likewise, secondly, when Idolatry prevailes. . . . Againe, thirdly, when divisions grow amongst a people union is a preserver; where there is a dissention of judgement, there will soone be dissention of affections; and dissipation will be the end if wee take not heed; for the most part Ecclesiasticall dissentions end in Civill. . . . It is a fearefull signe of some Judgement to fall upon a Church when there is not a stopping of dissentions; they may be easily stopped at the first . . . but when they are once gotten into the very vitall parts of the Church and Common-wealth, wee may see the mischiefe, but it is hardly remedied."

—RICHARD SIBBES, *The Saints Cordials*, 220-221

# CHAPTER 9

## THE ENGLISH PROTESTANT AND

## THE *VIA MEDIA*

✝ ✝ ✝

".... it will be requisite to a peaceable moderation, that we should give to every opinion his own due extent, not casting private mens conceits upon publick Churches, nor fathering single fancies upon a Community: All men cannot accord in the same thoughts. . . . In all waters . . . there are some sorts of fish that love to swim against the streams. . . ."

—JOSEPH HALL, *Works*, IV, 44

"From extreme to extreme, from east to west, the angels themselves cannot come, but by passing the middle way between; from that extreme impurity in which Antichrist had damped the church of God, to that intemperate purity in which Christ had constituted his church, the most angelical reformers cannot come but by touching, yea, and stepping upon some things in the way. . . . *It is the posture reserved for heaven to sit down at the right hand of God*: here consolation is that God reaches out his hand to the receiving of those who come towards him; and nearer to him, and to the institutions of his Christ, can no church, no not of the Reformation, be said to have come than ours does."

—JOHN DONNE, *Works*, IV, 485

✝ ✝ ✝

## I. The Problem of Variety in Unity

FROM THE BEGINNING of the history of Protestantism, the genius of this movement has pressed inexorably toward variety in the expression of the religious impulse. The qualities which have made for this tendency—the emphasis on a directness of relationship between the individual and God, for example, and the whole interiorization of the religious life—have been often cited by us in this book and by other students elsewhere. The Protestant drive toward the multiplying of creeds and churches has been so obvious, in fact, and so often pointed to and commented upon that it has been in a real sense overemphasized. Partly in consequence, the types and degrees of differences within Roman Catholicism have been insufficiently acknowledged and allowed to conceal themselves too completely behind the massive bulk of an institutional unity. Differences of emphasis, interpretation, and even of doctrine have existed within both of the great bodies of western Christianity, but the relative weakness of Protestant institutionalism has encouraged rather than suppressed or diminished these differences; it has rendered them overt and resolute rather than hidden and compromising. Where the central and essential viewpoint is that the true church is an invisible church, what power ultimately has a visible church to enforce even the pretence of absolute conformity and complete allegiance?

Yet there has been unity, too, in Protestantism. A common Protestant understanding has confronted the Roman Catholic understanding in all times and places where both have existed and where religious issues have been matters of importance. The individual Protestant is rare who even temporarily forgets that the divison between his own and another Protestant denomination is a mere gully in comparison with the chasm which yawns between the two primary branches of western Christendom. English Protestantism certainly shows surprising breadth and liberality in its willingness to recognize the complete validity of other Protestant churches in other nations. Repeatedly employed to illustrate this concept of unity in diversity and diversity in unity is the metaphor of the single ocean with many separate parts. Here Perkins invokes the image: "The Militant Church hath many parts. For as the Ocean sea which is but one, is devided into parts according to the regions and countries against which it lyeth, as into the English, Spanish, Italian sea, etc. so the Church dispersed over the face of the whole earth, is devided into other particular Churches according as the countries are severall in which it is seated; as into the Church of England and Ireland, the Church of France, the Church of Germanie, etc."[1]

1 Perkins, *Works*, I, 303.

Numbers of English Protestants exhibit impatience with the designation of particular Protestant churches by the names of particular leaders. The Roman Catholics, Airay observes, charge Protestants with being divided into a multitude of sects, Zwinglians, Lutherans, Calvinists, *et al.* "But I say unto them," he protests in return, "what doe they meane to note us by such termes? The memorie of these men we honour and reverence, as also we doe other notable lights which have beene in the Church, and are at this day. But if we be named after any other name then only the name of Christ Jesus, it is through their malice, not by our desire."[2] "Neither are the professours of the Gospell," Perkins similarly admonishes, "to be intituled by the names of such as have beene famous instruments in the Church, as to be called *Calvinists, Lutherans*, etc. . . . The . . . name of *Christian* was given to the disciples at Antioch not by the devise of man, but by divine oracle."[3]

"Particular Churches," as Carleton succinctly states, "are visible Assemblies who professe the true Faith, and holde the ordinances of Christ, and are governed by divers visible heads or governours. . . ."[4] The definition of this "true Faith" and the essential "ordinances of Christ" tends to be extremely minimal, at least in the abstract or the general statement. Thus Ussher argues that the "unitie of the faith . . . such as every true Christian attaineth unto . . . must consist but of few propositions" which are sufficiently basic and understandable to even the simplest Christian believer. Moreover, since it must be assumed that salvation depends upon the holding of "these radicall truthes," "it followeth thereupon, that the *unity of the faith,* generally requisite for the incorporating of Christians into that blessed societie [the Church of Christ], is not to be extended beyond those common principles." Ussher proceeds to suggest the Nicene Creed as the common basis for such a unified faith.[5]

There is, then, a clear and conscious distinction in English Protestantism between fundamental and minor aspects of Chris-

[2] Airay, *Lectures Upon the Whole Epistle of St. Paul* (1618), xxv, 2.
[3] *Works*, I, 445.
[4] Carleton, *Directions to Know the True Church* (1615), p. 2.
[5] Ussher, *A Briefe Declaration of the Universalitie of the Church of Christ* (1631), p. 23.

tian belief and practice; and both variation and error may occur in the latter without destroying or even weakening the former. Hence it follows that visible churches may differ in many points of ceremonial and doctrine and still equally remain branches of the one true church of Christ. As Carleton declares, "There may be some disagreements in some points of religion, and the sides disagreeing may both holde the true Church, so long as . . . they . . . holde one and the same rule of faith."[6] Perkins likewise declares that "though men differ in sundrie opinions in the true Church of God, yet they all agree in the Articles of faith, and in the foundations of Gods worship: their difference is in matters beside the foundation, and therefore it must hinder none from receiving and embracing true religion."[7]

Even where actual error enters in (indeed, it is generally assumed that visible churches, being human institutions, may and will err), the erring church continues to be a valid church so long as it maintains the fundamentals of the faith. Only when errors infect these few fundamentals and only when these fundamental errors are held not in frailty or ignorance but "in obstinacie"[8]—only then does a church, and still not necessarily all its membership, drop off into apostasy. Thus Perkins takes care to separate those errors which destroy from those which merely weaken faith: "A destroyer is that which overturneth any fundamentall point of religion . . . as the deniall of the death of Christ and the immortality of the soule, [or the assertion of] justification by workes, and such like: and the summe of these fundamentall points is comprised in the Creede of the Apostles and the Decalogue. A weakening errour is that, the holding whereof doth not overturne any point in the foundation of salvation; as the errour of free-will, and sundrie such like."[9] A man or church holding a "lighter" error—one that does not rase the foundation of salvation—is still a member of the "Church of God." ". . . The haie and stubble of mens errours that are beside the foundation, on which they are laid, doe not debarre them from being Christians or members of the Church."[10]

The breadth of approach to religious differences inherent in

[6] *Op.cit.*, p. 85.  [7] *Works*, III, 65.  [8] Perkins, *Works*, I, 305.
[9] *Ibid.*, p. 304.  [10] *Ibid.*, p. 305.

English Protestantism is further enhanced by yet another concept universally upheld: the concept of the complete reality of the invisible church and its omnipresence throughout the history of man. In all times, including, certainly, some among God's "chosen people" of the Old Testament, and in all Christian churches, whether true or false, it is assumed that there have been individuals who, while they might through ignorance have participated in certain errors of their visible community, nonetheless held firm to the fundamental truths essential to salvation and were therefore destined to share eternity with the saints. Beside what he considers the materiality and narrowness of the Roman Catholic concept of the church, Dering places the truly impressive scope of this ultimate Protestant idea: "Now let Rome go and boast herselfe, and pronounce her proud Decrees, that in her palaces the Church of Christ doth dwell. . . . The house of God is neither in Rome, nor in the Capital of Rome, no more than it is in Aegypt . . . but in everie nation and in everie countrie, the men that feare God and works righteousnesse, they are the Church, and the house in which God doth dwell."[11]

It then becomes readily possible for the English Protestant to admit that salvation is accessible even to the Roman Catholic whether of the past or present. Concerning Roman Catholics of the past, that is, of the period before the emergence of the churches of the Reformation, there is universal and emphatic affirmation of this point. Referring specifically to these Roman Catholics, Ussher declares that "where these things did . . . concurre in any (as wee doubt not but they did in many thousands) the knowledge of the common principles of the faith, the ignorance of such maine errors as did endanger the foundation, a godly life, and a faithful death: there we have no cause to make any question, but that God had fitted a subject for his mercy to worke upon."[12] "I believe," Adams similarly comments, "that many of our forefathers went to Heaven, though through blindness."[13]

Though none among the English divines we have read denies

[11] Dering, *Works*, p. 471.     [12] *Op.cit.*, p. 26.
[13] Adams, *Works*, p. 563.

completely the boon of salvation to contemporary members of a grievously erring church, they all exhibit greater caution in discussing the possibility. On this issue, moreover, there are some differences in viewpoint between one English Protestant and another—Hooker and Travers specifically quarrel about the matter, for example.[14] But the differences are insignificant beside the common ground, in which references to the readiness of God's mercy to the weak and ignorant are intermingled with warnings of God's wrath toward the willfully and obstinately apostate. "In the very midst of the Romane Papacie, God hath alwaies had a remnant which have in some measure truly served him."[15] Perkins would appear to include presently- as well as previously-living Roman Catholics in this all-embracing statement. And the warning to the willfully ignorant is as evident in Laud as in Adams. "The possibility [of salvation for Roman Catholics], I think, cannot be denied," writes Laud, "the ignorants especially, because they hold the foundation, and cannot survey the building. And the foundation can deceive no man that rests upon it. But a 'secure' way they cannot go, that hold with such corruptions, when they know them."[16] "Now indeed," Adams comments, "they [Roman Catholics] are more inexcusable, because our sound is gone out among them. . . . The wilfull blinde, leade the wofull blinde, untill both fall into the ditch. If they will not see, there is no helpe, no hope. If simple ignorance mislead, there is hope of returne: but if affected, it is most wretched."[17]

It is beyond question, therefore, that English Protestantism provides in the very nature of its logic a greater scope for the development and the acceptance of ceremonial, institutional, and even doctrinal variations than did Roman Catholicism. English Protestants are fully aware of this distinction between themselves and their major adversaries; indeed, they make of it a point of pride and superiority. Ussher, for example, complains of the Church of Rome that "instead of the Catholike Church which consisteth of the communion of all nations, they

14 The "Supplication" is in Hooker, *Works*, II.
15 Perkins, *Works*, I, 290.
16 Laud, *Works*, II, 316.      17 *Works*, p. 563.

obtrude their owne peece unto us; circumscribing the Church
of Christ within the precincts of the Romish jurisdiction, and
leaving all the world beside to the power of Sathan; for with
them it is a resolved case; that to every creature it is altogether
of necessitie to salvation, to be subject to the Romane Bishop."[18]
In conclusion, he observes that "they who talke so much of the
Catholike church but indeed stand for their owne particular,
must of force sinke as low in uncharitablenesse, as they have
thrust themselves deep in schism: we who talke lesse of the
Universalitie of the Church, but hold the truth of it, cannot
finde in our hearts to passe such a bloudy sentence upon so many
poore soules, that have given their Names to Christ, He whose
pleasure it was to spread the Churches seede so farre, said to
East, West, North, and South; *Give*: it is not for us then to say,
*Keepe backe* . . . wee for our parts doe not abridge this grant . . .
but leave it to his owne latitude, and seek for the Catholic
Church neyther in this part nor in that peece, but . . . among all
that in every place call upon the Name of Jesus Christ our
Lord, both theirs and ours."[19]

It is not possible, of course, to make of the ideas we have been
discussing a conscious and general program of religious toleration. To say that salvation may come to those who, through
lack of opportunity to do otherwise, remain caught in the
ignorance of Roman Catholicism, is not equivalent to toleration of Roman Catholicism, or of Roman Catholics as such, or
even to acceptance of the Church of Rome as a validly Christian
body. Indeed, the general sentiment embodied in the literature
of this period is, as we shall see, specifically intolerant both of
Roman Catholicism and of those radical sects which lay to the
left of the acceptable Protestant domain. As has been often
pointed out, the Christian humanism of the Renaissance had
a wider reach than this, and the deism of the Enlightenment
was to be sufficiently different as to move almost into another
dimension of thought.[20] Yet against the background with which

[18] *Op.cit.*, p. 10.
[19] *Ibid.*, pp. 11-12.
[20] The definitive study is that by W. K. Jordan, *Development of Religious Toleration in England. See also* J. Lecler, *Histoire de la Tolérance au Siècle de la
Réforme,* (2 vols.; Paris, 1955).

we are comparing it—the background of the Roman Catholicism of the middle ages and of the Counter-Reformation—English Protestantism appears remarkable in its generosity and
flexibility, and one or two exceptional individuals—Donne and
Chillingworth most notably—come at least close to speaking in
the voice of an Erasmus. In this passage from Donne, for instance, neither Erasmus nor Lessing seems to be so very far away:
"We must be so far from straitening salvation to any particular
Christian church of any subdivided name, Papist or Protestant,
as that we may not straiten it to the whole Christian church,
as though God could not in the largeness of his mercy, afford
salvation to some whom he never gathered into the Christian
church."[21]

The great majority of English Protestant divines were convinced, however, of the sufficient as well as peculiar soundness of
their own particular church, and they tended to view any considerable differences from it as passive imperfections at the least
or as active errors. The greatest difference and hence the greatest
error (within the Christian camp) was thought to be that which
was embodied in the Church of Rome, and it is with reference
to this error that the major defense of English Protestant rectitude proceeds. We have in previous chapters observed many
aspects of this defense. Here we wish only to make a few summarizing statements concerning its central mechanism: the
assertion that it is Protestantism as a whole and English Protestantism in particular which has held fast to the original verities
of Christianity while Roman Catholicism, through centuries of
repeated and multiplied defections, has betrayed the source and
wandered far afield. All Protestantism, after all, always saw
itself to be not a new faith based on a new revelation, but rather
a protest against novelties conceived by others and therefore a
re-formation of the original church of Christ. "*Renovatores
modo sumus*," Andrewes states, "*non Novatores*."[22] It is little
wonder, then, that in sermon after sermon in this literature,

21 Donne, *Works*, IV, 437. Cf. E. G. Lewis, "The Question of Toleration in the
Works of John Donne," *Modern Language Review* (April, 1938) R. W. Batten-
house, "The Grounds of Religious Toleration in the Thought of John Donne,"
*Church History* (September, 1942).
22 Andrewes, *Works*, III, 26.

when the question is raised, presumably by a Roman Catholic, as to where the Protestant church in general or the English Protestant Church in particular could be found before the time of Luther, the standard reply is the one presented here by Sibbes: "Therefore we say Our Church was before Luther, because our Doctrine is Apostolicall, as also is our Church that is continued thereby, because it is built upon Apostolicall doctrine. . . . Our positive points are grounded upon the holy Scriptures; we seek the Old Way, and the best way, as Jeremy adviseth."[23]

To its apologists, moreover, the English Protestant Church is not simply a resurrection or revival of the original church of Christ but more nearly an expression in a particular time and place of a truth of doctrine and a community of believers which have never ceased to be. The way it follows is not only the "old way" and the "best way"; it is also the permanent way which all the saints have travelled through all time. For whatever apostasy may have afflicted the visible church in western Christendom before the time of the Reformation, English Protestants universally agree that the invisible church at least has been and is eternal and omnipresent. This invisible church is thought to have existed even within and beneath the dark mass of the Church of Rome and to have reared itself up, like some continent rising and shaking off the waters of its long under-ocean burial, to become visible once more in the churches of Protestantism. Thus Adams comments that "the Church had a beeing in all ages, ever since the Promise was given to our first Parents in Paradise. If there had beene a time when no Church had beene on earth, the world should have then perished: for it stands for the Elects sake." On the basis of this eternality of the invisible church, Adams is able all the more readily and firmly to quiet the usual inquiry concerning the location of the true church before the time of Luther: ". . . before the dayes of Luther . . . an universall Apostacie was over the face of the world, the true Church was not then visible; but the graine of trueth lay hid under a great heape of popish chaffe."[24]

The Church of England is, therefore, an apostolical church

23 Sibbes, *Yea and Amen*, pp. 10-11.
24 *Works*, p. 556.

and a valid visible embodiment of the invisible church of the elect. It is also and finally a truly catholic or universal church, or at least a part of it. Thus Cosin declares that "the religion of the Church of England, in her article concerning the Holy Scriptures (whereunto the public Confessions of the reformed and protestant Churches abroad besides the Christians of the East and South parts of the world, be agreeable,) is truly Catholic." He speaks as well of the Church of England's adhering to "the ancient Catholic Faith and Doctrine of the Church."[25] Sibbes turns to those "Catholic" truths, saying that to hold them makes inviolate the catholicity of the church: ". . . here we may know what Truths are to be entertained as Catholic universall Truths; those that without question are received. Then, if the question be, which is the Catholike Truth; Poperie or our Religion: I say, not Poperie, but our Religion; I proove it from hence: That which without controversie, all Churches have held from the apostles times, (yea, and the adversaries and opposites of the Church) that is Catholike. But it hath beene in all times and in all Churches, even among the adversaries held, the positive points of our Religion. . . ."[26]

A declaration by Hildersam sums up this whole confidence of English Protestants in the verity of their creed and church: "the religion, and Doctrine that is at this day, and hath beene (through Gods mercy, now many, above sixty years without interruption) taught, and professed in the Church of England . . . is the only true ancient Catholique, Propheticall, and Apostolike faith."[27]

Of all this argument regarding the purity, permanence, and universality of the English Protestant faith, the real and central purpose was to prove, against the counter-claims of Roman Catholic polemicists, that the Church of Rome and not the Church of England was the product and the exponent of schism, innovation, and hence of human error supervening upon divine truth. English Protestant divines did not depart from this fundamental tenet that the separation of Protestantism from Roman

[25] Cosin, *Works*, III, 284-85.
[26] Sibbes, *The Fountaine Opened* (1638), p. 47.
[27] Hildersam, *CLII Lectures*, p. 110.

Catholicism had occurred because so many and such serious errors had through the centuries gathered around the older church and were so stubbornly maintained, despite the warnings of the reformers, that whoever knew of these errors and still persisted in allegiance to the institution was risking his salvation. Withdrawal from a Christian body under such circumstances did not constitute schism. The sin of schism adhered to the church which was in error and, being told of error, still continued in it. Chillingworth, one of the most moderate of the writers on this subject, presents the case in a series of ordered arguments. He contends, first, that there are errors in the doctrines of the Church of Rome; second, these errors are not merely held by the church but are imposed by it upon the faithful, since belief in them is an essential condition to membership in the church. But, Chillingworth next proceeds to argue, man can be obliged by man to do only that to which God also obliges him, and God "neither can nor will oblige us to believe any the least . . . falsehood to be a divine truth." Obviously, then, the demand by the Roman Church that man must believe error in order to retain membership in its communion automatically terminates the Christian's obligation there and thus to communicate. "And so the imputation of schism to us," Chillingworth concludes, "vanisheth into nothing: but lies heavy upon you for making our separation from you just and necessary, by requiring unnecessary and unlawful conditions of your Communion."[28]

As the English Protestant defines and analyzes them, the errors of the Roman Catholic Church (many particular examples of which we have noted in previous chapters) always represent the introduction of novelties and hence of departures from the foundation. We have observed in the discussion of Scripturalism (Chapter 8) that the English Protestant, in turning so directly to the Scriptures as the supreme source of religious truth, also attacked, both by implication and by frontal assault, the "Traditions, Councels, Fathers, Decretals, Constitutions, and

28 Chillingworth, *The Religion of Protestants a Safe Way to Salvation* (Oxford, 1638), pp. 16-17. Chillingworth was Laud's godson, a Douai-trained Catholic, and under Laud's influence was reconverted to Protestantism and wrote therefore from an unusual posture in religious affairs. See Jordan, *op.cit.*, II, for Chillingworth's importance in developing the rationale of toleration.

Legends" which Roman Catholicism had presumably intruded between the believer and the only proper basis of his belief. "I am to point," says Andrewes in introducing one such discussion, "at some of the superfluous and wicked ceremonies of the papists borrowed from the heathen."[29]

The major errors of the Roman Church, however—the errors which have in one sense or another destroyed its adequacy as a true church of Christ—tend to be dated fairly late in its history. Speaking of these major errors, Perkins contends: "No Apostle, no holy Father, no sound Catholike, for 1200 yeares after Christ, did ever holde or possesse that doctrine of all the Principles and grounds of Religion, that is now taught by the Church of Rome, and authorized by the Councell of Trent."[30] On these same Roman Catholic errors, Sibbes remarks that "their fooleries, wherein they differ from us, they are late inventions."[31] There is a certain concentration of English Protestant wrath indeed upon that most nearly contemporaneous of events in Roman Catholic history, the Council of Trent itself. Burton, for instance, notes particularly of the Council of Trent that it had broken with "the ancient Catholique doctrine."[32] Cosin writes at greater length in a similar vein: "Now . . . followed an assembly of a few men at Trent, (who took upon them the style and authority of a general and aecumenical council,) that made a decree among themselves, to control the whole world, and . . . to devise . . . new article[s] of Faith, for their own pleasure, whereof neither their own Church, nor any other Church of Christendom, had ever heard before.

"An assembly of men . . . that, by their magisterial and undue proceedings there, have done more hurt, and made a greater schism in the Church of God, than all the malice of wicked and unpeaceful persons was ever able to do, since Christ left His legacy of truth and peace among His disciples, and foretold the offences that would afterwards arise, to pervert and mislead others, who were not the better aware of them."[33]

That contemporary Roman Catholicism exhibited serious

[29] *Works*, XI, 370.   [30] *Works*, II, 602.   [31] *Op.cit.*, p. 48.
[32] Burton, *Baiting of the Pope's Bull*, p. 14.
[33] Cosin, *op.cit.*, p. 264.

corruptions of the original purity of the faith was the universal opinion of English Protestantism. But it was also generally conceded that something of the original truth remained. The literature shows some differences in interpretation and emphasis on this point—differences which to a certain extent, though by no means absolutely, can be tied to what is classically conceived as the party difference between Anglican and "puritan" in the Church of England. It is certainly true that those whom we have come to designate as the conservative group among the English clergy do grant a noticeably greater doctrinal and institutional community between Roman Catholicism and English Protestantism than do most other English divines. Hooker, for example, who shares in the strong institutional bias characteristic of the conservatives as a whole, concedes to the visible church something of the same eternality and universality which all English Protestants concede to the invisible. He speaks of "the Church of Christ which was from the beginning, is, and continueth unto the end: of which church all parts have not been always sincere and sound."[34] Hence the Church of Rome becomes, both in the past and in the present, a valid, though unsound, Christian church, and Hooker can finally state that "though with Rome we dare not communicate concerning her gross and grievous abominations, yet touching these main parts of Christian truth wherein they constantly still persist, we gladly acknowledge them to be of the family of Jesus Christ."[35] Summing up the agreements and disagreements between Roman Catholicism and English Protestantism on both "matters of opinion" and "matters of outward practice," Andrewes lists more than twice as many agreements as disagreements; in the process he supports the viewpoint, relatively dignifying of the Church of Rome, of the constant existence of the visible church.

One of the more important indications of the hardening and increased aggressiveness of the conservative vis à vis the "puritan" position in the period of Laud is the greater frequency and boldness of those arguments which assert the validly Christian, though imperfect, nature of the Roman Catholic Church.

[34] Hooker, *Polity*, III, 1, xx-xi.
[35] *Ibid.*

These arguments are in Laud's own writings and, above all, in those of Montagu. There is no genuinely new idea here, of course; but the stress which is placed upon certain old ideas is certainly not to be matched elsewhere in this literature. In his conference with the Jesuit, Fisher, Laud specifically grants to the Roman Church that its membership in the visible church of Christ was then and previously existent in the world. With notable and, to some, unquestionably shocking impartiality, he writes: ". . . the Roman Church and the Church of England are but two distinct members of that Catholic Church which is spread over the face of the earth. Therefore Rome is not the house where the Church dwells; but Rome itself, as well as other particular Churches, dwells in this great universal house. . . . Rome and other national Churches are in this universal catholic house as so many daughters, to whom, under Christ, the care of the household is committed by God the Father and the Catholic Church the mother of all Christians."[36]

At another point in his argument Laud observes that the Roman Catholic Church, though not a "right" church, is a "true" church. "For that Church which receives the Scripture as a rule of faith, though but as a partial and imperfect rule, and both the sacraments as instrumental causes and seals of grace, though they add more and misuse these, yet cannot but be a true Church in essence."[37] One passage from this Laud-Fisher Conference was, in Laud's "time of troubles" to cause him most particular difficulty: "If the religion of the Protestants be in conscience a known false religion, then the Romanists' religion is so too, for their religion is the same; nor do the Church of Rome and the Protestants set up a different religion, for the Christian religion is the same to both; but they differ in the same religion, and the difference is in certain gross corruptions, to the very endangering of salvation—which each side says the other is guilty of. . . ."[38]

Above all others, however, it is Montagu who, in his *Appello Caesarem*, represents a position defensive of Roman Catholic doctrine and the Roman Church, as opposed to what he at least advertises to be another and a minority position in the Church

[36] *Works*, II, 346.  [37] *Ibid.*, p. 144.  [38] *Ibid.*, p. 417.

of England of extremist antagonism and derogation. Again, the peculiarity of his treatise—indeed, its uniqueness—is created not by any genuine novelty in his ideas, but by the aggressiveness of his tone and the simple extensiveness of his argumentation. Certainly he says in essence no more than Laud has said; but he says it still more decisively and at greater length. The nature of his approach is summed up in the following remark: "I am absolutely perswaded, and shall bee till I see cause to the contrary; that the Church of Rome is a true, though not a sound Church of Christ, as well since, as before the Councell of Trent; a part of the Catholick, though not the Catholick Church; which wee doe professe to believe in our Creed; a Church, in which, among many tares, there remaineth some wheat. In Essentials and Fundamentals they agree, holding one Faith, in one Lord, into whom they are inserted through one Baptisme."[39]

This particular animus of Laud and Montagu may be limited to their own time and circumstances. But the logical core of their argument—that there are many and thoroughly justified agreements between English Protestantism and Roman Catholicism, and that the fundamentals of the Christian faith may still be found in the Church of Rome within or beneath accretions or sediments of error—is very widely, perhaps even universally, held by English Protestant divines. Chillingworth, as one might expect, follows a generous line on this matter. "These points of Christianity," he writes, "which have in them the nature of Antidotes against the poyson of all sinners and errours, the Church of Rome, though otherwise much corrupted, still retaines; therefore wee hope she erres not fundamentally, but still remaines a Part of the Church."[40] Hall argues likewise that the Roman Catholic religious society has not entirely lost "the claime of a true visible Church, by her manifold and deplorable corruptions." "If she were once the Spouse of Christ," he writes, "and her adulteries are knowne, yet the divorce is not sued out."[41] Even Ussher admonishes that "wee

---

[39] Montagu, *Appello Caesarem*, p. 13.
[40] Chillingworth, *op.cit.*, p. 163.
[41] Hall, *Works*, I, 2.

must distinguish the Papacie from the Church wherein it is," contending that the "foundation upon which the Church standeth . . . that common faith . . . in the unitie whereof all Christians doe generally accord" still exists in Roman Catholicism even though "upon this foundation Antichrist raiseth up new buildings; and layeth upon it, not hay and stubble onely, but farre more vile and pernicious matter."[42]

Among acknowledged "puritans," Sibbes grants that the Papists hold all the positive points of true religion.[43] In the previously quoted reference to the "graines of trueth" hidden under the "great heape of popish chaffe," Adams implies the continued survival of the fundamentals of faith despite the superimposition of corruption.[44] And in *The Reformed Catholike,* a long treatise devoted to the issues in dispute between Protestants and Roman Catholics, Perkins introduces the discussion of each issue with a section on the measure of agreement existing between the two religious groups.[45] He does insist, to be sure, in this treatise and elsewhere, that "the Papacy be not the Church of God" and "the doctrine of Poperie rase[s] the foundation"; but at the same time, as we have seen, he says that "in the very midst of the Romane Papacie, God hath alwaies had a remnant which have in some measure truly served him."[46] This is, after all, universal doctrine in the Church of England: that salvation has been and is available to certain individual members of the Roman Church who, though they may hold at least some of that church's errors and superstitions, continue to hold in sincerity the fundamentals of the faith. Hence it follows necessarily that it is universal doctrine in the Church of England that the fundamentals of the faith are also available in the Roman Church.

That this particular logic is universal in the Church of England does not, however, deny what we have previously maintained—that any emphasis on the continuity of viewpoint between Roman Catholicism and English Protestantism tends to cluster at the conservative end of the scale of English Protestant

[42] *Op.cit.*, p. 23.  [43] *Fountaine Opened*, pp. 47-48.
[44] *Works*, p. 556.  [45] See in Perkins, *Works*, I.
[46] *Works*, I, 290.

attitudes. We are, of course, dealing with a circular argument since the group of conservatives is defined in part by this very relative moderation on the Roman Catholic issue. Conversely, the antagonism—or at least the heat of the antagonism, the passion, the invective—should be less at the conservative than at what may be called the radical end of the scale. And in a general way this is the case. Certainly Hooker and Andrewes and, above all, Laud and Montagu are not to be cited as principal examples of emotional bitterness in their attacks on the Roman Catholic position. Yet, though one may make of this relative mildness a general conservative attribute, one can by no means make a general Anglican one. Carleton, the high Anglican, for example, proclaims that Satan himself is the head of the Roman Catholic Church[47] and that "the Popish Church as now it standeth can have no communion with Christ."[48]

Ussher is as passionate an opponent of the papacy and the church of the papacy as can be found in English Protestantism. Who, he asks, are the enemies of the church of Christ? "Such are al those, that hearing the name of Christians do obstinately deny the faith whereby we are joyned unto Christ, which are called Heretics; or that break the bond of charity . . . which are tearmed Schismaticks, or else adde tyranny to schisme and heresie, as that great Antichrist, head of the general apostasie, which the Scriptures forewarned by name." And who is Antichrist? "He is one who under the colour of being for Christ, and under the title of Viceregent, exalteth himselfe above and against Christ . . . a Man of sinne, a Harlot . . . a child of perdition, a destroyer establishing himselfe by lying miracles and false wonders: all which marks together, do agree with none but the Pope of Rome."[49]

What must always be remembered is that whether he tends to full or scant invective, no English Protestant divine—save perhaps Montagu—denounces any other Christian sect or heresy more seriously or strenuously than he denounces Roman Catholicism. Throughout this period the Church of Rome is seen consistently as by far the major doctrinal and ecclesiastical

[47] Carleton, *Directions*, p. 17.
[48] *Ibid.*, p. 12.    [49] *Divinitie*, p. 438.

opponent of the Church of England. English Protestant divines of every outlook devote incomparably more space and attention to combat with this first and oldest antagonist than to quarrels with groups and positions considered deviant within the Church of England or even to denunciation of separatist tendencies of Anabaptist sects outside. Moreover, during most of these decades, the political and national interest (in which English Protestant divines tend to be fully engaged) adds weight and pressure to the religious interest: and Roman Catholicism is seen not only as an enemy of the faith, but in terms of Gunpowder Plots and in its principal national embodiment, Spain, as an enemy of the state as well.

There is no friend to the Roman Church in the English Protestantism of this time. It can be argued that in the last years of this period the accommodations actually achieved at the political level pressed toward a measure of adjustment at the religious level, too, reflected, for example, in the relatively moderate tone of Laud and Montagu on the Catholic problem. Yet viewed objectively, Laud at least can surely not be called a friend of Roman Catholicism; he is only somewhat less violently unfriendly toward it than were his predecessors and many of his less administratively-involved contemporaries. Or perhaps his position is more accurately assayed by stating that the sharpness of his antagonism to Roman Catholicism—the rightward deviation from English Protestant rectitude—comes to appear less because it is so very nearly evenly balanced in him and his activities by sharp antagonism to any degrees of deviation toward the left. Thus he speaks of himself in his "time of troubles" and of his church as caught between the Papists and the Sectaries (which latter he defines most broadly) as between two millstones of equal weight and destructive capacity.[50]

Yet the major written work associated with him is the report of his long and exhaustive conference with the Jesuit, Fisher, in which he reveals his complete commitment to the Church of England as a Protestant church. He displays in this argument no willingness to compromise on any of the basic issues in dispute between the English and the Roman Church. "Besides,"

[50] *Works*, VI, 84-85.

he writes, "in all the points of doctrine that are controverted between us, I would fain see any one point maintained by the Church of England that can be proved to depart from the foundation. You have many dangerous errors about the very foundation, in that which you call the Roman faith; but there I leave you to look to your own soul and theirs whom you seduce."[51]

Even Montagu's mildness in regard to Roman Catholicism is a relative matter only: he moves simply a little farther in the same direction in which Laud was also going, and whatever degree of increasing accord with Roman doctrines and practices may be posited for him is largely a backwash of the intensity of his hostility to the opposite camp of so-called "puritans." And why is he so exercised with the "puritans"? Self-admittedly, it is in good part because they have ventured to fling at him that most opprobrious epithet of "Romanist," whose opprobrium, though not whose justifiability, he himself fully and freely acknowledges.

The breadth of English Protestantism, therefore, is sharply cut off on one side by the gulf which is seen to separate the English and the Roman Church. It is stopped on the side of sectarian radicalism as well by the terminus which is universally drawn for all toleration of varieties of valid Protestantism at the border of Anabaptism. The viewpoint on Anabaptism is nicely conveyed by an exchange between Whitgift and Cartwright. Troubled by the threat to constituted authority inherent in Cartwright's presbyterian proposals, Whitgift ventures to suggest the barest thread of connection between his ideas and the "manifold and horrible heresies" of the Anabaptists. To which charge Cartwright heatedly and self-righteously replies: "It is more than I thought could have happened unto you, once to admit into your mind this opinion of anabaptism of your brethren, which have always had it in as great detestation as yourself, preached against it as much as yourself, hated of the followers and favourers of it as much as yourself."[52]

In the further course of this argument, incidentally, Cart-

---

[51] *Works*, II, 362.
[52] Whitgift, *Works*, I, 76-77.

wright indicates his thorough approval of the application to "the camp of the anabaptists" of the power of the sword and of any and all "those punishments that some of that wicked sect received, for just recompense of their demerits."[53] Very little comment on the Anabaptists as such is to be found in this literature (save as the sect and their teachings come up in connection with the discussion of certain issues, that is, swearing and infant baptism), but whatever comment there is is always as strongly negative as is Cartwright's outburst.

Between Roman Catholicism and Anabaptism, two chasms of profound error on the right and left, extends the wide and relatively level plateau of valid Protestantism, the domain of the fairly numerous separate churches which English Protestant divines accept as sufficiently, though not necessarily perfectly, in accord with the doctrines and practices of the original Christian community. Differences obviously exist among these several churches, and every variation is by no means viewed by every English Protestant as equivalent in rectitude. Judgmentalism enters here, too, and even the plateau of relative truth is seen to be rutted with the tracings of fallacy and human willfulness. Yet these lesser differences are almost always seen in the perspective of the far greater ones which marked the boundaries of the plateau. Hence the sense of antagonism between Protestant and Protestant was hardly ever as severe or deep-reaching as that, for example, between Protestant and Roman Catholic. The mutual forbearance in this area is further enhanced by Protestantism's complete acceptance of the principle of the territorial or national church. Opposition to an international ecclesiastical jurisdiction had been one of the main springs of the Protestant revolt, and whatever the hope or intention of certain of its early leadership simply to reform and maintain the mammoth structure of Roman Catholic institutionalism, the territorial Protestant church so quickly appeared as the only possible practical achievement that what may have been forced of necessity on some shortly became a positive ideal for all. As indicated by the frequently-used metaphor of the single ocean and the several regional seas, though a universality of basic Protestant truth is

53 *Ibid.*

predicated, the variety of its national territorial expression is equally affirmed and approved.

The breadth of this general Protestant ideal does not prevent each area from setting up its own much narrower definition of the proper creed and polity for its own church. Thus English Protestantism, whose exact nature we have been attempting to define throughout this book, must be seen not only as a representative of general Protestantism, but also as a distinctive national entity. In fact, certain of its members, especially its ecclesiastical leadership, were inclined to defend its distinctiveness almost as vigorously as they defended its Protestantism. Because of the special history of the English Protestant Church, its involvement with the state is, as we have observed, notably close and pervasive.

Herein we find, then, for Protestant churches in general and perhaps especially for the English Protestant Church a source of strainings and disturbances. For, on one side is the wide scope of Protestant variability, which must be viewed with some degree of tolerance by all Protestants; on the other is the relatively narrow confinement of the boundaries established and maintained with some degree of firmness by the national church. Another factor contributes—again particularly in the case of the English church—to the tensions potential in this contradiction between breadth and narrowness. To the degree that Protestants are exercised about Roman Catholicism (their first and still major enemy)—to the degree, one might almost say, to which they are intensively Protestant—they tend to look other than dispassionately on the variabilities within Protestantism. They tend, that is, to judge these variabilities, and to judge them by the single obvious standard of their distance from the doctrines and practices of the enemy: the greater the distance the greater the truth; the less, the less. In these early days of Protestantism, Anabaptism does, to be sure, call a halt at one extreme point in the line of development; but clearly there is a tendency in all the branches of Protestantism for certain individuals and groups to be deeply involved with this standard of religious purity and with the effort to apply it within and (if forced so to do) then without their established churches.

In considering the history of any given Protestant church, many general factors must be taken into account, factors which more often work against than with one another. There is a factor for breadth and a factor for narrowness, for stability and for tension, for tolerance and for judgmentalism. When the specific historical events and personages are added to this already complicated mélange, one loses all hope for a simple kind of tale. Certainly the history of English Protestantism, even the few decades of it which we have surveyed, is no simple kind of tale; there are contradictions and tensions a-plenty, both such as are common to Christianity or to Protestantism as a whole and such as are peculiar to English Protestantism alone. We have, for example, observed at length in Chapter 8 that because of the circumstances of the origin of the Church of England, its institutional framework acquired and retained a relatively conservative cast (more Lutheran than Calvinist, one might say), while under the impact of later events its doctrines became thoroughly and aggressively Protestant (more nearly Calvinist, at least, than Lutheran). In this disproportion between institution and belief —the somewhat schizoid quality of the English church—there undoubtedly exists a tension-producing capacity which is fully exemplified in the presbyterian agitation associated with Travers and Cartwright; this capacity finds a diminished reflection in some subsequent disputes associated with the looser use of the term "puritan."

Quickly settling into its particular compromise with all the forces, political, economic, and religious, with which it had to deal, and closely integrated with the structure and functioning of the state, the Church of England resisted so radical a change as a change of government and continued to resist the emergence or the imposition of any line of doctrine or type of ceremonial which would greatly disturb its established ways or alienate sizable groups of its adherents. The Church of England was expected to be the church of all the English; it was also expected, by its leadership at least, to be another anchor for the state and for society, to hold all fast, a granite island in the midst of changing seas. Viewed from the standpoint of its life as an institution, therefore, the drive of the Church of England was throughout this period a drive for unity and stability.

Yet unity and stability are not always complementary nor even compatible goals. Stability is always accomplished merely by preventing further change (if it can be prevented), but unity must sometimes be accomplished by allowing it. Hence despite an undeviating pursuit of these twin goals, shifts and turns in policy occur, and the history of the Church of England is not, as we have said before, even during the seventy years of our survey, a simple story. There is never any doubt, however, of the disaster which must above all be avoided or prevented—the disaster of separatism. So long as the ideal of the national church is a living entity—and it is surely so through this entire period— the major effort of the leaders and the spokesmen of the Church of England is to maintain the seamless coat, the unbroken body of their society. The wiser leadership of the church, indeed, and the wiser spokesmen exhibit their wisdom principally perhaps by subordinating the goal of stability—at least as stability is translated into the mechanics of enforced conformity to a definite and undeviating pattern—to the goal of that broad kind of unity which allows for the co-existence of variations and for the slow change that usually accompanies such neighboring and mutually tolerated differences. The subordination of stability to unity in this manner and in this sense—the avoidance, in short, of the ultimately divisive policy of absolute conformity—is perhaps more than all else the central substance of the *via media*. And it is the *via media* which we have found to be the central substance of the English Protestantism of this era.

## II. The Puritans

To emphasize the *via media* is not, of course, to deny the existence of "puritan" thought, a "puritan" group, and a "puritan" problem in English Protestantism. We do strongly feel, however, that the separateness and rebelliousness of this mind and movement have been very much exaggerated by many modern students who have moved back into this period by way of the open and bitter conflicts of Gardiner's "Puritan Revolution," and have understandably tended to extend into these decades the clear lines of demarcation which they have found in 1640-1660. It is always dangerously and deceptively easy to trace on the basis of hindsight the beginnings of what you know is going to occur. But having plunged into the literature, trying to follow the thinking of these many divines in terms only of what they knew and appeared to feel at the time, we do not by any manner of means feel secure in interpreting what we have read as substantially a prelude to or preparation for the kind of revolt which actually took place. There are connections, yes; but they are devious. There are intimations, but, barring the concatenation of many other circumstances, they could easily, it appears to us, have come to nothing at all. The dynamic of what was to come in England must surely be sought, we feel, somewhere other than here.

Long before the "puritan" revolt, however, there were "puritans," or those called "puritans," in the English church. Completing our lengthy and involved pursuit of the various meanings which were attached in this literature to this term, we want finally to gather together the many strands of argument and to establish, if possible, a single valid definition for the group. From our continual emphasis upon the complex interrelationships of ideas in this body of religious thought and the shifting ground of time and circumstance which underlies them, it should already be amply evident how tentative, vague, and inclusive must be any statement concerning the "puritan"—his nature, his program, and his place in English Protestantism—which attempts to subsume the whole area of our research. Through a process of complete induction, however (since we started into this material with no preconceptions on the subject, or, if with preconceptions, then with opposite ones), we have come to at least one sharp and definite conclusion: that there is only one brief period in these seventy years when the "puritan" may be said truly to exist in the guise in which he is ordinarily portrayed—as a readily identifiable, markedly distinct, and unquestionably disturbing element in the Church of England. This is the period which lies, incidentally, at the farthest remove from the political and ecclesiastical crisis marking the terminus of our study, the period, that is, of the *Marprelate Tracts* and of the encounters between Travers and Cartwright and the established authorities of the church.

When the history of the English church is considered from the purely religious and ecclesiastical rather than the political standpoint, it appears only logical that its episode of clearest party division and most troublesome contention should be located precisely where it is. The memory of the Marian exile was freshest at this time; the thrust of anti-Catholicism was strongest; an enthusiastic and aggressive radical Protestantism felt most keenly the confinement of the ecclesiastical conservatism of the English church (more conservative then than it was later to become). Driving first at the "corruptions" in English Protestant liturgy and ceremonial—the remnants of "popishness," as they saw them —the proponents of this radical Protestantism moved quickly from here, as we have seen, to a broadside attack against the whole structure and constitution of the church. They advocated presbyterianism, in short; and to our mind this is the absolutely indispensable mark both of their distinctiveness and the degree of their hostility.

As befits the significance of the issue in dispute, this emergence of a presbyterian party and its engagement with the opposing officialdom of the church caused a debate that was highly acrimonious. If not in terms of its rancor (the *Appello Caesarem* is at least an equal contender on this score), then in terms of the number of clerics and clerical treatises involved, the acrimony cannot be matched again in this literature until the Revolution. Here, in these bitter presentations of charge and counter-charge, "puritan," as a word and concept, arises and acquires the quality of an epithet. "This . . . reforming consort with their followers," Bancroft complains of the presbyterian disturbers of the church's peace, "have divided themselves from all the rest of the ministerie, and Christians in England: and linked themselves into a newe brotherhood, with this lincke, viz. . . . the desire of the pure Discipline."[54] Pursuing the theme still further, Whitgift comes forth with the very word of "puritan" itself: "The name Puritan is very aptly given to these men;

[54] Bancroft, *Dangerous Positions and Proceedings* (1593), p. 121.

not because they be pure, more than were the heretics called Cathari; but because they think themselves to be *mundiores ceteris,* 'more pure than others,' as Cathari did, and separate themselves from all other churches and congregations, as spotted and defiled: because also they suppose the church which they have devised to be without all impurity."[55]

Like all such polemical words, however—like the word "popish," for example, as used by the presbyterian group—"puritan" even in its early uses was no rapier but a battle club: it did not pierce clean and straight to a point of disagreement, but was made to hit and smash as wide a surface as could possibly be demolished with a single blow. Even in the two brief passages we have cited, the effort is plain to bring to bear upon the group attacked the infamy attached to ancient heresies and to convict them also of the sin of schism and separatism. But, as we know, the presbyterians in question were actually not separatists; even in its defeat, this presbyterian agitation cannot be shown to have given rise to any major defections from the Church of England. To the full satisfaction of himself and to at least the partial satisfaction of the modern reader, Cartwright roundly refutes the applicability of the term "puritan" in its Catharist sense to the group he represents: "Albeit we hold divers points more purely then they do which impugn them, yet I know none that by comparison hath either said or writen that all those that think as we do in those points are more holy and more unblameable in life than any of those that think otherwise. . . . And therefore, as the name was first by the papists maliciously invented, so is it of you very unbrotherly confirmed."[56] It is all very amusing, very tragic, and very human.

Yet the term "puritan" as a label in this period for the presbyterian contingent in the Church of England does at any rate have a specific locale and some attachment, though prejudiced in its essence, to a definable reality. We bewail with Fuller, then, the continued employment of the term after the presbyterian issue has departed into the limbo of all lost causes. Fuller writes: "We must not forget that Spalato (I am confident I am

[55] *Op.cit.,* p. 171.    [56] *Ibid.,* pp. 171-72.

not mistaken therein) was the first, who professing himself a Protestant, used the word Puritan, to signify the defenders of matters doctrinal in the English church. Formerly the word was only taken to denote such as dissented from the hierarchy and church government, which now was extended to brand such as were anti-Arminians in their judgements. As Spalato first abused the word in this sense, so we could wish he had carried it away with him in his return to Rome; whereas now leaving the word behind him in this extensive signification thereof, it hath since by others been improved to asperse the most orthodox in doctrine and religious in conversation."[57]

Yet here is another reality to be confronted. For whether we or Fuller approve of it or not, the word "puritan" (and certain other related terms) was in fact used, though sparsely, throughout this literature. As time passed, it was used more and more loosely and broadly so that its initial anchorage to the presbyterian policy was first concealed and then entirely supplanted by a multitude of other issues and attitudes. As we have previously indicated, the most consistent and readily traceable of these issues in this literature is not Spalato's anti-Arminianism, nor any other doctrinal matter, but simply anticeremonialism. "Anti Ceremonian Brethren," Sanderson calls the "puritans,"[58] and thus defines them as adequately in brief compass (apart from their presbyterian origins and attachments) as any one has. Not that Sanderson's definition, though relatively satisfactory, can be accepted as either complete or altogether accurate. For he was throughout his career a stout antagonist to what he conceived to be the "puritan" position, and he packed even into this short phrase a considerable quantity of distaste. The word "brethren" in particular is a weighted word as he employs it, since it is consciously calculated to suggest the separatism toward which critics of the "puritans" were always quick to charge they were inclined. The "puritans," Sanderson observes in one of

[57] Fuller, *Church History*, v, 529. An amusing instance of the wild use of the word as a catchall of opprobrium is seen in the characterization of Royalist Inigo Jones, a man of no great religious feeling, by the papal legate Panzini as "puritanissimo fiero"! (See James Lees-Milne, *The Age of Inigo Jones* [1953], p. 52.)
[58] Sanderson, *XXXVI Sermons*, p. 78.

his earlier sermons, "say . . . they are despised in being scoffed and flouted, and derided by loose companions, and by profane or Popishly affected persons: in being stiled Puritans, and Brethren, and Precisions, and having many jests and fooleries fastned upon them whereof they are not guilty."[59] But refusing to yield upon the matter, Sanderson defends the justice of the attack and of the terminology: ". . . I see not but that . . . the Name of Puritan, and the rest, are justly given them. For appropriating to themselves the Names of Brethren, Professors, Good men, and other like; as differences betwist them and those they call Formalists: Would they not have it thought that they have a Brotherhood and Profession of their own, freer and purer from Superstition and Idolatry, than others have, that are not of the same stamp? And doing so, why may they not be called Puritans?"[60]

As an issue anticeremonialism is certainly less exact and determinate, and subject to a wider range of expression and interpretation, than presbyterianism. Even the exactness in Sanderson's definition of the "puritan" group tends to fade away as one pursues the reality of the "puritan"—not as this reality is given in the attacks of their opponents, but as it exists in their own writings and statements about themselves. Occasionally in these numerous sermons one does find that a "puritan" author uses the word "puritan," and that he sometimes even applies it self-consciously to himself. What meaning does the word take on for those English Protestant divines whom others designated as such? How do they defend themselves against the generally-recognized opprobrium of the word? In the process of using the word or defending themselves against it, do they perhaps define themselves a little more clearly, so that even if their more prejudiced and involved contemporaries did not truly comprehend them, we of the present may at least hope to do so?

In seeking to answer these several questions we shall turn first to Perkins. We find him lamenting at one point that "the *pure heart* is so little regarded, that the seeking after it is turned to a by-word, and a matter of reproach: who are so much branded

---

[59] *Ibid.*, pp. 15-16.
[60] *Ibid.* See *ibid.*, p. 96, for his list of "puritan" doctrines.

with vile tearmes of Puritans and Presitions, as those that most indeavour to get and keepe the puritie of heart in a good conscience?"[61] "For the practices of that religion," he says elsewhere, "which stands by the law of God, and the good lawes of this land, is nicknamed with tearmes of *Preciseness*, and *Purity*. A thing much to be lamented; for this bewraies that there is a great want of the grace of God among us."[62] Adams essentially rejects the relevance of the term "puritan" to any group or position which he represents. He ties it still to the presbyterian faction to whom it was originally affixed and with whom he has no sympathy: "Behold the exigent wee are in: the Papists say we have no ministers, because they are not made by Bishops; the Puritans say we have no Ministers, because they are made by Bishops. Which of these speake true? Neither. First to answere the Puritans; Bishops may make Ministers. . . . Now wee have true Bishops, therefore in Gods name allow us to have true Ministers."[63] He does acknowledge the broader use of the word, however. In a sermon devoted to the subject of the "wolves" (such as the "usurer," the "gay Gallant," the "flattering Sycophant," those who "keepe the poore away from their gates") who are wont to harass good ministers, the tender lambs of God, Adams includes among these wolfish persecutors "rurall ignorants, that blaspheme all godliness under the name of Puritanisme."[64]

Bolton, characteristically, is bolder than most "puritans," venturing to use and define the word positively and as a badge of honor to good Christians rather than as an epithet applied to them by their enemies. He carefully clears the word, of course, of many of the implications which commonly cling to it. "I meane not," he writes, "the superstitious Puritane who out of a furious selfe-love to his owne will-worship . . . thinkes himselfe to be the onely holy devout man."[65] His "puritans," then, are not Catharists; nor are they Donatists, for they are "not the furious Anabaptists of our times, who are as like the ancient Donatists, as if they had spit them out of their mouth." Neither are they "giddy" separatists nor "unwarrantable opinionist[s]

---

[61] *Works*, III, 15.   [62] *Works*, II, 304-05.   [63] *Works*, p. 561.
[64] *Ibid.*, p. 388.   [65] Bolton, *Works*, I, 85.

. . . because I am persuaded good men may differ in things indifferent without prejudice of salvation, or just cause of breach of charity, or disunion of affections."[66] Having by these and numerous other negatives and cautions stripped the word of any possible derogatory content, he proceeds at last to indicate the kind of person whom he intends it to signify and praise: "Mistake me not, I meane Christs puritans, and no other. . . . I meane onely such as Bellarmine intimates, when he cals King James puritan: for . . . if a man speak but holily, and name but reformation, Scripture conscience, and such other words which sting their carnal hearts, it is enough to make a man a puritan."[67] Analyzing in another treatise the hatred felt by the "notorious sinner" for the "puritan," he ironically observes: "You must know by the way, that these [puritans] are a very dangerous kinde of men, able to blow up whole houses, by their too fiery zeale against idlenesse, drunkennesse . . . and the like." In still another definition, he calls "puritans" those who "make conscience of study, and Religious education of Schollers; who are ready ever, and resolute to uphold goodnes in a House, though they be crusht, disgraced, and disofficed: who out of a gracious and ingenuous freedome of Spirit, will be their own men in Elections, and other Collegiate services; and not suffer their consciences to be led hood-winkt, to serve other mens humours and private ends; who chuse rather in a neglected state, sweetly to enjoy the continual feast . . . of a sincere heart . . . the society of Gods servants; then for many times full dearely bought favours and offices, to enthrall . . . both their judgements and affections. . . . In a word, who of the two, would rather save their soules, than prosper in the world."[68]

Thus even at his most extreme—and among the "puritan" writers of the post-presbyterian epoch whom we have read, Bolton is assuredly that most extreme—the "puritan" thinks of himself as simply more intensely religious, Christian, and Protestant (and specifically more English Protestant) than the ordinary churchgoer, and especially more than those who oppose him. Every religious reformer, to be sure, every sectarian, schismatic, and heretic in Christian history has thought of himself in such

[66] *Ibid*, pp. 86-87.　　[67] *Ibid.*, pp. 244-45.　　[68] *Works*, IV, 132.

general terms as these; hence we again have no real definition of the "puritan" as such. The point is, however, that in the true reformer and the identifiable schismatic this tone of superior and unappreciated religiosity is tied to definite issues of dispute and disagreement. Following these English "puritans" through the enormous bulk of their writings, we have found only a certain concentration of the tone in them; but we have found no issues to which it is consistently attached. Even anticeremonialism, which, as issues go, is as accurate a measure of the "puritan" as one can name, is by no means the absolutely consistent aspect of "puritan" thought that one might wish for the sake of easy analysis and the satisfying formula; it is, instead, a not infrequently fleeting and minor element in these writings and a matter more of deduction from other viewpoints than of straightforward statement.

In our effort to find a distinguishing line between "puritan" and Anglican, we have found no issue, doctrinal or ecclesiastical, of which we can speak in other than relative terms. The so-called "puritans" never either monopolize the concept or viewpoint in question or universally exhibit it; there is, as we have mentioned, never more than the certain concentration in their writings of a given type of thought or mood. In its more distinctive expressions—in Bolton or Adams, for example—the very tone of intense and misunderstood religiosity which we cited as a mark of the "puritan" is not characteristic of all "puritans." In its more general expressions it is not limited to "puritans," as we see, for example, in Perkins.

A sermon by Adams and particularly a certain passage from that sermon appear to us to condense and define, as well as it can be done, this "puritan" temper as an identifiable quality in the literature. The sermon conveys its "puritan" character in its very title, "The Gallant's Burden," and entrenches it further by the intensely direct and even ranting manner of the handling of the theme. There are pages of pointed criticism of the inadequacies of the ministry or of individual ministers in the Church of England (though the soundness and rectitude of the church itself are never questioned) and pages, too, of passionate attack on popery (though the soundness of certain individual Roman

Catholics is specifically allowed). As the culmination of the argument, good Christians are drawn apart from all this error and corruption to constitute a spiritual but not an institutional brotherhood and to become, since sin is an active force in the world, the objects of the hatred and the persecution of the carnal. At once protesting and lamenting the miseries of the godly, Adams at last proclaims: "But doe the Edomites [the Catholics] onely take up these weapons of scorne against us? No, I speake it betwixt shame and griefe, even the Israelites scorne the Prophets. There are some sicke of a wantonnesse in Religion so hot about the question, *De modo*, that the Devill states the matter of Religion from their hearts: if we cannot wrangle with Formes and Shadowes (i.e. do not accept and practice all the prescribed ceremonials) and shew our selves refractarie to established Orders . . . our Sermons shall be slighted, our persons derided. . . . One Arrow of these Israelites, wounds deeper than a hundred Cannon shot of Edomites. . . . Is it not enough for them, that they have drawne out the life-blood of our Livings, but they must expose our persons to contempt? So the Jewes spoyled Christ of his Vestments, and then mocked him with basenesse. . . . Surely, if repentance and restitution prevent it not, they shall have Tithe one day, which they have more right to, the tenth Sheafe of that Harvest, which is reserved for reprobates in Hell."[69]

This, then, undoubtedly is "puritanism." The sermon as a whole, the passage as a whole could have been written by no one other than a "puritan." Yet one cannot find its exact counterpart in manner and approach, if not in substance, in certain other English Protestant divines who are equally well-known as "puritans": neither in the moderate Perkins, for example, nor in the gentle Sibbes. Indeed, Bolton and perhaps Downame are the only other major "puritans" who come immediately to mind as being capable of much the same violence of language and tone. On the other hand, particular strands of thinking in this sermon—the attack on Roman Catholicism, the assumption that the godly will be persecuted by the ungodly, even some of the complaints about the inadequacies of the ministry of the Church

[69] *Works*, p. 13.

of England—can be traced through English Protestantism as a whole. Moreover, when one translates or transposes the negative complaints, criticisms, and protests even in this most "puritan" of sermons into a positive program for the Church of England, one finds that the program consists not of the assertion of one doctrinaire position as a replacement for another (as with the earlier presbyterian agitators); nor does it consist of the threat of separatism. Rather, it is essentially a plea for accomplishing the secure unity of the English church by enforcing a mutual forbearance upon differing groups. All that Adams really asks is that the leadership of the Church of England cease to discriminate against and to persecute (as he obviously feels they do) the "anti-ceremonian" godly. Thus even from this extremist "puritan" pronouncement the *via media* is the one genuine hope and policy which emerges.

We have spoken often of a group of representatives of the English church whom we have called conservatives. We have mentioned Hooker and Andrewes as being properly among their number, and Bancroft, Whitgift, and Sanderson should no doubt be cited too. Then at the end of our list in terms of time, but preeminently at its head in terms of his importance, there is Laud, to whom Montagu and Cosin must be added as particular affiliates and supporters of Laudian policies. To our mind these several men constitute a more distinctive group among English Protestant divines than do the "puritans." If it can be said that the function of the "puritans" is criticism of the established structure and practices of the Church of England, the function of these conservatives is defense. But whereas the criticism is various in approach and substance and in the number and identity of participants, the defense tends to be more narrowly focused around maintenance of the status quo, and to occupy particularly those whose institutional placement encourages their assumption of the role. Most of the conservatives we have listed hold bishoprics or archbishoprics in the course of their lives; most of the "puritans" do not. Relatively speaking, the "puritans" are the "outs" and the conservatives are the "ins," and the two groups are to be partly defined by their positioning in the hierarchy and the court's preference, which this positioning reflects, for those of conservative rather than critical mentality. But the hierarchy in itself and as such are neither "puritan" nor conservative, since the great majority by far are simply men of the *via media*.

Just as we have warned against an over-neat packaging of the "puritans" and against the too-frequent effort to define them absolutely and precisely, so here, with these conservatives, we find tight grouping and simple labelling unjustified by the always various and complicated facts of the case. Bancroft and Whitgift, for example, are wholly preoccupied by their encounter with the presbyterian contingent, and their procedures in controversy are shaped by the violent and crucial nature of the battle. Hooker's is a calmer mood and method, but the logic of his argument is still directed toward this one highly specific and militant opposition to the Church of England. Andrewes, on the other hand, finds himself in what is altogether a more peaceful age, and the moderateness of his conservatism, his tendency to equivocate and make the balancing, the turgid, sometimes the nearly meaningless statement, all reflect the confidence of the establishment in its security and the basically loyal and agreeable character of the adversary. Sanderson's early ecclesiastical career is spent in the same atmosphere, and the eminent rationality which characterizes his writings and which he maintains even into a period of stress and persecution for himself is of such a degree and depth that one hesitates to include him at all in the conservative category.

Yet all the conservative writers we have considered are committed to some degree to the basic concepts of the *via media*. Even Bancroft and Whitgift oppose presbyterianism, they say—and with more than the sophistry of debate to give substance to their claim—not to impose but to prevent a tyranny. And while Andrewes has the good fortune to be the principal representative among conservatives of this middle way in the age of its triumph, Sanderson proves the strength of the ideal in him by continuing to bespeak it in the age of its decline.

Such considerable and consistent adherence to the values of the *via media* by even conservative divines renders all the more puzzling their essential abandonment by Laud and the Laudian school. Laud, indeed, constitutes an uniquely exceptional figure among the throng of English Protestants whose works we have analyzed. That he belongs properly to the conservative group is not, of course, a matter of doubt or question. It is clearly evident in his attachment to the upper echelons of ecclesiastical administration and in his function as a champion of the established and of the hierarchy as an adjunct of the monarchy. Yet the process one watches in the series of Bancroft, Whitgift, Hooker, and Andrewes—the ultimate emergence, out of conflict with the threat of major change, of a policy of real ecclesiastical breadth—is reversed, as it were, in the single personage of Laud. Rather than unity through breadth, conformity through force becomes the goal of church administration, and the old techniques of defense acquire an active and intrusive quality more suitable to aggression. We are speaking of the reaching out of the disciplinary arm of the church—if not always in terms of effective enforcement, then at least in terms of harassment. There is the Laudian canon, for example, which commands for all what had hitherto been left to each particular minister's decision: the location of the communion table at the altar end of the church and obeisance to it by parishioners both on entering and departing from the place of worship.[70]

There is another, even more significant, Laudian canon which prescribes the formal equalization, in regard to the condemnation and the penalty provided, of any and all degrees of defection from the doctrines, the liturgy, or the ceremonial rules of the Church of England; this equalization applies whether the defection is a matter of Roman Catholicism, Anabaptism, Socinianism, Separatism, or merely of certain expressions of the "puritan" resistance to prescribed liturgy and fixed prayer. This canon, titled "Against Sectaries," reads as follows: "Whereas there is a provision now made by a canon for the suppressing of popery . . . this present synod well knowing, that there are other sects which endeavour the subversion both of the doctrine and discipline of the Church of England, no less than papists do, although by another way; for the preventing thereof, doth hereby decree . . . that all those proceedings and penalties which

---

[70] *Works,* v, 625.

are mentioned in the aforesaid canon against popish recusants, as far as they shall be appliable, shall stand in full force . . . against all Anabaptists, Brownists, Separatists, Familists, or other sect or sects, person or persons whatsoever, who do . . . obstinately refuse . . . (or) neglect to repair to their parish churches . . . for the hearing of divine service established, and of receiving the holy Communion according to law. And we do also further decree . . . that the clause contained in the canon now made by this synod against the books of Socinianism, shall also extend to the makers, importers, printers, and publishers, or dispersers of any book . . . devised against the discipline and government of the Church of England. And further, because there are sprung up among us a sort of factious people, despisers and depravers of the book of Common Prayer, who do not according to the law resort to their parish church or chapel to join in the public prayers . . . and worship of God with the congregation, contenting themselves with the hearing of sermons only, thinking thereby to avoid the penalties due to such as wholly absent themselves from the church. We therefore, for the restraint of all such . . . do ordain that the church or chapel wardens, and questmen, or redemen of every parish, shall be careful to enquire out all such disaffected persons, and shall present the names of all such delinquents at all visitations of bishops, and other ordinaries, and that the same proceedings and penalities mentioned in the canon aforesaid respectively, shall be used against them as against other recusants."[71]

That the shift in administrative policy under Laud is real and decisive the above canon is sufficient to indicate. Where is the source, however, of such a signal change? We have not here the space or the resources to reply to such an inquiry. Our only contribution from the work we have done is the conviction— indeed we feel, the proof—that, though the shift with which we have been concerned occurs within the church, the explanation for it must be sought outside. Though he has deserted the spirit and program of the *via media*, Laud on occasion wistfully employs its verbiage, and he himself appears to us to be more a

71 *Ibid.*, p. 622.

product than a prime mover, more a victim of historical circumstances than a maker of them.

## III. The Broad and Middle Way

The peculiarity of a Laud would not appear so great if the English Protestant literature of these decades had not impressed upon us first the growing strength and then the overwhelming dominance in it of the ideology and the temper of the middle way. We cannot conclude this chapter, therefore, devoted as it has been to summations and definitions, without an effort fully to penetrate the meaning of the philosophy of the *via media* and to observe its expression through the wide range of its spokesmen. This philosophy, to begin with, does not mean what it might superficially appear to signify—an expectation of the end to all contention in the church. Contention is accepted as a permanent aspect of the life of a unified church, accepted with reluctance by some but almost with approval by others. Such contention is, indeed, an inevitable consequence of the universally acknowledged nature of the church as a mixed company of godly and ungodly. The expression of this positive view of the necessity and even of the value of contention is, as one might expect, most frequent and emphatic in the writings of "puritans." Thus Preston exhorts: "My brethren, Contend for the faith once delivered to the Saints. Marke it, the worke must be to contend for it, you must be men of contention, let the world say what they will of you, it is the dutie that lyes on you, it is that which the Spirit calls for from you. . . . Let not pretence of indiscretion hinder you, for discretion when it is right, teacheth a man not to doe lesse but more, and better than another man. . . .

"So againe, let us not say we must be moderate, for what is that moderation? Indeede the moderation that keepeth from actions, wherein is excesse, is good; but if you meane by moderation to goe a slow and easie pace in the wayes of God, that is coldnesse, idlenesse, carelesnesse. . . . For . . . it were better there should bee great offences committed in the Land, great and notorious crimes, than that there should bee any losse in the matter of

Faith. . . . Errours in opinion are matters of great moment,
therefore it belongs to everie one to looke to it, to us that are
Preachers in our places, to every Man to contend for the common Faith."[72]

Even the gentle Sibbes proclaims: ". . . they are . . . scoffing
Atheists that trifle with Religion, as if it were no great matter
what it bee. They will bee earnest in all things else . . . but for
Religion it is no matter what it be, it is a thing not worthy the
seeking after, the old Religion or the new or both or none. . . .
There will be a faction in the world while the world stands,
Christ and Anti-Christ, Good and evill, light and darkenesse,
but a man cannot be of both, he must shew himselfe of one side
or other in case of opposition. Therefore the temper of the true
professor is to be earnest in case of opposition to Religion, and
in case of opportunity to advance his Religion. . . . in the
course of Christ, in the cause of Religion, he must be fiery and
fervent."[73]

Another "puritan," Dering, maintains the same inevitability
of religious contention and asserts though less militantly than
Preston or Sibbes, a clear line of demarcation between truth and
error in these differences; simultaneously, he makes of these
facts a basis both for the right to speak what he conceives as
truth and for the necessity of tolerating error. "I beare him witnesse who speaketh trueth," he says, "and beare with his errour
who is deceived, acknowledging my selfe more unworthy than
either of both." He proceeds to urge his readers: "I beseech you
to consider but this with mee: hath not God given us gifts
diversely, to one more, to one lesse. . . . Must wee not of necessity
one know more, another lesse . . . and hath not God given this
diversitie unto us for a good purpose, that thus standing in
neede one of another, we should all more effectually love and
helpe one another: looke not for it therefore, we should all
agree, in everything, for it shall never be till we doo all see the
Lord Jesu, who onely is perfect wisedome and trueth."[74]

Both the militancy of Sibbes and Preston and the optimistic

72 Preston, *Breast Plate of Faith*, pp. 211-13.
73 Sibbes, *Beames of Divine Light*, pp. 247-48.
74 Dering, *Works*, pp. 602-04.

receptivity of Dering are lacking from some other statements on the subject of religious differences and contentions: such divisions are noted instead with reluctance, though their absolute unavoidability is admitted and accepted. "And therefore," Chillingworth remarks, "though we wish heartily that all controversies were ended as we doe that all sinne were abolisht, yet we have little hope of the one or the other, till the world be ended."[75] Broadening his approach to speak of the whole scope of human contentiousness, Sanderson sadly comments that one should "never marvel to see so many scandals and divisions everywhere in the world . . . so long as their is Pride and Self-love in every mans own bosome, or indeed any other lust unsubdued. . . . Our comfort is, the time will come (but look not for it whilst this world lasteth;) when the Son of man will cause to be gathered out of his Kingdom . . . all things that minister occasion of stumbling or contention. But in the mean time . . . we must be content to want that peace; which we desire, but cannot have without God; till he be pleased to grant it. . . ."[76] With specific reference to religious differences, he argues: "If we look into the large Volumes that have been written by Philosophers, Lawyers, and Phisicians we shall find the greatest part of them spent in Disputations. . . . And we allow them so to do, without prejudice to their respective professions: albeit they be conversant about things measurable by Sense or Reason. Only in Divinity, great offence is taken at the multitude of Controversies, wherein yet difference of opinions is by so much more tolerable than in other Sciences; by how much the things about which we are conversant are of a more sublime, mysterious, and incomprehensible nature, than are those of other Sciences. . . ."[77]

Whether militantly championed by those who felt that continued contention would help them achieve a more general appreciation of their concepts of true religiosity, or regretfully conceded by those who identified more closely and completely with the status quo, the recognition of the inevitability of certain religious differences within the unified church was essential to

[75] Chillingworth, *op.cit.*, pp. 83-84.
[76] Sanderson, *op.cit.*, p. 465.
[77] *Ibid.*, pp. 485-86.

the viewpoint of the *via media*. But since these disagreements are expected to occur within the content of a civil and ecclesiastical unity, it was urged on every side that they be pursued in a spirit of Christian moderation and charity. The "puritans," interestingly enough, those who were presumably altogether extremist, contribute as frequently and fervently as any others to this type of argumentation. Sibbes, for example, urges that "we should not smite one another, by hasty censures, especially in things of an indifferent nature . . . where most holinesse is, there is most moderation. . . ."[78] He continues in the same broad and charitable vein: "The Church of Christ is a common Hospitall, wherein all are in some measure sicke of some spirituall disease, or other; that we should all have ground of exercising mutually the spirit of wisedome and meeknesse.

"This that wee may the better doe, let us put upon our selves the spirit of Christ. . . . The weapons of this warfare must not be carnall. . . . The Spirit will only work with his owne tooles. And we should think what affection Christ would cary to the party in this case; that great Physitian . . . had . . . a gentle hand and a tender heart."[79] Even that firebrand Bolton, the extremist "puritan" *par excellence*, warns that "it is the naturall humour of an hypocrite, to be supercilious and censorious and forward in finding faults."[80] "For all sound Converts," he continues, "desire and labour to be very charitable . . . in their censures. Consciousnesse of their owne corruptions makes them compassionate towards others in this kinde."[81]

Numbers of non-"puritans," or Anglicans, also argue for a policy of charity toward dissidents and dissidences within the English church. "Zeal is directed upon God," Donne admonishes, "and charity upon our brethren; but God will not accept anything for an act of zeal to himself that violates charity towards our brethren by the way."[82] Morton develops the same theme more fully: "It is but folly to looke for in mortall . . . man a heavenly and angelical harmonie void of all jarring. It is rather our partes to labour in repressing that pride and selfe

[78] Sibbes, *The Bruised Reede*, pp. 83-85.
[79] *Ibid.*, pp. 88-90.   [80] *Works*, IV, 126-27.   [81] *Ibid.*, p. 130.
[82] Donne, *Works*, IV, 374.

love of our corrupt natures, whereby men carnally minded and affected, are made to swell in anger and hatred against those who doe not in everie respect daunce after their pipe: being more alienated from their brethren for some fewe contradictions, then joyned together in Christian love, by their consente in all the points of religion beside. Milde and modest dissenting worketh out the trueth. . . ."[83]

Sanderson likewise urges that "good heed should be taken lest by the cunning of Satan . . . difference in judgment should in process of time first estrange by little and little, and at length quite alienate our Affections one from another. It is one thing to dissent from, another to be at discord with, our brethren."[84] Since there is little hope that all controversies in the church and between churches will end "till the world be ended," it is, contends Chillingworth, "best to content our selves with, and to persuade others unto an Unity of Charity and mutuall toleration; seeing God hath authoriz'd no man to force all men to Unity of Opinion."[85]

Another necessary element in the viewpoint of the *via media* is the distinction in religious beliefs and practices between lesser and greater issues; this we have previously discussed in a general way. Again and again by both those who are and who are not known as "puritans," this principle is invoked to make more readily possible the peace and unity of the English church. One of the most eloquent expressions of this particular argument and appeal is to be found in Donne; he writes: "And truly it is a lamentable thing, when ceremonial things in matters of discipline, or problematical things in matters of doctrine, come so far as to separate us from one another in giving ill names to one another. . . . There are outward things, ceremonial things, in the worship of God that are temporary, and they did serve God that brought them in, and they do serve God also that have driven them out of the church because their undeniable abuse had clogged them with an impossibility of being restored to that good use which they were at first ordained for. . . . Such another

---

[83] Morton, *A Treatise of the Threefolde State of Man*, Preface.
[84] *Op.cit.*, p. 471.
[85] *Op.cit.*, p. 85.

wall . . . the devil hath built now in the Christian Church; and both mortered it in the brains and blood of men in the sharp and virulent contentions arisen and fomented in matters of religion. But yet . . . for all this separation, Christ Jesus is amongst us all, and in his time will break down this wall too, these differences amongst Christians, and make us all glad of that name, the name of Christians, without affecting in ourselves, or inflicting upon others, other names of envy and subdivision."[86]

From Donne one expects this sort of broad and generous approach. But there is an element of surprise in discovering in Bolton, too, much the same idea, if not altogether the same eloquence. Bolton warns the overenthusiastic believer that Christianity "doth not consist, as too many suppose . . . in holding strict points, defending precise opinions."[87] Such are lesser things and are to be clearly distinguished from the greater. "It is too true," he additionally admonishes, "that those who are more fierce, and forward about the ceremonials, and circumstantials, then truely hot and zealous in the essentials, and substantials of Christianity, prove too often vaine-gloriously . . . mounted upon that foule hellish fiend, Hypocrasie, and posting apace towards some fearefull Apostasy, or Anabaptisticall phrensie."[88] Yet another "puritan," Sibbes, declares that godly ministers should not trouble their flocks "with curious or doubtfull disputes." "That age of the church which was most fertile in nice questions," he counsels, "was most barren in Religion."[89]

Fuller, a notable proponent of the *via media* and the unity of the church, finds the essence of the moderate man in religion to consist in this very capacity to distinguish between fundamental and minor issues. For moderation "is a mixture of discretion and charity in one's judgement." And discretion serves to put a difference "betwixt things absolutely necessary to salvation to be done and believed, and those which are of a second sort and lower form wherein more liberty and latitude is allowed." None is more zealous than the moderate man, he assures the reader, "in matters of moment." But in maintaining the truth or propriety of the lesser elements of religion, "the stiff-

---

[86] *Works*, IV, 373-75.   [87] *Works*, IV, 57.   [88] *Ibid.*, p. 60.
[89] Sibbes, *Bruised Reede*, p. 67.

ness of the judgment is abated, and supplied with charity towards his neighbor." Moreover, the moderate and the lukewarm man are not to be confused, for "the lukewarm man eyes only his own ends and particular profit; the moderate man aims at the good of others, and the unity of the church."[90]

It is the whole-souled pursuit of the unity of the church, however, which is above all the mark of the *via media*. The abhorrence of separatism, an opinion we have found to be virtually universal, is one side of this viewpoint; but there are also many direct and wholly positive expressions of it in the literature. Sibbes expresses well the depth and sincerity of the hope which was involved: "This mercy of Christ likewise should moove us to commiserate the estate of the poore Church torne by enemies without, and renting it selfe by divisions at home. It cannot but work upon any soule that ever felt comfort from Christ, to consider what an affectionate intreaty the Apostle useth to mutuall agreement in judgement and affection. If any consolation in Christ, if any fellowship of the Spirit, any bowells and mercies fulfill my joy, be like minded. As if he should say, unless you will disclaime all consolation in Christ . . . labour to maintaine the unity of the Spirit in the bond of peace."[91]

The extraordinary valuation which Sibbes places on the unity of the church is perhaps more adequately indicated in the following brief statement than even in the emotional passage we have cited. "In some cases," he asserts, "peace by keeping our faith to our selves, is of more consequence, than the open discovery of some things we take to be true, considering the weaknesse of many mens nature is such that there can hardly be a discovery of any difference in opinion, without some estrangement of affection."[92] There can be, it should be remembered, no greater sacrifice for the religious man than the sacrifice of even a little truth.

Thus in the great majority of its spokesmen and in the largest part of the seven decades of its life which we have surveyed, the Church of England had exhibited a remarkable capacity to express the general Protestant genius for a community of differ-

[90] Fuller, *Holy and Profane States*, pp. 254-57.
[91] *Op.cit.*, pp. 197-98.
[92] *Ibid.*, p. 200.

ences. The opposition of those forces always at work in Christianity—the force of the church with its drive for unity and uniformity and the force of the individual believer eternally seeking his own unique intimacy of contact with the source of his salvation—had been brought to a degree of balance as seemingly stable as any ever achieved in the history of Christianity. England may add to her other triumphs in this triumphant Elizabethan and Jacobean age the success of the *via media*. Why this adjustment failed so signally and so shortly is the question we leave at the end of this study to be the possible subject of another. Perhaps we have at least cleared away some of the obstacles confounding the scholar's long quest for illumination of the issues which generated revolution in England.

———————————————— ⸸ ⸸ ⸸ ————————————————

The sources we have used are in print, but they are numerous and widely scattered on the shelves of great libraries. We should like therefore to provide a comprehensive guide to them and a general survey of the critical literature related to the problems explored in this study.

The major corpus of English Protestant thought is in the library of the British Museum and is catalogued there; no other single collection is comparable and the published catalogues are not an adequate substitute for the thousand-odd volumes of the working catalogue in the library. Other libraries with important collections are Dr. Williams' Library in London, the Bodleian in Oxford, the Huntington in San Marino, California, the Folger in Washington, D.C., the Houghton Library of Harvard University, and the library of the Union Theological Seminary in New York City.

To aid our use of these gigantic collections for the purpose of a manageable and satisfactory sampling of Protestant religiosity, we have found the following helpful: A. W. Pollard and G. R. Redgrave, *A Short Title Catalogue of Books Printed in England, Scotland, and Ireland and of English Books Printed Abroad, 1475-1640*, 1948; C. H. Cooper and T. Cooper, *Athenae Cantabrigiensis*, 2 vols., Cambridge, 1858-1861; John Venn and S. A. Venn, *Alumni Cantabrigiensis*, 4 vols., Cambridge, 1922-1927; Joseph Foster, *Alumni Oxoniensis*, 4 vols., Oxford, 1891-1892; Anthony à Wood, *Athenae Oxoniensis*, 4 vols., ed. Philip Bliss, 1813-1820; William Jaggard, *Catalogue of Such English Books As Lately Have Been, or Now Are, in Printing*, 1618; William London, *A Catalogue of the Most Vendible Books in England*, 1658; William Crowe, *The Catalogue of Our English Writers on the Old and New Testament*, 1668; John Wilkins, *Ecclesiastes*, 1646; and Richard Baxter's *A Christian Directory*, 1673.

Among the printed sources most generally available to the serious student, special mention should be made of the Parker Society publications, in 55 volumes, 1843-1855; the collections of John Strype, in 23 volumes, 1821-1840; and the often useful publications of the Camden Society, the Surtees Society, and the Anglo-Catholic Library of Theology.

The best bibliographical guides to the English Reformation will be found in the book lists and critical notes in the monographs that follow, in the fine bibliographical articles in *Church History*, in the *Bulletin of the Institute of Historical Research* of the University of London, and the helpful *Thesis Supplement* published annually; and, of course, there are the Oxford bibliographies for the Tudors and Stuarts, *Bibliography of British History: Tudor Period, 1485-1603*, ed. Conyers Read, Oxford, 1959, and *Bibliography of British History: Stuart Period, 1603-1714*, ed. Godfrey Davies, Oxford, 1928.

The *Dictionary of National Biography*, 22 vols., ed. Sir Leslie Stephen and Sir Sidney Lee, 1921-1922, with supplements, is the most indispensable reference work we have used; Le Neve's *Fasti Ecclesiae Anglicanae*, 1716, has much valuable reference material for the student of English church affairs; and one should certainly mention the superb Herzog and Hauch, *Real-encyklopädie für Protestantische Theologie und Kirche*, 24 vols., Leipsig, 1896-1913.

In the following catalogue of sources and studies of Reformation England, we have abbreviated titles so that the student will have no difficulty checking references for his own purposes. There are several editions of many of the works cited; the differences are seldom important, and so we have noted only the editions used in this study. To avoid needless repetition, the place of publication will be understood to be London unless otherwise specified.

## Primary Sources of Protestant Thought

Adams, Thomas, *The Works*, 1629.
Airay, Henry, *Lectures Upon the Whole Epistle of St. Paul to the Philippians*, 1618.
Ames, William, *Conscience with the Power and Cases Thereof*, 1639.
Andrewes, Lancelot, *Works*, 11 vols., ed. J. P. Wilson and J. Bliss, Oxford, 1841-1854.
———. *XCVI Sermons*, 1629.

Bancroft, Richard, *Daungerous Positions and Proceedings*, 1593.
———. *A Survey of the Pretended Holy Discipline*, 1593.
Barrowe, Henry, *A Brief Discovery of the False Church*, s.l., 1590.
———. Grenewood, J., and Penrie, J., *The Examination of H. Barrowe, J. Grenewood, and J. Penrie . . . Penned by the Prisoners Themselves Before Their Deaths*, s.l., 1593.
Bastwick, John, *A Briefe Relation of Certaine Speciall and Most Materiall Passages and Speeches in the Starre-Chamber . . . June*

*the 14th, 1637 at the Censure of Those Three Worthy Gentlemen,*
*Dr. Bastwicke, Mr. Burton, and Mr. Prynne, 1638.*

———. *Elenchus Religionis Papisticae*, 1627.

———. *The Letany*, 1637.

———. *The Severall Humble Petitions of D. Bastwicke, M. Burton,*
*M. Prynne and of Nathan Wickins . . . to the Honourable House*
*of Parliament, 1641.*

Baxter, Richard, *The Practical Works*, 23 vols., ed. W. Orme, 1830.

Baynes, Paul, *Briefe Directions Unto a Godly Life*, 1618.

———. *Christian Letters*, 1620.

———. *A Commentarie Upon the First and Second Chapters of*
*St. Paul to the Colossians*, 1634.

———. *An Entire Commentary upon the Whole Epistle of St. Paul*
*to the Ephesians*, 1643.

Beard, Thomas, *The Theatre of God's Judgment*, 1597.

Becon, Thomas, *Works*, 3 vols., 1560-1564.

Benefield, Sebastian, *A Commentarie . . . Upon the First Chapter*
*of . . . Amos . . . in XXI Sermons*, 1613.

Bernard, Richard, *Christian See to Thy Conscience*, 1631.

———. *A Guide to Grand-Jury Men*, 1627.

———. *Isle of Man*, 1627.

———. *Plaine Evidences: the Church of England is Apostolicall*,
1610.

———. *The Ready Way to Good Works*, 1635.

Beveridge, William, *The Works*, 12 vols., Oxford, 1842-1848.

Bilson, Thomas, *The Effect of Certaine Sermons Touching the Full*
*Redemption*, 1599.

———. *The True Difference Betweene Christian Subjection and*
*Un-Christian Rebellion*, Oxford, 1585.

Bird, Samuel, *The Lectures Upon the Second Chapter of the Epistle*
*unto the Hebrewes, and upon the 38 Psalme*, Cambridge, 1598.

Bolton, Robert, *The Workes*, 4 vols., 1631-1641.

Bradshaw, William, *English Puritanism*, s.l., 1605.

Bramhall, John, *The Works*, 5 vols., Oxford, 1842-1845.

Brinsley, John, *The True Watch and Rule of Life*, 1614.

Broughton, Hugh, *The Works*, 1662.

Browne, Robert, *A Treatise of Reformation without Tarying for*
*Anie*, Middleburgh, 1582.

Buckeridge, John, *A Sermon Preached at Hampton Court*, 1606.

Burnet, Gilbert, *An Exposition of the Thirty-Nine Articles of the*
*Church of England*, 1699.

Burton, Henry, *The Baiting of the Popes Bull,* 1627.
———. *A Censure of Simonie,* 1624.
———. *Conflicts and Comforts of Conscience,* 1618.
———. *For God and the King,* 1636.
———. *Grounds of Christian Religion,* 1636.
Burton, Robert, *The Anatomy of Melancholy,* Oxford, 1621.


Carleton, George, *Directions to Know the True Church,* 1615.
———. *An Examination of those Things Wherein the Author of the Late Appeale Holdeth the Doctrines of Pelagians and Arminians, to be the Doctrines of the Church of England,* 1626.
Cartwright, Thomas, *A Directory of Church Government,* 1872.
Chillingworth, William, *The Religion of Protestants: A Safe Way to Salvation,* Oxford, 1638.
———. *The Works,* 3 vols., ed. T. Birch, Oxford, 1838.
*The Confession of Faith of those Churches which are Commonly (though falsely) called Anabaptists,* 1646.
Cooper, Thomas, *An Admonition to the People of England,* 1589.
Cosin, John, *The Correspondence,* Surtees Society, 1869-1872.
———. *The Works,* 5 vols., ed. J. Sansom, Oxford, 1843-1845.
Coverdale, Myles, *Writings and Translations,* 2 vols., ed. George Pearson, Parker Society, 1844-1846.
Crakanthorp, R., *Defensio Ecclesiae Anglicanae Contra M. Antonii de Dominis,* 1625.
Culpepper, Sir Thomas, *A Tract Against Usurie,* 1621.
Culverwell, Ezekiel, *A Treatise of Faith,* 1623.


Dent, Arthur, *The Plaine Mans Path-Way to Heaven,* 1601.
Dering, Edward, *M. Derings Workes,* 1614.
Dod, John, *Old Mr. Dod's Sayings,* 1661.
Dod, John and Robert Cleaver, *A Godlie Forme of Householde Government,* 1612.
———. *A Plaine and Familiar Exposition of the Ninth and Tenth Chapters of the Proverbs of Salomon,* 1608.
———. *A Plaine and Familiar Exposition of the Eleventh and Twelfth Chapters of the Proverbes of Salomon,* 1608.
———. *A Plaine and Familiar Exposition of the 13th and 14th Chapters of the Proverbs of Salomon,* 1609.
———. *A Plaine and Familiar Exposition of the 15th, 16th, 17th Chapters of the Proverbes of Salomon,* 1609.

———. *A Plaine and Familiar Exposition of the Ten Commandments*, 1619.

———. *Ten Sermons*, 1609.

———. *Two Sermons*, 1608.

Donne, John, *XXVI Sermons*, ed. John Donne, 1661.

———. *Fifty Sermons*, ed. John Donne, 1649.

———. *LXXX Sermons*, ed. John Donne, 1640.

———. *The Complete Poems*, 2 vols., ed. A. B. Grosart, 1872-1873.

———. *Devotions Upon Urgent Occasions*, 1624.

———. *Essays in Divinity*, ed. A. Jessopp, 1855.

———. *Ignatius His Conclave*, 1611.

———. *The Works*, 6 vols., ed. Henry Alford, 1839.

Downame, John, *The Christian Warfare*, 1633-1634.

———. *The Plea of the Poore*, 1616.

———. *A Treatise of Anger*, 1609.

———. *A Treatise of Swearing*, 1609.


Edwards, Thomas, *Gangraena or a Catalogue and Discovery of Many of the Errours, Heresies, Blasphemies and Pernicious Practices of the Sectaries of this Time*, 1646.


Fenton, Roger, *A Treatise of Usurie*, 1611.

Field, Richard, *Of the Church*, Oxford, 1628.

Foxe, John, *Actes and Monuments*, 2 vols., 1610.

———. *Narratives of the Days of the Reformation Chiefly from the Manuscripts of John Foxe and Martyrologist*, ed. John Gough Nichols, Camden Society, 1859.

Fuller, Thomas, *The Church History of Britain*, 6 vols., ed. J. S. Brewer, Oxford, 1845.

———. *The Holy and Profane States*, Boston, 1865.


Gataker, Thomas, *Certaine Sermons*, 1637.

———. *A Funerall Sermon*, 1637.

———. *God's Parley with Princes*, 1620.

———. *A Good Wife Gods Gift*, 1637.

———. *Marriage Duties Briefly Couched Together*, 1637.

———. *A Marriage Prayer*, 1637.

Gifford, George, *A Dialogue Concerning Witches and Witchcraftes*, 1598.

———. *Fifteen Sermons Upon the Song of Solomon*, 1598.

———. *A Short Treatise Against the Donatists of England*, 1590.

Goodwin, John, *The Saints Interest in God*, 1640.
Goodwin, Thomas, *Aggravation of Sinne*, 1637.
———. *A Childe of Light Walking in Darkness*, 1638.
———. *The Returne of Prayers*, 1636.
———.*The Vanity of Thoughts Discovered*, 1638.
Gouge, William, *The Dignitie of Chivalrie*, 1626.
———. *Of Domesticall Duties*, 1626.
———. *The Extent of Gods Providence*, 1631.
———. *Gods Three Arrowes: Plague, Famine, Sword*, 1631.
———. *A Guide to Goe to God*, 1636.
———. *The Saints Sacrifice*, 1632.
———. *A Treatise of the Sinne Against the Holy Ghost*, 1626.
———. *The Whole Armour of God*, 1627.
———. *The Worlds Great Restauration*, 1621.
Greenham, Richard, *The Workes*, 1612.

Hall, Joseph, *Heaven Upon Earth*, 1627.
———. *Holy Observations*, 1607.
———. *The Works*, 10 vols., ed. P. Wynter, Oxford, 1863.
———. *The Works*, 4 vols., 1628-1662.
Harrison, Robert and Robert Browne, *The Writings*, ed. Albert Peel and L. H. Carlson, 1953.
Herbert, George, *The Works*, ed. F. E. Hutchinson, Oxford, 1941.
Heylyn, Peter, *Ecclesia Vindicata or the Church of England Justified*, 1657.
Hildersam, Arthur, *CLII Lectures Upon Psalme LI*, 1635.
Holland, Henry, *The History of Adam*, 1606.
———. *A Treatise Against Witchcraft*, Cambridge, 1590.
Hooker, Richard, *The Works*, 3 vols., ed. John Keble, 3rd ed., Oxford, 1845.
Hooker, Thomas, *The Saints Guide*, 1645.
Hutton, Mathew, *The Correspondence*, ed. J. Raine, Surtees Society, 1844.

Jewel, John, *Works*, 4 vols., ed. John Ayre, Parker Society, 1845-1850.

Lake, Arthur, *Sermons*, 1629.
Laud, William, *The Works*, 9 vols., ed. W. Scott and J. Bliss, Oxford, 1847-1860.
Leighton, Alexander, *An Appeal to the Parliament, or Sions Plea Against the Prelacie*, 1628.

Leslie, Henry, *A Treatise of the Authority of the Church*, Dublin, 1639.

*The Marprelate Tracts, 1588, 1589*, ed. William Pierce, 1911.
Maynwaring, Roger, *Religion and Alegiance*, 1627.
Montagu, Richard, *Appello Caesarem. A Just Appeale from Two Unjust Informers*, 1625.
Morton, Thomas, *A Catholike Appeale for Protestants Out of the Confessions of the Romane Doctors*, 1609.
———. *A Treatise of the Threefolde State of Man*, 1596.

Overall, John, *Convocation-Book MDCVI Concerning the Government of God's Catholic Church*, Oxford, 1844.

Parker, Henry, *A Discourse Concerning Puritans*, 1641.
Perkins, William, *The Workes*, 3 vols., 1612-1613.
Pocklington, John, *Altare Christianum*, 1637.
Preston, John, *The Breast-Plate of Faith and Love*, 1634.
———. *The Golden Scepter*, 1638.
———. *Life Eternall*, 1631.
———. *The New Covenant*, 1630.
———. *The Saints Qualification*, 1634.
Pricke, Robert, *The Doctrine of Superioritie*, 1609.
Prideaux, John, *Twenty Sermons*, 1636-1641.
Prynne, William, *Canterburies Doome*, 1646.
———. *Histrio-Mastix*, 1633.
———. *The Sword of Christian Magistracy Supported*, 1653.

Rainolds, John, *The Prophecie of Obadiah*, Oxford, 1613.
———. *The Summe of the Conference Betweene John Rainolds and John Hart Touching the Head and Faith of the Church*, 1584.
Randall, John, *Three and Twentie Sermons*, 1630.
Robinson, John, *Works*, 3 vols., ed. R. Ashton, 1851.
Rogers, John, *The Displaying of an Horrible Secte of Gross and Wicked Heretiques, Naming Themselves the Familie of Love*, 1578.
Rogers, Richard, *Seven Treatises*, 1630.

Sanderson, Robert, *XXXVI Sermons*, 1689.

Sandys, Edwin, *Sermons*, 1585.

Scott, Thomas, *Vox Populi, or Newes From Spayne*, 1620.

Scudder, Henry, *The Christians Daily Walke*, 1631.

Sibbes, Richard, *Angels Acclamations*, 1638.

———. *Beames of Divine Light*, 1639.

———. *Bowels Opened*, 1639.

———. *A Breathing After God*, 1639.

———. *The Bruished Reede and Smoaking Flax*, 1620.

———. *The Christians End*, 1639.

———. *The Christians Portion*, 1638.

———. *The Churches Riches by Christs Poverty*, 1638.

———. *The Fountaine Opened*, 1638.

———. *A Fountain Sealed*, 1637.

———. *A Glance of Heaven*, 1638.

———. *The Rich Poverty*, 1638.

———. *The Riches of Mercie*, 1638.

———. *The Saints Cordials*, 1637.

———. *The Spirituall Mans Aime*, 1637.

———. *Two Sermons*, 1637.

———. *Yea and Amen*, 1638.

Sibthorpe, Robert, *Apostolike Obedience*, 1627.

Smectymnuus, *An Answer to a Booke Entitled, an Humble Remonstrance in which, the Originall of Liturgy, Episcopacy is Discussed*, 1641.

Smith, Henrie, *Gods Arrow Againste Atheists*, 1607.

———. *The Sermons*, 1625.


Tooker, William, *Charisma, siue donum sanationis*, 1597.

———. *Of the Fabrique of the Church and Churchmens Livings*, 1604.

Travers, Walter, *A Full and Plaine Declaration of Ecclesiasticall Discipline*, Zurich, 1574.

*Two Elizabethan Puritan Diaries* by Richard Rogers and Samuel Ward, ed. Marshall Knappen, Chicago, 1933.


Udall, John, *The State of the Church of England*, ed. Edward Arber, Westminster, 1895.

Ussher, James, *A Body of Divinitie*, 1645.

———. *The Whole Works*, 17 vols., ed. C. R. Elrington and J. M. Todd, Dublin, 1847-1864.

Whitaker, William, *A Disputation on Holy Scripture, Against the Papists*, ed. William Fitzgerald, Cambridge, 1849.
Whitgift, John, *Works*, 3 vols., ed. John Ayre, Parker Society, 1851-1853.
Wilson, Thomas, *A Discourse Upon Usury*, ed. R. H. Tawney, 1925.
Wren, Matthew, *A Sermon Preached Before the Kings Majestie*, Cambridge, 1627.

Yates, John, *Ibis ad Caesarem Or a Submissive Appearance Before Caesar; In Answer to Mr. Mountague's Appeale*, 1626.

Selected Sources and Studies of Ecclesiastical History
and Religious Biography

Barnes, Thomas C., "County Politics and a Puritan Cause Célèbre: Somerset Churchales, 1633," *Transactions of the Royal Historical Society*, Fifth Series, vol. 9, 1959.
Burnet, Gilbert, *History of the Reformation of the Church of England*, 3 vols., 1679-1715.

Calder, Isabel M., ed., *Activities of the Puritan Faction of the Church of England, 1625-1633*, 1957.
*Calendar of State Papers, Domestic Series*, 26 vols. through 1649, 1857-1897.
Cardwell, Edward, ed., *Documentary Annals of the Reformed Church of England*, 2 vols., Oxford, 1844.
———. ed., *A History of Conferences and Other Proceedings Connected with the Revision of the Book of Common Prayer*, Oxford, 1849.
———. ed., *Synodalia, A Collection of Articles of Religion, Canons, and Proceedings of Convocations in the Province of Canterbury from the Year 1547 to the Year 1717*, 2 vols., Oxford, 1842.
Collinson, Patrick, *The Puritan Classical Movement in the Reign of Elizabeth I* (unpublished Ph.D. thesis, University of London).
Cox, J. C., *Churchwarden's Accounts from the Fourteenth Century to the Close of the Seventeenth Century*, 1913.
———. *The Parish Registers of England*, 1910.

Davis, C. H., ed., *Constitutions and Canons Ecclesiasticall Treated Upon by the Bishop of London . . . and Agreed Upon With the Kings . . . Licence*, 1869.
Dugdale, William, *Monasticon Anglicanum*, 3 vols., 1665-1673.

Foster, Charles W., ed., *The State of the Church in the Reigns of Elizabeth and James I as Illustrated by Documents Relating to the Diocese of Lincoln*, Lincoln, 1926.

Frere, W. H., *The English Church in the Reigns of Elizabeth and James I*, 1904.

Fulbecke, William, *A Parallele or Conference of the Civil Law, the Canon Law, and the Common Law of this Realm*, 1601.

Fuller, Thomas, *Church History of Britain*, 6 vols., ed. J. S. Brewer, Oxford, 1845.

Gardiner, Samuel R., ed., *Documents Relating to the Proceedings against William Prynne in 1634 and 1637*, 1877.

Gee, H., and Hardy, W. J., *Documents Illustrative of English Church History*, 1896.

Gibson, Edmund, ed., *Codex Juris Ecclesiastici Anglicani*, 2 vols., Oxford, 1761.

Gosse, Edmund W., *The Life and Letters of John Donne*, 2 vols., 1899.

Habakkuk, H. J., "The Market for Monastic Property, 1539-1603," *The Economic History Review*, April 1958.

Hale, W. H., ed., *A Series of Precedents and Proceedings in Criminal Causes, 1475-1640, Extracted from the Act Books of Ecclesiastical Courts in the Diocese of London*, 1847.

Hart, A. Tindal, *The Country Clergy in Elizabethan and Stuart Times, 1558-1660*, 1958.

Heylyn, Peter, *Aerius Redivivus or the History of the Presbyterians*, Oxford, 1670.

———. *Cyprianus Anglicus*, 1668.

———. *Ecclesia Restaurata*, 1661.

Higham, Florence, *Lancelot Andrews*, 1952.

Hill, Christopher, *Economic Problems of the Church*, Oxford, 1956.

Hughes, Philip, *The Reformation in England*, 3 vols., 1950-1954.

Hutton, W. H., *The English Church from the Accession of Charles I to the Death of Anne*, 1903.

Kennedy, W. P. M., ed., *Elizabethan Episcopal Administration*, 3 vols., 1925.

Kinlock, T. F., *The Life and Works of Joseph Hall, 1574-1656*, 1951.

Larking, Lambert B., ed., *Proceedings Principally in the County of Kent in Connection with the Parliaments Called in 1640, and Especially with The Committee of Religion*, Camden Society, 1862.

Maitland, F. W., *Essays On Subjects Connected With the Reformation in England*, 1849.

———. *Roman Canon Law in the Church of England*, 1898.

Maycock, Alan, *Chronicles of Little Gidding*, 1954.

Messenger, E. C., *The Reformation, the Mass, and the Priesthood*, 2 vols., 1936-1937.

More, P. E., and Cross, F. L., *Anglicanism: the Thought and Practice of the Church of England Illustrated from the Religious Literature of the Seventeenth Century*, Milwaukee, 1935.


Neal, Daniel, *The History of the Puritans or Protestant Nonconformists from the Reformation 1517 to the Revolution in 1688*, 1732-1738.

Neale, J. E., "The Elizabethan Acts of Supremacy and Uniformity," *English Historical Review*, July 1950.

Notestein, Wallace, Frances H. Relf, Hartley Simpson, eds., *Commons Debates, 1621*, 7 vols., New Haven, 1935.

Notestein, Wallace, Frances H. Relf, eds., *Commons Debates for 1629*, Minneapolis, 1921.


Owen, H. G., *The London Parish Clergy in the Reign of Elizabeth I* (unpublished Ph.D. thesis, University of London).


Pollard, A. W., ed., *Records of the English Bible*, Oxford, 1911.

Procter, F., and Frere, W. H., *A New History of the Book of Common Prayer*, 1901.

Purvis, J. S., *An Introduction to Ecclesiastical Records*, 1953.


Reidy, Maurice F., *Bishop Lancelot Andrewes: Jacobean Court Preacher*, Chicago, 1955.

Richie, C. I. A., *The Ecclesiastical Courts of York*, 1956.

Ridley, Thomas, *A View of the Civile and Ecclesiastical Law*, 1607.

Robinson, Hastings, ed., *Original Letters Relative to the English Reformation, 1531-1558*, 2 vols., Parker Society, 1846-1847.

Rushworth, John, *Historical Collections*, 7 vols., 1659-1781.


Schaff, Philip, ed., *The Creeds of Christendom*, 3 vols., New York, 1877.

Selden, John, *The Historie of Tithes*, 1618.

Shaw, William A., *History of the English Church During the Civil War and Under the Commonwealth, 1640-1660*, 2 vols., 1900.

Smith, Lacy B., *Tudor Prelates and Politics*, 1953.

Soden, G. I., *Godfrey Goodman, Bishop of Gloucester*, 1953.

Sparrow, A., ed., *A Collection of Articles, Injunctions, Canons, Orders, Ordinances, and Constitutions Ecclesiastical . . .* , 1661.

*Statutes of the Realm*, 11 vols., ed. T. E. Tomlins *et al.*, 1810-1824.

Strype, John, *Annals of the Reformation*, 4 vols., Oxford, 1824.

——. *Life of John Whitgift*, 3 vols., Oxford, 1822.

——. *Ecclesiastical Memorials*, 3 vols., Oxford, 1820-1840.

Sykes, Norman, *The Church of England and Non-Episcopal Churches in the Sixteenth and Seventeenth Centuries*, 1948.

——. *Old Priest and New Presbyter*, 1956.

Thompson, A. Hamilton, *The English Clergy and Their Organization in the Later Middle Ages*, Oxford, 1947.

Trevor-Roper, H. R., *Archbishop Laud, 1573-1645*, 1940.

——. "King James and His Bishops," *History Today*, September 1955.

Usher, Roland G., *The Presbyterian Movement in the Reign of Queen Elizabeth as Illustrated by the Minute Book of the Dedham Classis, 1582-1589*, 1905.

——. *The Reconstruction of the English Church*, 2 vols., 1910.

——. *The Rise and Fall of the High Commission*, Oxford, 1913.

Walton, Isaak, *The Lives*, 1825.

Whiteman, Anne, "The Re-establishment of the Church of England, 1660-1663," *Transactions of the Royal Historical Society*, Fifth Series, vol. 5, 1955.

Wilkins, David, ed., *Concilia Magnae Britanniae et Hiberniae*, 4 vols., 1737.

## Modern Studies of the Protestant Ethos

Addison, James T., "Early Anglican Thought, 1559-1667," *Historical Magazine of the Protestant Episcopal Church*, September 1953.

Bahlman, Dudley W. R., *The Moral Revolution of 1688*, New Haven, 1957.

Bailyn, Bernard, *The New England Merchants in the Seventeenth Century*, Cambridge, Mass., 1955.

Bainton, Roland, "Ernst Troeltsch—Thirty Years Later," *Theology Today*, April 1951.

Barker, W. A., *Religion and Politics, 1559-1642*, 1957.

Baron, Hans, "Calvinist Republicanism and Its Historical Roots," *Church History*, VIII, No. 1, 1939.

——. "Rice's Renaissance Idea of Wisdom," *Journal of the History of Ideas*, January-March 1960.

Beard, Charles A., *The Reformation of the Sixteenth Century in its Relation to Modern Thought and Knowledge*, 1927.

Biéler, A., *La Pensée Économique et Sociale de Calvin*, Genève, 1959.

Brauer, Jerald C., "Puritan Mysticism and the Development of Liberalism," *Church History*, September 1950.

——. "Reflections on the Nature of English Puritanism," *Church History*, June 1954.

Brentano, Lujo, *Die Anfänge des Kapitalismus*, München, 1916.

Brodrick, James, *The Economic Morals of the Jesuits, An Answer to Dr. H. M. Robertson*, London, 1934.

Burrage, Champlin, *The Church Covenant Idea*, Philadelphia, 1904.

Cassirer, Ernst, *The Platonic Renaissance in England*, trans. James P. Pettegrove, New York, 1953.

Chenevière, M. E., *La Pensée Politique de Calvin*, Paris, 1937.

Choisy, Eugène, *L'État Chrétien Calviniste à Genève au Temps de Théodore de Bèze*, Genève, 1902.

Cohn, Norman, *The Pursuit of the Millennium*, Fairlawn, New Jersey, 1957.

Cunningham, William, *Christian Opinion on Usury*, Edinburgh, 1884.

Davies, Godfrey, "Arminian versus Puritan in England: ca. 1620-1640" *Huntington Library Bulletin*, April 1934.

——. "English Political Sermons, 1603-1640," *Huntington Library Quarterly*, October 1939.

Davies, Horton, *The Worship of the English Puritans*, Westminster, 1948.

Demant, V. A., *Religion and the Decline of Capitalism*, New York, 1952.

Dickens, A. G., *Lollards and Protestants in the Diocese of York, 1509-1558*, 1959.

Doumergue, E., *Jean Calvin: Les Hommes et les Choses de son Temps*, 7 vols., Lausanne, 1899-1927.

Emerson, Everett H., "Calvin and Covenant Theology," *Church History*, June 1956.

Fanfani, Amintore, *Catholicism, Protestantism and Capitalism*, New York, 1955.
Fellows, E. H., *English Cathedral Music from Edward VI to Edward VII*, 1941.
Foster, H. D., "The Political Theories of Calvinists Before the Puritan Exodus to America," *American Historical Review*, XXI, No. 3, 1916.
French, Allen, *Charles I and the Puritan Upheaval*, 1955.

George, Charles H., "English Calvinist Opinion on Usury, 1600-1640," *Journal of the History of Ideas*, October 1957.
———. "A Social Interpretation of English Puritanism," *The Journal of Modern History*, December 1953.
George, Charles and Katherine, "Protestantism and Capitalism in Pre-Revolutionary England," *Church History*, December 1958.
Gilbert, Felix, "Political Thought of the Renaissance and Reformation," *The Huntington Library Quarterly*, IV, No. 4, 1941.

Harbison, E. Harris, *The Christian Scholar in the Age of the Reformation*, New York, 1956.
Harkness, R. E. E., "The Development of Democracy in the English Reformation," *Church History*, VIII, No. 1, 1939.
Hauser, Henri, *Les Débuts de Capitalisme*, Paris, 1927.
Herr, A. F., *The Elizabethan Sermon, A Survey and Bibliography*, Philadelphia, 1940.
Hill, Christopher, *Puritanism and Revolution*, 1958.
———. "Puritans and the Poor," *Past and Present*, November 1952; and V. Kiernan on the same subject, *Past and Present*, February 1953.
Holden, William P., *Anti-Puritan Satire, 1572-1642*, 1954.
Hooykaas, R., "Science and Reformation," *Cahiers D'Histoire Mondiale*, III, No. 1, 1956; comment by Roland Bainton in the same issue, with an answer by Hooykaas, *op.cit.*, No. 3, 1957.
Hopf, Constantin, *Martin Bucer and the English Reformation*, Oxford, 1946.
Howell, W. S., *Logic and Rhetoric in England, 1500-1700*, Princeton, 1956.

Hudson, Winthrop, "Puritanism and the Spirit of Capitalism," *Church History*, March 1949.

Hughes, Philip, *Rome and the Counter-Reformation in England*, 1942.

———. *The Reformation in England*, 3 vols., 1950-1954.

Hyma, Albert, *Renaissance to Reformation*, Grand Rapids, 1951.

Jones, Rufus M., *Spiritual Reformers in the 16th and 17th Centuries*, New York, 1914.

Jordan, Wilbur K., *The Development of Religious Toleration in England*, 4 vols., 1932-1940.

———. *Philanthropy in England, 1480-1660*, 1959.

Ketton-Cremer, R. W., *Norfolk Assembly*, 1957.

Knappen, Marshall M., *Tudor Puritanism*, Chicago, 1939.

Kolko, Gabriel, "A Critique of Max Weber's Philosophy of History," *Ethics*, October 1959.

Lockwood, D. P. and Bainton, R. H., "Classical and Biblical Scholarship in the Age of the Renaissance and Reformation," *Church History*, June 1941.

Maclear, James F., "Puritan Relations with Buckingham," *The Huntington Library Quarterly*, February 1958.

McLachlan, Herbert J., *Socinianism in Seventeenth-Century England*, 1951.

McNeill, John T., *The History and Character of Calvinism*, New York, 1954.

———. "Natural Law in the Teaching of the Reformers," *Journal of Religion*, July 1946.

Maitland, F. W., "The Anglican Settlement and the Scottish Reformation," *The Cambridge Modern History*, II, New York, 1934.

Mercier, Ch., "L'Esprit de Calvin et la Democratie," *Revue D'Histoire Ecclésiastique*, vol. 30, 1934, pp. 5-53.

Miller, Perry, *Orthodoxy in Massachusetts, 1630-1650*, Cambridge, Mass., 1933.

Mitchell, W. F., *English Pulpit Oratory from Andrewes to Tillotson*, 1932.

Mosse, George L., *The Holy Pretence: A Study in Christianity and Reason of State from William Perkins to John Winthrop*, Oxford, 1957.

Mosse, "The Assimilation of Machiavelli in English Thought: the Casuistry of William Perkins and William Ames," *Huntington Library Quarterly*, xvii, No. 4, 1954.

――――. "The Importance of Jacques Saurin in the History of Casuistry and the Enlightenment," *Church History*, September 1956.

――――. "Puritan Political Thought and the 'Cases of Conscience,' " *Church History*, June 1954.

――――. "Puritanism and Reason of State in Old and New England," *William and Mary Quarterly*, 3rd Series, ix, No. 1, 1952.

Nelson, Benjamin N., *The Idea of Usury*, Princeton, 1949.

Noonan, John T., Jr., *The Scholastic Analysis of Usury*, Cambridge, Mass., 1957.

Nuttall, G. F., "Law and Liberty in Puritanism," *The Congregational Quarterly*, January 1951.

Parsons, Talcott, *The Structure of Social Action*, New York, 1937.

Rice, Eugene F., Jr., *The Renaissance Idea of Wisdom*, Cambridge, Mass., 1958.

Robertson, H. M., *Aspects of the Rise of Economic Individualism*, Cambridge, 1933.

Roover, Raymond de, "The Concept of Just Price: Theory and Economic Policy," *The Journal of Economic History*, December 1958.

Rupp, E. G., *Studies in the Making of the English Protestant Tradition, Mainly in the Reign of Henry VIII*, Cambridge, 1947.

Salin, Edgar, "Kapitalbegriff und Kapitallehre von der Antike zu den Physiokraten," *Vierteljahrschrift für Sozial-und-Wirtschaftsgeschichte*, vol. 23, Stuttgart, 1930.

Sayous, André, "Calvinisme et Capitalisme; L'Éxperience Genèvoise," *Annales D'Histoire Économique et Sociale*, viii, 1935.

Schenk, Wilhelm, *The Concern for Social Justice in the Puritan Revolution*, 1948.

Siegel, Paul N., "Shylock and the Puritan Usurers," *Studies in Shakespeare*, Miami, 1952.

Simpson, Alan, *Puritanism in Old and New England*, Chicago, 1955.

Solt, Leo F., "Anti-Intellectualism in the Puritan Revolution," *Church History*, December 1956.

Sombart, Werner, *Le Bourgeois*, trans. S. Jankélévitch, Paris, 1926.

Sykes, Norman, *The English Religious Tradition*, 1953.

Taeusch, Carl F., "History of the Concept of Usury," *Journal of the History of Ideas*, June 1942.

Tawney, R. H., *Religion and the Rise of Capitalism*, 1936.

———. "Religion and Economic Life," *The Times Literary Supplement*, January 6, 1956.

Trinterud, Leonard J., "The Origins of Puritanism," *Church History*, March 1951.

Troeltsch, Ernst, *Protestantism and Progress*, Boston, 1958.

———. *The Social Teaching of the Christian Churches*, 2 vols., trans. Olive Wyan, New York, 1931.

Tulloch, John, *Rational Theology and Christian Philosophy in England in the Seventeenth Century*, 2 vols., Edinburgh, 1874.

Walker, Gordon, "Capitalism and the Reformation," *The Economic History Review*, November 1937.

Weber, Max, *General Economic History*, trans. Frank H. Knight, Glencoe, Illinois, 1927.

White, Helen C., *English Devotional Literature, 1600-1640*, Madison, Wisconsin, 1931.

———. *Social Criticism in Popular Religious Literature of the Sixteenth Century*, New York, 1944.

———. *The Tudor Books of Private Devotion*, Madison, Wisconsin, 1951.

Whitney, E. A., "Erastianism and Divine Right," *Huntington Library Quarterly*, II, No. 4, 1939.

Wilmer, Richard H., Jr., "Hooker on Authority," *Anglican Theological Review*, January 1951.

Wolin, Sheldon S., "Calvin and the Reformation: The Political Education of Protestantism," *American Political Science Review*, LI, No. 2, 1957.

Wood, Herbert G., "Puritanism and Capitalism," *The Congregational Quarterly*, April 1951.

Woodhouse, A. S. P., *Puritanism and Liberty*, 1938.

Woodhouse, H. F., *The Doctrine of the Church in Anglican Theology, 1547-1603*, 1954.

Wright, Louis B., *Religion and Empire: The Alliance Between Piety and Commerce in English Expansion, 1558-1625*, Chapel Hill, N.C., 1943.

Wright, "William Perkins: Elizabethan Apostle of 'Practical Divinity,'" *Huntington Library Quarterly*, January 1940.

Yule, George, *The Independents in the English Civil War*, Cambridge, 1958.


Some Principal Sources of Foreign
and Roman Catholic Theological Influences

Aquinas, Thomas, *De Regimine Principum*, trans. G. B. Phelan, Toronto, 1935.
———. *Summa Contra Gentiles*, English Dominican translation, 4 vols., 1923-1929.
———. *Summa Theologica*, English Dominican translation, 21 vols., 1912-1925.


Bard, Thompson, "Zwingli Study Since 1918," *Church History*, June 1950.
Baro, Peter, *A Speciall Treatise of Gods Providence*, trans., J. L (udham), 1588.
Bellarmino, Roberto, *An Ample Declaration of the Christian Doctrine*, trans. R. Hadock, Rouen (n.d.).
———. *De Laicis*, trans. Kathleen Murphy, New York, 1928.
———. *Opera Omnia*, 7 vols., Cologne, 1617-1620.
Bèze, Théodore de, *A Briefe and Pithie Summe of the Christian Faith*, trans. R (obert) F (yll), [1565?].
———. *A Discourse Conteyning the Life and Death of John Calvin*, trans. I. S., 1564.
———. *A Discourse of the True and Visible Marks of the Catholique Church*, trans. T. W (ilcox), 1582.
———. *An Excellent Treatise of Comforting Such as are Troubled About Their Predestination*, 1591.
———. *An Exhortation to the Reformation of the Churche*, [1568?]
———. *Propositions and Principles of Divinitie*, trans. John Penry, Edinburgh, 1595.
———. *Tractationum Theologicarum*, 3 vols., Geneva, 1570-1582.
Birnbaum, Norman, "The Zwinglian Reformation in Zurich," *Past and Present*, April 1959.
Bucer, Martin, *De Regno Christi*, Basle, 1557.
Bullinger, Henry, *The Decades*, 4 vols., Cambridge, 1850.

Cajetan, *Secundae Summae Theologica . . . cum Commentariis*, Venice, 1593.

Calvin, Jean, *Joannis Calvini Opera Quae Supersunt Omnia*, ed. G. Baum, E. Cunitz, E. Reuss, P. Lobstein, A. Erichson, 59 vols., Berlin and Brunswick, 1862-1900.

————. *The Institutes of the Christian Religion*, 7th ed., rev., 2 vols., trans. J. Allen, Philadelphia, 1936.

————. *The Institution of Christian Religion*, trans. with notes by Thomas Norton, 1634. This was the popular translation of our period, and at least managed to render the title more accurately than have recent translations!

————. *Lettres Anglaises, 1548-1561*, ed. A. M. Schmidt, Paris, 1959.

————. *Sermons . . . Upon the X Commandementes*, trans. I. H., 1579.

————. *Thirteen Sermons*, trans. John Fields, 1579.

————. *Two and Twentie Sermons*, trans. T. S., 1580.

————. *Works*, 51 vols., Edinburgh, 1844-1856.

Gardiner, Stephen, *De Vera Obedientia*, Roane, 1553.

Hopf, Constantin, *Martin Bucer and the English Reformation*, Oxford, 1946.

Huber, R. M., "Recent Important Literature Regarding the Catholic Church, 1500-1648," *Church History*, March 1941.

Kidd, B. J., ed., *Documents Illustrative of the Continental Reformation*, Oxford, 1911.

Knox, John, *Works*, 6 vols., ed. David Laing, Edinburgh, 1846-1864.

Law, T. G., ed., *The Archpriest Controversy: Documents Relating to the Dissentions of the Roman Catholic Clergy, 1597-1602*, 2 vols., Camden Society, New Series, vols. 56, 58, 1896-1898.

Luther, Martin, *The Chiefe and Pryncypall Articles of the Christen Faythe*, 1584.

————. *Special and Chosen Sermons*, trans. W. G (ace), 1581.

————. *A Treatise Touching the Libertie of a Christian*, trans. J. Bell, 1579.

————. *Works*, 6 vols., ed. Henry E. Jacobs, Philadelphia, 1915-1932.

McNeill, John T., "Thirty Years of Calvin Study," *Church History*, September 1948.

Meyer, A. O., *England and the Catholic Church under Elizabeth and the Stuarts*, trans. J. R. McKee, 1916.

Parsons, Robert, *A Christian Directory*, s.l., 1585.

Ramus, Petrus, *The Art of Logick, Gathered Out of Aristotle and Set in Due Forme*, 1626.
———. *P. Ramus . . . His Dialectica*, trans. R. P (age), 1632.
Robinson, Hastings, ed., *The Zurich Letters, 1558-1602*, 2 vols., Parker Society, 1842-1845.
Ryan, John K., *The Reputation of St. Thomas Aquinas Among English Protestant Thinkers of the Seventeenth Century*, Washington, 1948.

Smith, Preserved, *The Life and Letters of Martin Luther*, Boston, 1914.
Southern, A. C., *Elizabethan Recusant Prose, 1559-1582*, 1950.
Suárez, Francisco, *Opera Omnia*, 9 vols., Paris, 1856-1858.

Thompson, Bard, "Bucer Study since 1918," *Church History*, March 1956.

Wycliffe, John, *An Apology for Lollard Doctrines, Attributed to Wicliffe*, ed. James H. Todd, Camden Society, 1842.

Zwingli, Ulrich, *A Short Pathwaye to the Ryghte and True Understanding of the Holy Scriptures*, trans. J. Veron, 1550.

## Selected Sources and Studies of Political, Legal, and Social Thought

Allen, John W., *English Political Thought, 1603-1660*, 2 vols., 1938.
Aubrey, John, *Brief Lives*, ed. Oliver L. Dick, 1950.

Bacon, Francis, *Works*, 7 vols., ed. James Spedding, R. L. Ellis, and D. D. Heath, 1857-1859.
Barclay, William, *De Potestate Papae*, 1609.
———. *De Regno et Regali Potestate*, 1600.
Bodin, Jean, *The Six Bookes of a Commonweale*, trans. Richard Knolles, 1606.

Coke, Edward, *Institutes of the Laws of England*, 1797.

Collier, J. Payne, ed., *The Egerton Papers*, Camden Society, 1840.

Cowell, John, *The Institutes of the Lawes of England*, 1651.

———. *The Interpreter*, 1607.

Craigie, James, ed., *The Basilicon Doron of King James VI*, 1944.

Davies, E. T., *The Political Ideas of Richard Hooker*, 1946.

D'Ewes, Simonds, *The Autobiography and Correspondence*, 2 vols., ed. James O. Halliwell, 1845.

Dunham, W. H. Jr., and Pargellis, Stanley, *Complaint and Reform in England, 1436-1714*, New York, 1938.

Filmer, Sir Robert, *Quaestio Quodlibetica*, 1653.

Firth, C. H., "Ballad History of the Reign of James I and Charles I," *Transactions of the Royal Historical Society*, Third Series, vols. 5 and 6, 1911-1912.

Fox, Levi, ed., *English Historical Scholarship in the Sixteenth and Seventeenth Centuries*, Oxford, 1956.

Fuller, Thomas, *The Soveraign's Prerogative and the Subject's Priviledge*, 1658.

———. *The Worthies of England*, ed. John Freeman, 1952.

Gardiner, Samuel R., ed., *The Constitutional Documents of the Puritan Revolution, 1625-1660*, Oxford, 1906.

Gierke, Otto von, *Natural Law and the Theory of Society, 1500-1800*, 2 vols., trans. Ernest Barker, Cambridge, 1934.

Gilbert, F., "Political Thought in the Renaissance and Reformation," *Huntington Library Quarterly*, iv, No. 4, 1941.

Gooch, George P., *Political Thought in England From Bacon to Halifax*, New York, 1914.

Gough, John W., *Fundamental Law in English Constitutional History*, Oxford, 1955.

Greenleaf, W. H., "James I and the Divine Right of Kings," *Political Studies*, v, No. 1, 1957.

Harrison, G. B., *The Elizabethan Journals*, New York, 1939.

———. ed., *A Jacobean Journal*, 1946.

———. *A Second Jacobean Journal*, 1958.

Haskins, George L., *Law and Authority in Early Massachusetts*, New York, 1960.

Hearnshaw, F. J. C., ed., *The Social and Political Ideas of Some Great Thinkers of the Sixteenth and Seventeenth Centuries*, 1926.

Holdsworth, William S., *A History of English Law*, 13 vols., 1922-1952.

Kocher, Paul H., "Francis Bacon on the Science of Jurisprudence," *Journal of the History of Ideas*, January 1957.

Laski, Harold J., ed. and trans., *Vindiciae Contra Tyrannos*, 1924.

Legg, L. G. Wickham, ed., *A Relation of a Short Survey of the Western Counties*, in *Camden Miscellany Vol. XVI*, Camden Third Series, vol. 52, 1936.

Maitland, F. W., *English Law and the Renaissance*, Cambridge, 1901.

McClure, N. E., *Letters of John Chamberlain*, 2 vols., Philadelphia, 1939.

McIlwain, C. H., *The Growth of Political Thought in the West*, New York, 1932.

———. ed., *The Political Works of James I*, Cambridge, Mass., 1918.

Nichols, John, *The Progresses, Processions, and Magnificent Festivities of King James the First*, 3 vols., 1828.

Notestein, Wallace, *The Winning of the Initiative by the House of Commons*, 1924.

Rollins, H. E., ed., *Old English Ballads, 1553-1625*, Cambridge, 1920.

Salmasio, Claudio, *De Modo Usurarum Liber*, Leyden, 1639.

Salmon, J. H. M., *The French Religious Wars in English Political Thought*, Oxford, 1959.

Saunders, H. W., ed., *The Official Papers of Sir Nathaniel Bacon*, Camden Third Series, vol. 26, 1915.

Schofield, Bertram, ed., *The Knyvett Letters, 1620-1644*, 1949.

Scott, Walter, ed., *A Collection of Scarce and Valuable Tracts . . . Particularly that of the Late Lord Somers*, 13 vols., 1809-1815.

Selden, John, *Table-Talk*, 1689.

Tanner, Joseph R., *Tudor Constitutional Documents*, Cambridge, 1930.

———. ed., *Constitutional Documents of the Reign of James I: 1603-1625*, Cambridge, 1930.

Vinogradoff, Paul, "Reason and Conscience in Sixteenth Century Jurisprudence," *Law Quarterly Review*, XXIV, No. 96, 1908.

Willson, David Harris, ed., *The Parliamentary Diary of Robert Bowyer, 1606-1607*, Minneapolis, 1931.
Wilson, Sir Thomas, *The State of England (1600)*, ed. F. J. Fisher, in *Camden Miscellany, Vol. XVI*, Camden Third Series, vol. 52, 1936.
Wormuth, *The Royal Prerogative, 1603-1649*, Ithaca, N.Y., 1939.
Wotton, Sir Henry, *Reliquiae Wottonianae*, 1651.
Wright, Louis B., *Middle-Class Structure in Elizabethan England*, Chapel Hill, N.C., 1935.

Zagorin, Perez, *A History of Political Thought in the English Revolution*, 1954.

## Modern Studies of English Society in Elizabethan and Jacobean Times

Bowen, Catherine D., *The Lion and the Throne: the Life and Times of Sir Edward Coke (1552-1634)*, Boston, Mass., 1957.
Bush, Douglas, *English Literature in the Earlier Seventeenth Century, 1600-1660*, New York (with a superb bibliography).

Davies, Godfrey, *The Early Stuarts, 1603-1660*, Oxford, 1937.

Firth, Charles H., ed., *Stuart Tracts, 1603-1693*, Westminster, 1903.
Fisher, F. J., "The Development of London as a Center of Conspicuous Consumption in the Sixteenth and Seventeenth Centuries," *Transactions of the Royal Historical Society*, Fourth Series, vol. 30, 1948.

Gardiner, Samuel R., *History of England from the Accession of James I to the Outbreak of the Civil War, 1603-1642*, 10 vols., 1883-1884.
Gibb, M. A., *Buckingham, 1592-1628*, 1935.

Haydn, Hiram, *The Counter-Renaissance*, New York, 1950.
Hill, Christopher, "La Révolution Anglaise du XVIIe Siècle, *Revue Historique*, Janvier-Mars, 1959.

Hinton, R. W. K., "The Decline of Parliamentary Government Under Elizabeth I and the Early Stuarts," *The Cambridge Historical Journal*, XIII, No. 2, 1957.

Hobsbawm, E., "The Crisis of the 17th Century," *Past and Present*, May 1954, November 1954.

Hulme, Harold, *The Life of Sir John Eliot, 1592-1632*, New York, 1957.

Jordan, W. K., *Men of Substance*, Chicago, 1942.

Lees-Milne, James, *The Age of Inigo Jones*, 1953.

Lewis, C. S., *English Literature in the Sixteenth Century Excluding Drama*, Oxford, 1954.

Mason, S. F., "Science and Religion in 17th Century England," *Past and Present*, February 1953.

Mathew, David, *The Jacobean Age*, 1938.

———. *Sir Tobie Mathew*, 1950.

Mattingly, Garrett, *The Armada*, Boston, 1959.

Mitchell, William M., *The Rise of the Revolutionary Party in the English House of Commons*, New York, 1957.

Morris, Christopher, *Political Thought in England, Tyndale to Hooker*, New York, 1953.

Mosse, George L., *The Struggle for Sovereignty in England*, East Lansing, Michigan, 1950.

Neale, J. E., *Elizabeth I and Her Parliaments, 1559-1601*, 2 vols., New York, 1953-57.

———. *Essays in Elizabethan History*, New York, 1958.

Notestein, Wallace, *The English People on the Eve of Colonization, 1603-1630*, New York, 1954.

———. *Four Worthies*, New Haven, 1957.

Polišenský, Josef, *Anglie Bílá Hora: The Bohemian War and British Policy, 1618-1620*, Prague, 1949.

Prothero, George W., ed., *Select Statutes and Other Constitutional Documents Illustrative of the Reigns of Elizabeth and James I*, Oxford, 1849.

Ranke, Leopold von, *A History of England Principally in the Seventeenth Century*, 6 vols., Oxford, 1875.

Rowse, A. L., *The England of Elizabeth: the Structure of Society*, New York, 1951.

———. *The Expansion of Elizabethan England*, New York, 1955.

Tillyard, Eustace M. W., *The Elizabethan World Picture*, 1943.

Trevor-Roper, H. R., "The General Crisis of the Seventeenth Century," *Past and Present*, November 1959.

Wedgwood, C. V., *The King's Peace, 1637-1641*, 1955.

———. "The Causes of the English Civil War," *History Today*, October 1955.

Willey, Basil, *The Seventeenth Century Background*, New York, 1953.

Willson, David H., *King James VI and I*, New York, 1956.

# INDEX

*445*

schools, and Protestant ethic, 157

Schramm, Percy E., 178n

Scott, Thomas, 248, 253

Scripture, as center of Protestantism, 341f; Protestantism rejects Catholic use, 342; superiority over ecclesiastical authority, 342; and tradition, 343; into vernacular, 344; interpretation of, 344f; and Scripturalism, 345f

sectarianism, 187, 205, 235; Protestant, and radicalism, 85

Sée, Henri, 145

Selden, John, 188

separatism, 187, 245, 370f

servitude, 295-304; Aquinas on, 296f; practice, 298-299; association with sin, 299; master's duty in, 302-305. *See also* slavery

sex, Protestant attitude toward, 271-275; in marriage, 272; extra-marital, 272-275

Shakespeare, William, 13

Sibbes, Richard, 35, 47f, 62, 65, 99f, 110, 117, 125, 129, 136, 140, 162, 164 202n, 234, 240, 281f, 317, 321, 325, 347, 357, 374, 383ff, 406, 416f

Sibthorpe, Robert, 203, 207n, 213f, 227, 337n

sin, Protestant emphasis on, 31-36; and justified man, 59f

slave trade, attacked by Sanderson, 301; rejected, 302

slavery, Aristotelian concept, 295; accepted by Christianity, 295; Aquinas on, 295ff; chattel slavery, 300-302

"Smectymnuus," 269

Smiles, Samuel, 169

Smith, Henrie, 135, 156, 158, 295n, 303

Smith, Thomas, 177, 226

social contract, use of by Protestants and Catholics, 183; new version emerges, 183; Locke's debt to Protestant clergy, 183; Hooker as proponent of, 183f; Calvin on, 184; Manegold of Lautenbach, 184; Marsiglio of Padua, 184; Protestant clergy, 184ff

socialism and Protestantism, 163

soldiers, and conduct of, 255. *See also* calling, chivalry, war

Sombart, Werner, 119n, 145, 147n

sovereignty, 176; idea distasteful to clergy, 214; Maynwaring on, 215; Dickinson on, 215f

Spain, 251, 253, 392

Spalato, Archbishop of (Marco Antonia de Dominis), 400f

stage plays, as moral problem, 141n; indicted, 274

Star Chamber, Court of, 208, 224

statutory law, *see* common law, positive law, Parliament

Stone, Lawrence, 360n

Stoughton, William, 225

Stow, John, 170n

Stuart monarchy, 218-20; view of kingship, 218; tribute to, 219, 220

Suárez, Francisco, 174ff, 183

Tawney, R. H., 14n, 145, 158, 158n

Tertullian, 39

theocracy, English, 183; monarchist, 189-194

Thirty-nine Articles, on predestination, 54; on inefficacy of human nature, 57

Thomas Aquinas, 166, 176, 280, 283ff, 290, 295ff, 303; on human nature, 33f; purpose of Thomism, 34; on manual and servile arts, 131; estimate of labor's value, 138; view of marriage, 261f; status of women, 262f; woman as companion, 263; *Summa Theologica*, 263, 284; on purpose of marriage, 269; inferiority of women, 280, 284; the relation of virtue and authority, 283; corporal punishment of wives, 283f; wife's right to give alms, 285; women as parents, 286; on children's rights, 290; on slavery, 295; and Aristotle, 296. *See also* Thomism

Thomas, K. V., 289n

Thomism, 105; as representative of Catholic theology and social theory, 9f; permeated by inequalities, 45; view of charity, 155

Thrupp, Sylvia, 119n

tithes, defended, 153; impropriations, 153f

toleration, 376-378, 381

transubstantiation, repudiated, 348-349

Travers, Walter, 152, 185, 188, 196n, 328, 330f, 351ff, 361, 363f, 369, 371, 380, 396

Trent, Council of, 386

Trevor-Roper, H. R., 14n, 241
Troeltsch, Ernst, 132n, 144, 145, 149

Udall, John, 364, 369
Usher, R. G., 15, 179n, 224n
Ussher, James, 35ff, 43, 43ff, 51, 55, 57,
  65, 71, 97, 103, 186, 222, 234, 317, 324,
  331, 333, 336, 341f, 345, 348f, 359ff,
  377, 379ff, 389f
usury, Protestants against, 167ff; money
  lenders condemned, 168f

vestiarian issue, 351-352. *See also*
  ceremonies
*via media*, 311f, 320, 363, 397, 407f;
  Laud's relation to, 409ff; contention
  as element, 413f; tolerance within,
  414f; and distinction between lesser
  and greater religious issues, 415-417;
  unity of Church as mark of, 417
Virgin, cult of, 264
vocations, *see* calling

war, and Protestant ethics, 254-256; as
  just, 254; Protestant attitude toward,
  254; and morality of soldiery, 256
wealth, and Protestant piety, 122-126;
  as a complement of calling, 137f;
  adverse opinion of, 161; Protestant
  position on, 160, 162
Weber, Max, 74n, 142, 173. *See also*
  Weber thesis
Weber thesis and social scientists, 145;
  and spirit of capitalism, 146, 148; and
  profit system, 146; and calling to
  profit, 147f; criticized, 148ff; and
  Protestant ethic, 149
Wedgewood, Josiah, 147
Wedgwood, C. V., 8n

Whitaker, William, 342ff
Whitelocke, James, 177
Whitgift-Cartwright controversy, 66,
  352; church-state relations, 194ff;
  Cartwright's theory of government,
  238. *See also* Whitgift and Cartwright
Whitgift, John, 152, 194ff, 204, 208, 232,
  236, 238f, 273, 323, 336, 351, 353f, 362,
  364, 366, 393, 399, 407ff
Whitney, E. A., 211n
Whyte, William, 169f
Willey, Basil, 13n
Witchcraft, 39n
Wolin, S. S., 250n
women, status exalted by Christianity,
  259; spiritual equality of, 259; inferior position, 259f; nunneries and
  asceticism, 260f; in the Catholic
  Church, 261; Thomas Aquinas on,
  261-264, 280, 283ff; as mother, 263f;
  cult of the Virgin, 264; as companion,
  269, 286ff; functions of good wife,
  270f; status of wife, 275-289; subordinate to husband, 277-282; as based in
  nature, 244f; due to Eve, 278; institutional nature, 278f; spiritual equality,
  281ff; obedience to husband, 284;
  corporal punishment of, 284f; and
  property rights, 285; equality as
  parent, 286; ecclesiastical role, 288f
Woodhouse, A. S. P., 86n
Woodhouse, H. F., 189n
works, good, Protestant emphasis on
  intent, 47-50; treasury of rejected,
  156. *See also* predestination
Wormuth, Francis, 214n
Wright, Louis B., 13n, 172n

Zagorin, Perez, 175n